THE ROYAL TREASURE

THE ROYAL TREASURE

Muslim Communities under the Crown of Aragon

in the Fourteenth Century

JOHN BOSWELL

New Haven and London   Yale University Press   1977

Published with assistance from the foundation established in memory of
Philip Hamilton McMillan of the Class of 1894, Yale College.

Library of Congress catalog card number: 77–76303
International standard book number: 0–300–02090–2
Printed in the United States of America by
The Vail-Ballou Press, Inc., Binghamton, New York.

Published in Great Britain, Europe, Africa, and
Asia (except Japan) by Yale University Press,
Ltd., London. Distributed in Latin America by
Kaiman & Polon, Inc., New York City; in
Australia and New Zealand by Book & Film
Services, Artarmon, N.S.W., Australia; and in
Japan by Harper & Row, Publishers, Tokyo Office.

11-21-78

for Jerry

CONTENTS

TABLES AND CHARTS

PREFACE

Since it would be impossible to express my gratitude to
all those who have in some way contributed to this volume, I limit
myself here to acknowledging only the most direct indebtedness.

Professor Giles Constable of Harvard University prepared me
for the task and saw me through it, and it was to his unfailingly
exquisite historical judgement that I turned for help in matters
of doubt. To Professor Jocelyn Hillgarth, now of the Pontifical
Institute, I owe my acquaintance with the particulars of medieval
Spanish history, and to him also enormous thanks for practical
assistance of every sort at each stage of preparation of this
study. These two men have been responsible for much of this
book through their inspiration and help.

Professor Thomas Glick of Boston University read the manuscript
and made many valuable suggestions, and Professor David Herlihy of
Harvard read and criticized portions of it.

Harvard University provided the funds for the year in Spain
during which I completed the bulk of my archival research, and I
am extremely grateful for its generosity to me. The directors of
the Archive of the Crown of Aragon in Barcelona were extremely
kind and helpful to me, as were the archivists and staff. To all
of them I am indebted not simply for the relative ease with which
I was able to conduct my investigations, but for the pleasantness
of my residence in Barcelona.

Finally, I wish to extend the most heartfelt thanks to Ralph Hexter and David Frusti for practical assistance in the preparation of the manuscript. Their cheerful generosity contributed as much as their actual labor to lightening tasks which would otherwise have been burdensome.

New Haven, August 1, 1977

ABBREVIATIONS

AHDE: Anuario de Historia del Derecho Español

BRABL: Boletín de la Real Academia de Buenas Letras de Barcelona

BRAH: Boletín de la Real Academia de la Historia

C: indicates a document from the Chancery of the Archive of the Crown of Aragon, as distinguished from documents of the Royal Patrimony from the same archive; the number following indicates the register and folio, thus: C 702:114 = Chancery Register 702, folio 114. The date in parentheses is the date of execution of the document as recorded in the register.

d: diner; see note on currency values, p.25

RP: indicates a document from the Royal Patrimony (Real Patrimonio) section of the Archive of the Crown of Aragon; citations follow the same form as those for Chancery documents, thus: RP 1701:8 = Real Patrimonio Register 1701, folio 8. The date in parentheses is the date of execution of the document as recorded in the register.

s: sueldo or solidus; see note on currency values, p.25

In addition, four collections are cited as follows:

Costums refers to the late thirteenth-century collection of laws of the city of Tortosa, known as Costums in Catalan and Costumbres in Castilian. The best modern edition is that of Ramón Foguet and José Foguet Marsal (Código de las Costumbres escritas de Tortosa [Tortosa, 1912]), with parallel Catalan and Castilian columns of the text, notes and apparatus in Castilian. The original Catalan is difficult, and the older edition of Bienvenido Oliver in Volume IV of his Historia del derecho en Cataluña, Mallorca y Valencia (Madrid, 1876-81) (4 vols), contained errors of text and commentary.*

---

* For example, in Volume II: on p.63 Oliver misreads IX.4a.2 of the Costums as prohibiting one converso from recalling to another their old faith, whereas it actually prohibits Christians from calling converts "renegades." On p.81 he wrongly interprets VI.1a.14 as declaring the son of a Christian and a Jewish slave to be free; what the text actually stipulates is that the offspring of a Christian and the slave or captive of a Jew should be free if baptized. Other errors of content are frequent (e.g., p.82, his comments about Muslims as property--cf.

Fueros   refers to the thirteenth-century collection of laws and
    privileges of Aragon. In this study these are all quoted from
    the excellent edition of Gunnar Tilander, Los Fueros de Aragón
    según el manuscrito 458 de la Biblioteca Nacional de Madrid
    (Lund, 1937).

Furs   refers to the collection of laws and privileges of Valencia
    begun in the thirteenth century, and known in Latin as Fori, in
    Catalan as Furs, and in Castilian as Fueros. A modern Latin edition
    has been published in the series of Textos of the Escuela de estu-
    dios medievales of the Consejo superior de investigaciones cientí-
    ficas (Fori Antiqui Valentiae, ed. Manuel Dualde Serrano [Madrid-
    Valencia, 1950-1967]), but the Catalan text in the series Els Nos-
    tres Clàssics (Furs de València, ed. Germà Colon and Arcadi Garcia
    [Barcelona, 1970]) is somewhat more thorough in preparation and
    annotation.

Viage   refers to the collection of texts published by Joaquin and
    Jaime Villanueva, Viage literario a las iglesias de España (Madrid,
    1802-1851). The first six volumes were edited by Joaquin, the
    remainder by Jaime.

Costums, VI.1a.9, and his interpretation of IV.11.21 on p.73), and
citations are extremely careless and inaccurate, especially p.69, notes
1 and 2; p.80, note 3; p.87, note 1; etc.

Introduction

An important and far-reaching change in the political and
ethnic constitution of the Iberian peninsula took place in the
eighth century of the Christian era. Contemporaries of this change,
and most historians writing before the last decade, described it as
the conquest of the Christian population of Spain by the forces
of Islam. This description is no longer considered entirely accurate; it is now apparent that what seemed to the Christian populations of the North of Spain as a "conquest" may actually have
been no more than a shifting of alliances among a population of
highly disparate religious and ethnic constituents, and that even
the purely Christian elements of this society quite likely collaborated with as much as they resisted the populations who crossed into
Spain from North Africa, perhaps more as settlers than conquerors.

Two aspects of the previous understanding of this period remain
intact, however: there is no doubt that most of the Iberian peninsula underwent an erratic but increasing process of Islamization from
the eighth century through the eleventh, nor that the Christian populations of the North saw this as a usurpation of their rights to the
peninsula, and were traumatized by it. It would, however, be inaccurate to imagine a Christian North holding at bay the Muslim hordes
of the South. Huge Christian populations remained in the South throughout the period of Muslim rule, and in many so-called Muslim areas the
only real sign of non-Christian dominance was the transfer of tax payments from Christian to Muslim lords. Intermarriage among all the
elements of the population--Berber, native Iberian, Hispano-Roman,

Visigothic, Arab—was common, and four centuries after the establish-
ment of Muslim dominion a Muslim writer observed that among the Islamic[1] population of Huesca there was not a single man who could prove
purely Arab descent.[2]

The fact that most southern populations were not wholly—perhaps
not even primarily—Muslim did not, however, deter the northern kingdoms from nursing rancor and bitterness toward the infidel "invaders."
Through the eleventh century, this rancor expressed itself largely in
raids, and the boundaries between the Christian and Muslim-ruled areas
of Spain fluctuated relatively little: a line drawn from the Catalan
coast between Barcelona and Tarragona and running northwest between
Pamplona and Tudela, then southwest between Segovia and Toledo, and
finally due west to Coimbra on the Atlantic, would delineate the approximate boundaries between the two factions in 1060.

Owing largely to population pressure from the North and the general disintegration of Muslim unity in the South, however, rapid
progress was made by Christians in the twelfth and thirteenth centuries. Two hundred years later, the line described above would be
drawn just above Granada, across the very bottom of the Iberian pen-

---

1. Although I am conscious of a distinction between "Islamic" and
"Muslim," I have chosen not to employ it consistently in the text of
this work. A great many institutions and aspects of Mudéjar life were
not, in fact, Islamic, in the sense of arising from the law or religion
of Muhammad; they would have been unrecognizable to Muslims in Damascus,
and were in some cases specifically repudiated by other parts of the
Islamic world, yet they were nonetheless the institutions of a group
of Muslims. Distinctions between the two words are thus of minimal value
in discussing Mudéjares, and have been largely ignored.

2. José María Lacarra y de Miguel, Aragón en el pasado, in Aragón
(Zaragoza, 1960), I, p.131.

insula, and the Christians under the Crown of Aragon had only Castile
to their south. The Muslim threat had been removed.

The Muslims themselves, however, had mostly not been removed, and
this study is an effort to discover what in fact happened to them.
Unlike the shadowy circumstances leading to Muslim hegemony over most
of Spain prior to the thirteenth century, the Christian recovery of
the Southeast of the peninsula was clearly a military conquest, and
the Muslim armies opposing the Christian forces either were vanquished
or surrendered. Much of the Muslim population was thus abandoned to
the invading Christians, and although some may have fled, the majority,
long used to shifts of power and rule, stayed on and bore the dominion
of new rulers.

Surprisingly little is known of these people. Contemporaries
called them "moros" in Castilian and Aragonese, "sarrahins" in Catalan, "sarraceni" in Chancery Latin.[3] Modern historians have tended
to call them "Mudéjares," from an Arabic word for "allowed to remain."[4]
In northern areas like Aragon and Catalonia, where the countryside

---

3. The word _morisco_, generally used to describe Spanish Muslims at
a later date, was used in the fourteenth century to describe objects,
but not persons: see in the Chancery registers of the Archive of the
Crown of Aragon, Register 683, folio 26 (such registers and folios
hereinafter cited as C 683:26, etc.), dated November 10, 1355: "...
una nau enombrada Santa Maria, cargada de cueros de Sevilia i de
moriscos i de otros mercaderies...." Cf. C 1075:66 (Jan.19, 1363),
C 1571:187 (Dec.10, 1363), and from the _Real Patrimonio_ of the same
archive, Register 1708, folio 19 (such documents hereinafter cited as
RP 1708:19, etc.). _Moro_ is derived from the Latin _maurus_, generally
assumed to have been inspired by the Mauretanian provenance of some
Spanish Muslims. The word _maurus_ is rarely encountered in fourteenth-
century documents, but see C 898:222, in the Appendix. _Agarenus_ also
occurs: see C 1570:36 (Sept.23, 1360).

4. Robert Ignatius Burns, in his _Islam under the Crusaders_ (Princeton,
1974), touches on the origin of _Mudéjar_ on p.64, n.1. For a more de-

was quickly overrun by the overflow populations of the crowded
Christian lands beneath the Pyrenees, they tended almost inevitably
to be congregated into "aljamas," or communities, in cities or villages. In the South they also formed municipal entities, but the
majority probably continued to reside in the countryside throughout
the thirteenth and early fourteenth centuries.

This book represents an effort to provide a detailed study
of the nature and situation of the Muslims living under Christian
rule at some distance from the reconquest, when they had been as
thoroughly absorbed into the Christian culture as they were ever to
be, and when relations between them and the Christian society which
ruled them were as "normal" as human relations ever are. The Crown
of Aragon was chosen to delineate the area of study, since it ruled
the largest proportion of Iberian Muslims, and left the richest depos-
its of documentation. The fourteenth century was adopted as the temporal focus of the book both because no previous study had undertaken to examine Mudéjares during this century, and because it fell
almost exactly in the middle of the period between the last major
conquests of Muslim-held lands (other than Granada) and the first official expulsions of Muslims from the Iberian mainland. Considerations
of scholarship narrowed the period further: the untapped archival resources of the Crown of Aragon are staggering. Even limiting the study
to the middle reign of the century (Peter the Ceremonious, 1336-1387)

---

tailed and cautious analysis, see Isidro de las Cagigas, Los Mudéjares
(Madrid, 1948-9), I, pp.58-64.

would have required a close scrutiny of about 2,000 registers, each comprising hundreds of folio pages. To maintain the broad geographical basis of the study, essential because no modern investigation had compared data for the three kingdoms under the Crown, it was therefore necessary either to sacrifice completeness or to limit the time parameters further.

The period from 1355 to 1366 seemed ultimately to constitute a particularly suitable unit of time. During these eleven years the population of Aragon-Catalonia-Valencia as a whole was under tremendous stress owing to a costly and extremely destructive war with Castile, which affected all levels of society. These years thus afford a unique opportunity to study the role of Mudéjares during a period of enormous social tension unrelated to their peculiar status. In many ways the immediately preceding crisis--the plague of 1348-9-- affected Muslims peculiarly, since they were accused along with the Jews of somehow being behind it, and had to be specially protected by the monarchies of Spain.[5]   Later in the century much social stress was directly related to the Muslims themselves, and led to attacks on morerías, pogroms, and much later, expulsion. But in the very middle of the fourteenth, during a war with Castile which could not be blamed on the Muslims, and with which they were involved just as much as the Christian population, the Mudéjares were as much a part of

---

5. See Amada López de Meneses, "Una consecuencia de la peste negra en Cataluña: el Pogrom de 1348," Sefarad, XIX (1959), 92-131, 321-364, and her Documentos acerca de la peste negra en los dominios de la Corona de Aragón (Zaragoza, 1956).

Aragonese society as they would ever be. The disruptions of ordinary life occasioned by the war afford unusually detailed accounts in royal registers of efforts to restore conditions to normal, and thus provide a rare glimpse into every aspect of mid-fourteenth-century Spanish life; at the same time, the oppression, exploitation, beneficence, favoritism, and indulgence visited upon the Muslims during this period can be studied and analyzed with great precision, allowing the historian to probe deeply the extent to which the Mudéjares were, in fact, a part of the society and its stress.

The "Crown of Aragon" in the fourteenth century was actually the union in one person of dominion over numerous political entities. The County of Barcelona and the kingdom of Aragon had been united through marriage in 1137, and remained so thereafter. This resulted in a rather anomalous numbering system for the kings of Aragon-Catalonia, so that Peter the Ceremonious, for example, was Pedro IV of Aragon and Pere III of Catalonia. The kingdom of Valencia was annexed from the Muslims by military conquest, as were the "marquessates" of Tortosa and Lérida. Each kingdom or county had its own law and Corts, or parliament. Each had its own civil service, courts, and clergy. In most of Aragon Aragonese was spoken; in Catalonia and Valencia the Christians spoke Catalan. The languages used by the Muslims are discussed below, in Chapter VIII.

Most of Aragon-Catalonia had been reconquered from the Muslims in the twelfth century (Zaragoza in 1118, Tortosa and Lérida in 1148, Teruel in 1170, etc.), while Valencia and its environs did not fall

until well into the thirteenth.   This made a pronounced difference
in the extent of acculturation of the Muslim inhabitants of the
several lands, as well as in the attitude toward them of the Crown
and ruling classes.   Population differences also had an effect.
Catalonia was by far the most populous region, with a 1365 population
of about 470,000.[6]   Aragon's population was probably about half this,
and Valencia's about half that of Aragon.   The Muslim populations
of the kingdoms were--significantly--reversed.   Valencia had by far
the largest proportion of Muslims, and Christians were actually in the
minority;   in Aragon Mudéjares were in the minority, though how small
a minority is practically impossible to guess.   The author would estimate their proportion of the total population at about thirty percent.
In Catalonia the Muslim population was very heavy around and south of
the Ebro, but there were few if any Mudéjares north of Tarragona.

Specific population figures for Aragonese Mudéjares are wanting
for the kingdoms as a whole, but for some aljamas there are data.   The
relatively small aljamas of Alborga and Gata had forty and sixty taxable persons respectively, if the king's informants can be believed.[7]

---

6. Ramón d'Abadal i de Vinyals, *Pere el Cerimoniós i els inicis de
la decadència política de Catalunya* (Barcelona, 1972), p.16. (For
the numbering of kings, see above.) This indispensable work was originally published in Castilian, which may be more accessible to many
readers than the later, annotated Catalan translation noted above.
The original is in Volume XIV of the *Historia de España* (Madrid, 1966),
under the title *Pedro el Ceremonioso y los comienzos de la decadencia
política de Cataluña*.   For other population figures see J.C. Russell,
"The Medieval Monedatge of Aragon and Valencia," *Proceedings of the
American Philosophical Society*, CVI (1962), 483-504.

7. The king accused the local Muslim leaders in these two towns of
"conspiring to defraud the Crown," by lying about their population
figures.   They claimed there were only twelve taxable persons in Al-

Teruel had ninety-two taxable males.[8] Ariza normally had a population of some 200 Muslim households.[9] Before the depopulations of
the war with Castile, the aljama of Huesca comprised 540 persons,
but in 1363 it had been reduced to 410.[10] Tax records from the aljama
of Zaragoza indicate a population of about 500 persons, including
women and children.[11] It is difficult to extrapolate from these figures
to other areas, or even to include women and children where only tax-

---

borga in 1356, when the morabetí was being collected, and only twenty-
five in la Gata, whereas the king asserted that there were certainly
40 and 60, respectively: C 1068:111 (May 4, 1356). The aljamas incurred a fine of 4,000s for this "fraud."

8. This was disputed: the aljama claimed to have forty-two taxable
persons, and at first the king believed them (C 701:140 [September
21, 1360], and C 701:141 [September 20, 1360]), but he later accused
them of lying, and finally assessed them for ninety-two taxable persons: C 1383:239 (Jan.2, 1361). Such population disputes between the
Crown and local government were legion after the plague and during
the war: cf. note 7, above, and C 1383:233 (Nov.22, 1360), where the
king disputes with Borja over the matter.

9. C 702:91 (Jan.18, 1361).

10. C 1384:40 (Jan.3, 1362).

11. From C 711:131 (1363) it is clear that the annual peyta in Zaragoza during this time was 6 sueldos per person, including women and
children. C 1205:68 (1365) indicates an annual total peyta of the aljama at 3,000 sueldos, which implies a total population of about 500
persons. This would seem to be about the right figure in any event.
Other indirect evidence of population exists for a few aljamas: the
Valencian aljama of Játiva was the largest, though precisely how large
is not clear. The aljama of Espada could send 300 men to help the
king in the war effort as late as 1365 (C 1204:55-6); the Muslims of
Calatayud provided one-third of the infantry and matériel for the war
in 1360 (C 700:144), which would imply that this was their proportion
to the general population of the city, since the king was scrupulous
about such things (see, for example, C 910:118 [1366]); on the other
hand, there were more Jews in Borja than Muslims, and the Muslims were
still required to pay a greater share in the war levies: "...vos tamen
ut fertur non attento quod numerus domicelliorum dictorum judeorum ex-
cedit numerum incolatorum sarracenorum predictorum, compellitis et compellere sarracenos ipsos nitimini ad contribuendum et solvendum in dicto solido quantitatem maiorem illa qua ex eadem causa per judeos sol-

able males are listed (as in Teruel):   in Elda in 1366 there were,
for instance, only 92 men, but a total of 451 persons, which would
imply a ratio of about five to one;[12]   in Aspe, on the other hand,
there were 225 males, 238 "households," and 624 persons--a ratio
of about three to one.[13]

These figures undoubtedly represent the Muslim population at
a rather low ebb. The plague had reduced the population of the
kingdoms as a whole only a decade before, and the terrible effects of
a war with Castile (beginning in 1355) lowered the Muslim population even further. Ariza was reduced from 200 families to ten by
1362;[14] the entire Muslim population of Orihuela was gone in 1366,
as was that of Alicante;[15] and the king considered Aspe at 624
persons to be "ad depopulationem maximam deductus propter occasionem
guerre Castille."[16]

The war with Castile was, in fact, a special hardship on the
Muslim population of Aragon. This will be discussed in greater detail
below. The precise causes of the war are not easy to fix. Peter the

---

vitur antedictos..." C 1384:22 (May 30, 1361). For a few population
indications for the fifteenth century, see Francisco Macho y Ortega,
"Condición social de los mudéjares aragoneses (siglo xv)," Memorias
de la Facultad de filosofía y letras (Universidad de Zaragoza), I (1923),
pp.161, 259, and idem, "Documentos relativos a la condición social y jurídica de los mudéjares aragoneses," Revista de ciencias jurídicas y sociales, V (1922), p.157.

12. RP 1711:3.

13. RP 1711:12ss.

14. See C 702:91, in Appendix.

15. RP 1711:3, 7.

16. C 913:91 (Nov.25, 1366).

Ceremonious considered that it began in 1356 as the result of a
naval contretemps between Catalan and Castilian ships, aggravated
by a letter of direct challenge from Peter the Cruel of Castile.[17]
Perhaps it was this simple in the minds of the combatants; in retrospect it is easy to see that both Aragon and Castile chafed at the
arbitrary boundaries drawn between them and were anxious to alter
them, and that the instability of both royal houses--the Castilian due
to dynastic uncertainties, the Aragonese due to the weakening effects
of its long struggle with the Union and exhausting foreign involve-
ments--invited external interference.

The exact progress of the war is difficult to trace, especially
in the absence of any thorough study. Peter of Aragon considered
the war over in 1361, after a peace treaty was signed in May of that
year ("la pau de Deça," May 18, 1361), but hostilities erupted again
before the summer was out, and by September Calatayud had fallen to
Castile. Peace was signed again in 1363, after Peter the Cruel had
taken Valencia and very nearly reached Tortosa, but this proved to be

---

17. The only modern biography of Peter the Ceremonious is that of
Rafael Tasis, Pere el Cerimoniós i els seus fills (Barcelona, 1962),
which can best be described as useful. For the importance of Peter's
reign and the political events which took place during it, on the other hand, there is the superb essay by Ramón d'Abadal i de Vinyals,
Pere el Cerimoniós i els inicis de la decadència política de Catalunya
(see note 6, above). We are particularly fortunate to have Peter's
own account of his reign in the Crònica de Pere el Cerimoniós, most
recently edited by the eminent Ferran Soldevila in Les Quatre Grans
Cròniques (Barcelona, 1971), 1003-1225. The notes and indices alone
make this the most desirable edition. Chapter six deals almost exclusively with the war with Castile, but unfortunately from a very
personal standpoint. The chronicle is--alas!--not useful for exam-
ining Peter's attitude toward the Mudéjares, whom he mentions rarely
and in tones of absolute indifference. There is also a collection of

an even shorter truce than before. In the sense of cessation of hostilities, the war ended in 1366. Neither party can be said to have
won--Peter the Cruel was eventually deposed by the ally of Peter of
Aragon, Henry of Trastámara, but the latter then declined to honor
almost all of the terms of their alliance. Certainly the lands of the
Crown of Aragon suffered more.

Many scholars believe that the reign of Peter the Ceremonious
marked the beginning of the decline of Catalonia, which had long been
the most prosperous and influential section of the Iberian peninsula.[18]
This argument has recently encountered persuasive opponents, but no
controversy attaches to the idea that the first part of the reign of
Peter constituted a watershed in Aragonese history. During this period the authority of the Crown was challenged and upheld in the revolt
of the Union, permanent and disastrous changes in demography and economy were effected by the plagues of 1348 and thereafter, the royal
house of Castile was replaced with Aragonese collusion, Majorca and
the Balearics were returned to the direct control of the kings of Aragon, and even Athens came briefly under the rule of the Aragonese

Peter's correspondence published by Ramón Gubern, Epistolari de Pere
III (Barcelona, 1955), in the series Els Nostres Clàssics. Only volume I has appeared to date.

18. Most notably, Ramon d'Abadal i de Vinyals, in Pere el Ceremoniós;
Pierre Vilar, "Le déclin catalan du Bas Moyen-Age. Hypothèses sur sa
chronologie," Estudios de historia moderna, VI (1956-9), 3-68; and Carmen Batlle Gallart, La Crisis social y económica de Barcelona a medi-
ados del siglo xv (Barcelona, 1973). Opposing and more modern views
are those of M. Del Treppo, I Mercanti catalani e l'espansione della
Corona Aragonese nel secolo xv (Naples, 1968), and Claude Carrère,
Barcelone, centre économique à l'époque des difficultés, 1380-1462
(Paris, 1967).

monarchy.

The early reign of Peter IV, in fact, witnessed the ostensible ascendance of royal power in nearly all areas of Aragonese life: if the period marked the beginnings of Catalan commercial and political decline, and saw the foundations laid for the ultimate submission of Aragon-Catalonia to León-Castile, it also witnessed the triumph of the Aragonese Crown over some of the forces which had opposed it within its own realms.

This was particularly true in the case of the Mudéjares.

> ...from the time of Peter the Fourth...the monarch recovers in fact those attributes which until then he had possessed in name only; he demands fairness in the treatment of the Moors; he reprehends and threatens nobles who abuse their rights; he collects taxes, such as the _cena_ and the _morabetí_, even in [the nobles'] aljamas; he reserves to himself supreme authority in criminal cases, and becomes the protector of each and every one of the Muslims.[19]

In the following chapters the mechanisms, causes, and effects of this consolidation are studied, as an approach to the general condition of the Muslims as a minority group. The question of _convivencia_, the living together of the various Iberian religious and ethnic groups, is intensely complicated, and the task of a scholar trying to understand and describe this symbiosis is rather like that of a man attempting to reconstruct a broken and crumpled spider's web.

For the present study, well over a thousand royal letters were extracted from the registers covering the years in question. No indi-

---

19. "...desde Pedro IV...el monarca recobra de hecho los atributos que hasta entonces sólo nominalmente poseía; exige blandura en el trato a los moros; reprende y amenaza a los nobles que abusan de su derecho; cobra en las aljamas de éstos algunos impuestos, como la cena y el maravedí; se reserva la apelación suprema en las causas criminales, y se

ces exist for these registers, and this had to be accomplished by

the tedious process of simply reading through all of the royal regis-

ters for the eleven years. A table of the types of registers involved

is presented, and many of the documents are published--all for the first

time--in the Appendix.[20] The study is, thus, almost exclusively a

documentary one. Secondary material has been used sparingly and only

to shed further light on unpublished materials. Bibliographical infor-

mation is provided as a help to the reader, but references to or compar-

isons with previous studies of Mudéjares have been kept minimal, both

to avoid blurring the documentary focus of the essay, and because it

is impossible, in the present state of research on the subject, to

account for many of the disparities between such studies.

   For the most part, previous efforts to study the Mudéjares and

their communities have not been extremely fruitful. A series of gen-

eral studies of the question in the latter half of the nineteenth

century sketched some broad outlines of the picture, and put into

print the major known treaties of capitulation and their terms, but

tended to be polemical and unscholarly.[21] In the first half of this

---

convierte en protector de todos y cada uno de los sarracenos" Macho
y Ortega, "Condición," p.192.

   20. Excluding individual citations in secondary works, the only efforts to publish materials from the Aragonese Chancery have been those
of Próspero de Bofarull y Mascaró, Colección de documentos inéditos
de la Corona de Aragón (Barcelona, 1847-1910), 41 volumes, and Eduardo
González Hurtebise, Libros de tesorería de la Casa Real de Aragón
(Barcelona, 1911). Specialized collections, of course, have published
documents relating to specific subjects, such as the Corts, the plague,
commerce, etc.

   21. In order of publication: Albert de Circourt, Histoire des Mores
mudejares et des morisques, ou des arabes d'Espagne sous ·la domination
des Chrétiens (Paris, 1846); Florencio Janer, Condición social de los

century, even fewer books appeared on the subject, and they were far
from adequate. Perhaps the most ambitious was that of Cagigas, in
the series on Minorías étnico-religiosas de la Edad Media española,
which was scholarly and largely dispassionate, but attempted to deal
with the issue on such an enormous scale that it, too, managed only
to suggest the bare outlines of the situation of the Mudéjares.[22]

On the other hand, a number of highly informative articles have
appeared during the twentieth century. Because conditions for the
Muslims as well as others varied from one Iberian kingdom to another,
these monographs have generally tended to concentrate on a particular
time period within one kingdom.

Francisco Macho y Ortega was the first Spaniard to attempt to
provide a really detailed analysis of Mudéjar life in Aragonese cities,
and his two major studies, published in 1922 and 1923, remain as crucial today as when they were first published.[23] By combing the notarial archives of Zaragoza, Macho y Ortega was able to glean an immense
wealth of information about many aspects of fifteenth-century Muslim
life in Aragon at its most basic level. Certain reservations, however,

---

moriscos de España (Madrid, 1857); A. Delgado Hernández, Memoria sobre
el estado moral y político de los mudéjares de Castilla (Madrid, 1864);
Francisco Fernández y González, Estado social y político de los mudéjares de Castilla (Madrid, 1866); J. Pedregal y Fantini, Estado social
y cultural de los mozárabes y mudéjares españoles (Seville, 1898).

22. See note 4, above, for Cagigas. Some other twentieth-century
works, in order of publication, are: Pascual Boronat y Barrachina, Los
moriscos españoles y su expulsión (Valencia, 1901); Pedro Longas, Vida
religiosa de los Moriscos (Madrid, 1915); Julio Caro Baroja, Los moriscos del reino de Granada; ensayo de historia social (Madrid, 1957).
For a more complete listing of modern works, cf. Burns, Islam, p. xviii,
n. 7.

23. See note 11, above.

must be expressed in regard to his results. Although he avoided the
pitfall of polemicism into which many fell both before and after him,
and managed to escape the temptation to treat treaties of capitulation
as constituting real guarantees of what their texts stipulated, Macho
y Ortega did display a certain naïveté about royal edicts. He assumed, for instance, that royal decrees enjoining nobles or others to
respect the rights of Mudéjares achieved their end, and cited them as
proof of the extent to which Mudéjares were well-treated by Crown and
society, when in fact the constant repetition of these edicts makes
quite clear that they almost invariably failed of effect, and the
issuance of them in the first place really proved nothing other than
the Crown's intention to placate the Muslims at the moment. Moreover,
many of Macho y Ortega's assessments and descriptions of aspects of
the organization and internal structure of the aljama were inferences
from a single document; corroborating evidence from other kingdoms,
or even other cities in Aragon, is wholly wanting.

An extremely important study of Valencian Mudéjares during the
first century after the conquest of Valencia (1238-1338) was published
in 1952 by Francisco Roca Traver.[24] Though relatively short, this
work was effected with enormous erudition, and quickly became the
standard reference for discussions of Mudéjares and their communities.
Unfortunately, this study, too, suffered from notable defects. Unlike
that of Macho y Ortega, it did not rely heavily on local or detailed

---

24. Francisco A. Roca Traver, "Un siglo de vida mudéjar en la Valencia medieval (1238-1338)," Estudios de edad media de la Corona de
Aragón, V (1952), 115-208.

material, but attempted to give a rather broader picture. While it
did draw some interesting parallels between Muslims in the North and
South, it was limited basically to the Valencian Muslims, whose condition could scarcely reflect that of Mudéjares generally, since they
were the most recently conquered, existed in the largest numbers,
and were the closest to lands still controlled by Muslims. Moreover,
Roca Traver's otherwise laudable work was severely marred by his stri-
dent efforts to demonstrate the extreme tolerance of the ruling Christian classes in regards to the Muslims and their religion.

Other notable regional monographs on Mudéjares are those of Cabezudo Astraín for Aragon, Grau Monserrat and Gual Camarena for Valencia,
and Torres Fontes for Murcia.[25] Winfried Küchler published in 1968 the

25. José Cabezudo Astraín, "Noticias y documentos sobre moriscos,"
Miscelánea de estudios árabes y hebraicos, V (1956), 105-117 (for Aragon see also Jean-Guy Liauzu, "La condition des musulmans dans l'Aragon chrétien aux xie et xiie siècles," Hespéris-Tamuda, IX [1968],
185-200, and the article by Ma. L. Ledesma Rubió, in the Miscelánea José Ma. Lacarra, Estudios de historia medieval [Zaragoza, 1968], 63-
79); Manuel Grau Monserrat, "Mudéjares castellonenses," Boletín de
la Real Academia de Buenas Letras de Barcelona (hereafter BRABL), XXIX
(1961-62), 251-73 (for Castellón, see also Arcadio García Sanz, "Mudéjares y moriscos en Castellón," Boletín de la Sociedad Castellonense
de Cultura, XXVIII [1952], 94-114); Miguel Gual Camarena, "Mudéjares
valencianos, aportaciones para su estudio," Saitabi, VII (1949), 165-
199, and idem, "Los mudéjares valencianos en la época del Magnánimo,"
IV Congreso de la historia de la Corona de Aragón, I, 467-494; Juan
Torres Fontes, "Los mudéjares murcianos en el siglo xiii," Murgetana,
XVII (1961), 57-90. For the Balearics, see Elena Lourie, "Free Moslems
in the Balearics under Christian Rule in the Thirteenth Century," Speculum, XLV (1970), 624-649. Ms. Lourie's dissertation, Christian Attitudes towards the Mudéjares in the Reign of Alfonso III of Aragon (1285-
91), D.Phil. thesis, Oxford, 1967, has unfortunately not yet been published. Many other articles could be cited, but this literature is
exhaustively covered by Burns in his Islam, and the list does not demand reiteration here. Of special interest, however, are two articles
with a slightly different approach and unusual excellence. These are
Thomas F. Glick and Oriol Pi Sunyer, "Acculturation as an Explanatory

first modern and scholarly attempt to analyze the tax liabilities
and duties of Aragonese Muslims.[26] This work has received less attention than it deserves: although it deals with the fifteenth century, it is indispensable for any understanding of royal tax policy
in regard to Jews or Muslims.

The first major work on the subject in English is the second
volume of a projected series by Robert I. Burns, S.J., called _Islam
under the Crusaders_.[27] This scholarly and erudite work deals with
many of the subtler issues involved in the Iberian symbiosis, and is
remarkably free of the bias which has so unfortunately infected earlier
studies. Moreover, the completed series of Burns' work promises to
be the most comprehensive treatment of Mudéjares anywhere, with minute analysis of every aspect of their existence and social structure.
Because of this, a comment on the present study in relation to the
work of Burns seems desirable.

Concept in Spanish History," _Comparative Studies in Society and His-
tory_, XI (1969), 136-154; and Pierre Guichard, "Le peuplement de la
région de Valence aux deux premiers siècles de la domination musulmane," _Mélanges de la casa de Velázquez_, V (1969), 103-158. The latter article is especially useful as a background to Mudéjar studies
in Valencia; the former as an approach to the problem of _convivencia_
in general.

26. Winfried Küchler, "Besteuerung der Juden und Mauren in den
Ländern der Krone Aragons während des 15 Jahrhunderts," _Gesammelte
Aufsätze zur Kulturgeschichte Spaniens_, 24 (1968), 227-256.

27. See note 4, above. Other works by Father Burns include "Christian-Islamic Confrontation in the West: The Thirteenth-Century Dream
of Conversion," _American Historical Review_, LXXVI (1971), 1386-1434;
_The Crusader Kingdom of Valencia: Reconstruction on a Thirteenth-Cen-
tury Frontier_ (Cambridge, Mass., 1967), 2 vols; "How to End a Crusade:
Techniques for Making Peace in the Thirteenth-Century Kingdom of Valencia," _Military Affairs_, XXXV (1971), 142-148; "Irrigation Taxes in
Early Mudéjar Valencia: the Problem of the _Alfarda_," _Speculum_, XLIV

The area--both temporal and geographical--of Burns' published works is clearly delineated: he deals only with the kingdom of Valencia, and only with the thirteenth century. His study is, therefore, one of a society just beginning to establish its internal organization; indeed, what primarily interests Fr. Burns is the mechanism and dynamics of the <u>establishment</u> of Christian hegemony over a Muslim population. The following study, on the other hand, is an effort to examine the position of Muslims once this hegemony was securely in place, i.e., what life was like for an established dissident minority. This thesis is more narrowly defined in temporal scope than Burns' works (or any previous study)--being limited in large measure to eleven years of documentation--but broader than his (or other modern studies) in geographical comprehension, since it deals with Aragon, Catalonia, and Valencia.

In many areas Burns' findings and those presented subsequently are in accord; in others they differ. It is not yet clear, due to the spotty and limited nature of studies published to date, and the consequent dearth of comparable data, whether such divergences as occur represent the effects of temporal factors, geographical variables, variant interpretation of unevenly biased documents, or

---

(1969), 560-567; "Journey from Islam: Incipient Cultural Transition in the Conquered Kingdom of Valencia," <u>Speculum</u>, XXXV (1960), 337-356; "Le royaume chrétien de Valence et ses vassaux musulmans (1240-1280)," <u>Annales, économies, sociétés, civilisations,</u> XXVIII (1973), 199-225; "Social Riots on the Christian-Moslem Frontier: Thirteenth-Century Valencia," <u>American Historical Review,</u> LXVI (1969), 378-400; "Immigrants from Islam: the Crusaders' Use of Muslims as Settlers in Thirteenth-Century Spain," <u>American Historical Review,</u> LXXX (1975), 21-42; <u>Medieval Colonialism: Postcrusade Exploitation of Islamic Valencia</u> (Princeton, 1975).

simply differences of opinion. In Burns' discussion of "the Law and its Interpreters," for example, he describes a system of justice far more organized and stable than that which this writer infers to have existed in the fourteenth century, with officials such as the zabaxorta, who do not occur in fourteenth-century documents, and with more specific roles for officials such as the çalmedina, who do. The passage of a hundred years would account for many of these differences, and the fact that Fr. Burns has limited himself to Valencia, whereas the present findings were derived from three kingdoms, would account for many more. Methodological variations play a part as well: Islam relies heavily on pre-reconquest Muslim archetypes (especially as described by Tyan), which were undoubtedly more important in the years immediately following the reconquest, and in the lands where Muslim rule was longest and strongest, than in areas of greater acculturation and considerable distance in time and place from Muslim rule. Islam under the Crusaders is less concerned with possible divergences between royal proclamations and actual practice, again quite likely the result of chronological considerations: such edicts were more apt to be live issues within a relatively short time of their promulgation than a century or two later. Moreover, the issues in the two works are largely different, despite the similarity of subject matter. Where Burns, for instance, addresses himself to the development of Mudéjar juridical practice from previously purely Muslim forms, the study at hand analyzes the gradual erosion of Mudéjar judicial independence under the steady encroachments of Christian authority, custom, and influence.

The point here is certainly not to throw stones at other authors, many of whose works far exceed the present offering; rather, it is to clarify the issue of what, precisely, is being treated, whether well or ill. The most excellent studies to date, such as those of Lourie on the Balearics and Burns' Islam under the Crusaders, have been addressed to the position of the Muslim minority in recently conquered societies, where their position was in its formative years and all aspects of convivencia were in flux. The few studies available for later periods are severely limited in scope, and, unfortunately, rather biased.

It is unlikely that there was ever any conflict between the Muslims and Christians themselves as pitched as the scholarly debate which has raged over the issue of Iberian tolerance of Semitic religious practices. While nothing could be less fruitful than to stoke the tired flames of this ancient conflagration, it is simply impossible to ignore the patent bias of Roca Traver, Macho y Ortega, and others who—for understandable reasons—have struggled mightily to counteract the equally biased picture painted by earlier Hispanophobic historians such as Circourt. Indeed, without a scrap of evidence to the contrary, such a statement as Roca Traver's "The Mudéjares were never for a moment the objects of intolerance or lack of understanding; very much to the contrary, they were given every opportunity to fulfill the rites and precepts of their own religion "[28] would strike any student of

---

28. "Los mudéjares en ningún momento fueron objeto de incomprensión o intolerancia; muy al contrario, se les dieron toda clase de facili-

history, or of human nature, as incredible. It is simply inconceiv-
able that after centuries of bloody fighting over the lands on which
they lived—fighting which, albeit not altogether motivated by religious fervor, was nonetheless organized largely along religious lines—
the peoples who had so long been exhorted to take part in these "holy
causes" should have instantly come to a complete understanding of
their erstwhile enemies, and that those very differences of "rite
and religion" which were the driving force of slaughter and carnage
from the steppes of Asia to the moors of England should have been
simply ignored after the thirteenth century in a land where the battle
for orthodoxy was fought more consistently and virulently than anywhere else in the Middle Ages.

To begin to cope with such paradoxes, a great many distinctions
must be made: between the attitudes of the ruling class of Aragon-
Catalonia-Valencia, concerned with establishing and maintaining a
peaceful and productive population base, and a lower class struggling
to support itself on a war-torn and oft-endangered land,.comforting
itself with ethnic pride and religious fanaticism; between a professional military element dependent on and committed to the destruction
of the "other side"—whatever it happened to be—and an agricultural
element interested mainly in enough social stability and organization
to allow for the planting, harvesting and marketing of its crops;
between a natural tendency of the human mind to fear what is different
and strange, and an equally natural desire to live at peace with one's

---

dades para que pudieran cumplir los ritos y preceptos de su propia
religión" ("Un Siglo," pp.25-6).

neighbors.

One way of approaching these issues would be to apply to the medieval Spanish situation the findings of modern disciplines in regard to systems and structures of ethnic pluralities. Certainly no one any longer doubts that inter-group relations in such societies do not occur randomly: they develop according to patterns which have analogues, if not exact parallels, in other ethnically plural socie- ties, and the study of such patterns will no doubt clarify the struc- tures within an individual society as well as the relations between several different ones.[29]

---

29. Thomas Glick ("The Ethnic Systems of Premodern Spain," Comparative Studies in Sociology, I [1977], in press) has suggested that a particu- larly valuable model for such analysis of Spain is provided by Pierre van den Berghe's conceptual dichotomy between paternalistic and competi- tive systems of ethnic stratification. Paternalistic systems are charac terized by a horizontal division of vertical stratification, with very little mobility: i.e., the society is organized from the bottom of the lower ethnic group to the top of the higher one in vertical succession, and the line dividing the two groups clearly defines the relationship of those in one group to those in the other, largely precluding mobility across the line. Such a system, while obviously "oppressive" from an egalitarian point of view, tends, in societies where it has been observe to minimize violence, since expectations match realities, and since ther is virtually no compettition between the ethnic groups for the same posi tions or status. In a competitive system the ethnic dividing line may be conceived of as bifurcating the class system vertically, with members of either group theoretically occupying the same positions on either si of the line. In reality, among those competitive systems studied, one group almost invariably occupies the upper strata to a greater extent, and this gives rise to discontent among the other groups, for whom expec tations of equal status are unfulfilled. The Muslim system of protected minorities (dhimmis) would, in Glick's view, be an example of a paternal istic system: no matter how high a dhimmi might climb within his own com munity, he could not officially aspire to compete in the upper levels of the larger society, open only to Muslims. The situation prevailing after the forced conversion of the Jews in Spain would represent a competitive system: though still ethnically distinct, the conversos were officially

Since, however, not even the bare facts of Mudéjar existence are
as yet well documented or understood, the rigorous application of such
conceptualizations to the following study might obscure many nuances
which are better left to the analytical preferences of individual
readers.[30] The aim of the work is not to present a case for any particular system of analysis of Iberian ethnic stratification, but simply
to give a clearer understanding of the historical reality of Mudéjar
life in fourteenth-century Spain.

---

entitled to enter any levels of the Christian society they might wish
to. The possibilities for hostility and violence arising from competition for status in the latter system are obvious; the likelihood of
violence in the former system would seem to depend largely on the size
and status of the protected minority, socio-economic conditions, and
the extent to which their exclusion from the larger society constituted
an economic or practical hardship.

In terms of these dichotomies, the relations between Christians and
Mudéjares in fourteenth-century Aragon would seem to be primarily cate-
gorizable as paternalistic. The systems are not, however, mutually exclusive: historical realities are always more complex than conceptualizations of them. In most areas of their lives the Mudéjares had "separate but equal" institutions—a characteristic of paternalistic ethnic
systems—but in some, such as law, there seems to have been such over-
lap of Muslim and Christian access and jurisdiction that one might view
the system as either competitive or midway between paternalistic and
competitive. Similarly, relations between Mudéjares and Christians
seem for the most part to have been peaceful and friendly—as one would
expect in a paternalistic society with a relatively well-treated subject
minority. But in particular areas and times, violence, hostility, and
bitterness are visible among both Christians and Muslims: whether this
was due to aspects of the Aragonese situation which more approximate a
competitive model than a paternalistic one, or to variations in basically paternalistic relations which caused discontent among some members
of the society, is not determinable until the mechanisms for such struc-
turing and stratification have been more thoroughly studied in historical
contexts.

30. It will, nonetheless, be obvious that a basically paternalistic
system of ethnic stratification is being described in this study, and
a number of parallels with other paternalistic social organizations will
be drawn in passing.

An appreciation of the relation of Muslim-Christian interaction i
medieval Spain to the broader fabric of Spanish history in particular
and to human relations in general, is badly needed, but it must be
reserved for another time and place, when the Muslims' own story is
more fully understood. The present volume is intended to pave the
way for such an enterprise by filling in some of the last missing
pieces of the puzzle of the Mudéjares themselves.

Prefatory note on currency and metric values

The basic unit of currency in Aragon was the _sueldo_ of Jaca.
During the period of this study seven of these made up one _morabe-_
tín (or _maravedí_).[1] The Aragonese _florin_ circulated in all three
kingdoms at about eleven _sueldos,_ though it was occasionally worth
up to 12 _sueldos_ and two _diners_ (hereafter written 12s 2d).[2] The
diner (or _dener_) was apparently worth about one-tenth of a _sueldo_
during the mid-fourteenth century, at least in Valencia.[3] Twenty
sueldos made up an Aragonese pound (herein designated £).[4]

In Catalonia the official unit was the _sueldo_ _real_ of Barcelona,
but _sueldos_ of Jaca and _reals_ of Barcelona are used interchangeably
in most documentation. Piles Ros estimated the difference between
them at less than one _sueldo_ in the fifteenth century, evaluating a
florin as eleven _sueldos_ _reales_ and ten _sueldos_ _jaccenses._[5]

---

1.   The _Usatges_ of Barcelona describe the _morabetín_ as being worth
four and one-half _mancus_ (about 225s) at the time of their drafting.
In the late thirteenth century it may have been equal to as much as
10s 6d in some areas: see _Códigos de las Costumbres escritas de Tor-_
tosa, ed. Ramón Foguet and José Foguet Marsal (Tortosa, 1912), p.12,
note 3.   For fourteenth-century values, which were fairly consistently
around 7s, see RP 2412:23, but cf. RP 992:39.   For the fifteenth century, see E.J. Hamilton, _Money, Prices and Wages in Valencia, Aragon,_
and Navarra (1351-1500) (Cambridge, Mass., 1936), p.84.

2.   Hamilton, _Money,_ p.15; cf. C 1570:122 (Aug.12, 1361), C 1076:112
(Apr.5, 1365).   In the last-mentioned document the king consciously
sets the value.   See also RP 1710:21.

3.   C 1569:29 (Nov.10, 1359).

4.   RP 993:45, C 1188:107 (July 26, 1363).

5.   Leopoldo Piles Ros, "Situación económica de las aljamas aragonesas a comienzos del siglo xv," _Sefarad,_ X (1950), p.83.

Valencian currency was based on the _sueldo real_ of Valencia.
Efforts to determine the relationship between the Aragonese and
Valencian _sueldos_ have so far been inconclusive; they are used
interchangeably in some documents and carefully distinguished in
others. My own opinion is that the Valencian _sueldo real_ was closely
allied to the _real_ of Barcelona in value, but there is insufficient
evidence to establish this certainly.

The economic value of these units is more difficult to express.
A fine horse was worth about 700s in the mid-fourteenth century;
a Muslim slave brought about 650s on the open market; post-plague
legislation set salaries for skilled craftsmen at a maximum of 70s
per annum, for infantrymen at 30s,[6] but actual salaries exceeded
these figures considerably. The most powerful civil servants under
the Crown, the general bailiffs of each kingdom, received annual
salaries of 2,000s. In 1357 six pounds of crude silk sold for 24s
6d.[7]

The _cafiç_ (or _cahiz_) was the basic dry metrical unit. Estimates of its modern equivalent range from 179.52 liters to well over
660 liters.[8] A _barchilla_ or _barcella_ was approximately 16.75 liters;

---

6. Gunnar Tilander, "Fueros aragoneses desconocidos promulgados a
consecuencia de la gran peste de 1348," _Revista de filología española_,
XXIII (1935), p.24.

7. C 693:46 (October 23, 1357). Three _sueldos_ would still buy a
pair of hens in the fifteenth century: Macho y Ortega, "Condición,"
p.243.

8. See note by Ferrán Soldevila in _Les Quatre Grans Cròniques_, p.
198, number 6. Cf. Hamilton, _Money_, pp.48, 99.

a _fanega_ about 33.5 liters; an _almud_ about 4 liters; a _robo_ was one-fourth the current value of the _cafiç_.[9]

---

9. Hamilton, _Money_, p.48. The accuracy of weights was guaranteed by the Crown through the official known as the _almotacén_ (Leopoldo Piles Ros, _Estudio documental sobre el Bayle General de Valencia_ [Valencia, 1970], p.86); this may have applied to measures of volume as well, but I have seen no direct evidence of this.

Chapter I

The Mudéjar Population: Its Constituents and Rulers

> Nonetheless, the persons of Muslims--male and female--in
> regard to any of the things so far mentioned, may not be held
> by any lord or any person except with the consent of the king
> or his bailiffs, because it is certain that all Muslims, wher-
> ever they reside, belong to the king, except for slaves and
> those whom the lord may bring to dwell on his lands from areas
> which are not under the jurisdiction of the Crown, in which
> case such Muslims and their descendants should by law belong
> to the lord and his family. Fueros of Aragón: VII.277.

Although for the sake of convenience Mudéjares are frequently
spoken of as being either the king's Muslims, or a noble's Muslims,
or subject to ecclesiastical jurisdiction, these designations do
not correspond to any clear distinction in the reality of fourteenth-
century life. All Muslims were in a sense royal Muslims: the Crown
of Aragon claimed ultimate jurisdiction over every Muslim living
in lands under its rule, and described them as "our royal treasure,"
"subject to our whim," "servants of our household."[1] There was, in
fact, a constant tension between lords and ecclesiastics who exer-
cized immediate, local control over large segments of the Mudéjar
population and a monarchy which saw itself as the protector and
lord of all Muslims living in its domains.

Since it was the Crown which had contracted with falling Muslim
governments for surrender and co-existence, there were substantial
grounds for its claims to ultimate authority over all Mudéjares.
Individual monarchs, however, displayed a general tendency to ali-
enate these rights by granting away financial or judicial preroga-

---

1. "...thesauri regii speciales..." C 913:33 (Sept.16, 1366);
"...son nuestro tresoro e estan a nuestro voler..." C 1210:83 (Apr.
24, 1365); "...judei et sarraceni servi sunt camere nostre..." C
699:161 (Feb.11, 1360). Cf. for later in the century C 1239:73
(July 21, 1376): "...fur d'Arago diu generalment que los corsos
de los moros son nostres propris...."

tives over aljamas and individuals either as rewards, bribes, or
payment of debts, and eventually a large segment of the Muslim population had passed out of direct royal control into the hands of
nobles and churchmen.

Precisely what authority was delegated and what authority was
inalienably royal remained a perplexing question throughout the
fourteenth and fifteenth centuries, and was further aggravated
by the importation of Muslims from areas still under Muslim control,
who thus had no clear relation to the Aragonese monarchy. A wel-
ter of conflicting claims and jurisdictions resulted, and there was
no static reality at any moment which can be accurately described.
Instead, there was a variegated pattern of constantly shifting
authority and jurisdiction, in which the figure of the Crown assumed
more or less importance as royal power waxed or waned, but which
was ultimately resolved by the development of absolute monarchical
power. The consolidation (or re-consolidation) of royal control
over Mudéjares can be seen most clearly during the reign of Peter
the Ceremonious, and particularly during the disruptive era of the
war with Castile when the Crown seized upon the opportunity to
extend war-time powers, taxations, and judicial arrangements and
make them permanent, and when Mudéjar aljamas which were conquered
by or defected to the King of Castile came back into Aragon as
vassals of the king, regardless of whose vassals they had been previously (see p. 166).

A more detailed discussion of the effects of the war with
Castile and the resulting changes in Mudéjar lifestyles comprises

part of the final chapter of this study. What is at issue here
is the general meaning of a Muslim's being subject to the king
as opposed to nobles or churchmen. Given that the reality was
fluid, certain general observations can nevertheless be offered.
All Muslims, no matter how effective local rule or control might
be, had recourse to royal officials for notarial services and for
final appeal in criminal cases.[2] Most, if not all, taxes were
collected from all Mudéjares, regardless of their relation to a
lord other than the king. On the other hand, there was separate
legislation for "royal" Muslims, i.e., those living under no authority except that of the king: an example of such legislation in
regard to minor criminal penalties is produced in the Appendix of
Documents at C 898:222, where the king prescribes in minute detail
what fines and punishments are to be exacted for various offenses
committed by Muslims in his aljama at Ricla. Where the king did
not enjoy sole jurisdiction, he might still set or prescribe the
penalties, but did not usually receive the entire fine collected,
so that, for instance, Mudéjares under the jurisdiction of the monastery of Roda paid part of any fines to the monastery, even though
subject ultimately to royal justice.[3]

Muslims subject to the king received much lighter fines for
violating dress codes (a privilege which nobles could sometimes
purchase for their Muslims), but were also subject to taxes, such

---

2. C 698:50 (Apr.7, 1362). Cf. C 1073:95 (July 8, 1361) and C 1068:
56 (Dec.4, 1355).

3. C 687:84 (July 12, 1356).

as the besant, which other Muslims did not regularly pay, so it
is questionable whether they were significantly better off economically.[4] They were generally free to transfer to areas subject to
clerics or nobles,[5] but no gross trends in such mobility are discernible during the fourteenth century, except a slight shift away from
lands held by clerics or orders towards those of the king.   There
was, however, no theoretical fluidity of property: Mudéjares who
changed lords lost all real property and all but personal movable
goods.   When the king sold property to which his Muslims were bound,
they were transferred with the property.[6]   The property of Muslims
subject to the king who died could not be inherited by Muslims living under noble or ecclesiastical jurisdiction, nor could royal Mudéjares inherit from the latter.[7]

Obviously, the looseness of the system would create problems
in adjudicating disputes about such matters as inheritance; the
complexities involved were enormous.   No one seems to have been
certain, for instance, whether the Muslim aljama of Algar (in Valencia) was royally or ecclesiastically ruled, neither the Muslims,
who claimed to be but could not prove that they were royal, nor the
monastery of Arguinis, which asserted but could not establish con-

---

4. On the besant, see C 1209:44 (1365); on dress codes, see Chapter
VII, pp.330ss.

5. Or vice versa, subject to general limitations on mobility, for
which see Chapter VI, pp.286ss.

6. C 694:127 (May 8, 1358).

7. See Chapter VI, pp.273ss.

clusive lordship, nor the king, who finally foisted the whole
matter off on subordinate officials.[8] The issue was further complicated by three subsidiary points of confusion: various towns
legislated on the matter independently of the king and sometimes
in conflict with him;[9] some towns had two or more separate aljamas;[10] some Muslims appear to have fallen under no jurisdiction.[11]
From 1359 on, moreover, the position of royal aljamas became even
more confused due to the transfer of numerous aljamas to the queen's
household, which is discussed at some length under Chapter VI.
This very important fact has been overlooked by many historians,
especially in regard to the fifteenth century.[12] It probably made
relatively little difference to the Mudéjares themselves, since
they were still "royal," but it made bookkeeping enormously more
intricate for the Crown, and left records for the historian which

---

8. C 713:182 (Mar.6, 1363).

9. E.g., from the Fuero of Calatayud (1131): "Et vicino de Calataiub qui poterit tenere homines in suo solare, christianos aut
mauros, aut iudeos, ad illo respondeant, et non ad nullo alio sen-
iore" J.M. Ramos y Loscertales, "Documentos para la historia del
derecho español: Fuero concedido a Calatayud por Alfonso I de Aragón en 1131," AHDE, I (1924), p.410. Cf. the early fourteenth-
century edict of Valls prohibiting change of jurisdiction, in Francesch Carreras y Candi, "Ordinacions urbanes de bon govern a Catalunya," BRABL, XII (1926), p.370.

10. E.g., Cuarte and Cuadrete, which each had two (Macho y Ortega, "Condición," p.157).

11. They were sometimes called "franchi," although this had other
connotations as well: see C 683:114 (Feb.24, 1356).

12. Macho y Ortega, for example, completely ignores it in his
treatment of fifteenth-century royal aljamas, although he publishes
in two of his studies documents which clearly allude to the transfer ("Condición," p.166, n.1, and "Documentos," pp.148, 156).

are often confusing and misleading.[13]

The primary distinction between noble and royal Muslims was, in the long run, the fact that the former owed their feudal[14] service--i.e., specified term of seigneurial labor, some military duties, and certain agricultural taxes--to the lord rather than the king. Even in these matters the lord's jurisdiction was not supreme: while there is no doubt that he could demand some military service of Muslim dependents,[15] the right of Muslims to bear arms was regulated by the Crown, and the king could demand service from any Mudéjar in the country when he wished. The right to collect major

---

13. This fact might explain, for instance, the otherwise bewildering sequence of events described in Macho y Ortega, "Condición," pp. 166-8. When the same author lists, moreover, Zaragoza, Huesca, Teruel, Daroca, Calatayud, Borja, Belchite, and Tarazona as the only aljamas remaining to the king in the fifteenth century, one wonders whether he is excluding from the royal patrimony Sagunto, Alcira, Morella, Montblanc, Tarrega, Villagrassa, Torella, Burriana, etc., simply because they do not appear in records for the king's household, although they might be listed for the queen.

14. I am conscious of the looseness with which the words "feudal," "serf," "vassal," etc., are used in this chapter, and that some historians may find this objectionable. One of the aims of this study, in fact, is to determine the extent to which such terms can be applied to Muslims. Refraining from using the words themselves until a rigid definition of them in context could be devised might well defer discussion of the place of Mudéjares in feudal society indefinitely, and there is urgent need for some guidelines in the area, however general they may have to be at first. It is well to bear in mind, moreover, that--especially in Spain--fourteenth-century feudalism was not a rigid concept, but a flexible reality, and one simply cannot find enough spaces in modern paradigms to accommodate neatly every class of fourteenth-century person. In general, the term "serf" as used in regard to Mudéjares should be understood by the reader as connoting what it would in relation to a medieval Christian. This is discussed in greater detail, below.

15. C 1402:147 (Feb.1, 1359). Cf. p.181.

taxes, such as the peyta, was enjoyed by the lord of an aljama
only when specifically granted him by the monarchy,[16] and all
efforts by lords--even the powerful counts of Trastámara[17]--to
obtain criminal jurisdiction over their Muslim vassals failed
utterly. Even in matters where all agreed that the lord enjoyed
theorètical authority, such as the regulation of mobility of Muslim vassals, the actual exercise of such authority was dependent on
the king's will, since he could not only ignore such privileges
by virtue of superior might, but was also the final arbiter of
any disagreement about them.

The king could also simply confiscate any Mudéjares he wished
to have, by right of ultimate judicial authority. The entire
Muslim populace of many areas of the kingdoms came under direct
royal control when the King of Castile occupied and then abandoned such areas: the King of Aragon was then able to grant them
back as a sort of largesse to those (previous) owners who had been
faithful to him during the war.

> Although both for the castle of Artana and for your own
> persons you have submitted to us and sworn fealty and homage to
> our noble and beloved counsellor and majordomo, the knight En
> Gilabert de Cencelles [=Scintilles], acting in our stead, ac-
> knowledging that you are our men and our own vassals,...never-
> theless, since in the Corts we recently convoked among the Val-
> encians we agreed to return to them those castles and places
> which were seized by the King of Castile and since among others
> we have ordered returned to our noble and beloved knight, En Ro-
> drigo Diaç, the said castle and valley of Artana, we therefore
> absolve you of all homage and duties of fealty which you have
> sworn to us.... We direct and command you that henceforth you
> have as lord the said En Rodrigo Diaç, and that you do homage
> to him and [render to him] such other things as you were liable

---

16. See, for instance, C 1205:68 (Apr.2, 1365); cf. Chapter V.
17. C 983:188 (Feb.20, 1359).

for before the castle was occupied by the King of Castile.[18]

Mudéjares as individuals or in communities came under ecclesiastical authority in various ways. Many clerics in the Middle Ages
were, of course, feudal lords in their own right, and as such might
have Muslim serfs as well as Christian ones. Military orders were
often granted Mudéjar communities in areas which they conquered or
defended. Orders of all types obtained Muslim slaves through confiscation for violation of laws or dress codes, either directly in
their own jurisdiction (though this was rare and of dubious legality),[19]
or indirectly through royal concession.[20] Orders also frequently
bought slaves.[21] The most common method of aquiring Mudéjares as
serfs, vassals, or slaves was undoubtedly through bequest of the
faithful, although there seems to have been a marked tendency on the
part of the Aragonese faithful to bequeath only a portion of Mudé-

---

18. C 986:43 (Sept.10, 1365), addressed to the Muslims of Artana;
text in Appendix. It was not at all unusual for even minor knights
to have Muslim vassals: Francèsch Desplugues, described merely as
miles, was lord of Muslims in Ondara, Verger, Real, Beniharb, Eig (=
Ejea), Miraflor, Pamies, and Vinyals (C 720:145 [Sept.25, 1365]).
For other cases of property being returned to its pre-war owner, see
C 720:89 (Eslida, Ahin, Veyó), C 1204:88 (Alfara), and C 1206:117
(Xinguer), all from 1365. For noble vs. royal aljamas and Mudéjar
individuals in the fifteenth century, see Macho y Ortega, "Documentos,"
p.153, and "Condición," pp.191-3, 228. Macho y Ortega was somewhat
confused by the lack of concrete distinctions between the types of
Muslims, but concluded that royal power became increasingly extensive
in the fifteenth century.

19. In C 1149:23 (Nov.12, 1356) the king upholds this right, but
this cannot have been typical.

20. E.g., C 983:24 (Dec.20, 1358), C 1070:23 (under Chapter VII,
p.348, and note 79), and C 1209:114 (May 21, 1365).

21. E.g., C 720:45 (Sept.4, 1365).

jares or their holdings rather than their whole interest; so that,
for example, one finds the Fratres Minores with one-third interest
in Muslim vineyards, the monastery of St Peter being the lord of a
portion of the Muslim population of Calatayud, the queen and the
Sorores Minores sharing equally the rights over the Mudéjares of
Bartaxell and Xirillent, and the monastery of San Cugat del Valles
owning one-half of a Muslim whose other half was unclaimed (res vac-
cans).[22] It is probably accurate, in fact, to say that the majority
of cases of ecclesiastical jurisdiction over Muslims overlapped with
some other type of authority and that in relatively few cases--such
as the Hospitallers in Monzón, Ripoll, and Puig[23]--did they have
sole authority.[24] Muslims living under the authority of a secular
bishop appear to have come under the delegated authority of local
priests by virtue of this arrangement, although this was occasionally
disputed.[25]

As with the Muslims subject to nobles, there were no hard and
fast rules about fiscal obligations of those subject to clerics.
Most clerical holders of Mudéjares received some income from the Mus-

---

22. C 684:196 (Apr.2, 1356); C 700:144 (Jan.30, 1360); C 1567:124
(Sept.10, 1359); C 688:64 (Sept.16, 1356): the "unclaimed" half in
this case was granted to a favorite of the Crown, who was then obliged
to buy the monastery's half.

23. C 695:82 (Apr.1, 1359).

24. Cases of overlapping authority: C 982:33 (Mar.21, 1357); C 983:
5 (Dec.3, 1358); C 1073:95 (July 8, 1361); C 1183:124 (Nov.21, 1362);
C 1209:25 (Mar.4, 1365); C 1381:34 (June 22, 1357).

25. C 713:182 (Mar.6, 1363) and C 1209:108 (May 13, 1365).

lims, but there was enormous variation.[26] Mudéjares belonging to the Hospitallers, for example, were exempt from war taxes, while those belonging to the Order of Calatrava were not.[27]

Macho y Ortega considered that Mudéjares "almost always preferred clerical lords,"[28] and it is true that some clerics, such as the Archbishop of Zaragoza, were traditionally patrons and protectors of Muslims in general, as well as those under their immediate control,[29] but it is equally common to find prelates who made it a habit to harass and oppress Mudéjares: the Bishop of Tortosa, who had Muslim dependents as far away as Eslida,[30] tried to force Muslims to pay tithes in defiance of established practice to the contrary, was involved in the illegal enslavement of more than thirty Muslims whom he had personally pardoned, and tortured and extorted money from Mudéjar officials.[31] The Bishop of Valencia was best

---

26. The monastery of St Peter in Terrer, for instance, received the lezda and pedagium of the Muslims (C 862:24 [Sept.5, 1337]); that of Sta Gratia received annually 800s from taxes on the Múdéjares of Carçre (C 1068:139 [June 6, 1356]). Cf. RP 990:13 (1357), RP 992:15 (1359), and succeeding entries for Catalan equivalents.

27. Hospitallers: C 695:82 (Apr.1, 1359); Calatrava: C 1401:60 (Apr. 10, 1355).

28. "Condición," p.180: "...los moros preferían casi siempre a los investidos del sacerdocio...."

29. C 900:42 (Mar.7, 1358), C 1205:68 (Apr.2, 1365). The Archbishop of Zaragoza was still seen as a Mudéjar patron in the fifteenth century: see Macho y Ortega, "Condición," p.180. The Hospitallers of Jabut interceded for Muslims over whom they had no jurisdiction in 1361: see C 705:68 in the Appendix; it was an official of an Order who saw to the protecting of the rights of Faraig de Belvis against local Christians in Nabal (C 1206:44 [Aug.20, 1365]).

30. C 1210:46 (July 6, 1365).

31. C 711:161 (Feb.27, 1363), C 986:13 (Aug.23, 1365), C 1208:78 (Sept.6, 1365).

known to the Muslim population there by his jail, in which very
large numbers of Muslims were kept awaiting trial or sale as slaves.[32]
The convent of St Clare, also in Valencia, invoked royal authority
to prevent the Muslims from building a new meat market, since the
nuns owned the sole rights over the existing one.[33]

There seems, in fact, to have been a tendency for Mudéjares
to flee ecclesiastical jurisdiction when possible: the Muslim vassals of the Abbot of Valldigna, including the officials of the aljama, defected en masse to surrounding nobles in 1365, and repeated
letters by the king threatening harsher and harsher penalties
against the Muslims and those who harbored them failed to get them
back.[34] This may have been due to the fact that while the monarchy
was anxious to intervene against and override nobles who abused their
Mudéjar dependents, it displayed considerable reluctance to meddle
in the affairs of the Church and its Muslim vassals and serfs; the
queen flatly refused, for instance, to force the Bishop of Valencia
to act against the rector of the church at Seta, who was abusing the
Muslim serfs of the parish.[35]

Although the term exaricus is generally employed in Spanish
documents to designate Muslims in land-holding servitude, it

---

32. C 724:157 (Jan.20, 1365), C 986:121 (Oct.17, 1365), and C 720:
77, in the Appendix.

33. C 1189:212 (July 13, 1363), cf. C 603:5 (Oct.27, 1355).

34. This included publishing a list of the names of the Muslims,
offering them for sale, and threatening a penalty of 7,000s for
harboring them: see C 986:93 (Oct.3, 1365 [repeat of order of July
13, 1364]), and C 1207:145 (same date).

35. C 1209:108 (May 13, 1365); cf. C 704:51 (July 7, 1360).

should not be understood as indicating a distinction in status
between Mudéjar serfs and Christian ones.[36] For the most part the
exarici occupied positions of traditional servitude: they passed
with the land when it was alienated or sold, their servitude was
hereditary, and they were mentioned in documents in the same terms
as Christian serfs. The distinction drawn by Burns and others
between free farmers as exarici and those in servitude is not apparent in the documents of the fourteenth century, when the (very
few) Muslims not in some form of servitude were ambiguously called
"franchi."[37]

As Burns points out, during the thirteenth century free Muslim
farmers lived under conditions generally similar to those they had
known under the weak and shifting Muslim rule of the previous century, and the maintenance of a prosperous class of free farmers
was still possible. The Aragonese monarchy, however, was markedly
more stable and its power more consolidated and better exercised
than that of the crumbling Almohad dynasty which had preceded it
in Valencia, and it was not long before the untidy remnants of the
"free" Mudéjar population were swept aside into one category or

---

36. The etymology of the word is uncertain, though it probably de-
rives from the Arabic sharika, "to share." On the meaning of the
term in Catalan law, see Costums of Tortosa, IV.26.33. For a more
general discussion, see Burns, Islam, pp.102-4.

37. See above, note 11, for "franchi." On the general status of
exarici see the long dispute (beginning in 1250) chronicled in C
905:219 and C 905:231 (both of 1361) concerning the hereditary status of a "free" Muslim and his family. On the equality of Christian and Muslim serfs, see, for example, C 912:142 (Apr.20, 1366).
In the fifteenth century the term exaricus was applied to Christians,
too: see Macho y Ortega, "Condición," p.150, note.

another of feudal servitude. Lords, kings, and clergy collaborated in this effort, and the hapless Muslims were in no position to resist. Intricate codes of dress and behavior were established which they might violate, thereby becoming slaves or incurring ruinous fines. The fines themselves could lead to loss of freedom, since a Mudéjar who could not pay might either be confiscated by the Crown or be forced to put himself into the service of a lord to gain protection from creditors. The Crown and local nobles, moreover, made servitude as attractive as possible by offering free land, remissions of taxes and rents, and protection from creditors or legal penalties to those who would inhabit their lands. Even other Muslims conspired against Mudéjar liberty, as the insolvent aljamas, pressed by the king to meet steadily increasing tax payments, reached further and further into the hinterlands to establish their tax base and used royal power to constrain "free" Muslims to contribute with the aljama.

By the mid-fourteenth century, a large class of free farmers was a fond memory. In the cities, Mudéjares were gathered into morerías, where they could be easily taxed and regulated by local and royal officials. The only Mudéjares who enjoyed anything like broad personal liberty were foreign mercenaries and the wealthy élite in the king's service. The class of Muslim military aristocracy described by Burns for the thirteenth century had vanished without a trace. Only a prosperous commercial class survived in the cities, and, at the very top of the Mudéjar social scale, the civil service.

Although it is possible to detect the presence of an élite

stratum of Mudéjar civil servants in the king's employ, only a few

personalities emerge with clarity: Abraham Abenxoa, meneschal of

Queen Eleanor, envoy to Granada, and qadi of Játiva, Elche, Crevillen-

te, Seta, Granadell, Bartaxell, and Xirillent; his cousin, also

Abraham Abenxoa, meneschal of the queen's son, Alfonse; Ali Abenco-

mixa, ambassador to Morocco and Granada; Çaat Alcafaç, purveyor

to the Crown and qadi of the kingdom's largest aljama; the Ballis-

tarius family, masters of the work on the royal residence in Zara-

goza.[38]

Undoubtedly the most powerful Mudéjares under the Crown of Ara-

gon were the Belvis family. Faraig de Belvis[39] had been intimately

---

38. Abraham (or Abrafim) Abenxoa (†1363) was allowed by the king
to have two wives: one in Onda and one in Valencia. A law in Valencia prohibited anyone not residing in the city from inheriting the
property of deceased Muslims, but when Abenxoa died the Crown came
to an agreement with the wife in Onda over a fair share of the estate
for her and her child. This unusual concession is clear demonstration of the high regard the king held for his Mudéjar employees (RP
1719:25 [1363]). For other material on Abenxoa the qadi, see C 905:
177 (May 31, 1361), C 966:139 (Nov.11, 1363), C 1208:85 (Sept.12,
1365), C 1569:82 (Feb.16, 1363), and under Chapter II, pp.81ss.
For his cousin, see C 1208:85, ut supra. For Abencomixa, see C 1211:
41 (Apr.4, 1365) and C 1404:53 (Feb.17, 1365). For the Ballistarii,
see C 1205:69 (Apr.7, 1365), and below, Chapter V, pp.214-216.
Alcafaç's career suffered as a result of charges brought against him
by other royal favorites (C 700:60 [Nov.15, 1359], and below), but
he retained some power in Valencia: see RP 1708 and 1709, passim.

39. Faraig was the surname of a prominent Mudéjar family in Borja
(C 692:205 [Sept.16, 1357]), where F. de Belvis held his first official post. I infer from this that he came from Borja, but there is
no further evidence. The name Belvis belonged to Mudéjar families
south of Valencia, but there is no certain connection with the Aragonese family, and numerous Christians also bore the name, including the lieutenant-procurator of the southernmost Valencian province
in 1284 (Roca Traver, "Un Siglo," p.84, n.16), and at least one other
member of the royal household of Peter himself (González Hurtebise,
Libros, p.24 and passim). It was such a common Christian name, in

associated with Peter the Ceremonious since well before the accession
of the latter to the throne of Aragon.[40]   His brother, Jahia de Belvis, was a wealthy and prominent Mudéjar in Castile,[41]   and his son
Ovechar was a member of the household of Peter's eldest son, John.[42]
Faraig himself was married to Fatima Fuster, the daughter of one of
the wealthiest merchants in Valencia and widow of another prominent
Muslim, Ali Alasrach, a relative of the Abenxoas mentioned previously.[43]

Faraig was extremely wealthy in his own right. He frequently
lent the Crown large sums of cash, for which he received various
privileges or land-grants: a female Muslim slave in 1364,   10,000s
worth of property in 1365.[44] He also maintained at his own expense

---

fact, that Verlinden failed to recognize it as belonging to a Mudéjar in a document relating to Faraig himself: see below, p.52. The
fact that Faraig's brother lived in northern Castile also militates
to some extent against linking the family with the Valencian Belvis.

40. C 575:149 (June 1, 1332).

41. C 685:44, in Appendix.

42. C 1183:124 (Nov.21, 1362).

43. For Faraig's marriage to Fatima, see C 1204:86 (Apr.24, 1365);
for her relation to Alasrach, C 693:100 (Jan.22, 1358) (two documents);
for her relation (through her first husband) to the Abenxoas, see C
1204:86, ut supra, C 1206:84 (Sept.12, 1365), C 1208:85 (Sept.12,
1365). It was a second marriage for Faraig as well: his first wife
was Mahometi d'Alazera. Since there is no clear indication that Mahometi died between the last mention of her (C 904:232 [Nov.13, 1360])
and the first mention of Fatima (1365), it is conceivable that Faraig
had more than one wife at a time; Jews were frequently allowed to
take more than one wife, as was a Mudéjar relative of Faraig himself:
note 38, above.

44. The slave (one of several the Crown gave the Belvis) is mentioned in C 1203:178 (Aug.20, 1364) as being worth 300s. The property, granted in C 1210:85 (Apr.25, 1365), was seized from Muslim trai-
tors in Daroca. Faraig rented it out, since he travelled with the
Court, and it was twice seized by local Christians (C 1206:44 [Aug.
20, 1365], C 723:158 [Dec.20, 1365]), who ejected the Muslim renter.

a number of horses in the royal cavalry; since he was ultimately
reimbursed for this outlay (nearly 1,000s in 1365 alone) by the
Crown, it must have been a type of indirect loan rather than a service.[45] He apparently displayed his wealth in his clothing: five
Valencian Christians went to an inordinate amount of trouble (drill-
ing a hole through one building to another) to steal his wardrobe
from an inn where he was staying in Monzón.[46] The source of his
wealth is not apparent; undoubtedly he earned considerable money
in fees from his various judicial posts--1,050s from one case in
Daroca[47]--and the king occasionally granted him some income from
the royal revenues. From 1336 on he received 300s annually from
the cena of Borja, which was to belong to his son Ovechar after
his death, and which was still collected when Borja changed lords
in 1366.[48] This is a rather modest income, however; the bulk of
the Belvis fortune must have been inherited or derived from rents
and salaries. Although Faraig's father-in-law, Maymo Fuster, was
a merchant, there is no indication of any member of Faraig's own
family engaging in commerce.

The Belvis were specifically exempted from codes regulating
Muslim appearance, and from all feudal duties of hospitality, even
to the royal family.[49] Royal officials and even officials of

---

45. C 1207:4 (May 30, 1365), RP 1710:47 (1365).
46. C 711:194 (Mar.4, 1363).
47. C 1183:118 (Nov.18, 1362).
48. C 1518:6 (June 30, 1366); cf. C 1168:129 (Jan.8, 1360).
49. C 981:22 (Feb.12, 1355); C 904:232 (Nov.13, 1360). ·

religious orders were instructed by King Peter to favor the affairs of the Belvis family "so that they may praise you and your
kindness [to them], since in this you will give us pleasure and
service, and since the contrary would displease us greatly."[50]
The king, moreover, personally oversaw the well-being of Faraig
and his family. When a procurator mismanaged Faraig's Borja property, the king personally appointed a prominent Mudéjar judge from
Zaragoza to handle the case;[51] when Faraig was unable, as qadi,
to bring charges against the present lieutenant-qadi and former
qadi of Valencia regarding property belonging to his wife Fatima,
the king placed Çaat Alcafaç in charge of the case and granted him
the full vices of the Crown.[52] During the war with Castile, the
Crown issued a safe-conduct for the Castilian fiancée of Ovechar
de Belvis and her party, and when the bride-to-be hesitated before
the final plans were made, actually forbade her to marry anyone else.[53]
When she defied him, he had her sequestered and ordered the qadi of
Brea to decide what should be done about the promised dowry, but
thought better of this and decided to rule on the case himself,
taking the qadi as counsel.

---

50. "...de guisa que ellos se puedan loar de vos et de vuestras
favores, sabiendo que en esto nos faredes plazer e servitio, e el
contrario nos desplazeria muyto..." C 1183:124 (Nov.21, 1362). Note
that in this document, as in the vast majority of those dealing with
Faraig and his family, there is no mention whatever of their being
Muslims.

51. C 692:182 (Aug.18, 1357). This judge is the only Mudéjar
addressed in any royal letter as "vos."

52. C 1204:86, 1206:84, 1208:85, as above, note 43.

53. C 901:288 (Feb.16, 1358), C 700:188 (Mar.6, 1360).

54. C 700:214 (Apr.8, 1360), C 699:207 (Apr.11, 1360).

Faraig united in his person an astounding number of official positions in the most important aljamas of Aragon and Valencia. In Borja he was the faqi (from 1339), royal notary, and çabiçala (=imām, or prayer leader).[55] In Huesca he occupied the positions of qadi, amin, royal notary, and cavalquinus, the latter three for life.[56] He was the qadi of Játiva and Valencia--the first and second largest aljamas of the kingdom--for life, and the royal notary of Játiva, as well.[57] He held all of these offices in absentia, appointing substitutes to do the actual business. While this was not unusual in itself, it did cause problems in some areas, such as Valencia, where the king had to intervene almost constantly to protect Faraig's interest against encroachment by his substitutes and others.[58] There is, moreover, evidence that Faraig sometimes obtained these positions through somewhat dubious means. In 1365 Faraig bluntly asked the king for the offices of qadi and notary of Játiva, which the monarch had only recently granted another Mudéjar notable, Çaat Alcafaç.[59] Casting about for some pretext to eject Alcafaç, the king decreed that if Alcafaç was not actually resident in Játiva he would grant the offices to Faraig on grounds of being "more competent." Alcafaç, in fact, lived in Valencia, so Faraig

---

55. C 965:233 (May 8, 1354), C 966:104 (Aug.20, 1357). See pp.510-11.

56. C 968:37 (Nov.28, 1360), C 715:56 (Oct.15, 1363).

57. C 966:138 (Dec.28, 1363).

58. C 685:61 (Oct.16, 1355), C 1183:119 (Nov.18, 1362), C 711:161 (Feb.27, 1363).

59. This sequence of events is recorded in C 1209:106 (May 11, 1365).

was granted the office a month later. Faraig--who naturally
exercised the office in absentia himself--then appointed Alcafaç
as his deputy. It is difficult to understand how this maneuver
was justified to the Muslim population of Játiva, which was already upset about having incompetent or absent qadis appointed
for it.[60]

Faraig de Belvis was also the "alcaydus sarracenorum totius
regni Aragonie," i.e., qadi of all the Muslims of Aragon.[61] The
exact prerogatives of this position are never specified, but it
seems likely that it was principally the ultimate appeals court
for Aragonese Mudéjares. There is evidence of this in the fact
that Faraig regularly heard cases in localities where he occupied
no official judicial position, such as Lérida and Borja, and that
cases could be removed from his jurisdiction only by the king
himself, and usually only at Faraig's own request.[62] Macho y Ortega
describes such a position in fifteenth-century Aragon as well, noting that the post was still associated with the Belvis family. He
termed the office the "tribunal del alcadi general de los reinos
de Aragón y Valencia y principado de Cataluña."[63] In Valencia Far-

---

60. See Chapter II, pp.85ss.

61. C 1068:56 (Dec.4, 1355).

62. E.g., C 699:131 (June 13, 1360), C 703:43 (Jan.13, 1360).
For other examples, consult the table under Chapter III, p.149.

63. "Condición," p.178. Macho y Ortega describes the Belvis family
as being from Zaragoza, but does not support this, and I am inclined
to believe he is mistaken: there is as much reason to believe the
family lived in Valencia in the fifteenth century as in Zaragoza.

aig exercised this authority under the simple designation <u>alcadius</u>

<u>regis</u>,[64] as did his fifteenth-century descendants, who inherited

the life-time position along with the name.[65]

At the opposite end of the social scale of Muslims living

under the Crown of Aragon in the fourteenth century was the slave.

Because excellent studies of slavery in general, and of Aragonese

Mudéjar slavery in particular, already exist, no attempt will be

made here to examine the question in great detail.[66] Certain

aspects of the enslavement of Moors during the particular years

covered by this study, however, deserve mention, and one or two

findings which conflict with those of earlier scholars cannot be

---

64. C 685:61 (Oct.16, 1355).

65. E.g., Ali de Belvis: Piles Ros, <u>Estudio,</u> p.157, #150 (1424); p.238, #501 (1432); p.241, #516 (1433).

66. In particular, the reader is referred to Charles Verlinden, <u>L'Esclavage dans l'Europe médiévale</u> (Brugge, 1955), I, and José María Ramos y Loscertales, <u>El cautiverio en la Corona de Aragón durante los siglos xiii, xiv, y xv</u> (Zaragoza, 1915). The study by Ramos y Loscertales is, unfortunately, only concerned with prisoners of war, and is therefore of more limited value than it might have been had the author applied his considerable talents to considering servitude in general. It is nonetheless extremely useful, despite this limitation and a rather disproportionate reliance on the <u>Costums</u> of Tortosa. Verlinden's study, too, relies generally on laws rather than indications of actual practice, which undoubtedly accounts for some of the differences between his findings and my own. Verlinden was, of course, covering an enormously broader area-- both geographically and temporally--than the present enquiry, and could hardly be expected to consider the question with the same degree of detail. It is nevertheless a bit disappointing that his comments on the fourteenth century are so limited, and based entirely on judiciary and published documents. The fifteenth-century material is largely derived from primary sources, but these are predominantly from the Balearics, which were, by Verlinden's own admission, atypical in their extraordinary dependence on slaves. The most disappointing aspect of this indispensable study is the author's grouping of the fourteenth and fifteenth centuries together and treating them

passed over.

Slaves were extremely numerous in the lands under the Aragonese monarchy during the fourteenth century; so numerous, in fact, that the Crown felt constrained to limit their number during the latter half of the century, when individuals were known to hold as many as sixty male slaves in their households.[67] It is impossible to determine with accuracy the provenance of such large numbers of slaves. From Muslim times there had been a thriving slave trade throughout eastern Spain, and this trade simply changed hands when Christians reconquered coastal cities. In 1356 all foreign Muslims except subjects of the King of Granada were considered de bona guerra, i.e., fair game for slave traders.[68] In 1360 the subjects of the King of Tunisia were put "off limits" by virtue of a treaty signed by the Aragonese Crown with that king, but other Muslims remained legally enslavable.[69]

Verlinden believed that "the enslavement of free nationals within the realm was no longer encountered" in the fourteenth century,[70] but this was manifestly not the case. Any Muslim found by Christians who could not or would not identify his lord or owner was automati-

---

as a whole, skipping back and forth through two hundred years as if there were no important historical trends intervening.

67. Verlinden, L'Esclavage, p.434. Slaves were most numerous in Majorca and Catalonia.

68. C 1403:6 (undated, presumably 1356).

69. C 703:25 (May 28, 1360). Some recently sold slaves were even sent back to Tunisia in fulfillment of the terms of this treaty.

70. L'Esclavage, p.426.

cally enslaved by the Crown:

> ...a certain Saracen captive called Abdulla was seized by
> some pilgrims in our realm and detained for a long time in the
> village of Aqualet by the local bailiff as an unclaimed object
> and a lordless person. During this time, although a public
> announcement was made, no one came forward to claim any rights
> over him, as a consequence of which he belongs to us and to
> our Court as an unclaimed object or lordless person....[71]

Even a free Mudéjar who was not an "unclaimed object" could be

enslaved for violating laws or dress codes.[72] This sort of enslave-

ment was so regular that, as Verlinden himself notes,[73] it was

common practice to grant to a favorite "the next Saracen confiscated

to the Crown" for such-and-such a reason:

> ...we therefore direct and command you to grant and release
> to the said Stephen one of the first female Saracens to be con-
> fiscated by you for our Court in the manner mentioned before,
> with which Saracen he may do as he wishes....[74]

---

71. "Attendentes quidam [sic] sarracenum captiuum vocatum Abdaylla
in dominio nostro per quosdam peregrinos captum fuisse, et in villa
Aqualate per baiulum eiusdem ville tamquam rem vaccantem [sic] et
sine domino per longum tempus detentum extitisse, infra quod licet
preconitzatum extiterit, nullus comparuit ius habere asserens in
eodem, et per consequens nobis et curie nostre tamquam rem vaccantem et sine domino ut prefertur pertinere..." C 899:68 (July 15, 1356).
Other Moors confiscated as res vaccantes are mentioned at C 688:64
(Sept.16, 1356), and C 1068:147 (July 12, 1356).

72. E.g., for violation of dress code: C 703:55 (1360) (cf. Chapter
VII) ; for failure to pay back a debt: C 901:260 (1358); for hiding
Muslims accused of some crime: C 1154:56 (1356); for rebellion: C
1205:91 (1365); for an unspecified crime: C 1569:26 (1359).

73. L'Esclavage, p.423, adduces two instances in the early 1330's;
cf. note 720.

74. "Ideo vobis dicimus et mandamus quatenus unam de primis sar-
racenabus per vos ut premittitur nostre curie confiscandis detis et
liberetis Stephano predicto, de qua suas proprias voluntates facere
valeat" C 1183:159 (Dec.1, 1362). Cf. Chapter VII, pp.346ss.

At least 59 Mudéjares can be shown to have been enslaved for no
stated reason between October of 1355 and October of 1365, in all
three kingdoms and by all classes of society.[75] While it is true
that in one instance the king fined a number of Christians very
heavily for illegally selling into slavery in Ibiza two free
Valencian Mudéjares, his attitude was far from clear-cut on the
issue, and there is some reason to believe that after the captors
and their collaborators in this case had paid fines in excess of
600s at least one of the enslaved Muslims was not released.[76]

The king did have a certain interest in the freeing of slaves,
since freedmen paid an annual tax of 5s in Catalonia, and a sort of
licensing fee called the dobla in Valencia (see below, pp.202-203),

---

75. By order of documentation: one Muslim by a noble in Valencia,
C 683:114 (Feb.24, 1356); one by peasants in Aragon, C 685:44 (Oct.
14, 1355); one by a noble in Valencia, C 703:241 (Dec.24, 1360);
ten by a noble in Valencia, C 708:37 (Oct.13, 1361); one by an official in Aragon, C 908:154 (Mar.23, 1363); thirty-odd by a noble
in Catalonia, C 986:13 (Aug.23, 1365); one by knights in Valencia,
C 1188:30 (Oct.3, 1363); two by unspecified Christians in Valencia,
C 1208:95 (Sept.18, 1365); two by mercenaries in Valencia, C 1208:
150 (Oct.14, 1365); seven by "townsmen" in Aragon, C 1537:66 (Dec.
7, 1363); cf. RP 1710:21 (1365).

76. The men who actually captured and sold them were fined 1,100s
jointly; the merchant who bought them was fined 660s; various collaborators were fined amounts of 110s and 220s; the man who transported
them to Ibiza paid 110s (RP 1710:21 [1365], cf. C 1208:95). Because
entries in the Real Patrimonio are not dated by month, and because
the corresponding entry in the Chancery register was sent long after
the event, it is impossible to be certain exactly when this incident
took place. In July of 1365, however, a Valencian Mudéjar woman was
given permission by the Crown to remarry because her husband, a slave
in Ibiza, was effectively "dead" (C 1207:124). Since the most likely
date for the enslavement of the two Muslims was the summer of 1365,
it seems possible that the woman's husband was one of the two, and
that he was thus allowed to be kept by the new owner. Ibizans had
been granted a special commission to enslave persons of any religion
who were at war with Aragon on a "no-questions-asked" basis: C 1413:
11 (Mar.10, 1349), published in López de Meneses, Documentos, p.55.

but Roca Traver's contention that all slave-related legislation reflects "the Crown's preoccupation with fomenting the personal liberty of his Mudéjar subjects" is unconvincing.[77] Not only the Crown's actions (as described above) but the economic facts as well argue indisputably against this. The prices for Muslim slaves rose steadily throughout the thirteenth and fourteenth centuries. For thirteenth-century prices, Verlinden suggests a range of from 45s to 340s, and for the fourteenth century from 260s-400s at the opening of the century to 600s-800s at the end.[78] Chancery documents for the period 1355-1365 indicate an average price for a Muslim slave of about 552s. (Male slaves were more valuable than females, the former averaging about 649s as opposed to 516s for the latter.)[79] Considering that the monarchy received at the very least one-fifth of the sale price of every Saracen sold, and in many cases the whole value, it was obviously in the king's interest to see as many Muslims as possible confiscated and enslaved.

In view of the rising value of such slaves, it seems, in fact,

---

77. "Un Siglo," p.59. For the Catalan tax, see RP 994:13 (1363); for the dobla, see RP 1711:11 (1366).

78. For the thirteenth century, see Verlinden, L'Esclavage, pp.282-4, and cf. prices given in Roca Traver, "Un Siglo," p.58, n.160; p.63, n.186; and p.83, n.14. For the fourteenth century, see L'Esclavage, p.449.

79. A sampling of such prices, in order of documentation: C 685:44 (1355): a male sold for 700 morabetins; C 697:141 (1359); a female sold for £33; C 703:211 (1360): a black male sold for 52s; C 903:107 (1359): a male sold for £37; C 986:59 (1365): a male sold for £60. By way of perspective it seems worth noting that horses were often worth more than Muslim slaves: see C 720:53 (Sept.8, 1365), where a trade is effected to the disadvantage of the party receiving the Muslim slave ("estimatio facta de dicto equo est major precio dicti sarraceni...").

remarkable that they had any opportunity at all to become free,
but it is certain that very many Muslim slaves were allowed to
buy their freedom, either by working or begging alms, and that
free Mudéjares considered it their pious duty to give money to those
trying to gain freedom through begging.[80] Escape was relatively common, and even though aiding or abetting runaways was often severely
punished, very prominent Mudéjares and even some Christians did co-
operate with escaping slaves,[81] possibly preferring Deuteronomic
law ("Non trades servum domino suo qui ad te confugerit" 23:15) to
Aragonese ordinances.

Verlinden was convinced that Mudéjares could not themselves own
slaves, either Muslim or Christian, and criticized Roca Traver for
implying the reverse. None of Roca Traver's documents, he averred,
demonstrated the existence of slaves owned by Mudéjares, and several
of the Valencian Furs specifically prohibited this.[82] In fact, however, the particular Furs adduced by Verlinden (I.8.1-2) only prohibited Muslims' owning Christian slaves, and said nothing about
their possessing non-Christians. This was generally the case with
medieval Spanish law codes: the Costums of Tortosa, for instance,
prohibit absolutely Jews and Muslims having Christian slaves or
servants (I.9.1), but strongly imply that Muslims might own other

---

80. E.g., C 688:97 (Dec.17, 1356); RP 1708:18 (1362).

81. E.g., the faqi of Borja: C 705:150 (June 26, 1361). For Christians, see C 720:45 (Sept.4, 1365). Twelve Mudéjares were pardoned
for helping runaways in 1365: see C 1209:17Q (Jun3 17). Cf. C 983:
24 (Dec.20, 1358).

82. See L'Esclavage, pp.317, n.264; 533; 534, n.1003. The Furs are
published in Roca Traver, "Un Siglo," p.45, n.114.

Muslims (VI.1.18). The earliest Aragonese and Catalan treaties
and laws (e.g., those of Alfonso with Tudela, or of Ramón Beren-
guer with Tortosa) proscribed Jews owning Muslims, but were silent
or ambiguous about Muslims owning Muslims.

In fact, though Verlinden attempted to explain away one document he published which cast doubt on his theory (p.317, n.264),
he unwittingly used another document which categorically disproved
his assertion: on pp.863-4 he reproduced a grant by the Aragonese
Crown of a Muslim slave to Faraig de Belvis, apparently unaware
that Faraig de Belvis was himself a Muslim (this fact is, indeed,
often excluded from Chancery materials relating to the Belvis family:
see p.46, n.50).[83]

Several members of the Belvis family owned Muslim slaves: Faraig's
brother, Jahia, who was in the service of the King of Castile, purchased a Muslim slave in Daroca for the exorbitant price of 700 morabetíns and used him extensively to conduct his business affairs in
lands under the Aragonese Crown. When this slave was captured by
Christians and illegally sold again in Barcelona, Fáraig intervened,
and--with the help of royal officials--had the slave returned to his
brother in Castille.[84] Faraig himself was granted another female
Muslim as a slave by the king in 1364,[85] and the king even granted
a Jewish favorite in Valencia a Muslim slave.[86] Foreign dignitaries

---

83. This document is C 575:149 (June 1, 1332); the Muslim woman had
been confiscated for sleeping with a Christian.

84. C 685:44 (Oct.14, 1355), in Appendix.

85. C 1203:178 (Aug.20, 1364), in Appendix.

86. C 907:61 (Apr.10, 1362): "Cum nos in excambium et permutationem

from Muslim countries often purchased Muslim slaves in Barcelona,
and sometimes Muslims captured by pirates had slaves with them
whom they had themselves bought from pirates.[87] There is, in short,
no doubt at all that Muslims under the Crown of Aragon not only
could but did possess other Muslims as slaves.[88]

In addition to civil service, local government, and butchering,[89]
Mudéjares appear to have engaged in every possible profession except the priesthood. Outside the aljama most were farmers and/or
serfs. In Valencia they raised mostly grain and fruits, generally
for sale. In Aragon and Catalonia they were subsistence farmers.
Within the aljamas in all three kingdoms a thriving urban culture
demanded craftsmen, laborers, and professionals of all types.[90]

Salamoneti Abbu, iudei civitatis Valentie, et ad quorundam familiarum nostrorum supplicationem, qui pro infrascriptis nobis humiliter
intercesserunt, dari et tribui concesserimus Jacob Abbu, iudeo Valentie, Abdalla Alminxar, sarracenum regni Castelle, ipso Jacob dante
et solvente precium pro quo emerunt [illum] illi penes quos erat
dictus sarracenus."

87. RP 1002:40 (1360) ("...Na Axa, que compra Scidi Boltacim, moro
missatger del Rey de Tuniç, qui le s'en mena...."); C 698:128 (Oct.2,
1359).

88. Cf. RP 997:68 (1366). Although in the early fifteenth century
Muslims could still own Muslim slaves (see Piles Ros, Estudio, p.243,
#523), this was absolutely prohibited shortly before the close of
the century (ibid., p.285, #730).

89. See Chapter II, pp.95ss.

90. These professionals apparently organized guilds comparable to
those common among medieval Christian merchants and skilled craftsmen, with obligations to oversee the burial of members, etc.: "...
collectores illius juris quod exigitur et levatur in dicta civitate
[Valentie] ab omnibus confratriis ipsius civitatis in auxilium guerre Castelle...compellere nituntur dictam aljamam et singulares eiusdem ad solvendum certum jus confratrie, vigore cuiusdam ordinationis
et statuti inter sarracenos facti quo cavetur in efectu quod siquis
sarracenus menestralis ipsius civitatis decesserit, per alios sarracenos, qui sunt illius officii quo utebatur dictus decedens dum vi-

The table appended to this chapter presents the occupations most
frequently encountered in the documentation for this study. Its
variety speaks for itself and for the economic sophistication of
the aljama. No document contains specific figures relating to the
percentage of Mudéjares who engaged in any profession or trade.
Nevertheless, cautious inferences can be drawn from wide reading
in archival material. The most common occupation of all aljama
Muslims was retail merchandizing. Second to it, in Valencia, was
the pottery industry, which was wholly run by the Muslim community.[91]
In Aragon the second most common occupation was probably construction. The aljaferia (royal residence) of Zaragoza was a converted
Muslim stronghold, and it was built and maintained entirely by Mudéjar craftsmen, stonemasons, carpenters, laborerers, etc. Artistic
consistency was probably not the only motivation: for some reason
Muslims dominated the construction industry in Aragon. The adverse
effects of the war on the Mudéjar population, in fact, created a
critical shortage of construction workers, and hence, of housing.[92]
Muslims were crucial in other areas also: they were major arms-makers
in Aragon, and were forcibly recruited during the war years to ply

---

vebat, haberi sepeliri sub incursu certarum penarum..." C 714:115
(Aug.29, 1363).

91. Roca Traver, "Un Siglo," pp.54ss.

92. C 1069:55 (cf.:5) (Jan.20, 1357). In the fifteenth century,
Aragonese Muslims travelled as far as Granada to do construction
no one else could (or would?) do: see the safe-conduct issued by the
General Bailiff of Valencia to 28 Aragonese Mudéjares who were on
their way to repair the Alhambra of Granada in 1492 (Piles Ros,
Estudio, p.314).

their trade.[93]   Aragon also depended on Muslims for the importation
of salt, so much so that the king protected the personal safety
of the Mudéjares involved in the trade.[94]   Valencia depended on Mudéjar skill and labor for grain, salt, and, of course, the maintenance of the systems of irrigation developed (if not invented) by
the Muslims.   The paper the royal Chancery used was provided by
Valencian Muslims exclusively.[95]

Muslims formed "companies" recognized by the Crown, and it was
not at all uncommon for Christians and Muslims to co-operate in
business ventures as equal partners.[96]

Muslims and Jews seem to have played an important--perhaps
disproportionate--role in the practice of medicine under the Crown
of Aragon in the fourteenth century.   The practice of medicine was
strictly regulated by the Crown and Curia.   Physicians were required
to have studied medicine for three years, and to display a thorough
knowledge of standard medical textbooks ("libros ordinarios scien-
tie medicine").   Christian aspirants to the profession were examined
by a board of Christian physicians to make certain they met these
requirements.

> Jewish and Saracen physicians, however, are to be examined
> by physicians of their own law and sect, if any are available,
> but with one Christian physician present at their examination.
> In the absence of physicians of their own law and religion they
> shall be examined by two Christian physicians; after this examin-

---

93. C 1075:91 (Feb.15, 1363); cf. C 1170:160 (May 9, 1360).

94. C 1402:147 (Feb.1, 1359).

95. RP 1709:50; 1719:60; 2469:58; see also the table on occupations,
p.62, under "paper miller."

96. RP 1711:34 (1366); cf. C 1170:160 (1363).

ation, if they are found acceptable, they shall have to swear
publicly to practice well and legally before they are admitted
to the profession.[97]

Though the provisions of this edict appear to place Muslim

physicians on a slightly lower plane than Christian ones (a Chris-

tian must be present at examination of Muslims and Jews), such

was manifestly not the case, and some purely religious concern

must have prompted the disparity in procedure. Muslims were per-

mitted to treat Christians on an equal footing with Christian

physicians, even though foreign (Christian) physicians were not,[98]

and both the king and queen had Muslim physicians in their households,

in the case of the former a noted eyesurgeon.[99]

---

97. C 985:70 (Mar.8, 1363). "Judei autem et sarraceni medici exam-
inari habeant per medicos eiusdem legis vel secte, siqui fuerint, uno
tamen medico in eorum examine adhibito christiano. Et medicis eiusdem legis vel secte non existentibus, habeant per duos medicos christianos; qua examinatione habita, si sufficientes reperti fuerint,
iurare publice habeant bene et legaliter practicare, antequem ad
praticam admittantur."

98. C 909:154 (1364). On foreigners not being allowed to practice medicine, see Lopez de Meneses, Documentos, pp.14-15. On e-
quality before the law, see also the regulations about Christian,
Jewish, and Muslim physicians in the ordinances of Valls, in Carreras y Candi, "Ordinacions," XII, pp.202 and 281. The Bishop of
Moncada had inveighed against Christians who employed Muslim or
Jewish physicians in the late thirteenth century (Villanueva, Viage,
V, pp.314-15), but there was in general no official opposition to
this form of convivencia.

99. "Ad supplicationis instantiam aliquorum domesticorum et familiarum nostrorum cum presenti carta nostra recipimus te, Abdarramen
Muhameti, sarracenum cirurgicum, in familiare nostrum, et aliorum
familiarum et domesticorum nostrorum consortio liberaliter agrega-
mus. Volentes et tibi specialiter concedentes ut illis de cetero
honoribus et favoribus gaudeas, quibus alii domestici et familiares
nostri potiri vel perfrui dinoscuntur. Ceterum quare te ut cirurgi-
cus [sic] ad diversas mundi partes et loca declinare contigit..."
(ordinary safe-conduct for members of royal household follows) C
1573:29 (May 1, 1364). Note that Abdarramen is to continue his regular practice. On the king's eye surgeon, see J. Rius, "Mes documents

Mudéjares also seem to have been disproportionately represented in the entertainment industry of the northern lands: the royal household employed Moorish jongleurs, dancers, and musicians; Muslims were used on board ships as trumpeters, jongleurs, and jesters; references to Muslim troubadors, musicians, and jesters of both sexes and all conditions abound.[100] Possibly the Christian majority found such positions unappealing and gladly left them for the Mudéjares.

---

sobre la cultura catalana medieval," Estudis universitaris catalans, XIII (1928), p.162. The king also had a Jewish physician, Master Boniuda, who attended his soldiers and knights (C 683:240 [Aug.8, 1356]). For fifteenth-century Muslim medicine, see Piles Ros, Estudio, pp.172, 184, 226 (n.b. the Muslim here described as "moro negro"), and passim.

100. C 1402:153-4 (1359); C 1958:22 and 25 (June 11 and Sept.9, 1389); González Hurtebise, Libros, pp.233, 402; Macho y Ortega, "Condición," pp.308-9.

TABLE OF MUSLIM OCCUPATIONS

The following table lists occupation found in various Chancery documents of the fourteenth century. Beside the occupation is a letter corresponding to the kingdom in which the trade or profession was practiced: i.e., "A" for Aragon, "C" for Catalonia, "V" for Valencia; the number represents the document in which the reference is found. Previously published documents are included only where they shed some light on the material in unpublished ones: the list is intended to be indicative rather than exhaustive. Only one reference is given for a particular occupation, even when there are many in the registers. Second or third references indicate information about different aspects of the trade, not the frequency of its occurrence in charters and letters. Civil servants are included only where the evidence indicates civil service was their profession rather than a civic duty or a temporary position. Nearly all Mudéjares outside the morería were farmers, and this profession is listed only as a reminder of this fact.

accountant (A)	C 1170:62
archer (A-C-V)	C 688:91, 905:972, 908:79
arms maker (A)	C 1075:91
bailiff (V)	C 702:59
brick maker (A-V)	C 692:205, RP 1708:50
cableman (C)	C 1402:153
carpenter (A)	C 899:195
civil servant (A)	C 986:48, 1203:135
contractor (A)	C 687:7
cooper (A)	C 982:55
dyer: general cloth (V)	RP 1710:47-8
silk (V)	Verlinden, L'Esclavage, p.877.
farmer (A-C-V)	C 686:218, 721:135, 1573:148
inn-keeper (A)	C 711:194
ironworker (A)	C 702:195, 713:160
jester (C)	C 1402:154
jongleur (A-C-V)	C 1402:154, Gonzalez Hurtebise, Libros, p.233
kiln owner and operator (C)	RP 994:40
"machine maker" (A)	C 1069:5, 55
merchant: general (V)	C 714:165
grain (V)	C 714:965
leather (A)	C 688:160
salt (A)	C 1402:147

paper miller (V)	RP 1708:18
potter (V)	Roca Traver, "Un Siglo," p.54
sheep shearer (A)	C 908:233
shoemaker (A)	C 688:160
silversmith (V)	RP 1706:18
stonemason (A)	C 1069:5, 55
surgeon: general (A-C)	C 909:154, 985:70, 1573:29
eye (C)	see note 99, above
tambourine player (A-C-V)	C 1402:154
tanner (A)	C 702:195
tax collector (A)	C 703:12
transporter (C-V)	RP 1711:34
trumpeter (A)	C 1402:154, Gonzalez Hurtebise, *Libros*, p.4(
vintner (A)	C 684:196

Chapter II

The Aljama and the *Morería:*
Internal Organization of the Mudéjar Community

The morería, or Muslim quarter, was a distinct geographical
and political entity. Generally outside the walls of the city in
the early years of Christian rule, it had become in most cases
a part of the city enclosure by the mid-fourteenth century, and
was usually set apart by walls from the Christian and Jewish quarters. Many morerías did not have dividing walls, and there was
apparently no requirement that there be any, since in a letter
of 1360 the king himself assumed that there was no clear division
between the Muslim and Christian houses of Ariza, and his subordinates had to inform him that the Muslim section was indeed geographically distinct.[1] It is clear, nonetheless, that it was
thought desirable to have the quarters divided by a wall, as is
evidenced by an order of June 3, 1361, establishing a new judería
and morería for the city of Tarazona within (n.b.) the city walls
but segregated by a walled enclosure:

> ...we direct you to go personally to the city of Tara-
> zona and to establish there in our name and on our authority
> a judería, within the walled portion of the city if possible,
> or in the quarter of St Michael, or in any other part there,
> i.e., wherever seems most suitable. Within this judería all
> Jews dwelling in the city, presently or in the future, will
> and must dwell, and it is to be separated from the Christian
> section by walled enclosure. You will establish a morería in
> the same way....[2]

---

1. "...repererimus hereditates sarracenorum predictorum esse ab
aliis hereditabus christianorum et judeorum separatas..." C 700:
238 (Apr. 28, 1360).

2. Addressed to the Justice of Aragon and his treasurer, Guer-
aldus de Spelunca, this letter is published in its entirety in the
Appendix under C 905:205. The aljama of Alcira was not walled in
till after 1426, when the Muslims requested a wall to separate them
from the Christians (Piles Ros, Estudio, pp.185-6). The wall sur-

During the reconquista the Muslim population had generally been moved out of the central city to morerías outside the walls, e.g., in the case of Huesca in 1096.[3] But in the fourteenth century, influenced either by humanitarian motives or practical considerations, the king ordered the Christians to move out instead, and guaranteed them compensation for their property, or real estate of equal value in other parts of the city.[4]

As private citizens Christians had free access to the morerías. The documents of the Real Patrimonio are filled with cases of Christians being arrested for misconduct inside the morería of Valencia, and there is no reason to suspect that the Christians of that city enjoyed any peculiar privilege in this regard.[5] Christian officials, on the other hand, had no authority within the morería unless it was specifically delegated them by the king, and could not even enter it unless accompanied by the amin and

---

rounding the aljama of Játiva was torn down by Christian officials in the fifteenth century, but the king ordered it entirely rebuilt, since the aljama suffered "grave harm" without it (ibid., pp.248-9, #544). The synonym for morería, ravale, reflects the originally suburban nature of morerías, but came to be used indiscriminately of the Muslim quarter, regardless of its relation to the city walls. Cf. modern Castilian arrabal, "suburb."

3. Macho y Ortega, "Condición," p.152. Cf. the agreement between Alfonso el Batallador and the Muslims of Tudela in 1115: "...completo anno quod exeant ad illos barrios de foras cum lure mobile..." (Tomás Muñoz y Romero, Colección de fueros municipales y cartas pueblas de los reinos de Castilla, León, Corona de Aragón y Navarra [Madrid, 1847], p.415).

4. C 905:205, ut supra, n.2.

5. See, for example, the entries in RP 2911:1 and passim (1355), where Christians are accused of attacking a blacksmith within the morería, throwing stones at moros, attacking moras, etc., and ibid., 47-48, where two Christian women are fined for fighting in the morería. Cf. the question of tafureries, below.

adelantati of the aljama.[6] Though this privilege was occasionally
violated, the sanctity of the morería was much prized by the Muslims, and this right was one of the least often abused of all those
enjoyed by the Mudéjares.[7]

It is commonly assumed that Christians could not actually live
in the morería, or Muslims in the Christian quarters, and it would
seem, indeed, that to permit such mingling would have frustrated
the whole point of the enclosure. Many treaties of capitulation
specifically prohibited such intermingling of dwelling places.[8]
But the evidence indicates that such prohibitions were not respected in practice. In Teruel, for instance, numerous Muslims were
renting their homes from Christians, and therefore presumably living in the Christian sections of the city, since it is unlikely
that so many Christians would own property in the morería (see below
on this point).[9] It is even possible that this document refers to

---

6. This privilege was often granted and confirmed by rulers, e.g.,
Alfonso I (1115): "Et non intret nullus christianus in casa de moro
nec in horto per forza..." (Muñoz y Romero, Colección, p.415). Cf.
C 1570:23 (1273). The Costums of Tortosa prohibit a Christian official's even entering a private Muslim home to retrieve a runaway
slave without being accompanied by two Muslims of the qadi's choosing (VI.1a.2). In this regard the Muslims were notably better off
than the Jews of Tortosa, whose homes could be entered by the Veguer
and other Christians under the same circumstances (ibid.).

7. It was therefore necessary for Muslim authorities to oversee
the repair of city walls which lay within the morería; this was sometimes held to fulfill the Muslims' feudal duties regarding the walls
(C 693:9 [Aug.5, 1357], C 699:66 [Nov.26, 1359]), but there were frequent attempts by Christian officials to compel them to contribute
more: C 699:66, ut supra.

8. E.g., that of Chivert.

9. "Cum pluries et diversi sarraceni civitatis nostre Turoli habi-

Muslims' occupying rooms in Christian homes, though this was generally prohibited (note 13, below). In 1365, when Játiva was threatened by the war, all Muslims who lived "among the Christians of the city" were specifically ordered to move into the morería,[10] but they must not all have obeyed, since in the following year the Crown felt constrained to declare that Muslims living outside the morería were affected by decrees relating to its internal affairs just as much as those dwelling inside it.[11]

The opposite occurred as well: in 1359, during the reconstruction of the walls of Calatayud, Christians whose homes had been destroyed during the reparations moved into the homes of Muslims and established residence in them. The king ordered them to move out, since they had occupied the Muslim dwellings by force, and were seriously discomfiting the still-resident owners, but no mention is made of any general principle's being violated.[12] It was, more-

---

tent in aliquibus domibus christianorum eiusdem civitatis, quas tenent certis loqueriis ad certa tempora ab eisdem..." (C 693:56 [Nov.26, 1357]). This letter was sent by the king to prevent the Christian landlords from evicting some Muslims before their leases expired in order to charge higher rents. On the right of Muslims to sell property to Christians, and vice versa, see Chapter VI.

10. C·1206:151 (Oct.15, 1365).

11. C 910:120 (Sept.16, 1366).

12. "...aliqui christiani quorum domus de nostri mandato in dicta villa pro operibus murorum eiusdem diruuntur, non attento quod alie domus fuerunt christianorum ubi se possent collocare, per vim ac contra voluntatem sarracenorum predictorum non sunt vel fuerunt veriti intrare domos dictorum sarracenorum et inibi havitare, in ipsorum sarracenorum evidens periculum atque dampnum" (C 983:149 [Jan.22, 1359]).

over, common for Christians to stay at inns operated by Muslims
within the morería,[13] and in Borja Christians and Saracens
jointly operated an inn located in the judería of the city.[14]

That the Muslim and Christian populations were not kept
separate, and that this was a matter of concern to the former as
well as the latter, are both well attested by the demand of the
returning moros of Castro and Alfandequiella that "no Christian
or Jew be allowed to settle among them."[15] On the other hand,
the financial advantages of convivencia in such a literal sense
were many, and as in many aspects of social interaction, they
seem to have triumphed in the end. Sales of property by Muslims
to Christians were frequent, especially when war or other disasters
had reduced the number of Muslim buyers, and the records even show
instances of the sale of factories in the morería to Christians.[16]
Christian buyers were not wanting, and the turnover in real estate held by Christians within the morería seems to have been quite
brisk: see document 904:73 (and :85) in the Appendix, where property in the morería of Zaragoza worth 800s changes hands from Muslim

---

13. O 711:194 (Mar.4, 1363). This in spite of the fact that popes
and secular legislators alike saw in this sort of convivencia a grave
threat to the Catholic faith. Cf. the carta puebla of Vallibona: "No
estiguen mesclats moro et christia en una casa, com no sia ocasio de
molts mals e perill de mort et violentament de la fe catholica" (Roca
Traver, "Un Siglo," p.8).

14. C 689:153 (Jan.31, 1358).

15. C 1204:63, in Appendix; cf. English version under "Problems."
In the fifteenth century Christians were specifically forbidden to
rent homes in the morería of Valencia: Piles Ros, Estudio, p.126.

16. See, for example, C 689:71 (Dec.20, 1356), where Juceff Çalem

to Christian, Christian to Christian, and Christian to Muslim within the space of a few years. In fact, the trade in morería property was so extensive that the monarchy, whose interests suffered when Muslim lands passed into Christian hands, took steps to discourage it in September of 1363 by penalizing such sales.[17]

Curiously, the integrity of the judería seems to have been more assiduously maintained than that of the morería. Both buyer and seller lost their interest in Jewish property if it was sold to a Christian or a Saracen,[18] and in at least one case the king agreed to force Muslims off land they had owned for many years and grant them property of equal value elsewhere, apparently to prevent Muslims and Jews from living in close proximity.[19] On the other hand, both Christians and Muslims were allowed to own property in the judería of Borja,[20] and the king himself granted property formerly held by Jews to loyal Saracens during the war.[21]

Within the confines of the morería were all the necessities of fourteenth-century life: markets, workshops,[22] mosques, homes

---

sold "quoddam repertorium sive fecceriam cum camera superiori" to Martinus de Cortes Asterius.

17. C 1571:159. For more detail on the subject of property sales between Muslims and Christians, see Chapter VI.

18. C 904:21 and C 1071:93 (Nov.24, 1359).

19. C 721:135 (Jan.22, 1365). This curious document is printed in the Appendix in its entirety.

20. See above.

21. C 903:290 (May 7, 1360), in the Appendix.

22. The workshops along the interior wall of the morería of Huesca occupied a space of about one hundred feet (C 908:233 [Sept.1, 1363]).

and public facilities. The morería of Zaragoza had iron-works and
tanneries and its own water supply to operate both.[23] All aljamas
of any size had baths, supported at public expense, charging nomin-
al admission fees, and liable to taxes collected by the Crown.[24]
Most morerías maintained their own cemeteries.[25] The markets of
the morerías of Aragon, especially the meat markets, drew not only
Muslims from the surrounding countryside, but also Christians from
the city, who seem not to have minded paying the higher rates
charged for meat slaughtered by specially licensed Muslim butchers.

The morerías' main attraction for the Christian populace
seems to have been as centers of low life. Prostitution, which
was perfectly legal (see under Chapter VII, below) flourished
there, and Christian and Saracen women plied their trade side by
side. Between January of 1354 and January, 1355, no fewer than
seventy-one prostitutes of the city of Valencia were fined for
rendering services after hours (the crida, or curfew, was the cut-
off hour), and paid an aggregate fine of 1,186s to the Crown. Considering that these were only the prostitutes prosecuted for a

---

23. C 702:195 (June 23, 1361).

24. Ibid.; cf. RP 994:40 (1363). The aljama of Azp paid about 400s
annually for their baths, in return for which the king maintained
them (RP 1711:3ss). The tax was not direct: the king rented the
baths to one Muslim, who then charged admission himself. During the
war years the lessee was allowed to deduct for days when the city was
under seige and the baths could not be used. In Tortosa Christians,
Jews and Muslims all used the same publi: baths (Costums, I.1.15);
it is not clear whether this was the general practice in Aragon-Catalonia. In Valencia, separate bathing facilities seem to have been
the rule.

25. C 1188:50 (Oct.7, 1363).

particular crime, the number involved in the trade must have been enormous. Most of the names recorded were Christian ones, but all the women involved conducted their operations within the morería.[26]

Even more important was the game called tafureries.[27] Every large morería had a place where this game was played, legally by Muslims, illegally by Christians. There is a certain irony to this, since games of chance were specifically forbidden to Muslims by the Prophet,[28] while there is no specific injunction against them among the words of Jesus. Neither divine nor secular laws, however, had much effect on the popularity of the game. In Huesca the fine for Christians was 100s, and an official was appointed whose sole duty was to collect this fine (the tafurarius).[29] In 1358, when the office fell vacant, a bitter struggle over it ensued, and again in 1363 a dispute arose: Christians had held the office for at least ten years, but in March of 1363 the Saracen çalmedina of the city had seized the post for himself. The income must have been considerable.[30] Indeed, if Valencia was typi-

---

26. · These statistics are in the RP Register 2911:35ss. A typical case is that of Mari Sanchez: "Item de Mari Sanchez, mala fembra qui estaua en l'ostal d'En Palma, prop la carniceria dels moros...." She was fined 20s for her first offense and 30s for the second.

27. Backgammon? The evidence about its exact nature is scanty.

28. Surah II ("The Cow"):219, V ("The Table"):90.

29. C 965:232 (May 3, 1354).

30. C 966:80 (1358) and C 714:30 (Mar.25, 1363). On the income, see C 965:232, ut supra.

cal in this regard, tafureries were second only to prostitution
as money-makers for the Crown. During the year 1354-55 the fines
collected from those Christians and Jews illegally joining the
Muslims at their game amounted to well over 1,500s. This is especially remarkable in view of the fact that in Valencia the fine
averaged only about 3s3d per person, which would indicate that
over 500 people paid the fine within one year. The problem of
detection was made simple by granting the informer one-third of
the fine collected. The Crown and the city divided the remaining
two thirds. Those found guilty in the year mentioned ranged from
the chief butcher of the city's major Christian meat market to one
of the "public women" (who were in the neighborhood anyway).[31]

The internal affairs of the aljama were--theoretically--in the
hands of the adelantati, elected officials roughly corresponding to
the Christian jurados. Originally these were to be four: "...we wish
you to have four Saracen adelantati, whomever among you you may choose
to elect; these shall have care and maintenance of you and your affairs and finances [jura]."[32] In practice, their number seems to have
varied from one to four, according to the needs and desires of the
aljamàs.[33] Methods of election also varied widely; in some places
they were elected by the heads of families, in others by the outgoing

---

31. This information is all derived from RP 2911:11ss. Of 1006s 10d
reported as "collected," the Crown received 522s 4d, which means the
informer's third had already been deducted from the figure.

32. Archivo Real de Valencia C 658:15, published in Roca Traver,
"Un Siglo," p.18, n.29.

33. See Macho y Ortega, "Condición," pp.158ss, and Roca Traver, "Un
Siglo," p.14.

adelantati.[34] The position was honorary and carried no salary. In

the early fourteenth century the Crown prohibited the practice of

adelantati hiring others to perform their duties under fine of

100s;[35] by the fifteenth century this fine had to be raised to

200s, and the term of office reduced from one year to two months--

apparently the position was extremely undesirable.[36] This is not

hard to understand: in reality the adelantati had no power, and

did little more than bear official responsibility for fiscal ar-

rangements imposed on the aljama by the Crown and its officials.

Even officially they could decide nothing without the consent of

the Christian mayor of the city.[37] Their real importance lay in

their function as mouthpiece for the king: it was to them he gave

orders to be carried out within the aljamas, and in their name that

fiscal arrangements were made. They were, in effect, the king's

unwilling official agents in the Muslim communities: hence the un-

popularity of the position.[38]

The adelantati did, however, appoint a host of minor officials,

---

34. Macho y Ortega, "Condición," p.158, describes an interesting
method used in Zaragoza in the fifteenth century.

35. C 860:6 (1335).

36. On the plight of the adelantati in fifteenth-century Zaragoza,
see Macho y Ortega, "Condición," passim.

37. C 899:179 (Jan.10, 1357). Macho y Ortega, "Condición," p.158,
mentions this fact, but seems not to grasp its significance. They
could not even appoint a substitute for themselves without the may-
or's approval: C 860:6 (April, 1335).

38. Burns considers the adelantati unimportant for the thirteenth
century as well: see Islam, pp.394-7. His discussions of the internal structure of thirteenth-century Valencian aljamas, while not directly relevant to the present study, provide invaluable background

the civil service of the aljama. These included the sagio, carnifex,[39] magister cantorum, torcimana, scribanius,[40] cavalquinus, mostaçafus, andator, acompanyat,[41] and the official tutor appointed by the community to guard orphans.[42] It was not uncommon for Christian offi-

---

material, especially pp.374ss.

39. See below.

40. See below.

41. Most of these were permittted to draw a maximum salary from the receipts of their office. On the sagio, a sort of police officer, see Burns, Islam, p.237, and cf. C 1207:145 (1365) and C 699: 202 (Mar.25, 1360); for the carnifex, see below; the magister cantorum was the çabiçala (from sāhib aṣ-salāt, "prayer leader"), or heir to the position traditionally held by the imām in Muslim communities, i.e., that of ceremonial religious head; torcimana is Romance for turjiman, from the Arabic tarjamana, "translate": see below, n.116; for the scribanus, a very important office, see below; for the cavalquinus, see C 968:50 (Apr.7, 1362); the Muslim mostaçaf corresponded to the Christian one (collector of market taxes): see C 699:202 (Mar.25, 1360); the andator and acompanyat were tax collectors: for the former see C 699:202, ut supra; the latter's function appears to have been as a combination translator and scribe, since acompanyats were employed only in Muslim areas where Romance was not spoken, and always accompanied Christian collectors: see RP 1711:27ss. In the fifteenth century large aljamas had lawyers--most often Christian--appointed for them by the court for the term of one year. Their salary was quite low (50s a year). The aljamas of Zaragoza, Teruel, and Borja had consellers as well as .adelantati, and those of Zaragoza, Borja, and Huesca had financial officials known as clavarii (Macho y Ortega, "Condición," pp.159ss). The same author posits the existence generally of an office of "messenger" between the aljama and the king, paid by the Crown (ibid., p.162). This was certainly not the case in the fourteenth century. Messages to the aljama from the king were carried by royal officials and read aloud to the qadi, amin, and adelantati, or to the population as a whole. Sometimes the aljama's crier was employed; occasionally the qadi was summoned to court. References to nuncii in documents are clearly using the word in its ordinary Latin sense, not as a designation for an office. Messages from the aljama to the king were taken personally by the qadi, or, more frequently, the adelantati, who were always sent with grievances of the aljama: see C 903:203 in the Appendix. Macho y Ortega himself publishes a document ("Documentos," pp.445-6) regarding an edict read aloud to the officials of the aljama of Zaragoza in 1432 with no mention of nuncii.

42. Hamet de Faraig, for instance, was appointed the tutor of Ma-

cials to try to intervene in or override the appointment of such
officials by the Muslims, but the monarchy usually upheld the
right of the aljama to appoint its own officials.[43]

It is, however, impossible to agree with Roca Traver that
"the intervention of the seigneurial representative was limited to
private interests of the lord, in regard to aspects which affected
him directly...,"[44] or that the aljamas enjoyed "an absolute freedom and autonomy in their officials, in their internal government,
in the creation and election of the former, and, finally, in their
own administration and government."[45] In fact, the aljama was not
really independent at all in those matters of most pressing concern,
either financial or juridical. During a period of crisis, the
Crown did not hesitate to pre-empt all the functions of the aljama's
government by appointing a Christian official with absolute power
over every aspect of life in the morería. This official was various-

---

oma de Peno, the orphan of wealthy parents (C 692:205 [Sept.16,
1357]). His duties included both the personal guardianship of the
child and the management of his business interests. Cf. the case
of the orphans of Mahomat del Rey, whose tutor used his office
to bring justice on the murderer of his wards' father (C 688:160
[1357]; printed in the Appendix). The guardianship of orphans is
regulated by the Koran: Surah IV ("Women"): passim.

43. E.g., in the case of Aranda in 1360, where the "justicia,
jurati, et mostaçafus universitas christianorum" tried to wrest
this right from the aljama, though the latter had enjoyed it "a
tanto citra tempore quod memoria hominum in contrarium non existit."
The king upheld the aljama: C 699:202 (Mar.25, 1360).

44. "Un Siglo," p.17.

45. Ibid., p.13. Cf. Burns' comments on Roca Traver and other
early students of aljama govenment: Islam, pp.377ss.

ly designated as commissarius, administrator, or rector. The

aljama of Zaragoza was continuously ruled by such an official from

1358 throughout the war years, and though the holder of the position

changed, its absolute powers did not; the commission granted to

Dominicus Luppus Sarnes in December of 1362 was identical to that

awarded Sanctius Martes in May, 1358:

> ...we therefore commit and commend to your care the
> governance and administration of the said aljama of Saracens,
> as well as the allotment of its royal taxes, tributes,
> subsidies, and other exactions, for as long as shall suit
> our intention. You are thus to be rector, or administrator,
> of the aljama, and to rule and administer it lawfully and
> wisely, and to apportion prudently among them [the Saracens]
> their shares of the royal taxes, tributes, subsidies, and
> other exactions or duties of any type in whatever way seems
> best, so that each one is taxed (for whatever purpose) ac-
> cording to the means he possesses, and so that through the
> diligence of your supervision this aljama, now in great want,
> may be able to improve its state. You may impose whatever
> penalties or means seem appropriate to compel the said Sara-
> cens to observe and comply with your directives and assign-
> ments concerning these things, and you may either collect
> and receive the taxes and [?] on behalf of our Curia your-
> self, or cause them to be levied and collected by someone
> else of your choosing.... Furthermore, in all civil cases
> and litigations in any way concerning this aljama and its
> members, you shall be judge, and you will bring them to a
> just conclusion in accordance with the dictates of. law and
> reason. And you will oversee and arrange every single de-
> tail which seems to you necessary or desirable for the wel-
> fare and recovery of the said aljama....[46]

Both men were mayors of Zaragoza at the time they were appointed

to rule the aljamas, which made the usurpation almost a simple

extension of the traditional power of the mayor over the adelantati,

and also facilitated considerably the problem of getting Muslims

---

46. C 968:56 (Dec.10, 1362); reproduced whole in the Appendix.
The grant to Sarnes of May 23, 1358, occurs in C 966:82, and is
identical in wording.

and Christians to co-operate in the defense of the city. That

the rectorship was generally a mere extension of the mayoralty,

however, seems unlikely in view of the fact that rectors were

sometimes appointed to aljamas in other cities (Martes was

rector of Tahusc at the time of his appointment to that of

Zaragoza), and that persons who were not mayors were also ap-

pointed rectors (e.g., Eximen Perez de Salanova, the rector

of Tahusc after Martes).[47] Most rectors do seem to have been

mayors, but even when the same person was rector and mayor the

two functions were kept quite separate.[48]

It is significant that the grant of power to the rector did

not impinge on the authority of the qadi in criminal cases. A

Koranic institution, the office of qadi was the most enduring of

all Muslim institutions under Christian rule. The qadi was, in

fact, the central figure in Mudéjar life.[49] More than any other

person or force he represented for the Muslim minority of Aragon

---

47. C 966:86 (June 27, 1358). This document states specifically
that the rectorship of Tahusc was not a prerogative of the mayor of
Zaragoza. During the fifteenth century the aljama of Zaragoza was
rarely permitted to rule itself without a rector (usually the
mayor):·see Macho y Ortega, "Condición," pp.157, 176.

48. In a letter to the aljama of Zaragoza dated Aug.18, 1362,
the king points out to the Muslims that they must obey Sarnes in
his capacity as commissarius (= rector) within the aljama, and
in his role as mayor in regards to the defense of the city (C
1075:17). For a case of a fifteenth-century· rector in Valencia,
see Piles Ros, Estudio, p.247, #538.

49. Burns draws a clear distinction between qa'id and qadi for
thirteenth-century Valencia. While interesting, this distinction
is not intelligible in fourteenth-century documents, since the position of qa'id had effectively ceased to exist. Occasionally a dicho-

a connection with the Muslim world from which they were cut off.
Unlike Christianity, Islam made no effort to separate the secular
from the spiritual. From the earliest days all power had been
lodged in one person, whether Muhammad or his successor, and
every question--legal, financial, moral, military, juridical,
spiritual, theological--was referred to him. The local qadi was
this all-in-one power at its lowest and most indestructible level.
While struggles over the caliphate sundered the Muslim world, and
Christians separated Muslims from the temporal organization established in central cities, while theological warfare splintered
the already fragmented Islamic state, the qadi continued in each
little town to administer justice, decide moral issues, settle theological disputes, oversee good works, and do very nearly all those
things the Prophet himself had done for his followers. Allah was
the Judge of all things in all times, Muhammad had been the judge
of all aspects of Muslim life while he lived, and the qadi was the
judge of all that happened in the community.

In most areas of the Muslim world--the Mamluk empire, for
instance, or Ottoman Turkey--the qadi was the only continuity between successive regimes, and therefore the only stability at the
village or town level many Muslims ever knew. Under the Crown of
Aragon, although the jurisdiction of the qadi was probably less
impinged upon than that of any other Muslim official in the king-

---

tomy is apparent between alcadius as a Muslim qadi and alcaydus as
a Christian judge (e.g., C 910:118 [Sept.16, 1366]), but far more
often the two are used indiscriminately according to the loose orthography of the period with no semantic distinction.

dom, the continuity of qadi rule was severely threatened by the
political uses to which it was put by the monarchy and its repre-
sentatives. Nearly every conquered Muslim city had been promised
the right to choose its own qadi,[50] yet by the mid-fourteenth century, few if any aljamas in the kingdom enjoyed this right. Alfonso IV had, in 1329, provided for the appointment by royal officials of qadis in Valencian aljamas under direct royal control;[51]
by the reign of Peter the Ceremonious royal control over the appointment of qadis was ubiquitous, exploitative, disruptive, and extremely inconsistent.

Peter had on his accession instituted a series of laudable
and much-needed reforms among the qadis of Valencia. On January
13, 1337, in response to complaints by the aljama of Valencia
that the Crown and General Bailiff of Valencia were appointing
qadis ignorant of Islamic law, to the manifest detriment of the
community, he decreed that henceforth the elders of the aljamas
must be consulted concerning the knowledge and suitability of any
prospective appointee before any final decision was made, and
even ordered the bailiff to consult Muslim jurists and wise men
about those already holding office to make sure they were competent. There should be, he decreed, only one qadi for the mor-

---

50. "Et volumus quod vos, predicti sarraceni et successores vestri,
possitis eligere et ponere alcadi inter vos, quem volueritis, qui
judicet et determinet causas vestras et quod vos possitis illum mutare, si bene et fideliter non se habuerit, in officio antedicto..."
Roca Traver, p.18, n.29; cf. "E que puxquen fer alcadi et alami per
si mateixos..." ibid., p.10, n.15.

51. Roca Traver, "Un Siglo," pp.70-1, and note 210.

ería of Valencia, and he must actually reside within the confines
of the morería, appointing a lieutenant only temporarily if he
had to go outside on business.[52]

These were important reforms, and if pursued would have put an
end to several crying abuses in the governing of the aljamas, such
as absentee rule and the appointment of favorites not qualified
for the positions. But on the very same day the king had enacted
these provisions he appointed more than one qadi for the morería,[53]
and within twenty-five years completely altered his position, not
only permitting all the abuses he had officially proscribed earlier, but actually encouraging--in fact, demanding--them by virtue
of royal authority. In 1355, for instance, he ordered the Governor
of Valencia to seek out and expel from office immediately any Muslim
exercising the office of qadi who was not appointed to the position
by the king himself.[54]

Throughout the war years the qadi of Valencia was Faraig de
Belvis (see preceding chapter), who exercised this and a great many
other offices in absentia. Faraig held the office for life,[55] and
hired substitutes to discharge his duties, since he did not reside

---

52. These provisions are contained in a series of documents in C
862:119ss. They also provide for the qadi's exemption from the peyta.

53. C 862:119ss (Jan.13, 1337). One of these is designated alcadi
maior; this could be the alcadi general de apelación referred to by
Macho y Ortega, "Condición," p.178. Both Roca Traver and Gual Camarena
complain of there being no evidence of such an official in Valencia,
but see preceding chapter for a contrary opinion.

54. C 685:61 (Oct.16, 1355). This was done at the request of Faraig
de Belvis.

55. C 966:138 (Dec.28, 1363).

in Valencia. One of these substitutes was so incompetent that he was fined 900s in 1357 for abuses of office,[56] and the confusion occasioned by this arrangement was so great that in some instances two qadis ruled on the same case.[57]

Other aljamas were no better off. Numerous Valencian morerías even had Christian qadis at one time or another, e.g., Játiva, Santa Cruce, Elche and Crevillente. In the case of the latter two (which shared a qadi), the appointment of a Christian qadi and scribanus in 1361 followed more than a year of battling between the Court and the aljama and the appointment or re-appointment of no less than four different persons during an eighteen-month period. It was not until five years later that a Muslim was appointed, following yet another Christian appointee of the same year. The Muslim was not a resident of either city.[59]

Alcadias were granted like livestock to favorites: the queen rewarded Abraham Abenxoa with those of Seta, Granadell, Bartaxell, and Xirillen in one fell swoop, and only three years later granted

---

56. RP 1704:23. This was Azmet Açaba. Other known substitutes were Fac Alvaremoni, 1362 (C 1183:119), and Açar Alcafaç (C 966:138). Cf. C 711:161 (Feb.27, 1363), where Faraig claims that his rights as qadi are being usurped by others.

57. E.g., that of Abraham Abenxoa and Ali Alcabba: RP 1708:18 (1362).

58. The dispute began in January, 1360, with the appointment of Mahoma Alguafiqui (Aljafiqui in some documents), and ended in July, 1361, with the appointment of the Christian Berengar Togores. The material is in C 1569:40, 72, 79, 92, 100, 108. The qadi received 3,000s annually from Crevillente alone: it is scarcely surprising the office should have occasioned controversy.

59. Çaat Alcafaç of Valencia (or Játiva): C 1572:66 (Nov.30, 1366). The Christian he replaced was Vincent de Vall, also of Játiva: C 1572: 51 (Sept.12, 1366).

someone else the same ones.[60]

Probably the most flagrant abuses of the office occurred in Játiva, the largest of all the Crown's aljamas. Petrus Dueso, a Christian, had held the office of qadi of the Saracens of Játiva (at an annual salary of 500s) from 1348 to 1356, when he was removed from the office for "incompetence."[61] He continued, however, to collect his salary, and in February, 1357, was re-instated in the office "for life."[62] In August of 1362, Dueso was replaced by another Christian,[63] but this one was shortly deposed in favor of Çaat Alcafaç, who retained it until 1365. Faraig de Belvis requested the alcadia of Játiva in that year, and was granted it on June 14.[64] He exercised it in absentia, through Çaat Alcafaç--even though he had been granted the post on grounds of his being "more competent" than Alcafaç--until the latter was tried and deposed for abuses of office in the following May.[65]

---

60. C 1570:86 (Fev.16, 1361); Axer Apartal was the second: C 1573: 5 (Jan.30, 1364). Note that Abenxoa had continued to hold office while on trial: see note 57, above.

61. C 966:89 (Apr.16, 1356). This salary represents 300s from the actual proceeds of the office, plus a subsidy of 200s granted by the king "quod assuetum salarium alcaydie ipsius morarie dicitur esse modici emolumenti." It is an extremely low figure for the largest and wealthiest aljama in the kingdom.

62. C 966:96 (Feb.19, 1357). He also held the esmenda of Penacadell, at a salary of 1,000s annually.

63. Bernard Rocha, bailiff of the city: C 1571:40.

64. C 1209:106, 157.

65. C 1210:94.

It might seem to those schooled in a tradition of the evils of
multiple benefices that Faraig de Belvis' holding the alcadias of
both Valencia and Játiva at the same time was somewhat questionable.
In fact, these were not his only titles: in addition to being qadi
of the two largest morerías in the kingdom, he was the faqi, scribanus, and çabiçala of Borja, the qadi, cavalquinus, scribanus, and
amin of Huesca, and the alcaydus totius regni Aragonie. He was also
court-appointed tutor to orphans of several wealthy Mudéjares.[66]
He held all of these offices concurrently and for life, and exercised them all in absentia. Nor was anyone scandalized by this;
indeed, many grants of morería offices by the king specified that
the office was to be held in absentia,[67] and there is some reason
to believe the monarchy was consciously trying to put Saracens
whom it knew to be loyal into positions of importance throughout
the realm, even if they did not exercise their jurisdictions directly.[68] Both multiple office-holding and absentee rule were common
in medieval Spain, and by no means limited to positions within the
morerías;[69]no one would have thought of objecting to them.

What the medieval Muslims did object to was royal interference,
and it is significant that in the northern kingdoms, where Muslims
generally enjoyed greater privileges, there was less of this type

---

66. E.g., to Mahomet el Baranco: C 1183:118 (Nov.18, 1362).

67. E.g., C 968:16 (Oct.10, 1359), which grants Bernard Arlouin
three offices in Jewish and Muslim quarters to be held in absentia.

68. Even the qadi of Lérida, though he resided within the city,
is described as being "of the king's household."

69. See Hamilton, Money, p.66; but cf. above, p.44.

of intervention and abuse, and the government of the aljamas was
much stabler. There were Christian qadis in the North--the important
aljamas of Aranda and Oriola both had them during the decade 1355-
65[70]--and the Crown exercised strict control over royal morerías,
but the over-all disruption of Muslim organization was much less.
The royal aljama of Lérida is a good example of this. In 1356 the
qadi of the aljama applied to the king for permission to resign.
He had held the post since the time of King James II of Aragon,
Peter's grandfather, and now, at 80 years old, he wished to retire
from the post granted him for life.[71] The king accepted his resig-
nation in September, and appointed a Saracen of his own household
to replace him temporarily.[72] Not long after, En Sulleyma Abenjumen became the qadi of Lérida.[73] Abenjumen had been an adelanta-
tus of the city before he was elected qadi (C 691:232), and his
accession demonstrates the existence of a class of Muslim civil servants which contributed to the relative stability of the Léridan
aljama's government. Only four years later, however, he was replaced
by Ali Minferre,[74] and the fact that after a rule of at least twenty nine years by a single qadi there were then three different occu-

---

70. Sanctius Sanctii of Torquemada in Aranda (C 702:167[1361]);
Domenicus de Costa, the bailiff of Tortosa, held the alcadia of
Oriola for life (C 1189:223 July 17, 1363).

71. C 685:100 (Mar.12, 1356).

72. C 967:166 (Sept.12, 1356).

73. RP 992:40 (1359). He paid (the Crown) 28s annually for the
post. See below for his own legal troubles.

74. RP 994:40 (1363).

pants of the position in the next seven years probably indicates
a certain disintegration of stable government even in the North
under the pressures of the decade.

Ironically, the stress of the war operated to the benefit
of the southern Mudéjares: in 1365, undoubtedly worried about
flagging Moorish loyalty in the war-torn city, Peter was induced
to grant the Muslim community of Játiva the right to choose their
own qadi--a startling concession in a period of increasing royal
control:

> ...Since we have learned from the aljama of Saracens of
> the city of Játiva that, according to their law and custom,[75]
> a qadi should not be chosen, either by us or anyone else, ex-
> cept on the recognition of the aljama itself, and that he
> should be someone knowledgeable and well-versed in their reli-
> gious and secular law,[75] and noting that we have previously
> disposed of the said position without the knowledge of the
> aljama and in violation of their law and custom (of which we
> were not unmindful), and since because of this the said aljama
> has humbly asked that we deign to provide for them the remedy
> for these [ills] which is described below, we therefore hereby
> concede to the aljama and are pleased to dispose that it may
> elect and remove its qadi whenever and howsoever often it shall
> deem expedient.
> This qadi shall be responsible for deciding and settling
> all litigation among the Saracens of the said aljama without
> pay. From the settlement of disputes, as was the former custom,
> he shall have 2d per pound and no more, and from certifications
> of indebtedness which he receives or makes between Saracens he
> shall earn 4d per certificate....[76]

Generous as this concession seems, it was not without its limitations. The king did not intend his favorite, Faraig de Belvis, to
be done out of any income through his high-minded largesse:

Nevertheless, since our intention regarding the provision

---

75. "Zuna et xara."

76. C 1206:138 (Oct.8, 1365); text in Appendix.

mentioned above neither was nor is to diminish any right of
Faraig de Belvis, our steward, who some time ago obtained
through our concession this very office of qadi, we therefore
expressly direct and specifically command you to accord and
force to be accorded to this Faraig (or his deputy in the
office) all rights customarily given or paid for this office
for as long as he lives, the letter given above notwithstanding in any way. After his decease, however, we wish the decree to be observed in both letter and spirit....[77]

Still, it was an improvement over even the theoretical dispositions
of the pre-war years, and represents one of the ways in which the
Muslim populations of the South managed to wring benefit from
the bitter fruits of the war.

It is clear from the foregoing letter what the king considered
to be the essential duties of the qadi. The qadi's legal jurisdiction was wide-ranging and unchallenged; even transient Muslims
were subject to him.[78] His jurisdiction could be extended at will
by the king.[79] In addition to legal affairs, he was responsible
in many cases for such matters as the safety of the morería (in
some places being required to supply the police force from among his
own personal retainers);[80] attending Court to counsel the king about
internal affairs of the aljama, or merely to give legal advice;[81]
leading troops into battle;[82] personally guaranteeing the aljama's

---

77. C 1206:138, ut supra.
78. C 715:50 (1363).
79. C 1205:45 (Mar.15, 1365).
80. C 1569:26 (Oct.17, 1359).
81. Ibid.:73 (Nov.12, 1360).
82. C 1211:31 (March, 1365).

compliance with royal edicts; and sometimes actually accompanying those summoned to Court to see that they showed up.[83] With all these obligations, nevertheless, the office remained attractive, both for its prestige and power and for its remunerative capabilities. There seems never to have been any want of applicants for the position.[84]

The aljama of Játiva had a Saracen official titled fiscalis sarracenorum Xative, who was paid 100s annually (the money being drawn from the receipts of the office), but it is unclear precisely what his duties were,[85] or whether other aljamas may have had the same official without leaving records of it. All communities had a çalmedina, the Saracen equivalent of the merino, or mayor. In the thirteenth century the çalmedina had been an extremely important official (see Burns, Islam, pp.234-8), but since in the fourteenth the functions of the mayor were nearly all exercised by the qadi and amin--indeed, the qadi frequently was the çalmedina--the office was largely superfluous. In individual aljamas the çalmedina sometimes retained signs of his former power: see Chapter III, p.140, below; and for Huesca, p.71, above. There is no sign of competition for the office, and no influential Mudéjares seem to have held it. The çalmedina's primary function seems to have been the supervision

---

83. C 1387:131 (Feb.3, 1465).

84. Alcadias were granted as rewards to Muslims who served faithfully during the war: C 1209:64 (1365); cf. below, last chapter. These grants were usually for life, but only in Valencia.

85. C 1203:63 (Dec.7, 1364); C 1209:125 (May 29, 1365).

of the market-place, but even here his jurisdiction was often
superceded by higher authorities. The position was for two years,
and beginning in 1356 was held only by Muslims.[86]

Both Roca Traver and Macho y Ortega mistakenly considered
the amin (Castilian alamín; Latin alaminus), to have been the
real power within the aljama, although the former admits that
within his purview lay only "the exercise of judicial authority
in small towns and in criminal matters of minimal significance,"
and the latter notes that Zaragoza, the most important aljama of
the North, did not even have an amin.[87] (Nor did that of Valencia,
the second largest of all the aljamas.[88]) And even Macho y Ortega concedes that the amin only exercised juridical power in towns

---

86. "Cum regimen dicte çalmedine officii per sarracenum et non per
christianum, ex quo ex ipsis aliqui idonei et capcis sit perpendimus
in dicta aljama existunt regi et exerceri jubemus et velimus." C 966:
89 (Apr.16, 1356). This letter was addressed to the aljama of Játiva, and a suitable Muslim was found and installed in the office made
vacant by the deposition of the Christian who had previously occupied
it. Four years later the Muslim was tried for abuses of the office:
RP 1706:18 (1360).

87. Roca Traver, "Un Siglo," pp.13-14: "...el alamín tenía dos
consideraciones: como presidente nato del consejo y como supremo
árbitro en las cuestiones judiciales...; ...era de su incumbencia
el velar por el cumplimiento de las leyes, la percepción de tributos
e impuestos (parte de los cuales debía entregar al señor), el reparto
de casas y haciendas, el llevar la discusión de los negocios públicos
y, además, el gobernar personalmente la aljama en toda la acepción de
la palabra." Macho y Ortega's statement ("Condición," p.197) is more
moderate, and applies only to the fifteenth-century aljamas of señorío. It is questionable, all the same, even on its own terms: the
aljama of Zaragoza was one of the señorío and did not even have an
amin.

88. The office was abolished by royal edict on January 13, 1337
(C 862:120), and a tax-collector--to be appointed by the General
Bailiff of Valencia--was designated to replace the functions of the

too small to have a qadi: wherever there was a qadi, his authority superceded that of the amin.[89] In fact, the amin was the tax collector and general financial officer of the morería, and no more.[90] In the fourteenth century amins were generally appointed by the lord of the community, and received a set salary from the receipts of the office.[91] Many communities had two or more amins.[92] In addition to collecting the "revenues and other incomes" owed to the lord of the aljama, the amin kept the accounts of the community and turned these books over to the bailiff of the city when he left office, along with any surplus funds he might have accumulated. In the South these accounts were kept in Arabic, and if the bailiff wished to read them he had to hire a translator.[94] The amin also represented

---

amin which could not easily be assumed by the adelantati: "...statuimus et ordinamus quod decetero non sit alaminus in dicta aljama, quinimo cessantes et annullantes officium illud, volumus quod alaminus qui nunc erat in peytis et aliis contribucionibus aljame illius partem sam prout ceteri sarraceni aljame eiusdem ponere ac contribuere teneatur...."

89. "Condición," p.157.

90. This is made perfectly clear in C 862:120, and wàs also the case in Muslim communities outside of Spain in the Middle Ages: see Ira M. Lapidus, Muslim Cities in the Later Middle Ages (Cambridge, Mass., 1967), pp.160, 285.

91. C 1567:124 (Sept.10, 1357); in 1400 Huesca and Fabara obtained the right to appoint their own amins (Macho y Ortega, "Condición," p.155). The amin of Eslida was appointed by the general bailiff in the fifteenth century: see Piles Ros, Estudio, p.333.

92. E.g., Segorbe: C 720:77 (1365).

93. C 1208:78 (Sept.6, 1365); C 1570:87 (Mar.10, 1361).

94. C 1569:75 (published in the Appendix).

the aljama in any suit brought against it bearing on its finances
or properties.[95] Because they were appointed by whoever had jurisdiction over the aljama, and were more directly responsible to him
than any other Muslim official, the amins enjoyed the special confi-
dence of Christian lords, and were frequently entrusted with nego-
tiations or messages betweeen Christians and Muslims.[96] During the
war quite a few amins distinguished themselves by faithful service
to the king, often personally effecting the return of whole communities to the royal service, and most were handsomely rewarded.[97] Often
amins ended up becoming stewards for the personal affairs of the
lords they were responsible to,[98] and it is the popularity they enjoyed
with nobles and kings which explains the frequent references to
them in royal documents, not any great authority within the morería.

It is important to remember that the Mudéjares of fourteenth-
century Spain were cut off from the mainstream of Muslim culture,
and subject to no central regulating authority other than the Crown
of Aragon. It is scarcely surprising that the organization of the
aljama should have become loose and confusing, and should appear
somewhat impractical to modern observers accustomed to the precise

---

95. C 686:172 (Mar.30, 1356).

96. C 1197:129 (1364); C 1211:37 (1365).

97. C 720:77, ut supra, and C 1573:127, 128 (May 6, 1365). There
were also occupational hazards. the amin of Benagar was captured
and tortured by the Bishop of Tortosa in an effort to extort the
money in his keeping: C 1208:78 (Sept.6, 1365).

98. E.g., in the case above: C 1208:78.

definition of duties of office. It is virtually impossible,

for instance, to delineate the nature of the office of faqi

(Castilian alfaquí; Latin alfaquinus).[99] The Arabic word faqih

(from faqiha, "to have legal knowledge") originally designated either

a legal expert, a theologian, a lay-reader, or an elementary school

teacher. During the period of this study, the office seems to have

included a bit of all these, and to have been primarily a legal-

aid position, overlapping but subordinate to both the qadi and

amin. Along with the scribanus (see below), the faqi drew up

"instruments" (i.e., public documents) for the Muslims of his com-

munity,[100] and the offices of faqi and scribanus were frequently

held by the same person.[101] His juridical duties involved principally

the arranging of trials (assigning scribes, etc.), but he could

also impose fines for offenses, such as failure to stand guard or

fortify one's home properly,[102] and had primary jurisdiction in

certain civil cases involving only Muslims.[103] The faqi seems always

---

99. The spelling faqih is preferred by Burns (e.g., Islam, pp.382-
384); it is certainly better Arabic, but less recognizable to those
familiar with Romance forms without the "h." Since he provides no
corroborating evidence, I am forced to conclude that Macho y Ortega
is guessing when he states that the faqi was the head of the mosque
in fifteenth-century Aragon ("Cóndición," p.197). In the fourteenth
century the çabiçala discharged this function: see above, note 41.

100. "Et nullus sit ausus nec posset conficere instrumenta sarracenica inter sarracenos nisi solum alfaquini et scriptores [=scriba-
ni] sarraceni ad id deputati..." C 968:50 (Apr.7, 1362). Cf. note
108, below.

101. C 1518:6 (June 30, 1366); C 1566:103 (Jan.16, 1357).

102. C 1566:115 (Mar.3, 1357). On the arranging of trials, see
C 1068:56 (Dec.4, 1355).

103. C 693:28 (Sept.16, 1357) implies that the faqi of Borja had
primary jurisdiction in all cases involving Muslims.

to have been appointed, often for life,[104] and to have paid in

many cases a certain annual sum for the privilege.[105] It was

probably lucrative; the salary was drawn from the _jura_ of the

offica.[106]

Two seemingly minor officials exercised enormous influence

over the _morería_--the notary and the butcher. The notary (_scri-_

banus or _scriptor_) very often held some other position in the

aljama as well--usually he was the _faqi_; sometimes even the _qadi_[107]

--but it was not from this that he derived his power. It was

simply that the drawing up and notarizing of documents was abso-

lutely indispensable for the protection of one's rights, and prior

to 1360 only court-appointed notaries could make documents for

Muslims with legal authority: "...no one can or should dare to make

public documents for or among Muslims except the _faqi_ and notaries

appointed for Muslims by us...."[108] (In spite of the apparent mean-

ing of the Latin in this document, the Muslims' _scriptor_ was gene-

rally not a Muslim before 1360, although this constituted a direct

violation of the law in Aragon, which prescribed in great detail

the religion of every notary who witnessed any document signed in

---

104. C 966:12 (Apr.5, 1356); C 1518:6, _ut supra._

105. C 1566:103, _ut supra_: in this case, 200s for the _scribania_
and _alfaquinatus_, which he held for a term of four years.

106. _Ibid._

107. C 968:50 (1362); C 1209:106, 157 (1365); C 1518:6 (1366).

108. "...aliquis non sit vel esset ausus nec posse conficere
instrumenta sarracenica inter sarracenos nisi solum alfaqui et scriptores sarraceni deputati per nos" (C 1073:95 [July 8, 1361]). Cf.
note 100, above.

the realm.[109]) The appointment was generally for life, which

made the granting of the crucial position to a Christian particular-

ly odious, and there was no limit on the salary he could draw by

setting prices for contracts and documents.[110] These abuses, plus

the practice of granting the office to favorites who did not even

reside in the city where the office was to be exercised,[111]finally

led to a series of protests and demands for reform in the 1350's

---

109. "En toda e dreita conueniença qu'el cristiano faga e sea
tenudo de conplir a iudío o a moro e la fiziere con carta, deue
la fer escriuano que sea cristiano, e si el judío fiziere carta con
conueniença al cristiano o al moro, escrivano iudío deue fer aquesta carta, e si moro fore tenudo po complir conueniença con carta al
cristiano o al iudío, escriuano moro deue fer la carta. E si entre
las personas de sus ditas fore feito priéstamo de dineros o de otras
cosas, el escriuano de aquella ley qui recibe el priéstamo deue fer
la carta. En pero esto deue seer sabudo que, si sobre alguna cosa
foren feitas cartas entre cristiano e moro e entre moro e iudío o
entre cristiano e iudío, dos testimonias deuen seer puestas en aquellas cartas, una de la una ley et otro de la otra, segunt de qual
ley foren aquellos qui fazen aquellas miercas, e si en aquellas
miercas oujere mester fiança, deue seer recebida de entramas las
partidas comunalment." Fueros de Aragón, II, 121. Cf. s.36 of the
Fueros de Calatayud (1131): "Et christiano firmet ad iudeo cum christiano et iudeo; et iudeos ad christiano similiter; et de mauros similiter fiet" (José Ma. Ramos y Loscertales, "Documentos para la historia del derecho español: Fuero concedido a Calatayud por Alfonso I
de Aragón en 1131," Anuario de historia del derecho español, I (1924),
p.412). I am inclined to disagree with Macho y Ortega, who contends
that the scribano was an official who heard cases between "colectivi-
dades moras y judías o cristianas" ("Condición, p.177). I have seen
no instance where a scribano heard any case, though in their capacity
as scribes they were required to be present at trials (C 1068:56
[1355]) to record oaths and decisions, as well as notarize the testimony of witnesses according to their respective religions (as above).

110. "...habeatis et recipiatis pro salario et labor[e] vestro
a contrahentibus juxta quantitatem et qualitatem contractium..."
C 966:22 (May 11, 1356).

111. A Christian from Jaca for instance, exercised the office
in Calatayud in 1356: C 689:71 (Dec.20). The two cities are almost
200 kilometers apart. In Jaca itself, which did not have a Muslim
aljama, the Jews had a Christian scriptor: C 966:54 (July 20, 1357).

and 1360's.[112] At the meeting of the Corts in Zaragoza in 1360 the
aggrieved Muslims obtained a concession from the Crown that they
be allowed to make their contracts with whomever they wished,[113]
and in 1364 the community of Daroca effected the actual removal of
the Christian scribanus appointed for them ten years before.[114] It
is true that he was reinstated two years later,[115] but in the long
run the Mudéjares' objections prevailed. By the end of the century
most aljamas could choose their own scriptor, and he was always a
Muslim.[116]

___

112. After vehement objections from the Muslims of Teruel in 1354,
the king's lieutenant revoked the appointment of Dominic Exi de Lidon
to the scribania of the Jews and Saracens of the city, which he had
received only six months before (C 686:220 [May 10, 1356]), but the
king subsequently re-appointed him (C 684:224 [May 19, 1356]).   The
following year the king had to give very forceful instructions to
the aljamas of Calatayud to honor his grant of the scribania to Ferdinand Diaz of Altarriba (C 966:58 [Sept.10]), yet he continued to
make such appointments: Bernard Arlouin was awarded the offices of
notary, rabbi, and butcher of the Jewish and Muslim communities of
Borja in October, 1359, for life, all to be held in absentia (C 968:
16). Holding the office for both Jewish and Muslim communities was
common, perhaps the rule: cf. Jacob Castillion, scribanus of both
aljamas of Daroca (C 966:22).

113. C 903:282, text in Appendix. Muslims did not attend and
were not represented at the Curia, but their demands were seriously
considered when war or some other crisis made their goodwill and
co-operation particularly necessary.

114. C 1203:196.

115. C 725:75 (Apr.2).

116. C 1918:73 (Mar.18, 1387). In Valencia the office of scribanus
was generally held conjointly with that of torcimana, or "translator."
Unlike their northern brethren, Valencian Mudéjares spoke little if
any Romance, and all documents had to be translated for them as well
as notarized. It is likely that there were not enough bilingual Muslims even to fill these posts: see concluding chapter. In 1358 a
Jew was appointed to the office in the town of Crevillente (he was
also the notary and customs-master). For three years the aljama

Forbidden unto you are carrion and blood and swine-flesh,
and that which hath been dedicated unto any other than Allah,
and the strangled, and the dead through beating, and the dead
through falling from a height, and that which hath been killed
by horns, and the devoured of wild beasts, saving that which
hath been immolated unto idols. Koran V ("The Table"):3; cf.
II:172ss, V:96; VI:119ss, 146ss; XVI:114ss; XXII:34, 36.

To those reared in the prosperous industrial nations of the

West since the world wars, where meat has been plenty and the mar-

ket system relatively free, the importance of the butcher in the

life of fourteenth-century Iberians may come as rather a surprise.

Throughout the Middle Ages in Spain it was common for livestock to

be strictly regulated by the Crown, nobility, and local officials,

and during the fourteenth and fifteenth centuries the sale of meat

itself was generally handled as a state monopoly rented to the high-

est bidder. The price was monitored minutely, the state's share of

the profits gathered inexorably, and the export of it prohibited

absolutely or taxed astronomically.[117] For the Muslim minority the

problem was aggravated by relatively detailed dietary laws enjoined

upon them by the Koran (above). In their details these were highly

---

struggled to have him removed from office, alleging every sort of
abuse of office against him, but the queen declined to alter her
appointment. Finally the Saracens complained bluntly that it was
not right for a Jew to hold the office among Muslims, and the queen
agreed to reconsider. In 1361 she replaced the Jew with a Christian.
The documents are in C 1547:18, C 1563:93, and C 1569:74, 80, 100, 121.

117. For such regulations see Francesh Carreras y Candi, "Ordinacions de bon govern a Catalunya (segles xiii a xviii)," BRABL, XI
(1923), p.307 ("Ordinacions" of Barcelona, 1301), and passim. Note
that at IV.24.2 of the Costums of Tortosa there is a strong implication of a free market, regulated by neither Crown nor city: "...en
lo qual mercat poden los homens de Tortosa e de sos termens vendre
totes lurs coses e lurs mercaderies, e comprar atressi francament e
sens tota exaction que aqui no son tenguts de donar, a pes ne a me-
sura, ne a leuder; ne a nuyl hom leuda, ne nuyl seruij, ne nulla

like those of the Jews. What the conjunction of the state monopoly on the sale of meat and the Muslim dietary laws meant in practice was that Mudéjares could purchase meat in only one place and
from only one butcher (appointed by the king), and at only one
price--set by the king and regularly one <u>obolum</u> per pound higher
than the price of the same meat in a Christian market (where the
price was set by local officials).[118] Fortunately for historians,
the aljama of Calatayud did not receive its own meat market and
butcher till 1354, and the text of the grant survives. Its provisions are detailed and revealing:

> As we are aware that in every city and town in the kingdom
> of Aragon where Saracens dwell, or there is an aljama of Saracens,
> the aljama or Saracens have their own meat market, separate and
> distinct, and a butcher who kills and prepares the meats they
> require according to their religion and custom..., but you, the
> aljama of Saracens of the town of Calatayud, do not have a sepa-
> rate butcher or market, and since you have asked us to provide
> you with a fitting solution to this problem, we therefore wish
> you to have and concede to you, the aljama of Saracens of the

---

cosa que nols deu esser demanat ne pres...ans en totes coses son
francs e liures e quitis...." But the market of Tortosa was actually regulated as thoroughly as all other markets of the day, as is
clear from the complex and detailed provisions of IX.16.1-8, which
even set prices for specific meats. Cf. for fifteenth-century practice, Macho y Ortega, "Condición," p.198.

118. In Valls the municipal code of 1299-1325 rather curiously
demanded <u>lower</u> prices for meat sold to Jews and Saracens: "Item,
etc., que tota carn de qualque bestia, que degolada sia per jueu,
o per sarray, ques uena la liura, meala menys que aquela daquela
natura que sia degolada per crestiá, e encara, que estía a la taula
hon se uendrá la dita carn degolada per jueu o per sarray, la taula,
o la post quey es acustumada de posar, per tal que sia manifest a
tuyt, que, aquela carn es juygua, o rebuyada per jueus, o per sarrayns. E si per auentura algun carnicer no ueu carn juygya, o rebuyada per jueus, o per sarrayns, ne aquela, o menys que laltra carn
daqueyla natura o menys daquela post damunt dita, que pach per cascuna vegada v. sous, sens tota mercé." Carreras y Candi, "Ordina-

said Calatayud and your successors forever, that you may construct and maintain your own separate meat market in the neighborhood which is called "de los Ferreros" (from St Mary's Hos-
pital to the gate of the juderia), in whatever one house or
shop shall seem best to you. We also wish that outside this
house or shop which you choose you shall not be allowed to
keep weights, [?], or a table.... If you wish to move this
table to your moreria or to a place or neighborhood where you
live, you may do so on the conditions previously given.

    With the proviso that the butcher must be a Christian and
a native of the town of Calatayud, you may choose whomever you
wish as your butcher.... We concede, moreover, that this Christian butcher whom you are to choose may demand and obtain for
all meat [he sells], of whatever type and at all times, one
obolum per pound more than other Christian butchers of the town
of Calatayud, who sell their meat publicly or in the market of
Calatayud.[119]

The requirement that the butcher be a Christian is slightly mislead-

ing. Obviously, a Christian was not apt to be knowledgeable about

Koranic laws or acceptable to the Muslim community as their butcher.

This grant was really no more than the issuance of a license to

slaughter and sell meat to the aljama. The license was to be held

by a Christian, in this case of the aljama's choosing, who would then

rent out the actual job. That this was the practice is made clear

in a similar grant of the carniceria of the aljamas of Zaragoza to

a Jew, Tedroç Aventilca: "...we grant and concede to you one but-

cher or meat-dresser, whomever you may choose to appoint.... This

butcher shall be responsible to you for the usual income [of the

---

cions," p.291. For thirteenth-century rates charged in the carniceria
of Tarazona, see de Bofarull y de Sartorio, Rentas, p.224.

   119. Paraphrase of C 907:56 (Apr. 9, 1362). The original grant
is contained in a later amendment (1362), which allowed the meat
to be prepared outside the market itself.

post]."[120] Although the Calatayud grant is unusual in assigning
the license to whatever Christian the aljama should elect to be-
stow it on, it was not at all unusual for the recipient to be a
Christian: in every documentable case (other than that of Zaragoza)
the license was held by a Christian, and actually exercised by a
Jew or Muslim.[121] The same person generally held both the Jewish
and Saracen licenses, and the office seems to have rendered its
occupant singularly unpopular with both communities:

> ...we order that no Jew or Saracen of either aljama
> may excommunicate or attempt to excommunicate in any way
> the said butcher, nor shall an aljama either impose any bond
> upon him or declare any sentence [against him], or lay any
> excommunication [on him].[122]

This hostility may have been due to the taxes the butcher collected
on an item as basic as meat, or to the fact that, though an official
of the aljama, he was largely free of supervision by any Muslim or
Jewish official.[123] Certainly the office was extremely lucrative,

---

120. C 910:22 (July 1, 1366): "...damus et concedimus tibi unum
carnificem seu talliatorem carnium quemcumque ad hec constituere
volueris.... Qui carnifex teneatur tibi ex iure solito repondere."
Cf. C 689:79 (Jan.14, 1357), where Çalema Biallarus sublets the
meat concession for the Muslims and Jews of Borja from Dominicus
Egidius de Cascellus.

121. D. Bienvenido Oliver wrongly asserts (Historia del derecho
en Cataluña, Mallorca, y Valencia [Madrid, 1878], II, p.62) that the
Costums of Tortosa prohibit a Jew from selling meat. He has clearly
misread IX.16.4, which merely prohibits Jews' slaughtering or dress-
ing it: "Negun jueu carn que en les taules se deja vendre, no deu
degoylar ni la ma dintre les besties metre." Possibly the ordinance
is merely intended to prevent the same Jew from slaughtering and
selling meat.

122. "...mandantes quod nullus iudeus vel sarracenus seu eorum aljama excommunicent vel excommunicare audeant ullo modo dictum carnificem neque etiam aliama vel ligamentum in eum imponere vel iactare
nec sententiam vel excommunicationem aliquam proferre" C 910:22.

123. Ibid. Note that in the case described in Chapter IV, p.176,

and this may have contributed to the ill-will of the aljamas.[124]

From all indications, nevertheless, the holders of the office were conscientious about the responsibility. Bernard Arlouin, for instance, held the license for the Jewish and Muslim carnicerías of Borja (a Jew, Jafudenus Amilus, actually did the butchering and selling),[125] and personally supervised the rebuilding of them after the war, interceding with the king for assistance.[126] In fact, carnicerías were almost always the first things reconstructed when a town began to recover from war damage, and even though other buildings were left in ruins when walls near them were refortified, meat markets were immediately rebuilt.[127] New ones, moreover, continued to be erected throughout the fourteenth century: the king's remark in his letter to Calatayud that every other aljama had a meat market in 1354 was far from accurate. The aljama at Barbastro did not have one till November, 1361,[128] and the community of Valencia did not receive theirs till 1376,[129] though the actual li-

---

the king personally overruled the judgement of the faqi against a Muslim butcher for not fulfilling his military duty as part of the aljama.

124. Note the enormous fine levied in the case of Mahoma Muferig Mançor (C 1566:115 [Mar.3, 1357]).

125. C 704:50 (July 7, 1360).

126. C 703:62 (July 2, 1360).

127. Ibid.; cf. C 1571:89 (Feb.4, 1363).

128. C 906:83 (Nov.14, 1361).

129. Compare the details of this grant with those of the grant above: "...possitis ac vobis liceat construere, facere et tenere infra limites morerie prefate, cui magis elegeritis, carniceriam, et in ea scindere et vendere carnes quascumque et quibuscumque volueritis, et in

cense to build one had been issued at least twice before.[130]

In fact, carnicerías were still being established in the
fifteenth century.[131] Though this may seem a bit curious at first--
what had the Muslims been doing for meat before?--it is actually
readily understandable. Despite royal rhetoric to the contrary, the
carnicerías were not established for the benefit of the Muslims: as
far as they were concerned a carnicería was merely a further restriction on their freedom and a greater financial burden. In a city
which had no Muslim butcher or meat market, capitalism would set the
prices and the sale of meat would be relatively untrammelled, i.e.,

---

et super carnibus nedum inter vos sed etiam quoscumque alios ementes
de dictis carnibus imposicionem quam volueritis, dum nobis placuerit, ponere et ordinare eamque exhigere et levare...." ARV, Real, 613:
158-9, quoted in Roca Traver, "Un Siglo," p.94, n.30.

130. C 1189:192 (July 5, 1363) (n.b. the postscript: non fuit per-
fecta); C 1189:212 (July 13, 1363). Játiva had a separate Muslim
meat market during the reign of Peter, but the arrangements regarding it were not settled: the Muslims protested a municipal tax
levied on non-resident Muslim butchers and meat vendors, and the
king duly revoked the tax in April, 1356. Then the city itself
complained that it was providing, free of charge, the market and
butcher employed by the Saracen aljama, and was entitled to collect
as much from the Saracens thus serviced as it did from the Christians who paid meat taxes to the University ("...ut cum ipsa universitas teneatur et peracta sit tenere sarracenis prelibatis carnificem et tabulam separatam pro parando et excoriando carnes ad eorum
proprios usus, ...dicti sarraceni exsolvant partem eos exsolvere
contingentem in impositionibus carnium predictarum..."). The king
was impressed by this argument, and ordered Garsia de Loriz to investigate to see if the claim of the city was accurate, and if so,
to compel the aljama to pay the tax. Why it should be levied only
on non-resident Muslims is not quite clear: cf. Chapter VI. Possibly
the city was concerned about the exploitation of municipal resources
and services by the apparently very large number of transient Muslims
who came to the city either because it was, in many ways, the most
Muslim of the conquered cities, or because it was a center of trade
for the whole kingdom of Valencia.

131. Macho y Ortega, "Condición," p.172.

it could be effected where and when the parties desired, and the
profits accrued to the Muslim butchers, merchants, and farmers.
Once the official butcher and market had been established, however, the prices, places, and times all came under official control, and since meat was a staple of Mudéjar diet, it provided
a ready medium for head taxes. These could be used, in fact, to
pay for the price of constructing the market, so that no royal
expense was incurred.[132] Taxes were imposed on meat for other,
special purposes as well. In Huesca, for example, a tax was
levied on all meat--whether Christian or Muslim--to support the
Studium Generale.[133]

From the royal point of view, in fact, the only conceivable
reason for not building a market for Saracens was the previous
issuance of a license to do so to someone else. Valencia's not
having its own Muslim market until 1376--though construction of
one had been started at least twenty years earlier--was the result
of the grant of an earlier license to sell meat to the Muslims to
the convent of St Clare, which license the nuns tenaciously protected.[134]

The taxes on meat, both royal and local, and fines for fraud
and other market offenses were collected by a specially appointed
official, the mustaçaf, but the market also lay under the juris-

---

132. C 703:62, ut supra; C 1571:89, ut supra.

133. C 1151:79 (Feb.19, 1357); this despite a royal edict prohibiting such practice: C 684:231 (June 7, 1356).

134. C 1189:212 (July 13, 1363).

dictions of the çalmedina, amin, and bailiff of the city.[135]

There was considerable co-operation between the aljama's butchers and those of the Christian markets: the livestock were pastured jointly,[136] and the Christian butchers were frequently allowed to use the facilities of the Saracen market.[137] Christians often bought meat in the morería, not only to avoid special taxes imposed on the Christian markets, but apparently because the Muslim cuts were desirable in themselves.[138] In the case of the

---

135. C 966:76 (Apr.5, 1358); C 1567:173 (Feb.10, 1360). In Valencia the Crown received 100s per annum from the market: C 1189: 192, ut supra. In Huesca the bailiff alone had jurisdiction over the market: C 704:42 (June 20, 1360); the fines all went to the king. On the election of Catalan mustaçafs, see the privilege of March 27, 1386, conserved in the cathedral archives of Lérida (Rafael Gras de Esteva, Catálogo de los privilegios y documentos originales que se conservan en el archivo reservado de la Ciudad de Lérida [Lérida, 1897], pp.24-5). An excellent study of the mustaçaf of Valencia has been published by F. Sevillano Colóm: Valencia urbana a través del oficio de mustaçaf (Valencia, 1957).

136. C 907:56 (1356).

137. Ibid.; C 899:133 (Nov.29, 1356); but not always: see C 683: 241 (Aug.5, 1356), where Christian butchers are specifically forbidden to sell in the Muslim market of Huesca.

138. Macho y Ortega, "Documentos," pp.451-2. Butchers for the aljama could not, by law, be constrained to sell meat intended for the morería to Christians at the lower price charged in Christian markets (C 907:56, ut supra), except in Barcelona, where an ordinance of 1301 required butchers to sell meat to Christians at Christian prices, whether specially slaughtered or not (Carreras y Candi, "Ordinacions," XI, p.307). Up until 1359 Christians under the jurisdiction of the Bishop of Tortosa were prohibited from eating meat prepared for Muslims or Jews, but the Synod of Tortosa in that year revoked the proscription: "'Revocatio constitutionis, quae incipit. Quamvis in concilio Agatensi.' Item dominus episcopus cum concilio et assensu dicti capituli absolvit, et revocavit ex causa sententiam excommunicationis promulgatam in constitutione synodali contra comedentes carnes et cibaria judaeorum et sarracenorum, prout in ea continetur, quae incipit, Quoniam in consilio Agatensi..." (Joaquin L. Villanueva, Viage literario a las iglesias de España [Madrid, 1806], V, p.358).

former, the Crown sometimes intervened to force the Muslim butchers
to collect a Christian tax from Christians,[139] and Christian offi-
cials--local and royal--generally showed no hesitation about intervening in any aspect of the Muslim market's operation which interested them.[140]

In conclusion, a few words about the aljama and the universitas
seem inevitable. The Christian universitas, the corporate municipal body, was even more important under the Crown of Aragon than in
most medieval states. A highly urban culture, coupled with Catalan
jealousy of and resistance to royal power, caused Catalan cities to
pride themselves on their autonomy and independence, and to invest
the municipal power structure with almost regal prerogatives. Other
areas under the same crown (Valencia, for instance) were quick to
emulate the pretensions of Catalan cities, and a tradition of civic
pride and municipal independence grew up in eastern Spain which in
many ways paralleled the rise of the Italian city-state. Contemporaries viewed the aljama of the Saracens as basically equivalent to
the universitas of the Christians. Many royal documents juxtapose
the two as if they were merely different names for the same institution, and sometimes the aljama is actually referred to as the
universitas sarracenorum.[141] They regulated all the inner workings

---

139. C 899:133, ut supra. In this case, when the latter measure
failed, the Crown prohibited Christian butchers from selling in the
Muslim market, which does not seem exactly to the point (C 683:241,
ut supra). Cf. note 130, above.

140. C 683:181 (1356), discussed at some length in Chapter VI.

141. C 904:59 (Apr.23, 1360).

of the community: commerce, trade, lands, construction and repair
of public buildings. Both established municipal ordinances for
the populations under their jurisdictions. Both oversaw the administration of justice. Both were the ultimate source of fiscal
responsibility for the community: contracting debts, raising the
taxes necessary to meet local needs and royal demands. Both were
theoretically responsible to the king alone, in a manner which
seemed to make his need for their cooperation almost as urgent as
their need for his protection. Both owned communal lands and buildings, and could borrow money as corporations for sudden needs.
Even in their details they were remarkably similar: both were run
by a council, generally plutocratic; both appointed a host of minor
judicial and fiscal officials to manage the quotidian affairs of
their respective municipalities; the physical plants subject to
them were similar, with like facilities for public bathing, similar
meat markets, and even jointly held pasturage.

But it is crucial for a proper understanding of the place of
Mudéjares in fourteenth-century Aragonese society to realize that
the aljama was really in no way the equal of the universitas. The
universitas was the basic, indestructible reality of urban Aragonese
political existence. It existed in accord with the monarch or in
defiance of him. It organized co-operation with his national policies or bore the brunt of his anger when the populace would not
support him. Its authority was self-contained and supported,
unjustified and unquestioned. It was the popular power of the
Corts at its most real and exertable level. It was, moreover, the

only government the average urban dweller ever knew directly or
was personally affected by. Citizens of Barcelona, Tortosa, Lérida, or Valencia obeyed royal edicts as they were relayed to them
through the public officials of the cities. If the public officials declined to concern themselves with the king's projects, the
projects languished. The king could threaten or cajole, even
march on the cities and conquer them, but the authority of the
universitas itself stood.

The position of the aljama was inordinately weaker. The Muslim communities existed by the sufferance of the monarchy. They
were directly dependent on the king for the preservation of their
most basic rights. Both his attitude and their daily lives made
this pellucidly clear to them. The authority of the aljama existed
only insofar as the king wished to protect and support it, or was
able to do so. The ordinances of the aljama could be quashed, its
organization dramatically altered or abolished altogether, its financial arrangements removed from its control or summarily cancelled,
its property confiscated or sold--all at the whim of the suzerain.
In fact, the very persons of the leaders of the aljama were by
universal assent of the Christian populace subject to arbitrary
seizure by the king or his officials, and, for any of hundreds of
offenses against laws regularly invoked, to being sold as slaves.
Even in its direct relationship to the universitas the aljama was
in a position of inferiority. Various municipal bodies could regulate aspects of life in the morería--e.g., the price of meat, the

export of grain or other goods, freedom to bear arms or travel
at night, the construction or repair of walls or public buildings--
while the aljama had no pretense to any control over the Christian
section of the city, even in heavily Muslim areas like Játiva.[142]
Even the traditional sanctuary offered--in practice if not in theo-
ry--by cities to runaways was denied to aljamas: runaways could be
and frequently were extracted from morerías.

In many ways the morerías of Aragon-Catalonia-Valencia (especially the last) were probably superior to the Christian portions of the cities they shared with their conquerors. Equipped
with extremely sophisticated irrigation and water supply systems,
large public baths, hospitals, beautiful mosques, and with artisans and craftsmen in great demand among the Christian populace,
they glittered with the abandoned gems of a more elaborate and
complex society. But politically they were children, allowed to
regulate their own affairs as it suited the king, and controlled
in minute detail when it did not. Ultimately, the aljama had no
rights, only privileges, granted by the king and valid at his pleasure. Such privileges were about as effective in guaranteeing the
autonomy of the aljama as the walls of the morería were in protecting its inhabitants from the pogroms of later years.

---

142. For an interesting fifteenth-century demonstration of this,
see Piles Ros, Estudio, p.197, #313 bis.

Chapter III

Mudéjares before the Law: Competing Systems of Justice

When, in 1115, the Saracens of Tudela signed a treaty of
capitulation with Alfonso el Batallador, it was agreed by both
sides that henceforth the Muslims, though subject to the king's
authority generally, should retain their own criminal courts
and judges, and that these should have final jurisdiction over
them even in cases involving Christians:

> ...that they be and remain in their litigations and
> trials under the jurisdiction of their qadi and his lieuten-
> ants, just as in the days of Muslim rule. And if a Muslim
> shall have litigation with a Christian, or a Christian with a
> Muslim, the Muslim qadi shall render judgement to the Muslim,
> according to Islamic law, and the Christian judge to the
> Christian, according to [Christian] law.[1]

In nearly every surviving treaty of capitulation between Muslims
and Christians similar guarantees were made of the perpetual inviolability of Muslim law and juridical process,[2] yet by the mid-fourteenth century, Muslim communities actually enjoying the legal privileges accorded them in preceding centuries were extremely few.

Although the Bailiff of Játiva was the only Christian official
within the kingdom of Valencia legally entitled to hear cases
between Muslims in the mid-fourteenth century, no less than eighty-

---

1. "...quod sint et stent illos in judicio et pleytos in manu de
lure alcudi, et de lures alguaziles, sicut in tempus de illos moros
fuit. Et si habuerit moro judicio cum christiano, vel christianus
cum moro, donet judicium alcudi de moros ad suo moro, secundum suam
zunam, et alcudi de christianos ad suum christianum secundum suum
foro" Muñoz y Romero, Colección, p.416.

2. E.g., that of Chivert: "...contencio vel querela inter christianos et sarracenos vel iudeos alfachinus alcaydus iudicet sarracenus,
secundum legem suam, et christianus baiulus templi iudicet christianos et iudeos" Roca Traver, "Un Siglo," p.73, n.217; cf., for Játiva: "Si aliquis christianus conqueratur de sarraceno recipiat iusticie complementum in posse çaymedine vestre, secundum çunam sarra-

nine percent of all such cases recorded during the decade 1355-1365
were heard by some Christian official. In fact, of the nineteen
cases between Muslims summarized in the table appended to this
chapter, fourteen of the trials were conducted in clear violation
of Muslim treaty agreements and the laws of Valencia.

In Aragon the disparity was slightly less pronounced, possibly
because the royal house had begun as early as 1316 to put a stop
to illegal interference in Muslim judicial matters by Christian
officials.[3] None of the cases recorded for Zaragoza violated the
rights of the aljama there, and only one of nine recorded for Borja
violated the privileges of that aljama. In Lérida, however, half
the cases reported were counter to the law and the rights of the
Muslims, and in Huesca more than two-thirds contravened the king's
own provisions for the Mudéjar community there.[4] The tendency in
all these cases was to remove jurisdiction from Muslim courts and
officials and to place it in the hands of Christian ones.

Though in each of the kingdoms under the Crown of Aragon some
Muslim officials had competence over cases between Muslims and
Christians, in only one case (in Catalonia) between the two peoples
during the entire period did a Muslim official exercise such jurisdiction. Only once did a Muslim official preside at a trial involving

---

cenorum" ibid., n.218. Cf., for Lérida (1228), Villanueva, Viage,
XVI, p.181.

3. C 907:58 (Jan.1, 1316).

4. One-third of the recorded cases violate the provisions of James
II, and another third the grant of Peter IV (both of these discussed
below), even though they take place within a few years of the issuance

Jews and Muslims, and then only jointly with the bailiff of the
city. Most surprising of all, though a majority of Mudéjar communities enjoyed the right to try civil cases between Muslims, in
Valencia they were able to exerci e this right only about ten percent of the time, and in Catalonia only about fifty percent. In
Aragon they did actually exercise the prerogative a majority
of the time, but even here well over half the cases (about 60%)
originally heard before Mudéjar officials were subsequently removed
or appealed to Christian ones, making the over-all competence of
the Muslim courts in Aragon even more limited than those in Catalonia.

The process by which this transition was effected, and the
reasons adduced by Christian authorities for their steady encroachments upon promised Mudéjar judicial independence, will be considered
in more detail subsequently. To facilitate the reader's understanding of the process, the following pages offer a description of the
Christian officials involved in the administration of justice to
Mudéjares and the general purview of their jurisdiction. As will
be shown later, such limitations as existed in theory on the competence of a particular official bear little relation to his authority
in practice. The list is thus intended merely to characterize
and introduce these officials and their offices, rather than to
define them. The offices themselves were not defined. The index

---

of the latter. Of all the cases recorded, only two (C 715:56 and
C 1197:9) seem to conform to the law. All of the data upon which
the observations on these pages is based are summarized in the table
at the end of this chapter.

of cases provided at the end of this chapter affords a better
look at the authority _actually_ exercised by them.

The KING himself intervened in relatively few cases, although
all authority over Muslims stemmed ultimately from him. He appears
to have concerned himself primarily with cases in which favorites
of his were concerned, such as suits involving Faraig de Belvis,
or the suit of Çaat Alcafaç against the king's own mercenaries.
In other cases, even those of major importance, he was generally
content to allow the general bailiff or some other official to
deal with the matter. In all cases, nonetheless, the king recéived
one-fourth of the penalty ("calonia") if it was financial,[5] and the
whole fine in capital cases such as sodomy or miscegenation.[6] Sometimes he granted his rights over the _calonias_ to others in reward
for services rendered or as a form of vassalage.[7] He could and
did transfer jurisdiction from one _qadi_ to anòther as well as from
one Christian official to another.[8]   There are more than a few

---

5. Roca Traver, "Un Siglo," pp.68-9.

6. Macho y Ortega, "Condición," p.179.

7. E.g., the grant to Blasius Acenarius de Lorau of those of Daroca
in return for two cavalrymen: "...concedimus vobis predictos denarios
quos pro nobis habeatis teneatis et percipiatis in et super dicta
aljama sarracenorum predicte ville [Daroce] et caloniis ipsius dum
vitam duxeritis in humanis, ac si et prout dictus Sanctius de Martes a nobis ipsos habebat et percipiebat, pro quibus servitium duorum
equitorum armatorum nobis facere teneamini juxta forum..." C 966:74
(Feb.23, 1358).

8. In 1365, for example, the king removed the Muslim population
of the valley of Almonacir from the jurisdiction of Segorbe and constituted a new jurisdiction for them within the valley, prohibiting
any further extradition of them to Segorbe: C 1205:69 (Apr.7). He
could not, however, grant an _elongamentum_ (prorogation) for a fine
already imposed by a _qadi_: C 719:106 (Feb.12, 1365).

cases in the registers of Muslims appealing to the king to intervene in Muslim proceedings, and it seems likely that he was thought
of by the Mudéjares as fair and impartial. Certainly in those cases
where he did rule (and a record is preserved) there seems to have
been no tendency toward favoritism, except perhaps a slight leaning
toward the Muslims.

The QUEEN was granted a great many aljamas during the course
of the war, primarily to supplement her dwindling income from other
sources. These included the Saracen aljamas of Tortosa, Torella,
Borja, Burriana, Eslida, and Játiva, and the Jewish aljama of Valencia. Many of these remained under the control of the Queen of
Aragon through the fourteenth century.[9] Eleanor, during the decade
in concern here, took possession of all fines collected through
judicial channels, but did not personally intervene any more than
her husband in juridical proceedings themselves, except in Valencia.
There she demanded that Peter Boyl, the general bailiff, immediately
terminate the inquisition in progress against the Muslims (see p.370)
and yield to her all jurisdiction over them.[10] She does not appear
to have heard cases herself thereafter, nonetheless, but to have
allowed the bailiff of the city and Muslim officials there to
supervise the administration of justice.

The GENERAL BAILIFF was the official who oversaw the ordinary functioning of the laws of the realm. As the king's deputy
he enjoyed particular authority over Muslims and Jews, "the king's

---

9. Macho y Ortega, "Documentos," p.148.
10. C 1534:129 (Dec.22, 1361); cf. C 1537:56 (Jan.1, 1363).

treasure." Each of the three kingdoms had a general bailiff, and
in each the office was for life and salaried at 2,000s annually,
plus "jura et castra."[11] The opportunities for increasing one's
personal wealth must have been enormous.   Each general bailiff
was supreme in his own kingdom, and co-operation between them was
effected through the king.[12] Mudéjares were subject to the bailiff
of the realm in which they found themselves at any given moment:
Saracens from Barcelona accused of a crime in Aragon were under
the jurisdiction of the General Bailiff of Aragon,[13] Valencian
Muslims leaving the country through Barcelona had to be certified
by the General Bailiff of Catalonia,[14] and Catalan or Aragonese
Mudéjares leaving through Valencia were certified by the General
Bailiff of Valencia.[15]

Particularly in Valencia, the rule of the general bailiff was
ubiquitous and all-encompassing. He issued licenses to bear arms,
beg alms, disregard dress codes, practice prostitution, change
residence, visit enemy countries, transport merchandise, and emigrate, and he prosecuted anyone caught doing these things without

---

11. C 1074:98 (May 21, 1362); RP 1704:50 (1357). For an excellent
detailed study of the General Bailiff of Valencia in the fifteenth
century, see L. Piles Ros, Estudio documental sobre el Bayle General
de Valencia (Valencia, 1970).

12. C 688:97 (Dec.17, 1356).

13. Ibid.

14. C 904:139 (Aug.13, 1360), in ppendix.

15. Registers of the Real Patrimonio, passim, provide examples of
these functions and the respective jurisdictions of the general
bailiffs.

one of his licenses.[16] He could bring charges against as well as try Muslims for any criminal act, and in most areas he was competent to hear civil cases involving Muslims and Christians (see below). He could seize and imprison Saracens suspected of crimes, and frequently did so, especially in cases of carnal relations between Muslims and Christians.[17] He determined the salaries of other officers of his courts,[18] and investigated the honesty even of Muslim legal officials. Numerous instances occurred during the decade of the general bailiff's prosecuting and fining qadis and çalmedinas for abuses of office or even simple incompetence.[19]

Peter Boyl, the General Bailiff of Valencia during most of the reign of Peter the Ceremonious,[20] made the office even more

---

16. His ability to license emigration and almsbegging were often limited or circumscribed by the king in response to special circumstances: see C 1506:20 (Mar.22, 1363), where the king forbids the issuance of further licenses to emigrate, and C 862:124 (1337), where the king removed the right to grant alms licenses from the purview of the General Bailiff of Valencia. In addition to these duties, the general bailiff of all kingdoms provided the king with financial information about the state of the aljamas (C 687:50 [June 8, 1356]), enforced royal edicts, supervised levying of troops on Muslim aljamas, and generally acted as the king's deputy in regard to Muslims. This latter function extended to the protection, in the king's name, of foreign Muslims visiting the king's lands: see C 720:8, in the Appendix.

17. RP 1710:23 (1365), for example.

18. C 966:96 (Feb.10, 1357).

19. E.g., the inquisition initiated against Azmet Açaba for abuses of the office of qadi, which culminated in Azmet's paying a fine of 900s (RP 1704:23 [1357]); cf. the fine imposed on the çalmedina of the morería of Játiva for incompetence ("errades que's deya ignoranter auer fets"): RP 1706:18 (1360).

20. The first General Bailiff of Aragon during the decade 1355-65 was Peter Jordan. He also held the post of General Bailiff of Cata-

powerful than it had been traditionally, through his close relationship to the king and tireless efforts to increase his own authority
at the expense of that of the Governor of Valencia, Garcia de Loriz.
Through Boyl's efforts a number of rights which had been removed
from the office in the early years of Peter IV's rule were restored
to it (e.g., the right to issue alms licenses),[21] and his personal
power extended far beyond the official prerogatives of the office.
The king granted him personally, for instance, absolute criminal
and civil jurisdiction over a number of areas of Valencia formerly
not subject to the general bailiff:

> We hereby grant and concede to you and yours forever,
> under the agreement following, with a free and irrevocable
> donation, all criminal jurisdiction which does or should belong
> to us over the living Saracens, present or future, in the place
> called Alcocer, which belongs to the heir of Raymund Castellano,
> situated within the term of the city of Valencia, as well as
> that in the place called Aledua, which belongs to Berengar
> Fabra and Jacob Scivamur, knights, within the term of the city
> of Alcira. [This applies to all] the inhabitants, either in-
> side the places and their environs, or on public roads where
> they do wrong, regardless of their status, or whether they are
> native or foreign..., saving only that [you] shall not inflict
> the death penalty, which we expressly reserve to ourselves....[22]

---

lonia until his death in 1362, when Blasius Acenarius de Borau replaced him as Bailiff of Aragon, and Jacob de Rocafort as Bailiff
of Catalonia (C 1074:98 [May 21, 1362], C 687:50 [June 8, 1356],
C 719:88 [Jan.31, 1365]). In 1364 a new general bailiwick was created "ultra Sexonam" for the area to the southwest of the bailiwick
of Valencia proper. This post was filled by Johannes Dolit (RP 1711,
preface).

21. C 692:154 (July 21, 1357). Cf. "Rights."

22. "Tenore presentis damus et concedimus vobis et vestris perpetuo sub pacto subscripto, donatione pura et irrevocabili, inter vivos
iurisdictionem criminalem nobis quomodolibet pertinentem et pertinere debentem in sarracenis nunc habitantibus et habitaturis in loco d'Alcacer, qui est heredis Raymundus Castellani, in termino civitatis Valentie situato, ac in loco d'Aledua, qui est Berengarii Fab-

This authority included the power to "burn or brand...ears, hands and feet, noses and other members, or to remove or amputate them, to incarcerate or banish, or [inflict] any other punishment or type of sentence...as should seem fitting, without any appeal, complaint, supplication or recourse" by the Muslims.[23]

Unlike the GOVERNOR OF VALENCIA, the GOVERNOR OF ARAGON was competent to hear Muslim cases in his courts.[24] In fact, it was so common for civil cases between Muslims to reach his court that Mudéjares began using the expense involved in travelling to and appearing in his court as a weapon against each other, bringing false accusations to bear against other Muslims they wished to incommode. In March of 1356, to put a stop to this, the king prohibited the governor from hearing any but really necessary cases between Saracens,[25] but this measure apparently failed of its effect, and in April of the same year he ordered the governor to prosecute the Moors who were using his court for their own personal vendettas.[26] In general his authority seems to have been directed

---

re et Iacobi Scivamur, militum, in termino ville Algezire constituto, et eorum terminis, sive infra ipsa loca et eorum terminos cuiuscumque conditionis existant, sive delinquant in caminis publicis sive non, et sive sint extranei sive privati..., dum tamen pena mortis, quam nobis expresse reservamus, non habeant condempnare" C 911: 28 (Oct.22, 1364).

23. "...fustigando, crucesignando...aures, manus et pedes, nares et alia membra auferendo et privando, relegando, exulando et quovis alio punitionis et condemnacionis genere..visum fuerit, absque aliqua appellatione, provocatione, et suplicatione vel recurssu..." ibid.

24. E.g., C 683:154 (Mar.31, 1356).

25. Ibid.

26. C 683:171 (Apr.2, 1356).

toward actually executing orders of the courts and guaranteeing
the personal rights of Muslims accused before the law.[27] His jurisdiction did not extend outside the kingdom of Aragon.[28] The Governor of Valencia, as has been seen, had rather limited jurisdiction. Officially, his primary duty in regard to the Muslim population of Valencia was probably the capture and prosecution of
runaway slaves (even those not vassals of the king), which was the
one area where there was no dispute between him and the general
bailiff.[29] Apart from these duties, the governors in both kingdoms
frequently dealt with Mudéjares simply as the deputies of the king.[30]

It is impossible to define clearly the duties or prerogatives
of the JUSTICE OF ARAGON.[31] Apart from records of his presiding
at certain trials, there is so little evidence that it is impossible
to infer the precise authority over Muslims enjoyed by the holder
of this office. In Aragon and Catalonia there were, in addition,
LOCAL JUSTICES, whose salaries were paid by the citizens of the

---

27. E.g., C 1402:147 (Feb.1, 1359).

28. C 691:163 (Jan.29, 1358) is a letter from the king to the Governor of Aragon, forbidding him to carry out an execution on the property of some Hospitallers' Mudéjares in Aztone "quia dicta loca non
intra regnum predictum Aragonie situata existunt, sed potius intra
Cathalonie principatum, ex quo in eisdem locis per vos executio non
debet fieri quavis ratione vel causa."

29. C 693:163 (Oct.18, 1357). In the fifteenth century there was
such a dispute: see Piles Ros, Estudio.

30. See, for examples: C 688:32 (Aug.21, 1356),   688:91 (Dec.17,
1356), 689:48 (Nov.30, 1456), 690:165 (Feb.16, 1357), 693:9 (Aug.
5, 1357), 908:233 (Sept.1, 1363).

31. There is no clear evidence of a Justice of Valencia in the
fourteenth century.

town,[32] and who seem to have acted generally (like the Justice
of Aragon) as the king's vicar in any given case involving Muslims.[33]

Outside of Valencia, the LOCAL BAILIFF seems to have played
a greater and greater role in the administration of Muslim justice
as the fourteenth century progressed, possibly because he was the
one official with clear jurisdiction in every Aragonese and Catalan
city or town. This is suggested both by the fact that during the
depopulation occasioned by the Great Plague many duties formerly
discharged by other officials devolved upon town bailiffs, the one
indispensable official,[34] and by the fact that the monarch made
use of the local bailiff as the repository of all cases not lying
under the specific competence of another judge.[35]

Whatever the causes of this tendency, it made a good deal of
sense. If Muslims were not themselves to have control of legal
proceedings concerning them, the local bailiff was certainly the
Christian official most apt to deal fairly with them: he had little
to gain from harassing them, and was uniquely familiar with life
in the morería, since his ordinary duties included supervision of
its physical upkeep and facilities, overseeing the erection of

---

32. C 1567:183 (Mar.23, 1360).

33. For the Justice of Aragon, see C 723:90 (Oct.22, 1365) and
C 900:42 (Mar.7, 1358); for the local justices, see C 683:241
(Aug.5, 1356), C 684:231 (June 7, 1356), and C 986:188 (Feb.5,
1359).

34. See López de Meneses, Documentos, p.65.

35. E.g., C 683:153-4 (Mar.31, 1356).

needed walls or buildings (such as <u>carnicerías</u>), assigning taxes

and assessing the property values of Muslim edifices, and safe-

guarding Muslims against unjust taxation by royal officials.[36]

The city of Valencia had separate bailiffs for its Christian and

Muslim populations,[37] as did Borja.[38] The duties of the latter

were seen by the king as comprising "the exercise, on our behalf,

...of law and justice among Jews and Saracens, [in cases] among

themselves or involving those who have claims against them...."[39]

Peter was adamant that the particular care of Muslims by the local

bailiffs should not be disturbed by other officials:

> ...we command that, keeping absolutely clear of all the
> aforesaid [duties] and similar ones which pertain to the juris-
> diction or the office of the said bailiwick, you shall in no
> way endeavor to intervene against the said aljamas or any of
> their members, singly or in groups, or [interfere] with the
> privileges and incomes of the said bailiwick....[40]

It is somewhat difficult to generalize about the judicial duties

---

36. For examples of such duties, see C 684:233 (June 8, 1356), C
711:135 (Jan.24, 1363), C 699:66 (Nov.26, 1359) (the protective
function of the bailiff vs. other officials is particularly evident
in this document), C 714:23 (Mar.22, 1363), C 908:233 (Sept.1, 1363),
and C 1571:89 (Feb.4, 1363).

37. RP 1708:18 (1362).

38. C 1566:129 (July 5, 1357). In this document Garsia M. de Bierlas is appointed to the office of the "bajulia judeorum et sarracenorum Burgie," although he already held the "bajulia civitatis Terolis
et aljamarum sarracenorum et judeorum eiusdem" as of April, 1356
(C 966:21). Cf. C 966:46 (July 26, 1356) and C 1566:157 (Nov.5, 1357).
There is some reason to suspect that de Bierlas was particularly associated with Muslim affairs: see Chapter VII, p.347, n.75.

39. "...exercendum pro nobis...jus et justiciam ipsis judeis et
sarracenis inter se et querelantibua de ipsis..." C 966:54 (June 27,
1357).

40. "...mandamus quatenus a predictis omnibus et similibus vos
penitus abstinendo de hiis qui ad cognitionem seu oficium [sic]
spectant bajulie predicte, contra dictas aljamas vel aliquem ipsarum

of the local bailiff. As the "ordinary" of the aljama,[41] he
was called upon to conduct many trials himself (see table), but
there does not seem to have been a type of case reserved specifically for his jurisdiction. The bailiff of Barcelona enjoyed sole
criminal jurisdiction over Muslims in the city, but this cannot
have been common; there was no aljama in Barcelona, and all the
Muslims under the bailiff's jurisdiction would have been captives.[42]
In general, Aragonese and Catalan local bailiffs seem either to
have performed the functions attributed to the General Bailiff of
Valencia [43] or to have acted simply as the king's direct representative or deputy in a given city.[44]

In Valencia the role of the local bailiff was minimized by
the enormous authority of the general bailiff of the kingdom.
As in Aragon-Catalonia, local bailiffs oversaw the physical upkeep
of the morerías (and even assigned lands to Muslim immigrés[45]),
granted licenses, and administered justice in purely municipal mat-

---

aut singulares earundem, vel de cognitione jurium et reddituum dicte
bajulie vos intromittere minime procuretis..." C 713:178 (Feb.28, 1363.

41. C 983:156 (Jan.21, 1359).

42. C 967:275 (Sept.12, 1358); cf. C 685:44 (Oct.14, 1355), in Appendix. Cf. also note 104, below.

43. E.g., the regulation of prostitutes: C 686:14 (Oct.14, 1355).

44. Cases where the bailiff deals with Muslims as the king's deputy:
C 683:240 (Aug.8, 1356), C 686:218 (May 10, 1356), C 686:220, ut supra
C 687:50 (June 8, 1356), C 688:122 (Jan.14, 1357), C 689:71 (Dec.20,
1356), C 689:79 (Jan.14, 1357), C 690:31 (Aug.12, 1356), C 705:178
(July 22, 1361), C 711:135 (Jan.24, 1363), C 721:135 (Jan.22, 1365),
C 1571:89 (Feb.4, 1363), C 1573:165 (Oct.4, 1365). For the bailiff's
role in the fifteenth century, see Macho y Ortega, "Documentos," p.
147 (but read for the date of this entry 1399 instead of 1339).

45. C 1569:102 (July 6, 1361).

ters, but the general bailiff jealously guarded his prerogatives
over the Mudéjares, and the local bailiffs of Valencia seem to
have heard cases mostly involving only Christians.[46] It is ironic
in a way that local bailiffs in Valencia did not hear Muslim
cases as often as their Aragonese counterparts, since, unlike the
latter, Valencian bailiffs were sometimes Muslims.[47]

The JURISPERITI were Christian lawyers assigned to hear
or assist in cases involving Muslims and Christians, or, occasionally
only Muslims. Muslims could not be lawyers (see Chapter VII), and
hence had need of expert legal advice in their suits before Christian authorities. There is some evidence that certain Christians
specialized in law relating to Muslims: Martin de la Torre appears
in at least seven cases involving Muslims during the decade, in
numerous localities.[48] Several of these cases are among the most

---

46. On licenses, see C 862:124 (1337); on his hearing of Christian cases, see C 1571:40 (Aug.26, 1362). Cf. the opinion of Roca
Traver that "los justicias de las villas intentaron sentenciar personalmente los litigios suscitados, mas el monarca cortó rápidamente
este abuso, ordenando que en estos asuntos fuera el bayle [general]
quien entendiera" ("Un Siglo," p.71). That the king upheld the
jurisdiction of the Christian general bailiff against that of the
Christian local bailiffs hardly justifies Roca Traver's subsequent
conclusion that the aljama was "a judicial entity completely separate from the Christian community" (ibid.).

47. RP 1704:2, 1705:2, 1706:2, 1709:2, 1719:2 are the lists of
payments for the office of Bailiff of Valencia (city) for the years
1357, '59, '60, '62, '64, and '63, respectively. The only year the
holder of the office is specified--1358--he is Ali Alfoxeni, who
paid 700s for the office (about average: for the salaries of Valencian bailiffs, see RP 1711:27ss, and for other remuneration, C 966:
96 [Feb.10, 1357]). As has been pointed out, there were separate
bailiffs for Muslims and Christians in Valencia, so Alfoxeni did not,
presumably, hold office over Christians.

48. C 708:213 (Apr.6, 1362), C 714:137 (Sept.14, 1363), C 723:158

celebrated of the time, e.g., the conspiracy of Cilim, or the robbery of the king's qadi, Faraig de Belvis. His name never occurs in trials involving only Christians.

It is not possible to determine exactly the distinctions between other officers of the courts, such as the ALGUATZIRUS (cf. Castilian "alguacil"), LICENCIATUS IN LEGIBUS, JUDEX, LEGUM DOCTOR , etc. The titles themselves explain as much as can be inferred from the documents.

Even in Christian courts the administration of justice to Muslims differed from that for Christians. Jews and Muslims could not be constrained to swear upon the Gospels, and elaborate provisions were made in Aragonese codes of law for the taking of oaths from them.[49] Nor could Christians be required to swear to or at the demand of a Muslim or Jew, but only at the behest of a judge, and only on the Gospels or the head of a Christian.[50]

The question of witnesses was rather perplexing, and official policy on the subject varied from time to time. Under the Fueros of Aragon Christians in criminal cases had to be convicted on the testimony of two Christians, while Muslims or Jews were to be convicted by one Christian and one person of their own faith.[51] In

---

(Dec.20, 1365), C 1197:19 (Feb.26, 1364), C 1207:4 (May 30, 1365), C 1208:77 (Sept.6, 1365), RP 2911:6. Garsia de Munyonis of Pamplona also specialized in Muslim cases (C 705:138, C 700:144, etc.).

49. See the very complex dispositions of the Fueros on the subject, where the oath is determined both by the religion of the swearer and the nature of the crime: II.134, 138. Cf. Ramos y Loscertales, "Recopilación," s.83; Carreras y Candi, "Ordinacions," XI, p.388.

50. Costums, IV.1.4; Villanueva, Viage, VI, p.185.

51. Fueros, VIII.315 (Tilander, p.186).

civil cases the plaintiff had to provide one witness of his faith and one of the defendant's.[52] This latter provision was included not from any concern for objectivity, but because, as the legislators commented, "if battle or ordeal were required by law of such witnesses, the Jew or Moor would never be able to find Christian witnesses to testify for them."[53] The Costums of Tortosa provided that a Christian must prove something against a Muslim with two or more Muslim witnesses, and a Muslim against a Christian with two or more Christians.[54] Nevertheless, the Costums also denied to both Jews and Muslims the right to testify in capital cases such as kidnapping,[55] and excluded many Muslims from court by denying freedmen generally the right to testify against their padrons, and prohibiting anyone with less than fifteen morabetíns in personal wealth from bringing suit in any court.[56]

In Majorca Saracen captives could not even bear witness against Jews, by special royal edict,[57] and in Valencia in the thirteenth

---

52. Fueros, II.107 (Tilander, p.53).

53. "...si batalla o torna fuesse iudgada por fuero contra tales testimonias, nunqua podría trobar el iudío o el moro testimonias cristianos qui testimoniassen por ellos" ibid. It is odd that this reason should be adduced, however, since the testing of Christian witnesses for Muslims by combat or ordeal is specifically prohibited later in the same chapter (II.114). Cf. the earlier version in Ramos y Loscertales, "Recopilación," and its significance, below, p. 368.

54. IV.11a.29. Note that in Jewish-Christian conflicts only one witness of the opposite faith was required (IV.11a.27-28).

55. IX.24.6.

56. IX.1a.13.

57. Llabrés y Fita, "Privilegios de los hebreos mallorquines," BRAH, XXXVI (1900), p.24 (document of July 21, 1269); cf. "Carta de la paería de Tortosa (1276)," in D. Bienvenido Oliver, Historia del

century a Muslim could be convicted of a criminal act on the testimony of two Christians alone.[58]   But in Aragon under the reign of Peter IV the provisions of the Fueros were strictly observed regarding witnesses in criminal and civil cases: "...it has always been the usage of the kingdom, according to law and custom, in civil and criminal cases involving Muslims to admit Muslim witnesses, and without the proof of Muslim witnesses never to rule on Muslim cases...."[59]

Although Muslims could not, as has been observed, practice law, they were free to bring suit before Christian judicial officials as plaintiffs in civil suits.[60]   It was common for Muslims and Christians to file suit jointly as co-plaintiffs, or to be named as co-defendants in civil or criminal action;[61]   this implies at least generally equal footing before the law.   The court sometimes

---

derecho en Cataluña, Mallorca, y Valencia (Madrid, 1878), II, p.498.

58. "Item stablim e ordenam que dos testimonis christians convinents de bona fama puguen fer testimoni e llur testimoni sia cregut contra iuheus e sarrahins en tot fet criminal que sia entre christians e iuheus o christians e sarrahins ho contrastants nenguns privilegis per nos o per nostres antecessors atorgats a iuheus o a sarrahins..." (privilege of James II [Aureum Opus, 12], published in Roca Traver, "Un Siglo," p.74, n.224).

59. "...de foro et consuetudine regni fuerit solitum in questionibus tam civilibus quam criminalibus sarracenorum recipi testes sarracenos et sine probatione testium sarracenorum questiones ipsorum nullatenus terminari..." C 705:134 (June 9, 1361). In fifteenth-century Aragon the Crown went even further, and granted to some Muslims the right to be accorded equal weight of testimony in legal process: see Macho y Ortega, "Condición," p.172.

60. As were foreigners: Costums, III.1a.29.

61. C 684:105 (Jan.22, 1356), C 686:16 (Oct.24, 1355), C 706:197 (Oct.21, 1361).

appointed public defenders for individual Muslims accused of some

crime,[62] and in at least one instance appointed a regular attorney

for an aljama:

> Since the Muslim aljama of the city [of Teruel] and its
> members have and intend to have numerous suits pending, both
> as plaintiffs and defendants, with the city and with various
> other persons, and since your advocacy may be extremely use-
> ful and necessary for them, we therefore direct and command you
> to act on their behalf in all these [cases], and in all mat-
> ters to assist them and to lend them in such suits advocacy,
> aid, counsel and support.[63]

With the exceptions noted above, Muslims enjoyed the same

privileges and suffered the same liabilities in the general proce-

dure of the court as their compatriots. They could be extradited to

stand trial, but not to give testimony, except by the king himself

or with reimbursement.[64] They had to pay court expenses when the

case was decided against them or dropped.[65] They were required by

law and royal edict to carry through to a conclusion any legal ac-

tion they began.[66] They could be—and frequently were—pardoned by

---

62. Such public defenders were called "caplevatores": C 686:92 (Jan.2, 1356).

63. "Cum aljama agarenorum civitatis eiusdem et eius singulares habeant et habere intendant diversas questiones agendo vel defend-endo cum universitate dicte civitatis et nonnullis aliis personis, sitque eis patrocinium vestrum plurimum necessarium et etiam opor-tunum, eapropter vobis dicimus et mandamus quatenus fovendo partem dicte aljame in omnibus, et per omnia assistatis eidem, sibique in dictis causis prestetis patrocinium, auxilium, consilium, et favor-em" C 1570:36 (Sept.23, 1360).

64. Fueros, II.110; C 720:39 (Sept.1, 1365).

65. Such expenses were often enormous: C 1183:118 (Nov.18, 1362) mentions court expenses of 1,150s; C 1566:154 (Nov.5, 1357) sets court costs at 2,000s.

66. Costums, III.1a.29.

the king, before or after a trial, for any crimes they might have committed,[67] or come to a "settlement" either with the presiding official or with the offended party or his family.[68]   Even the murder of Christians by Muslims was occasionally settled out of court.[69]

The king received all or part of fines collected for such offenses as assault, manslaughter, theft, adultery, fraud, malfeasance in office, etc., even when all parties involved were Muslims.[70]   Homicidia were collected from Muslims by the amin of the aljama, but turned over to the local bailiff to be employed at the king's discretion.[71]   Other fines were retained by the presiding official of the trial, or split between two when a dispute arose over jurisdiction.[72]   Enforcement of fines was generally the duty of the local bailiff, but as with other police functions of the courts (i.e., apprehending the accused, enforcing subpoenas, etc.), the king employed whatever officials might be handy in a particular case.[73]

The amount of fine and type of punishment for Muslims, or for

---

67. E.g., C 1205:45 (Mar.15, 1365). Cf. table, below.

68. E.g., RP 1704:23 (1357), where six Saracens accused of defrauding the city of Játiva with defective building materials settle out of court with the bailiff for the sum of 2,400s.

69. C 687:84 (July 12, 1356); C 900:27 (Feb.26, 1358).

70. RP 1705:22ss (1359); RP 1706:18 (1360).

71. C 1570:87 (Mar.10, 1361).

72. RP 1709:19 (1364).

73. E.g., the superadjuttarius: C 707:193 (Apr.9, 1362).

Christians committing crimes against Muslims, were established either by _fuero_ or by royal edict.[74] An example of such an edict is published in the Appendix (C 898:222). These fines varied enormously from place to place, and are not susceptible of generalization. In most cases it is apparent that every effort was made to safeguard the physical well-being of the Muslims, even if they were not accorded full equality before the law.

In at least one respect Mudéjares were better off than their Christian compatriots: they were theoretically exempt from torture, and any noble who tortured a Muslim incurred no less a penalty than the loss of his lands.[75] As in so many matters, however, there was quite a gulf between theory and practice, and there are numerous instances in the royal registers of authorization or tacit approval by the king of the torture of Muslims.[76] Even in cases

---

74. A certain inflationary tendency is notable in this regard: the _Fuero_ of Calatayud of 1131 demanded a penalty of 300s for the murder of a Muslim; the _Fueros_ of Aragon compiled about a hundred years later demanded 500s for the same offense (Ramos y Loscertales, "Fuero de Calatayud," s.35, p.412; Tilander, _Fueros_, VII.273, p.162). In Tortosa the general penalty for murder was death, but Christians who killed Muslims or Jews were liable only to a fine (_Costums_, I. 1.14) until the drafting of the _Costums_, at which time all murder was made punishable corporally (_ibid._; Aunos Perez [_El Derecho catalan en el siglo xiii_ {Barcelona, 1926}, p.134] is in error on this point). The fine for assaulting a Muslim in fourteenth-century Valencia was 12s (RP 2911:48 [1354-55]).

75. "...iuxta forum Aragonie si aliquis baro torserit aliquum sarracenum debet amittere locum suum" C 1073:161 (Jan.8, 1362). This was true in the thirteenth century as well: see Villanueva, _Viage_, VI, p.187 ("...nec tornantur judei nec sarraceni..."). Macho y Ortega is mistaken in assuming that this exemption from torture was a fifteenth-century innovation ("Condición," p.193).

76. The _jurisperitus_ of Huesca handling a murder case involving only Muslims was twice empowered to use torture in gathering infor-

where the monarch rebukes officials for violating the law in
this way the prescribed penalty is never inflicted.[77]

On the other hand, the king's general leniency toward the
Muslims was remarkable. He allowed them to bring suit in violation
of statutes of limitations, justifying this on the grounds of
their ignorance of the law.[78] And he granted pardons with amazing
frequency, for every sort of crime, even those one might have
thought the most execrable. Following is a table of the pardons
and amnesties granted by Peter to Muslims between 1355 and 1365,
with the crime for which they were granted indicated wherever
possible.

---

mation from Muslims (C 688:160 [Feb.16, 1357], C 690:232 [May 8, 1357])
The queen's procurator in Eslida received instructions to proceed
with torture "according to Muslim law" after the Mudéjares of the
community complained about the torture being used against them:
C 986:45, in Appendix.

77. In C 1073:161, ut supra, a fine was exacted, but in C 1208:
78 (Sept.6, 1365) and C 1211:63 (May 26, 1365) there was no penalty
at all, even though in each case the torture was patently inspired
purely by greed on the part of the official. C 1380:108 (Dec.19,
1356) is--to my knowledge--unique in manifesting compliance with
this law during the decade.

78. C 687:17 (Apr.15, 1356).

TABLE OF PARDONS AND AMNESTIES ISSUED TO MUSLIMS BY THE KING

All documents are from Chancery registers

Date Document	Recipient	Charge
Dec.24, 1356 1379:93	Muslim soldier in king's service	unspecified
July 1, 1357 901:104	Muslim from Zaragoza	murder and escape from jail
Aug.9, 1357 901:135	Muslim immigrants to Játiva	all crimes committed to date, including illegal emigration
Aug.11, 1357 901:137	two Muslims of Calatayud	murder
Nov.5, 1357 1566:154	Muslims of Teruel	murder
Feb.9, 1358 901:269	female Muslim of Valencia	unspecified
Sept.10, 1359 1567:128	aljama of Seta	all crimes to date
Feb.4, 1360 1170:186	aljama of Torrellas	treason
Apr.4, 1362 907:40	Muslim of Valencia	murder
Apr.5, 1362 907:62	aljama of Valencia	all crimes to date
Apr.14, 1362 907:64	Muslim of Valencia	murder*
Jan.9, 1362 911:51	female Muslim	illicit carnal relations

---

* This pardon was highly unusual in that it was of temporary duration ("quousque ipsum revocaverimus"), and covered only the personal safety of the recipient: after a year his goods could be inventoried and confiscated as penalty for the crime. During the validity of the pardon, moreover, the Muslim could make no effort to defend himself: "...non possis super crimine vel bonis aut aliter iudicaliter

TABLE OF PARDONS, CONTINUED

Date Document	Recipient	Charge
Feb.3, 1365 1387:131/ 1404:56	Muslim of Lérida	unspecified
June 17, 1365 1209:170	various Muslims	giving aid and counsel to runaway slaves

---

te defendere ullo modo, sed processus quivis iudicialis et extra iudicialis contra te et tua bona hoc guidatico suspendatur, excepta bonorum annotatione et confiscatione, que post annum possit fieri...."

Although the administration of justice to Muslims by the
Christian hierarchy of Aragon, both secular and ecclesiastical,
was generally lenient and equitable, there was one very serious
point of contention which created a fundamental dissatisfaction
among the Mudéjares. Muslim law ("çuna") was the foundation not
only of the Islamic state, but of the Muslim religion, just as,
during most of the Middle Ages, Christian law was seen as the
foundation of Christian states. References to Jews and Muslims
in medieval documents always refer to peoples not of differing
religions, but of different laws, and this concept of legal identity
was shared by the minorities themselves. In treaties of capitulation between Muslims and the conquistadores, therefore, there
was nearly always a clause guaranteeing the right of the conquered
peoples to their own law, the çuna, by which they regulated their
personal lives as well as their communal affairs. This right was
continuously upheld by the Aragonese monarchs, in theory if not
in practice, and one of Peter IV's own acts was to confirm the
right of all his Muslim subjects to their own law: "...in every
sort of case, civil or criminal, you shall be judged by and according to the çuna and not by the civil law or any other law or custom
of the land...."[79]

Yet Muslims were manifestly not judged according to the çuna in
a great many cases, as will be obvious from the table appended to

_____

79. "...in quibuscumque [ca]usis civilibus et criminalibus judice-
mini per et secundum çunam et non per forum seu aliam quamcumque
legem seu consuetudinem patrie..." C 906:177 (February, 1348). A

this chapter, unless one assumes that Christian judges were conver-
sant with Islamic law. This is, of course, the main reason for the
effort on the part of the aljamas to safeguard the prerogatives of
the qadi and to be able to nominate him themselves (see Chapter II).
If the majority of cases involving Muslims were not heard by
qadis or Muslim officials, the majority of cases were not decided
according to the çuna. It is true that some Muslims preferred civil
law to their own, either as a means of independence from the rule
of the aljama, or because the penalties under the çuna were more
severe than corresponding ones under the Christian fueros,[80] but in
the vast majority of cases Muslims found themselves subject to Christian law through simple usurpation by civil authorities. In a
few cases the monarchy intervened to protect Muslim rights in the
matter,[81] but the king himself constantly violated or overrode
Islamic laws in matters such as inheritance, public religious

---

fine of 1,000 morabetíns was to be imposed for violations. For
one of the very many treaties of capitulation which mention the
çuna, see that of the Muslims of Tudela, in Muñoz y Romero, Colección, pp.415ss.

80. Mahoma Ballistarius sought and received the right to be
tried according to the forum Aragonie rather than the çuna, either
as a plaintiff or defendant: C 705:170 (July 18, 1361). In addition, a Muslim of Lérida was fined 40s for declining to be tried
in a Muslim court ("qui no volch tenir juy de çuna donat per lo
çabiçala" RP 993:45 [1361]), and several female Muslims opted for
the Christian penalty of enslavement for carnal relations with
Christians rather than the Muslim punishment of stoning: e.g., RP
1710:22 (1365). Other than these cases, however, there is no indication that the vast number of cases involving Muslims and handled by
Christian officials (see table) represent the will of the Mudéjars.
Ironically, the practice of allowing Muslims to opt for a lighter
civil penalty violated the laws of Valencia: see Roca Traver, "Un
Siglo," p.75, n.225.

81. E.g., C 1569:26 (Oct.17, 1359).

observance, and sexual mores.[82]

James II was the first to alter the legal position of Muslims

on a general scale. In 1316 he issued an edict establishing new

guidelines for trials involving Muslims in all his kingdoms.

Briefly put, these provided that in the future all civil cases

involving only Muslims or Muslims and Christians should be heard

before Muslim judges and determined according to Islamic law

(çuna), but that criminal cases were to be heard by Saracen qadis

only when they involved a Muslim defendant and plaintiff; if the

plaintiff was a Christian and the defendant a Muslim, the case was

to be handled by Christian officials of the place where the crime

occurred, according to the laws of Aragon.[83] Although this decree

was confirmed by subsequent monarchs (e.g., Peter IV in April, 1362),

it had been superseded almost immediately by another disposition

of James himself in 1319, this time placing all jurisdiction over

Muslims in criminal cases in the hands of the Justice of Aragon,

and jurisdiction in civil ones under the general bailiff:

---

82. See the sections on travel and inheritance in Chapter VI;
cf. C 908:140 (1363). On sexual mores see Chapter VII, pp.343ss.
Sodomy, moreover, which was severely punished under the Christian
monarchs of Spain, is not a crime under Islamic law; that Muslims
were burned for it is certain: see Piles Ros, Estudio, p.288, #750.

83. "Quia super criminibus per aliquem vel aliquos sarracenos
comissis vel committendis contra aliquem vel aliquos christianos,
iudex sarracenus se nullatenus intromittat, sed per iusticias aut
alios officiales iurisdictionem exercentes locorum quibus dicta crimina commissa fuerint procedatur secundum forum Aragonie ad conservationem iusticie super eis. In causis vero tam civilibus quam
criminalibus que de sarraceno ad sarracenum ventilabuntur, quequidem
secundum çunam sarracenorum iuxta eorum predicta privilegia usitata
debuèrint terminari, volumus quod per iudices sarracenos procedatur
ac terminentur et ipse cause. Cause etiam civiles quas per christianos contra sarracenos moveri contingerit volumus quod per sarra-

...but the judging and sentencing of such crimes shall
be effected by you, the aforesaid justice, with proper recognition of [any] privileges granted to the Saracens which
have been in effect to date. In other cases the said bailiff
shall exercise jurisdiction over the Saracens, as properly
pertains to his office.[84]

Officially, this remained the royal policy regarding Muslims

until 1351, when all cases involving Muslims—civil or criminal—

were placed under the sole jurisdiction of the General Bailiff

of Aragon:

>...the said General Bailiff of the kingdom of Aragon, pres-
>ent or future, and no other official, shall hear all litiga-
>tions and cases, civil and criminal, brought to or due for
>trial in regular fashion and involving Christians, Jews, Mus-
>lims, or any combination thereof. He shall bring them to a
>just conclusion and rule on them as their merits demand,
>freely exercising absolute jurisdiction even over Jews and
>Saracens.[85]

The extent of divergence in practice from official norms of legal

procedure will be dealt with more fully below, but it is worth

noting here that even royal edicts betray severe discrepancies

between theory and practice. This disposition of 1351, for example,

was made necessary, according to the king's own words, by the

fact that "some question very frequently arises between the Gover-

nor and the General Bailiff of Aragon concerning the exercise of

jurisdiction over Jews and Saracens of the kingdom, and over the

---

cenos iudices terminentur" C 907:58 (Jan.1, 1316; confirmed Apr.11,
1362).

84. "Cognitio tamen et decisio dictorum criminum fiat per vos,
justiciam supradictum, salvis et servatis privilegiis concessis dictis sarracenis quibus usi sunt hucusque. In aliis enim bajulus mem-
oratus exerceat jurisdictionem in dictis sarracenis prout ad eius
officium noscitur pertinere" C 1567:172 (Mar.27, 1319).

85. "...dictus baiulus generalis regni Aragonie, qui nunc est vel
pro tempore fuerit, et non alius, de quibuscumque causis et questio-

[right of] ruling on cases which they bring either against each other or against Christians...."[86]   In theory, the Governor of Aragon had no right to judge such cases at all, and the fact that the king had to rule on such disputes is eloquent testimony to the irregularity of Aragonese judicial policies regarding Mudéjares.

To a certain extent this lack of consistency in application of juridical norms may have been due to genuine misunderstanding and confusion. Though the edict of 1351 may seem clear in retrospect, and was certainly widely disseminated,[87] there was controversy about its text as little as six years after its promulgation, and the king had to clarify its meaning to prevent abuses of authority and damage to Muslim interests.

> It has recently been pointed out to us on behalf of the
> said general bailiff that when Christians are the plaintiffs
> [in such cases], such Christians and some Jews and Saracens,
> ignoring the aforesaid provision and declaration [of 1351],
> obtain from us diverse letters of commission for officials and
> judges other than the general bailiff [to rule on] civil and
> criminal cases which these Christians have against Jews or
> Saracens, or which the Jews and Saracens have against each
> other. By this means the Jews and Saracens are oppressed with
> various injuries, and the authority of the bailiff, who ought
> to be regarded as their ordinary, is considerably demeaned

---

nibus, tam civilibus quam criminalibus, inter christianos et judeos seu sarracenos ac etiam inter se ordinarie [?] motis et movendis cognoscat, et eas fine debito terminet ac decidat prout earum merita duxerint exposcenda, in judeos et sarracenos ipsos iurisdictione omnimoda libere exercendo" C 707:70 (Nov.18, 1351).

86. "...sepissime inter gubernatorem et baiulum regni Aragonie generalem super iurisdictionis exercitio in iudeos et sarracenos regni ipsius et decidendis ipsorum questionibus quas tam inter se quam cum christianis habent questio aliqua exoritur..." ibid.

87. It was reconfirmed in 1357 (C 1070:48 [Oct.22]), in 1361 (C 707:70 [Dec.23]), and again in 1363 (C 1075:93 [Feb.18]).

and visibly diminished. We wish therefore...the said provision and declaration to be observed absolutely, and we hereby revoke any and all commissions granted by us or the Governor of Aragon in the past or future to any official or person... if they in any way seem to contradict the said provision and declaration, unless that letter is contained in them word for word.[88]

The provision of 1351, thus clarified, remained the official stand of the Crown on civil and criminal jurisdiction over Aragonese Muslims throughout the fourteenth century. There were, however, numerous qualifications, exemptions, and exceptions. Huesca had been granted by James II an exemption from the very first abridgements of Mudéjar legal autonomy, so that within the confines of the city criminal cases involving a Christian plaintiff and a Muslim defendant were supposed to be handled by the qadi rather than local officials (or the Justice of Aragon or the general bailiff).[89] This dispensation was not honored, however, even verbally, and in June of 1360 the king removed from the General Bailiff of Aragon the

---

88. "Et nunc pro parte dicti baiuli generalis nobis fuerit demostratum [sic] quia quando christiani sunt actores, iidem christiani et aliqui iudei et sarraceni, tacito de provisione et declaratione iamdictis, obtinent a nobis super causis, tam civilibus quam criminalibus, quas ipsi christiani contra iudeos et sarracenos et iidem iudei et sarraceni inter se habeant, diversas commissionum litteras ad alios officiales et judices pretercumque ad dictum baiulum generalem, ob quod iudei et sarraceni predictis diversis maliciis oprimuntur et iurisdictio dicti baiuli, qui inter eos pro ordinario est habendus, leditur non modicum et diminiuitur evidenter. Volentes igitur ex certa scientia et expresse quod provisio et declaratio iamdicte penitus observentur, commissiones quascumque per nos seu gubernatorem nostrum Aragonie quibusvis officialibus et personis s[epe?] predictis factas et faciendas, que in aliquo provisione et declarationi obviare videantur huius serie revocamus, nisi in eis tenor de verbo ad verbum preinserte littere insertus [sit]" C 707: 70 (Oct.22, 1357).

89. C 704:42 contains information about this grant, but does not give its exact date. James reigned from 1291 to 1327.

jurisdiction he had been exercising there and granted it to local officials in the first instance, with appeals still to go to the general bailiff.[90] Perhaps stimulated by this peremptory violation of a privilege long in desuetude, the Muslim community of the city immediately reminded the king of the privilege granted them by his grandfather, and on the twenty-first of the same month he issued a very strongly worded order to the officials he had lately put in authority, commanding them to relinquish all legal jurisdiction over the Muslims in accord with the ancient privilege or risk criminal prosecution and loss of their positions.[91]

Zaragoza also enjoyed particular municipal privileges. James had granted its qadi the same authority enjoyed by that of Huesca in 1298,[92] but as in the case of the latter, this concession had been officially ignored in later years. In 1346 Peter allotted the Christian merinus of the city the rights over Muslim criminal jurisdiction enjoyed by local Christian officials elsewhere in the realm, together with cases involving only Muslims.[93] This usurpation, unopposed by the Zaragoza aljama, was confirmed in 1358 and 1365, and extended to include the rector in the former year.[94] On the other hand, the city's Muslim inhabitants were exempt by royal decree from the jurisdiction of the governor and general bailiff,

---

90. C 1570:19 (June 2, 1360).

91. C 704:42 (June 21, 1360).

92. C 860:6 (Apr.15).

93. C 986:47 (Nov.10, 1346–Sept.1, 1365).

94. C 1070:134 (May 23, 1358); C 966:85 (May 25, 1358).

who had ultimate authority elsewhere in the kingdom,[95] and
lords in the areas of Zaragoza were prohibited from appointing
judges to rule on cases involving the city's Mudéjar population,
as they did in other places.[96]

The general lack of consistency in official policy in this
matter was further complicated for the Mudéjares (and historians)
by various specific royal decrees which indirectly impinged on the
authority of one official or other, as when, for instance, Daroca
was exempted from a general inquisition being conducted against
Muslims during the years 1361-1363, and no one but the bailiff of
the city was allowed to conduct trials involving Muslims unless
the king himself was present in the city;[97] or when the Jews and
Muslims of Ejea requested and obtained from the king a general
dispensation from the authority of the Governor of Aragon (n.b.),
since they had to travel to dangerous places on business and (presumably) needed more immediate attention. They were placed under
the personal jurisdiction of Luppus de Gurrea, a friend of the
Court. All cases involving them, whether with Muslims, Christians,
or Jews, were liable to him, and he was to deal with them "de foro
et ratione ac secundum ritum judeorum et çunam sarracenorum."[98]

---

95. C 703:40 (June 1, 1360). This was the case in Borja as well:
C 693:28 (Sept.16, 1357).

96. C 1073:95 (July 8, 1361).

97. C 906:11 (July 22, 1361).

98. C 793:58 (Aug.25, 1362); cf. C 707:70, ut supra. According to
Macho y Ortega the general practice in Aragon in the fifteenth century was for the amin to have primary jurisdiction in all civil cases
involving only Muslims, with appeals made to the qadi; in criminal

There is less information about this issue in Catalonia generally. In Tortosa a case between an _exaricus_ and his lord was decided by a Christian or Muslim judge depending on the religion of the plaintiff:

> And if there should happen to arise between the lord and his _exaricus_ a complaint or suit, the lord should file, lodge, witness and settle the suit under the authority of the Muslim _qadi_, both in its first hearing and in any appeals, and [likewise] any suits in reference to an original _exare-quia_ between them which the lord may bring against his _exaricus_.
> But if the _exaricus_ brings suit against his lord, it should be heard and decided in a Christian court, and brought to a conclusion [there].[100]

This was an unusual dispensation, and there is no evidence of its being applied elsewhere, but if the case of the large and influen-

---

cases the General Bailiff of Aragon ruled, advised by the _amin_ and _qadi_ ("Cóndición," p.177). He avers, moreover, that the bailiff "was the only Christian who intervened in the internal affairs of the Muslims, since, though it is certain that in the fourteenth century the justices and _almutazafes_ made certain inspections in the Muslim aljamas, John I put an end to this intrusion and decreed that no Christian official '...should presume or attempt to proceed or conduct any trials against you [Muslims] for any crimes or misdemeanors, no matter what his rank or station...'" (_ibid._, p.175). Simply assuming that this edict actually put an end to the practice seems to me unjustified, since such edicts were legion in the fourteenth century, and since Macho y Ortega himself publishes a document which clearly shows that just such abuses were taking place in Calatayud in the mid-fifteenth century: see his "Documentos," p. 451 (document of 1459).

99. I.e., an agreement of such a relationship dating from the time of the conquest of Tortosa: this is made clear in the text preceding.

100. "E si per auentura entrel senyor e son exaric sera pleyt ne demanda: quel senyor la demanda deu fer, termenar e examinar, e acabar en poder del alcayt dels sarrains, axi el principal com en les appellacions, e totes demandes que per rao de la exarequia veyla sien mogudes ne feyta entre ells quel senyor moua contra son exarich. Mas si lo exarich mou demanda contra lo senyor, deuse examinar e determenar en la cort dels crestians: e portar a acabament" _Costums_, IV.26,33.

tial aljama of Lérida is typical of Catalonia as a whole, the
Muslims of that area were considerably better off than their
co-religionists elsewhere under the Aragonese Crown. Peter II
had in 1202 guaranteed their judicial autonomy against the encroachments which were then affecting other Mudéjar communities,
and conceded them a privilege not then enjoyed by any other
Hispanic Muslims, i.e., that of ruling on criminal cases involving Christians and Muslims:

> I decree that if any Christian or Jew shall have litiga-
> tion with any Saracen of Lérida or with any Saracen who comes
> to Lérida, he shall take it before the çalmedina or qadi es-
> tablished for the Saracen aljama of Lérida, and shall make his
> case directly before them: no Saracen shall be summoned before
> a Christian or Jewish court except by the çalmedina or qadi
> of the aljama. And in case a contest or dispute should some-
> day arise or be brought up between the said adelantati and
> aljama and the Bailiff of Lérida about whether, by virtue of
> the words of the decision above, the aforesaid aljama is com-
> pletely exempt, or should be exempted from trial or judgement
> of the Bailiff of Lérida, it is just so: the said bailiff may
> not proceed against them for any crime or misdemeanor, nor
> interfere in any way with them, in civil cases or criminal
> ones.[101]

Unlike the case of the similar grants of James II to the aljamas
of Aragon, the judicial liberties of the aljama of Lérida (and
other Catalan aljamas?) were zealously protected by the royal house.
In the mid-fourteenth century (1355) Peter the Ceremonious not only
confirmed and upheld his ancestor's grant, but expanded on it at
some length and demanded the co-operation of local officials in
enforcing it.

...we hereby provide that henceforth the said aljama and

---

101. C 903:203, in Appendix.

its members shall try every case, civil or criminal, before the
qadi or çalmedina of the said aljama, present or future, so that
the said Bailiff of Lérida, present or future, shall not be competent to intervene in any of the aljama's cases, civil or criminal, or those of its members; rather, the said qadi and çalmedina, present and future, shall render justice in such cases according to their law, and punish as they shall deem fit. And
we wish this decree to be obeyed and observed exactly, whatsoever commissions, processes, customs, and practices to the
contrary notwithstanding in any way....

We therefore hereby command our Governor General and his
lieutenant in Catalonia, and the Vicar and Curia of Lérida, as
well as the said Bailiff of the city, and our other officials
and subjects, present and future, under penalty of 500 morabetíns of gold (to be collected by our treasurer as often as the
edict is violated), that they observe firmly and honor this concession, interpretation, declaration and confirmation of ours,
and that our officials cause it to be honored and observed in-
violately, and not transgress it for any reason.

And that the foregoing may enjoy greater vigor, we swear
before the Lord God and upon His four holy Gospels, touching
them at this very moment, to honor and observe forever all these
things in every detail, and to cause them to be observed,
just as they are set out above.

Moreover, since we desire this concession, interpretation,
and confirmation for the said aljama to be observed effectively
and always, particularly by the said Bailiff, present or future,
we command under the same penalty that the said Bailiff, either
the one now in office or those who shall hold the office after
him, shall have to swear on the said four holy Gospels of God
to observe all that which is disposed above before they may exercise their office. And we also wish the said officials and
their deputies to lend the said qadi, çalmedina, and adelantati
of this aljama their counsel, help, and favor in exercising their
aforesaid jurisdiction, if and when they shall have need of it.

It is, nonetheless, our intention that in whatever judgements or sentences pronounced or promulgated by the said qadi,
çalmedina, and adelantati of the aljama on any matter, as well
as in the trials hereafter conducted [by them], our Fiscalis
of Lérida, present or future, shall be obliged to watch out
for our interests and the maintenance of our rights, and this
Fiscalis shall receive any portion belonging to us from such
proceedings, in our name, and will not fail to be responsible
for it to [our] treasurer.[102]

These were not idle words. Shortly after the reconfirmation of

102. C 903:203, in Appendix.

the privilege in 1359 the bailiff of the city obtained from
the king a commission which violated the provisions of the concession, and when this was pointed out to the monarch he immediately
revoked the commission, stating emphatically that there were to be
no abridgements of the judicial autonomy of the aljama.[103] And in
1365, when a Muslim was arrested for theft and the murder of Christians and held for trial by the Vicar and Prohomens of Lérida, the
king ordered his immediate release into the custody of the qadi,
who alone could try such a case under the ancient privileges of the
city.[104]

In striking contrast to the situation in Aragon, the civil and
criminal jurisdiction over Valencian Mudéjares was very nearly uniform and clearly understood by all parties. Prior to 1298 the procurator general had exercised this authority, but in that year
James II constituted the General Bailiff of Valencia as permanent
and ultimate judge of all civil and criminal cases involving the
Muslim population of royal or ecclesiastical lands.

> Although the hearing and deciding of all litigations
> and cases, civil and criminal, of the Saracens of Valencia is
> considered to be the prerogative of the procurator general, we
> now think it desirable to establish that in all such cases of
> Saracens residing in our lands or those of the Church or an

---

103. C 903:214 (Nov.10, 1359).

104. C 721:142 (Jan.26, 1365). In Barcelona the bailiff of the
city had sole jurisdiction over Muslim inhabitants of the city,
which might indicate that the case of Lérida was not typical of
Catalan cities. But there was no Muslim aljama in Barcelona, and
in fact the jurisdiction of the Bailiff of Barcelona extended officially only to captives: "...bajuli civitatis predicte fuerunt
et sunt in possessione patefacta atque usu civiliter et criminaliter capiendi et puniendi quoscumque captivos et servos, neophitos

Order, the said general bailiff shall nevertheless hear and
rule and give sentence on them, and no other official may
hear them or intervene in any of them.[105]

Cases involving Muslims on nobles' or knights' lands were still

reserved to the Procurator General of Valencia.

On his accession to the throne, Peter the Ceremonious refined

slightly the claims of the office of the general bailiff, specify-

ing that he could conduct trials against Muslims only when he pro-

ceeded "without profit or salary, and with minimum expenses," and

allowing the qadi primary jurisdiction in civil cases involving

only Muslims within the aljama.[106] In 1355 he introduced further

---

seu babtitzatos, liberos necminus et alios sarracenos et sarracenas
captivos civitatis jamdicte" C 967:275 (Sept.12, 1358).

105. "Licet cognitio et decisio omnium negotiorum et causarum tam
civilium quam criminalium sarracenorum regni Valencie ad procuratorem generalem pertinere noscantur [sic] nunc taliter duximus ordinandum quod de causis omnibus supradictis sarracenorum sed habitancium
in locis nostris et ecclesiarum et religiosorum dictus baiulus generalis tamen cognoscat et eas determinet et decidat et nullus alius
officialis nec de eis cognoscat aut se in aliquo intromittat" Aureum Opus, priv.7 of James II (1298), published in Roca Traver, "Un
Siglo," p.74, n.214. Roca Traver found it difficult to offer an
over-view of the administration of justice to Valencian Mudéjares,
even though the role of the general bailiff makes it simpler than
that of Aragon. Burns' observation about thirteenth-century Valencia that "the average free Muslim, unless he had to bring charges
against a Christian or serve as witness against one, never entered
a Christian court" (Islam, p.270) is not applicable to the fourteenth
century in any of the Crown's lands. Burns also entertains the opinion that "A Moor haled into court by a Christian appeared before his
own judge...; in criminal cases he retained his own law. Nor could
the testimony of Christians or Jews condemn him. The requirement
of a witness from one's own religious group had become normal in Europe by the twelfth century" (ibid., pp.264ss). The requirement of
one type of witness does not preclude conviction on the testimony
of others. Moreover, these findings are markedly at variance with
thirteenth-century texts published by Roca Traver (see note 58, above).

106. "Super aliis vero negotiis civilibus dictam aljamam aut singulares eius tangentibus alcadius dicte morarie et in eius deffectum
dictum bajulum generalem vel eius locumtenentem procedi volumus et

modifications designating the king's <u>qadi</u> (cf. Chapter II) as the sole judge in criminal cases involving only Muslims.[107]

But in general the authority of the bailiff tended to increase rather than decrease, and the office was clearly the focal point of all legal transactions involving Moors. After a series of disputes, for instance, between the governor and procurator general over the right to try the Muslims of nobles, the king transferred jurisdiction over them from the procurator to the general bailiff in all cases where they committed crimes in areas under royal control.[108] As of 1357 the bailiff could try even civil cases between Muslims within the aljama of Játiva,[109] and from 1359 he alone could hear cases involving Jews and Saracens or Christian plaintiffs against non-Christian defendants.[110] In outlying towns Muslims en-

---

jubemus..." C 862:119 (Jan.13, 1337).

107. C 685:61 (Oct.16, 1355).

108. "...cognitio et punitio illorum sarracenorum locorum nobilium et militum qui committunt aliqua crimina infra loca et terminos regios spectant et spectare debent ad ipsum bajulum generalem et non ad vos seu alium officialem regni..." C 692:154 (July 21, 1357). For an example of the type of dispute that led to this change, see C 692:66 (Mar.15, 1357), where a Christian who fatally wounded a Muslim was taken to be tried by the men of the town where the incidént occurred. The governor protested that the matter lay under his competence, but the king finally assigned the trial to the procurator general.

109. This decree seems to have been aimed particularly at the overnor, whose constant efforts to interfere in Mudéjar justice were apparently annoying the monarch: "...aljama sarracenorum civitatis Xative et eius singulares, qui sepius per gubernatorem regni Valentie et alios officiales et commissarios nostros vexantur immensibus et immoderatis sumptibus et expensis..." C 901:134 (Aug.4, 1357)

110. C 966:121 (Nov.21, 1359).

joyed the privilege of not being judged outside their communities,
nor could the procurator, under whose jurisdiction they were
comprised if they were not royal or ecclesiastical serfs, enter
their courts. The bailiff, on the other hand, could exercise
his authority there without restriction.[111]

Other officials did retain some competence in the face
of the increasing concentration of power in the hands of the bailiff. Nobles in Valencia could hold trials of their own Saracens,
or appoint notaries to do so,[112] and in the larger cities both
Muslim officials and the Christian municipal bailiffs continued
to conduct trials and exercise juridical authority.[113] But the
balance of power in Valencia was clearly shifting to the general
bailiff throughout the century, and there seems to have been a
deliberate effort on the part of the Crown to strip both the governor and procurator general of all judicial authority over the Muslims, or at least to circumscribe their competence severely.

However, the disparity between official pronouncements and
actual practice was so great that the intention of the king was
a matter of scant importance in the legal affairs of Mudéjares.

---

111. C 1571:9 (Apr.9, 1362).

112. C 720:65 (Sept.13, 1365).

113. "Quia amodo nisi in casibus et criminibus delictis vel excessibus iam exceptis, in omnibus aliis et singulis quibusvis casibus, criminibus, excessibus et delictis serventur dicte aljame
suisque singularibus dicta çuna iuxta quam de ipsis cognoscant et
iusticiam faciant una cum dicto baiulo vel eius locumtenente aut de
eius licencia seu mandato predicti alcadius, alcaydus, çalmedina,
et sagio, prout hec ad singula eorum officia de antiqua consuetudine pertinent et expectant...; ...[et] dictus procurator fiscalis

The table appended to this chapter provides an index of cases involving Muslims which appear in Chancery registers from 1355 to
1366. Of the cases of civil and criminal litigation between
Christians and Muslims in Valencia the general bailiff heard only
one more than the governor: obviously the king's efforts to give
the bailiff predominance had little immediate effect, despite
the very clear intention of the law in enjoining the governor from
interfering in such cases. Moreover, in flagrant violation of
legal principles centuries old and continuously upheld by the
monarchy, both the general bailiff and the governor constantly
intervened in cases involving only Muslims, even civil suits.
They heard nearly a third of such cases in Valencia during the
period in question.

During the war, when the king was under constant stress and
badly needed the support of the Mudéjares, numerous aljamas took
advantage of the situation and wrested from the harried suzerain
guarantees of their right to be judged according to Islamic law.
The registers of the Chancery record such demands from the
communities of Paterna, Mericis, Crevillente, Elche, Artana, Valencia, Játiva, Castre, Alfandequiella, Aspe, Espada, Enveyo, Benicandut, Alcudia, Xenguer, and Ayhi.[114] It is undoubtedly significant that all of these aljamas are Valencian. In Aragon the usur-

---

se nullatenus intromittat, nam hoc sibi penitus inhibemus" C 910:
118-9 (Sept.16, 1366). Cf. C 910:120 (Sept.16, 1366).

114. In addition to the listings under "Demands" at the end of

pation of Mudéjar judicial authority was enormously less; in
Catalonia there was virtually no abridgement of legal autonomy.
Moreover, the war generally weakened the position of the Aragonese
aljamas, and even if they had wished to correct abuses they were
not in a good position to do so. The Valencian Muslims suffered
the greatest abridgement of their freedoms throughout the thirteenth
and early fourteenth century, and by a kindly turn of fate were the
segment of the population most able to take advantage of the war
between Aragon and Castile in the mid-fourteenth century. They
found themselves in a position to better their legal status, and
they took it.

The index of cases on the following pages provides a closer look
at the workings of Aragonese justice in regard to Mudéjares. It
should be obvious from this table that general pronouncements about
jurisdiction over the Muslims would be of limited value. This very
fact testifies to the very great degree of inter-dependence of the
Muslim and Christian communities generally, and to the necessity of
a system of justice loose and diverse enough to accommodate the com-
plexity of Iberian convivencia. It seems likely that the discrepancies between official theory and daily practice worked to the
advantage of the Muslims as much as to their disadvantage. There
are relatively few cases of complaints about usurpation of jurisdiction, and in quite a number of cases Muslims clearly preferred

---

Chapter VII ("Oppression"), these will be found at C 691:177 (Feb.
26, 1358), C 1569:26 (Oct.17, 1359), C 1205:36 (Mar.1, 1365), C 1204:
63 (Apr.8, 1365), C 913:91 (Nov.25, 1366).

Christian justice to Islamic courts, possibly due to procedural limitations on the administration of justice against Muslims by Christians. In short, despite the widespread violation of post-reconquest promises of judicial autonomy, the system of interlocking justice prevailing under the Crown of Aragon in the fourteenth century may represent a successful departure from the general pattern of institutional separation between Christians and Muslims, a departure which operated to the satisfaction of a considerable proportion of both communities.

CHRONOLOGICAL INDEX OF ALL CIVIL AND CRIMINAL CASES INVOLVING

MUSLIMS IN THE DOCUMENTS OF THE ROYAL CHANCERY BETWEEN 1355 AND 1366

It is likely that a number of civil cases involving only Mudé-jares in Catalonia did not find their way into Chancery records, since there was less Christian interference in Muslim judicial process in Catalonia than in the other lands of the Crown, and since some cases heard by local Muslim officials might have left no record outside the Muslim courts. That such was the case out-side of Catalonia, or even in Catalonia generally, does not seem at all likely. It would be a mistake to imagine the legal system of Aragon in the fourteenth century as comparable to the vast jungle of litigation known today, or even as similar to the far-ranging and relatively well-organized system of courts in France or England at the time of this study. The legal system of the Aragonese Crown operated less efficiently and on a much smaller scale. During the period in question the population of Aragon-Catalonia-Valencia, always small by comparison (even to that of Castile), was even fur-ther reduced by the plague. All cases involving any important crime, and very nearly all cases involving Christians or Jews as well as Muslims, necessarily drew attention and the notice of higher officials.

Moreover, the nature of the cases recorded argues strongly that nearly all cases left records in the Chancery. Those listed below, for example, are for the most part far from being in any way remarkable. Many of them were, in fact, heard by local Muslim officials, and need have left no record. In relatively few of the

cases is a specifically royal court involved, and even when the
king himself heard a case, it was scarcely of so dramatic or
urgent a nature that one might infer that only the most remarkable
or important cases found their way into the monarch's purview
(n.b. cases 711:133, p.153; 1070:50, p.158; 1210:85, p.162).
Quite to the contrary, the great diversity of officials involved
in the proceedings, and the enormous variety of cases presented,
testify to the very great percentage of cases which must have found
their way into Chancery records.

Furthermore, in the majority of cases the material used as a
basis for the table has been drawn from documents which do not deal
overtly with the trial or suit in question, but only mention it by
way of enforcing the decree of the presiding official, requesting
or demanding payment of the official's salary, ordering the original
trial to be reopened under new supervision, or instructing officials
to honor a property settlement arranged during the course of some
litigation. It is significant in this context that royal decrees
ensuring enforcement of judicial process were often issued for
cases involving only Muslims and ruled upon by qadis.

Perhaps most to the point, the evidence presented herein sup-
orts strongly the general picture drawn in the preceding chapter on
the basis of other types of records and documents: if Chancery
documents do not provide a complete list, it appears that they at
least give a representative sample.

EXPLANATION OF SYMBOLS AND ABBREVIATIONS

All documents are from the Chancery registers of the Archive of
the Crown of Aragon

"place" designates the location of primary jurisdiction, i.e.,
the scene of the crime or the residence of the parties bringing suit; it is not the point of execution of the document
cited

titles of officials in quotation marks are those employed in the
document itself

BGA = General Bailiff of Aragon

BGV = General Bailiff of Valencia

FdB = Faraig de Belvis, the "king's qadi." It is not clear whether
in all cases heard by de Belvis he acted as "king's qadi" or not:
wherever the document itself indicated the precise nature of his
authority in specific cases it has been noted.

GV = Governor of Valencia

JP = Jurisperitus

Just.Arag. = Justice of Aragon

"bailiff" without other designation refers to the bailiff of the
city of primary jurisdiction
"qadi" without other designation refers to the qadi of the aljama
of the city of primary jurisdiction

when two or more names appear as presiding official:

the sign → separating them indicates that jurisdiction was
removed from the first and granted to the second by
the king
the sign { joining them indicates they shared jurisdiction
equally
the sign × separating them indicates that jurisdiction was
disputed between them; the name following the sign →
is the name of the official who ultimately won the dispute
and heard the case
the numbers 1., 2., etc., before an official indicate primary
and secondary jurisdiction: the case was heard by 1. and
appealed to 2.; wherever the documents reveal the identity
of the appelant it has been noted

ARAGON

Cases between Muslims

Source Date Place	Presiding Official	Crime or subject of litigation
688:160* Feb.16, 1357 Huesca	JP	murder of one Muslim by another
691:34 June 21, 1357 Borja	faqi → "auditor curie"	civil suit between two Muslims
692:182 Aug.18, 1357 Borja	Abdalla de Galip	civil suit between FdB and his procurator
699:131 Jan.13, 1360 Borja (?)	FdB as faqi	civil case between two Muslims
700:188† Mar.6, 1360 Brea	qadi → {faqi king	breach of promise suit by Muslim against erstwhile fiancée
703:43 June 17, 1360 Borja	FdB → Merinus of Zaragoza → bailiff	unspecified suit between Muslims
704:68 Aug.19, 1360 Borja	Blasius Eximinus	suit by two Muslims vs. the faqi of the aljama
1073:5 Dec.17, 1360 Zaragoza	JP	Crown vs. aljama
706:122 July 12, 1361 Zaragoza	qadi → JP	suit over property between Muslims removed from qadi at request of plaintiffs
1183:118 Nov.18, 1362 Daroca	bailiff (?)	civil suit between two Muslims

* Text in Appendix.

† Cf. C 699:207 (Apr.11, 1360).

ARAGON

Cases between Muslims, continued

Source Date Place	Presiding Official	Crime or subject of litigation
711:133 Jan.20, 1363 Zaragoza	king	suit between Muslims
715:56 Oct.15, 1363 Huesca	1. FdB as qadi 2. JP	suit vs. Muslim adelantati by qadi
1197:9 Feb.23, 1364 Huesca	1. FdB as qadi 2. Çalema del Rey	suit between Muslim and his father-in-law
1197:19 Feb.26, 1364 Buruaguena	JP	suit against female Muslim by aljama over back taxes
719:106 Feb.12, 1365 Zaragoza	qadi	civil suit vs. Muslim and his wife by another Muslim

ARAGON

Cases involving Muslims and Jews

Source Date Place	Presiding Official	Crime or subject of litigation
686:180 Apr.1, 1356 Tarazona	{bailiff J. Ferdinand	property dispute between Jews of Tarazona and Muslims of Malon
1566:65, 106 June 8, 1356 Tarazona	1. queen's bailiff* 2. JP	unspecified suit aginst Jew by two Muslims
687:189 Nov.29, 1356 Ariza	BGA	dispute over property between Muslim couple and Jew
1566:115 Mar.4, 1357 Tarazona	bailiff	complaint by Muslims that Jews lent money in violation of royal ordinances
691:127 Oct.23, 1357 Zaragoza	Just.Arag.	carnal relations of Jewess with Christians and Muslims
701:16 May 6, 1360 Borja	local justice	financial dispute between one Jew and one Muslim
701:16 May 6, 1360 Borja	{faqi bailiff	financial dispute between one Jew and several Muslims
705:138 June 12, 1361 Calatayud	"judex curie regis"	disputed debts between Jews and Muslims
707:193 Apr.9, 1362 Borja	local justice†	murder of Jew by two Muslims

---

* The bailiff delegated his authority in this case to an official styled "eximius," who conducted the trial in the name of the bailiff and the procurator general.

† The widow of the murdered Jew had unsuccessfully attempted to obtain justice first from the qadi and amin of the town where the accused were living.

ARAGON

Cases involving Muslims and Christians

Source Date Place	Presiding Official	Crime or subject of litigation
686:16 Oct.24, 1355 Ricla	procurator	unspecified charges vs. Christian and Muslim
684:196 Apr.2, 1356 Borja	BGA	suit vs. Fratres Minores by aljama of Borja regarding property
687:84 July 12, 1356 Huesca	merinus*	murder of Christian by Muslim
688:145 Jan.31, 1357 Zaragoza	JP	civil suit by Muslim for exemption from taxes of aljama
691:31 June 2, 1357 ?	king	murder of Muslim by Christians
695:60 Jan.31, 1359 Huesca	king†	murder of Muslim and wounding of his companions by Christians
983:188 Feb.20, 1359 Ricla	Just.Arag. × lord of Ricla → king	murder of Christian by Muslim
696:184 Apr.5, 1359 Zaragoza	1. Just.Arag. 2. P. de Casseda, "miles"	complaint vs. Muslim by Christian; appeal by Muslim
1567:156 Jan.13, 1360 Huesca	bailiff*	unspecified prosecution of aljama by the city

---

* This document terminated the proceedings without a ruling.

† The investigation and preliminary hearings in this case were conducted by a local justice; the final ruling was given by the king.

ARAGON

Cases involving Muslims and Christians, continued

Source Date Place	Presiding Official	Crime or subject of litigation
1071:96 Jan.25, 1360 Aranda	"capitaneus of Aranda"	carnal relations of female Muslims with Christian males
699:169 Feb.15, 1360 Calatayud	bailiff	civil suit by tax collector to collect back salary from aljamas
699:217 Apr.18, 1360 Quadret	Lieut.Just.Arag.	civil suit vs. Christian and the Muslim aljama of Quadret by Christian plaintiff
703:77 July 8, 1360 Letun	Peter Avarchus	unspecified suit between P, Eximi d'Eleson and Muslim aljama of Letun
1071:192 July 17, 1360 Zaragoza	Peter de Salanova	carnal relations of Muslim and Jewish males with Christian females
702:163 May 4, 1361 Tamarit	JP	civil suit by domestic of the kin against the aljama of St Stephen
705:150 June 26, 1361 Borja	Vice-governor of Aragon → local justice	complaint of Christian vs. Muslim who aided in the escape of Muslim captive
706:197 Oct.21, 1361 Calatayud	Just.Arag.	civil suit with Muslim and Christian co-plaintiffs
705:157 July 5, 1361 Quartel	Justice of Sagunto	"state" vs. Muslim
711:194 Mar.4, 1363 Monzón	alguatzirus	robbery of Muslim by Christian

ARAGON

Cases involving Muslims and Christians, continued

Source Date Place	Presiding Official	Crime or subject of litigation
711:185 Mar.20, 1363 Barbastro	king	unspecified charges vs. Muslim by Christian
717:82 May 28, 1364 Huesca	1. judex 2. JP of Zaragoza	unspecified complaint vs. Muslim by Christian; appeal by Muslim
725:21 Feb.25, 1366 Monzón	alguatzirus	carnal relations of male Muslim with female Christian

CATALONIA

Cases involving Muslims and others

Source Date Place	Presiding Official	Crime or subject of litigation
684:196 May 19, 1356 Teruel	local justice	suit by Jewish and Muslim aljamas for the removal of court-appointed scribanus
1566:48 May 27, 1356 Teruel	bailiff	carnal relations of female Muslim with Christian males
688:18 Aug.2, 1356 Figueras	{ Prince John alguatzirus JP of Perpignan	assault against Muslims by Christians
1566:75 Sept.15, 1356 Teruel	bailiff	carnal relations of female Muslim with Christian males
1154:88 Feb.28, 1358 ?	"legum doctor"	carnal relations (?) of female Muslim with non-Muslim males
692:36 Feb.7, 1357 Lérida	"judex et auditor curie"	carnal relations of Muslim male with Christian female
1070:50 Oct.28, 1357 ?	king	carnal relations of two female Muslims with Christian males
983:5 Dec.3, 1358 Lérida	qadi	non-payment of debt owed to cleric by aljama
906:133 Dec.15, 1361 Barcelona	Guillelmus de Figaria	illegal seizure of emigrating Muslims (suit brought by the Muslims themselves)
909:154 July 11, 1364 Barcelona	king	criminal negligence charges vs. Muslim doctor in treating a Christian
721:88 Dec.3, 1364 Lérida	JP	murder of Jews by Christians and Muslims

CATALONIA

Cases between Muslims

Source Date Place	Presiding Official	Crime or subject of litigation
691:231 May 17, 1358 Lérida	bailiff*	wounding of one Muslim by another
1073:6 Dec.17, 1360 Teruel	{JP king's procurator	corruption in office
1183:139 Nov.26, 1362 Lérida	FdB	dispute over dowry, involving qadi of Lérida as defendant

---

* The bailiff was subsequently fined by the king 100 morabetins for violating the laws of Catalonia, which provided that all cases involving Muslims should be tried before the Muslim qadi.

VALENCIA

Cases involving Muslims and others

Source Date Place	Presiding Official	Crime or subject of litigation
683:5 Oct.27, 1355 Valencia	BGV	dispute over rights to Muslim market between Bishop of Valencia and the Abbess of St Elizabeth
1068:45 Dec.13, 1355 ?	BGV	selling of captured Christians and illegal arms to Granada by Muslims
686:92 Jan.2, 1356 Valencia	undecided	trespass and assault vs. Christian committed by Muslims
684:105 Jan.22, 1356 Chiva, Godela, Penxissa	1. GV 2. king	sentences vs. aljamas and universities of the cities by GV appealed; original charges not specified
687:17 Apr.15, 1356 Madrona-Borral	JP	suit by aljama vs. Christian for harassment suffered during revolt of the Union
1380:108 Dec.19, 1356 Valencia	king	carnal relations of Muslim male and Christian female
901:241 June 22, 1357 Castellón	GV	theft of a purse from Christian woman by two Muslims
691:84 Aug.14, 1357 Valencia	portarius	carnal relations of female Muslims with Christian males
691:114 Oct.11, 1357 Valencia	Lady Timbors × GV → ?	carnal relations of female Muslims with Christian males
1566:175 Jan.18, 1358 Penaquibus	bailiff*	theft by Muslim

---

* The bailiff was fined for unlawfully hearing this case, which

VALENCIA

Cases involving Muslims and others, continued

Source Date Place	Presiding Official	Crime or subject of litigation
691:153 Jan.18, 1358 Játiva	notary	civil suit between Muslim and Christian over property rights
693:100 Jan.22, 1358 Játiva	bailiff	civil suit between Muslim and bailiff regarding will
691:199 Feb.26, 1358 Valencia (?)	"legum doctor"	civil suit vs. female Muslim by Christian nobles
695:190 Sept.24, 1359 Sagunto	{"legum doctor" judex → Prince Ferdinand	murder and rape of Christian women by Muslims
1071:76 Oct.24, 1359 Valencia	BGV	carnal relations of Christian women with Muslim male
699:226 Apr.20, 1360 Valencia (?)	Luppus de Forbes	murder of Christian by Muslims
1569:76 Dec.12, 1360 Valencia	queen	suit against queen's procurator by Muslim
710:31 Mar.2, 1362 Valencia	BGV	murder of Muslim by Jew
707:140 Mar.18, 1362 Valencia	Justice of Alcira → 2 Valencian Christians → vice-GV → "legum doctor" → BGV → JP	dispute over Muslim accused of treason and claimed as captive by Christian plaintiff

---

belonged to the jurisdiction of the qadi.

VALENCIA

Cases involving Muslims and others, continued

Source Date Place	Presiding Official	Crime or subject of litigation
714:165 Nov.15, 1363 Valencia	GV*	illegal export of wheat by Muslims
1210:85 Apr.26, 1365 Artana	king	theft of mules by Muslim muledrivers
1209:108 May 13, 1365 Seta	BGV	suit by Muslims vs. the rector of the church of Seta
1209:128 June 3, 1365 Perpunxen	GV	capture of Christians by Muslims
1211:97 June 16, 1365 Valencia	scribe	capture of Christian scout by Muslims
720:39 Sept.1, 1365 Morella	king	robbery perpetrated vs. Muslims by Christians
1208:77 Sept.6, 1365 Valencia	Lieut.-justice of Valencia	dispute between Barcelona merchant and Muslim whom he claims as slave
986:66 Sept.19, 1365 Valencia	king	suit against two Christians by Muslims†
986:93 Oct.3, 1365 Valldigna	Abbot of Valldigna	treason of Muslim serfs of the monastery

---

* A suit was initiated against the governor by the lord of the Muslims, asserting that his prosecution of them was illegal; the king ruled against the governor.

† The accused Christians were summoned and appeared, but the Muslim plaintiffs did not; the king brought charges of harassment against the Muslims.

VALENCIA

Cases between Muslims

Source Date Place	Presiding Official	Crime or subject of litigation
684:207 Apr.16, 1356 Valencia	BGV	property dispute
1068:134 June 16, 1356 Valencia	GV	adultery of male Muslim
899:41 July 28, 1356 Valencia	BGV	adultery of female Muslim
692:155 July 20, 1357 Valencia	{ B. Vinus procurator fiscalis	unspecified charges vs. converso
692:182 July 20, 1357 Valencia	Abdalla de Galip	fraud perpetrated vs. FdB in property sale
901:276 Feb.11, 1358 Valencia	BGV	illegal alms-begging
693:110 Feb.12, 1358 Valencia	alguatzirus	murder of one Muslim by another
700:60 Nov.15, 1359 Válencia	king	civil suit vs. Çaat Alcafaç by Muslim mercenaries
709:37 Aug.9, 1361 Algar-Quartell	{ "legum doctor" JP → Justice of Sagunto	highway robbery
706:176 Aug.12, 1361 Mizlata	1. judex 2. licenciatus in legibus	unspecified charges vs. Muslim official; appealed on his behalf by notary

VALENCIA

Cases between Muslims, continued

Source Date Place	Presiding Official	Crime or subject of litigation
907:40 Apr.4, 1362 Valencia	BGV	murder
714:137 Sept.14, 1363 Zaragoza*	JP of Valencia	treason
986:86 Oct.2, 1365 Segorbe	alguatzirus	treason (?)
1204:86 Apr.25, 1365 Játiva	king	suit vs. former qadi and current lieutenant-qadi by wife of current qadi, FdB
1205:71 May 8, 1365 Valencia	king's treasurer†	unspecified charges vs. Muslim
1210:94 May 21, 1365 Valencia	GV → licenciatus in legibus	unspecified charges vs. Çaat Alcafaç
1206:18 Aug.8, 1365 Castre	licenciatus in legibus	theft
1206:84 Sept.12, 1365 Valencia	Çaat Alcafaç	civil suit between FdB on behalf of his wife and Hacen Alcomoch

---

* Although the Muslims imvolved were subject to the Archbishop of Zaragoza, the king apparently considered their place of residence (Onda, in Valencia) to constitute the most important criterion in assigning primary jurisdiction.

† The treasurer employed as his subdelegate Raymund Tolosanus, here styled "legum professor"; this same R. Tolosanus was the "licenciatus" referred to in the following entry.

Chapter IV

Feudal and Military Duties of the Mudéjares

Specifically feudal obligations of Mudéjares appear to have
been little different from those of Christians. Burns' contention
in regard to the Mudéjar population that the ceremonial of doing
homage was so restricted that only Muslim leaders were required to
perform it does not apply to fourteenth-century Valencia.[1] After
the Muslims of Eslida were accepted as vassals of the king in March
of 1365, they were required to come personally in groups of twenty
to swear homage, and when they were transferred to the queen (at
their own request), they were again required to swear homage personally to her procurator, even though they had done so to the king
himself only two weeks previously.[2]

Their duties--whether owed to the Crown, to nobles, or to the
Church--were the standard duties of Aragonese vassals or serfs.
Muslim vassals of the king in Ricla, for instance, owed him six days
service per year, with oxen or goats if they owned them, on foot if
they did not; the king was to feed them during this time.[3] For the
most part, however, feudal duties in the fourteenth century took the
form of payments, either in cash or kind, and military service. Military duties are discussed below; the question of payments is addresse
in a separate chapter. There is no reason to believe that, apart
from one or two special taxes of little consequence, and the two excep-

---

1. Burns, Islam, p.285. Much of his discussion of the nature of
thirteenth-century feudalism is, nonetheless, pertinent to the fourteenth as well, especially pp.273ss.

2. C 1211:11 (Mar.16, 1365); C 1205:60 (Mar.31,11365).

3. C 898:222 (Apr.1,11356), text in Appendix.

tions noted below, Mudéjar serfs were in any way distinct from Christian ones. Verlinden quotes a document published by Kovalevsky purporting to show a change in the status of some Muslim serfs after the plague years,[4] but the evidence to support this single document is wanting, and his conclusions are at variance with other materials at hand.

The one aspect of Mudéjar feudal duties which may have been different, and which was at any rate clearly burdensome to them, was their obligation to work on municipal walls. All Muslims, even those of outlying districts, were responsible for the upkeep of the walls of the city or castle to which they were subject or in which they took refuge in time of need.[5] The distinction in this regard between Mudéjares and Christians (who were also responsible for such duties) was that the former were responsible for the upkeep of the physical plant of the *morería* as well as that of the Christian *universitas*. The Muslims of Tarazona, for instance, complained bitterly in 1357 that they were being forced to work on the city's walls while the walls of the *morería* crumbled unattended.[6]   Moreover, Mudéjar

---

4. *L'Esclavage*, p.438, n.770.

5. E.g., C 689:48 (Nov.30, 1356); cf. C 1566:103 (Jan.16, 1357) and C 690:48 (Feb.2, 1357). For a castle, see C 1571:77 (Dec.30, 1363).

6. C 1566:107 (Jan.20, 1357). The complaints worked: in March the king granted the Mudéjares an *elongamentum* for debts, since they "continually serve us in the repair of the walls and fortifications of the city" (C 1379:162 [Mar.6, 1357]). Even so, the city had to hire Muslims at 2s per day to do this same work in 1363; possibly population decline among the Mudéjares rendered the former system impractical (C 713:160 [Feb.3, 1363]).

workmen were in special demand for their skills, and were often needed
to work long in excess of ordinary feudal obligations. In Játiva they
alone produced quicklime needed for the walls,[7] and in Zaragoza
they provided the entire labor force for the royal castle, the aljaferia. Conscious of the unfair burden on the aljama of Zaragoza
posed by this duty, the king tried various means of alleviating their
distress, first compensating the laborers for any loss in wages by
giving them tax relief,[8] and then adopting the unusual expedient
of arbitrarily extending the duty to surrounding aljamas:

> ...we expressly and deliberately order and command each one of
> you [royal officials], that according to the allotment which will
> be given you by the Mayor of Zaragoza, you shall force and con-
> strain whatever Saracens of Huesca, Calatayud, Daroca and other
> cities of the kingdom, who fall under the jurisdiction entrusted
> to you, and who are technically skilled, to take their share with
> the Saracens of Zaragoza in [the number of] days which the Zarago-
> zan Saracens shall assist in the said work....[9]

In Huesca the town authorities were empowered to gather the
Muslims and Jews into a compound with their goods until they agreed
to perform the needed repairs on the city walls;[10] and in Calatayud

---

7. RP 1704:23 (1357).

8. C 899:195 (Jan.25, 1357).

9. "...vobis et unicumque vestrum dicimus et mandamus expresse ac
de certa sciencia quatenus iuxta certificationem vobis tradendam per
merinum Ceseraguste compellatis et distringatis quilibet vestrum in
jurisdictione vobis commissa sarracenos civitatis Osce, ac villarum
Calataiubi et Daroche, et aliorum locorum regni, utentes arte mecanica, ad coequandum se dictis sarracenis Ceseraguste diebus quibus
ipsi sarraceni Ceseraguste interfuerint operibus antedictis..."
C 702:32 (July 6, 1360).

10. "...que mandedes, si menester sera, seer recollidos dentro
muro, judios i moros i biens d'ellos i que puedan seer costreytos a
treballar de sus personas en las ditas obras" C 982:33 (Mar.21,
1357); cf. C 1381:34 (June 22, 1357).

the Mudéjares were forced to provide materials as well as labor.[11]
Even under the severe duress of the war, when Valencian Mudéjares
wrung from the harassed monarchy enormous concessions for the price
of loyalty, Mudéjar serfs could not escape the burden of wall maintenance (see below, p.365, no.10).

On the other hand, in some communities, e.g., Borja,[12] the duty
was commuted to a small tax, and in a few areas the lord actually had
responsibilities to the Muslims in this regard: "...it was customary
for the lord of these places to give help to those building new homes,
both in overseeing the construction and [in providing?] new doors...."[13]

Mudéjares were also held liable for duties of hospitality. These
included accommodating not only the royal family, or a local lord and
his family, but also soldiers and their mistresses, even when the
latter were Christian. The fact that the mistresses alone could not
stay in Muslims' homes and had to be relocated when the soldiers were
away implies that Mudéjar homes were filled first and Christian ones
only when the Mudéjar homes did not suffice.[14] Prosperous individuals
or morerías were also called upon to lodge foreign Muslim dignitaries
visiting the king: see C 720:8 (Aug.18, 1365), in the Appendix. Although many feudal duties and customs were falling into desuetude

---

11. C 983:150 (Jan.22, 1359).

12. C 1381:33 (June 21, 1357).

13. "...illis qui domos novas in locis ipsis contstruhebant fiebat
per dominum locorum ipsorum auxilium in magistro eas operante et etiam in januis novis..." C 1567:124 (Sept.10, 1359). The "places" are
Bartaxell and Xirillent, in Valencia.

14. C 701:50 (June 6, 1360), in Appendix.

by the mid-fourteenth century, it seems likely that that of hospitality was still actually demanded, since the king granted as a signal
honor to his favorite, Faraig de Belvis, the privilege of exemption
from duties of hospitality even to the royal family.[15]

Mudéjares were also responsible, in many locales at least, for
providing the bedding and linens for the local castle and the troops
garrisoned there.[16]   Játiva even had an official styled the "collector
lectorum et azemilarum judeorum sarracenorumque."[17]   This odd liability may have been merely an extension of a previous obligation to
quarter troops, but it could also have been a quirk of the status
of minorities in a feudal society, comparable to the obligation placed
upon the Jewish aljamas of the Crown of Aragon to quarter the royal
menagerie.[18]   Like Christian feudal obligations, Mudéjar duties were
gradually reduced to purely financial arrangements: the obligation to
provide hospitality was dispensed with in the later fourteenth century,[1]
and the early fifteenth even saw the termination of dues owed the

---

15. C 904:232 (Nov.13, 1360).

16. For Tortosa, see C 724:55 (Nov.3, 1365).

17. C 1071:34 (July 12, 1359).

18. On this fascinating phenomenon, see C 901:86 (June 14, 1357),
where a single Jew is required to keep lions for the king, but reimbursed for their food (at the rate of 10d per diem); C 1073:25 (Feb.
3, 1361), where the Jewish aljama of Valencia is ordered to care for
the royal bear and leopard at its own expense; C 1076:69 (Jan.9, 1365),
where the passage of four royal lions from Perpignan to Zaragoza is
charged to the Jewish aljamas of Aragon-Catalonia; and C 1076:76 (Jan.
19, 1365), where the Jews of Catalonia are required to pay for the maintenance of the larger two of these lions in Tortosa. A forthcoming
study of Jews under the reign of King John by Jaume Riera will examine
this phenomenon for the later fourteenth century.

19. Macho y Ortega, "Documentos," pp.159-60.

municipal walls.[20]

It has long been assumed that the Muslim communities under the
Crown of Aragon were not liable to military service. Both Circourt[21]
and Macho y Ortega state or imply this, the latter quite positively:
"It is certain that Aragonese Moors were exempt from military duties...."[22] It is patent, however, that this was not in fact the
case--either in Aragon proper or in any of the realms under its
Crown--in the fourteenth century. While it is true that many of the
original treaties of capitulation between Muslim communities and
their Christian conquerors included provisions exempting the Muslims
from military duties (for obvious reasons), such provisions were almost universally ignored in succeeding centuries.[23] It is curious
that Macho y Ortega should have been deceived in this matter, since
he himself cited a dispensation from military service granted to

---

20. Macho y Ortega, "Condición," p.171. All the same, Muslim serfs
were still being inherited as property throughout the fourteenth century: see Ramos y Loscertales, Cautiverio, p.131, n.5.

21. Histoire des Mores, I, p.257: "...les Mores s'enrichissaient
plus vite que les chrétiens de basse condition, d'abord par leur in-
dustrie supérieure, ensuite parce que le service militaire, auquel
ils étaient rarement appelés, constituait une charge bien plus
ruineuse...." Macho y Ortega cites this passage (incorrectly) and
agrees with it, but denies the economic inferences drawn by Circourt:
see note following.

22. "Condición," p.188.

23. Viz., the macaronic agreement between Alfonso I, el Batallador,
and the Saracens of Tudela in 1115: "Et non faciat exire moro in ap-
pellito per forza in guerra de moros nec de christianos" Muñoz y Romero, Colección, p.416. Cf. the charter granted to Chivert: "Insuper
serraceni non teneantur facere hostem vel cavalcatam contra serracenos
alios aut christianos nisi forte aliqui sarraceni aut christiani fac-
erent aliquod malefficium vel forciam vel gravamen castro suo et
rebus suis" (April 28, 1234), in Manuel Ferrandis, "Rendición del Castillo de Chivert," Homenaje a Don Francisco Codera en su jubilación

fifteenth-century Aragonese Mudéjares.[24] Moreover, in the collection
of documents he published in the Revista de ciencias jurídicas there
is a letter from the king to the officials of Zaragoza, dated 1413,
asking them to refrain from collecting the 500s owed by the Muslims
of that city for archers, since the major part of the aljama was
already serving with the king's army at the siege of Balaguer.[25]

There can be no doubt that, prior to the fifteenth century, the
custom of using native Muslim troops to assist in the king's military exploits was widespread and unopposed. Burns discusses this
for the thirteenth century at some length.[26] The great-grandfather
of Peter the Ceremonious, during a war with the French in 1283, set
a precedent when he demanded a company of "well-appointed" archers
and lancers from each of the aljamas of Valencia designated by the
faqi Samuel.[27] According to Zurita, during Peter IV's struggle with

---

del profesorado (Zaragoza, 1904), p.31.

24. "Condición," p.172.

25. "...como la mayor partida de los moros de la dita aljama sean
de present en aqueste sitio en servicio nuestro, e sia razonable cosa
que pues aqui nos sirven, sean relevados del cargo e servicio que a-
quexa Ciudat nos deve fazer. Por esto vos rogamos que a la dita aljama hayades por escusada en la contribucion del servicio sobredito..."
"Documentos," p.158.

26. Islam, pp.289-90, and Chapter XII, passim.

27. "...us pregam eus manam que aquels de cascune de les vostres
aliames quel dit alphaquim nostre elegira a asso nos trametau ab companya de balesters et de lancers de cascuna daqueles aliames be apar-
elats et be adobats et nos darem a aquels bona soldada...." This document is published in Bofarull, Colección, VI, p.196. Roca Traver in-
cautiously assumes that the Saracens met the demand as stated: see
"Un Siglo," p.43, where for "p.190" read "p.196." On the general
circumstances of this incident and the actual Muslim contributions,
see Burns, Islam, pp.292-3. It may be significant that the Jews of

the Union, "Don Pedro de Exerica, and Don Gilabert de Centellas,
who was the qa'id of Játiva, gathered a great number of Moors of the
realm of Valencia and other areas" to come to his aid.[28]   In Aragon
itself, the Saracens of Borja were already paying as much as 1,500s
a year for cavallerías in 1347.[29]

In the waging of war as in many other matters, Aragon's Muslim
population proved to be useful mostly because they could be forced to
do what a king of Aragon could only request from his orthodox subjects. During the campaign in Sardinia, for instance, Christians
were so anxious to avoid military duty in a far-flung and unpopular
campaign that they abandoned royal lands they were inhabiting to
escape obligations attendant on them, and it was necessary to force
Jews and Muslims onto the waiting ships to fill out the depleted
forces:

> ...none of the subjects of the Lord King wished to go there
> [Sardinia], nor even to board the [king's] ships; rather,
> people fled from the lands of the king, ...and those who
> boarded were Jews and Moors, who did so through force....[30]

Certain positions on ships in the king's navy seem, in fact, to have

---

Catalonia, or at least of Gerona, also participated in the defense of
the realm against this French invasion, though apparently voluntarily:
see Yitzhak Baer, A History of the Jews in Christian Spain (Philadel-
phia, 1961), I, p.175.

28. "...don Pedro de Ejerica, y don Gilabert de Centellas, que era
alcaide de Játiva, ayuntaron gran número de gente de moros del reino
de Valencia y de otras partes..." Jerónimo Zurita, Anales de la Corona de Aragón, ed. Angel Canellas Lopez (Zaragoza, 1973), IV, xix,
p.92. Cf. p.299, below.

29. C 1382:67 (Mar.14, 1348).

30. C 980:95 (July 10[?], 1355). In the Capitula Gerunde of 1358
the Catalan Corts specifically prohibited the king's sending men from
Gerona to Sardinia by force (C 1381:237), but Gerona had no Muslim community in the fourteenth century.

been largely if not entirely held by Muslims, notably those of
cablemen and jongleurs, trumpeters, and tambourine players.[31]
During the war with Castile, as it became harder and harder to
impress even Muslims into naval service, the king arranged to have
Muslim prisoners released from Catalan and Aragonese jails to serve
on board his ships. Such an arrangement usually netted the Muslim
a grant of immunity from prosecution for the duration of his service
plus a specified period thereafter, ranging from enough time to get
home to a full year.[32]

Even without royal duress, however, the Mudéjares seem to have
felt that a certain share in the defense of the realm was incumbent
upon them. Christians and Saracens of Valencia voluntarily operated
a sort of vigilante guard against Castile at the start of the war.
This was prohibited by the king, however, and those found guilty of
engaging in such operations were fined, Muslims more than Christians.[33]

---

31. There were two cablemen ("palomers") on a ship, and both the fac
that they received a special allowance to eat outside the court ("han
de provisio cas[cun] en cas que no menjen vianda dé Cort, una libra"
[C 1402:153 {1359}]), and the following comment by Muntaner lead one
to speculate that they were usually Muslim: "El tramès un palomer que
sabia molt be sarrahinesch" (Chronicle, 85). Each ship had "juglars
que tocaran a la taula a metre e alevar, ço es, dos trompados, una
trompeta, una tornamusa e tabaler"; these, too, received a special allowance to eat outside the court (C 1402:154), implying that they followed special dietary laws, and hence were either Jews or Muslims. Cf.
Piles Ros, Estudio, p.148, #112, where a Muslim enlists in the navy
"to see the world."

32. In C 1387:131 (Feb.3, 1365), for example, a certain Mudéjar in
the Lérida jail is ordered released into the custody of the qadi, wh
is to bring him to Barcelona to join the navy. C 1404:56 (Feb.4) give
the man's name (Ayte Mugefiç), and indicates that he received a grant
of immunity for the duration of his service plus one year.

33. RP 2911:1.

Nevertheless, one of the primary military uses of Mudéjar communities was as local guards or militia. During the first year of real
fighting with Castile, whole populations of Valencian Muslims were
commandeered by the king to defend fortresses in endangered areas.
Garsia de Loriz was ordered, for example, to see whether the castle
at Ayora (belonging to Pere de Vilanova) was still defensible, and
if so to force the local Muslims into it and not allow them to leave,
the idea being (apparently) that thus put in danger of their lives
they would fight to prevent the castle's being taken no matter what
their loyalties in the war might be.[34] This same idea was behind the
king's order to his Valencian procurator in 1362 to have the Muslims
of Seta put all their movable goods in the castle and then to appor-
tion guard duty among them, either by the week or the day as he saw
fit.[35] On the other hand, the Saracens of Vilamalur, another small,
predominantly Muslim town, voluntarily guarded not one but two strategic castles for the king.[36] In general, it seems to have been the

---

34. "Dehim vos e'us manam que reconegats o façats regonexer si'l castell de Anna, que es d'en Pere de Vilanova e es en la frontera d'Ayora,
es tal que si'ls moros del loch hi acuraven lo porien defendre e guar-
dar, que no fos esuasit ne occupat per enemichs, e si'n es, forçats
los dits moros d'acurar en lo dit castell e que no'l desemparen" C
1379:24 (Sept.13, 1356). On the question of Muslim loyalty, see below,
pp. 391ss.

35. C 1571:47 (Sept.15, 1362): "Item uolem que ordonets que dels
moros de la villa de Seta, que son molts, sia fet compartiment, que
entre aquell nombre que a vos sera vinyars dins lo dit castell per
defensio de aquell, e que aço's faça per setmanes o per dies segons
qu'us sera semblant...."

36. C 1209:25 (Mar.4, 1365). They may have felt constrained to make
some gesture of loyalty after having first defected to Castile and
then returned to Peter IV's service.

task of the Saracens in any locality to guard their own section of
the town, plus exclusively royal castles in it. Heavy fines were
levied on those unwilling to comply. Even in 1357, a year of relatively little fighting, the butcher of Tarazona was fined about 1,000s
because he refused to stand guard "as was incumbent on him, along with
others deputed for the purpose, for the defense and protection of the
city...."[37]

A pool of Muslims from various surrounding towns was used to man
the aljaferias in Zaragoza and Huesca, and, at least in the earlier
stages of the war, this was seen as being in lieu of further military
service. Unlike the guard forces, or even the Saracen contingents
in the army, these aljaferia units seem to have been permanently
assigned to their posts, forming a sort of elite guard. Nineteen of
them are mentioned by name in a document exempting them from other
military duties in 1357.[38] When the Christians of Huesca tried to

---

37. "...prout [sibi] incumbebat cum aliis ad id faciendum deputatis
ad tuitionem et defensionem civitatis eiusdem..." C 1566:115 (Mar.4,
1365). This fine, later remitted, was imposed by the faqi of the aljama itself. The exact amount was 100 morabetíns and 200s. Under normal circumstances extra guards, such as nightwatchmen in excess of
the ordinary watch of the Muslim quarter, had to be provided by the
qadi at his own expense: see C 1569:26-27 (Oct.17, 1359), where the
qadi of Elche and Crevillente is ordered to desist from recruiting
eight extra watchmen from the aljama, since the latter is already
bound to keep night watch over itself, and to provide these men from
among his own personal retainers.

38. C 982:55 (Apr.1, 1357): "...Muçoc Barberus, Heyta Esguerre,
Abdulla d'Aroz, Mahoma Cernutho [et al.]...sarracenis civitatis Osce
gratiam suam. Dicimus et mandamus vobis quatenus cum vestris armis
et bonis ballistis, et aliis appartamentis ad tuitionem aliafferie nostre necessariis, remaneatis in ipsa aliafferia stablida, nobis ibidem
servitium legaliter impensuri. Nos enim harum serie ab eunde et seg-
uendo [sic] nostrum exercitum vos et vestrum quilibet tenori presentium excusamus." The aljaferias were closely associated with Mudéjar-

force the Saracens of the town to help pay for sending troops to the frontier, the queen intervened in their behalf, pointing out that the Saracens alone had to provide archers for the local aljaferia without any aid from the Christians, and that to force them to pay for border troops would be in effect double-charging them. Moreover, she observed, the Muslim community of Huesca had never been liable to help pay for such forces with the Christians.[39] In early 1363, aware of the strategic importance of the aljaferia of Zaragoza, the king ordered Francesch Sentliment, the merinus of the city, to put forty men, Jews and Moors, into the castle at night to guard it ("We expressly command the mayor of the city to place immediately in the aljaferia forty men, divided between Jews and Moors who are competent for such duty, to keep guard by night").[40] In December of that year the king learned to his dismay that this order had never been carried out, because the mayor was unwilling to force the city's non-Christian inhabitants to comply. In another letter the king reiterated his demand and insisted that force be used if necessary, but reduced the requirement to twenty men, to be apportioned equally between Jews and Muslims.[41]

---

es in other ways, too: see

39. "...cum numquam vobisquam in similibus contribuere consueverint" C 1567:174 (Feb.13, 1360).

40. "...manam espressament al merino de la dita ciutat que encontinent faza metre en la dita aljaferia xl homnes entre jueus e moros qui sien aptes en aytal fet, los quals de nits guayten..." C 1384:171 (Feb.22, 1363).

41. C 1385:178 (Dec.4, 1363).

Especially in Valencia, abuses grew up around this system of sharing guard duty, and Muslim communities were often unjustly imposed upon. The aljamas of Bartaxell and Xirillent complained to the king in 1359 that they were being forced to buy arrows and other armaments for the castle, and the Saracens of Seta protested against both the forced purchases of lances and arrows, and also unfair requirements of work on the castle.[42] In Aragon and Catalonia, on the other hand, co-operation was the rule, and in some cases, such as Sariñena, where neither the Muslims nor the Christians could provide enough men for the city's defense, the king provided troops in return for money provided equally by the two communities.[43]

Of those Muslims actually sent to join the king's army, the vast majority were certainly infantrymen, though the number of Muslim cavalry was not inconsequential (see below). It is extremely difficult to estimate the number of Mudéjares in the king's service, or even to approximate the percentage of the total they may have represented. At the beginning of the war with Castile their contribution was modest: the group of thirty men, ten archers and twenty rowers (remers), sent by the Crown's largest aljama, Játiva, in June, 1355, was probably typical.[44] As the war escalated, so did the numbers of soldiers required, and the demands made on the aljamas. In the general levy on the towns of Aragon-Catalonia of 1358, Teruel was assessed for 65

---

42. C 1567:124 (Sept.10, 1359).

43. C 986:98 (Oct.3, 1365). The sum mentioned is 85s for each group, but it is not clear for what amount of time.

44. C 1401:86 (June 2, 1355).

equites, for which the Moors and Jews were to be equally responsible with the Christians. Although quite a few Muslims served in the cavalry, few if any Jews served, and on the whole it seems to have been standard for the two minorities to provide infantry when they were subject to the same levy. It was agreed, therefore, that every 146 infantrymen provided by the Jews and Muslims would be equal to one cavalryman with his horse.[45] If this ratio were actually adhered to, it would have meant the two communities were responsible for about 5,000 infantrymen from Teruel alone—an obvious impossibility, since the entire body of infantry at the border numbered only about 6,000,[46] and they would surely not all be Muslims—so it seems likely that the actual contribution fell far short of the theoretical one.

Some of these Mudéjar troops fought in units under their lord,[47] but most were apparently mixed in with the other soldiers indiscriminately, and formed no separate body in regard to discipline. In 1357, when the king granted the troops from Daroca the right to retreat from the border without specific permission to do so, the order was directed to all soldiers, "whether cavalry or infantry, Christian or Muslim."[48] How well integrated these mixed bodies were must remain moot, but there

---

45. C 982:132 (June 29, 1358), in Appendix. On the general question of Jews and the military during this period, see Baer, History, I, pp. 59ss, 89 (and note, p.397), 113ss, 186, 359, 368, 369.

46. C 982:165 (Oct.18, 1358).

47. C 695:140 (June 15, 1359): in this case, for Johann Martín de Luna.

48. C 901:177 (Oct.22, 1357).

is evidence of efforts to train such groups at the local level,
albeit belatedly. The war had already been under way for about six
years when, in 1361, the king granted the inhabitants of Aranda a
three-year exemption from certain taxes on the condition that all
of them--Christian and Saracen--form a sort of militia, with regular
practice after dinner on Sundays and holydays, prescribed arms, and
obligatory weekly "manoeuvres."

> ...with, however, this condition attached and added,
> that all and sundry inhabitants of this village capable of
> acting as archers--Christians as well as Saracens--be held to
> retain in their own homes at all times a good and sufficient
> bow, strung and ready for use, and one hundred arrows or pas-
> sadors [a type of small, very sharp arrow], and to practice ar-
> chery with these after dinner on every Sunday and holiday they
> can, under pain of a fine of 15s.
>   The rest of those in the village shall in similar fashion
> be held by you to maintain a sturdy shield, a tancea (?), two
> [?] spears or good swords, and to carry a hat or cap or hel-
> met, all of which each of the aforesaid villagers has to procure
> within six months immediately following the date of this [letter].
> Moreover, both the archers and the [others] are to be strictly
> bound and obliged during the aforesaid triennium to make or cause
> to be made...one outing or day's march each week in the valley or
> the environs of the village, without salary or expenses, under
> pain of a fine of 15s.[49]

Naturally, as in every other matter under the Crown's jurisdiction,
there were exceptions, exemptions, extensions. Those Saracens guard-

---

49. "Tali tamen condicione opposita et adjecta, quod omnes et singuli vicini ville predicte tam christiani quam sarraceni abti [sic] ad
exerciari ballistarum, in eorum domo propria bonam vel suficientem bal-
listam cum eius corda cinta et encorda necnon centum viratores sive
passadors [sic] teneantur habere continue, et facere cum ipsis ballistis
exercitium omnibus diebus dominicis et festivis qui valeantur post pran-
dium sub pena quinque solidorum iaccensium.... Ceteri vobis ville
ipsius modo simili tenere habeant bonum pavesium, tanceam, duo telas
coreaceas seu bonas spaterias, et capellinam aut capellum seu galeam
ferre, que omnia quilibet ex vicinis ipsis procurare habeant infra
sex menses a datis huiusmodi quamprimo venturos. Et nichilominus
tam dicti ballistarii quam ipsi empevasati teneantur et sint astricti
durante dicto triennio qualibet septimana facere seu fieri facere sine

ing the _aljaferia_ in Huesca, as has been mentioned, were specifically
exempted from service in the army, not merely collectively but often
individually,[50] though not without contest.[51] The aljama of Pomario
in Aragon was completely excused from military service, either personal
or financial, because of its poverty and small numbers.[52] Rarely were
such exemptions agreeable to all parties. The king's needs for
certain Muslim subjects were liable to conflict with the needs of
nobles. The Saracen residents of Nabal (in Aragon) were vitally
necessary to the king's forces in their role as conveyors of salt
to much of Aragon, yet they made up the vassals on the basis of which
certain nobles were assessed for infantry. After a prolonged battle over the nobles' seizing much-needed mules from the Muslims and
insisting that the Mudéjares serve in the army contingents the nobles
were constrained to supply, the king ruled that the Saracens should
be exempt from all military service and "the field of battle."[53]

As in the case of the local guard units, numerous abuses and injustices occurred in the handling of these Muslim infantry contingents. Although technically bound to contribute with the monastery
of St Peter towards its share in 700 knights, the aljama of Calatayud was compelled by the city to contribute instead with it, and to

---

solucione seu logerio sub pena quinque solidorum...unam peonatam sive
jornal in vallo seu talliata ville iamdicte" C 906:23 (Aug.25, 1361).

50. C 982:55, _ut supra_.

51. See above, p.174.

52. "...qui ut percepimus estis pauci numero et non facultatibus
opulenti...non teneamini...ire vel quemquam mittere ad ipsos exercitus,
nec solvere aliquid pro redemptione eorum..." C 1402:146 (Feb.1, 1359).

53. C 1402:147 (Feb.1, 1359).

provide one-third of

> the mules, soldiers, provisions and armaments of the
> castles of the towns; what is worse, the city itself refused
> to grant any payment or remuneration to the said Saracens for
> these things, even though it put into its accounts the salaries
> and stipends which ought to have been allotted or paid the
> Saracens as if they actually had been; which monies they [the
> townspeople] wrongly retained for themselves and still possess.[54]

There is reason to believe that in addition to outright defrauding,
as in Calatayud, there was official discrimination against Muslim
soldiers in regard to salary and benefits. The king had assigned
fifty archers to the Valencian town of Crevillente, but the Queen,
who was responsible for the town's finances, discovered that the
rents of the town were not sufficient to pay the full complement of
fifty at the prescribed pay of two sueldos a day. She therefore ordered the recruiting of forty local archers, who, she understood,
would work for only 18 diners per diem. If the locals would not work
at a lower price, the official was to hire 25 Christian archers "at
whatever price he could," and fill out the original fifty with Saracen
archers to be paid eighteen diners a day. Of this amount, only six
of the diners were actually to go to the Muslims thus employed, the
remaining twelve to be given to their lord, Prince Martin, "on account."
To ensure the loyal performance of men employed under these terms, the
wives and children of the Mudéjares were held as hostages, and un-

---

54. "...azemilis, peditibus, et in victualibus ac munitionibus cast-
rorum aldearum, dicte ville renuendo, quod peius est, solidum vel stipendium aliquid prefatis sarracenis pro predictis exsolvere, licet solidum vel stipendium quod dari et solvi ipsis sarracenis debebat in compoto pro soluto reddiderit, quod penes se minus debite retinuerint et
etiam retinent" C 700:144 (Jan.30, 1360).

married men were therefore unacceptable for the position.[55] As

if this were not enough, a year later the queen found it necessary

to reprimand the procurator and bailiff of Crevillente for having

failed to pay the Muslim archers even the six _diners_ they were sup-

posed to receive for food.[56] One wonders, all the same, whether the

royal expedient of taking hostages was really necessary, since some

of the archers hired at 45s per month subsequently managed to engage

others to take their places at 25s.[57]

While it is scarcely surprising, considering their numbers, that

the Mudéjares furnished a considerable portion of the king's infantry,

it is something of a surprise to find that they also constituted a

substantial share of the royal cavalry. From the very first levy of

troops for the war with Castile (1356),[58] Muslims were expected to

contribute their share of cavalry in all three kingdoms. Contrary to

what one might expect, moreover, a financial contribution was not

necessarily sufficient to discharge this obligation, and in most cases

where they were liable for it, Saracens and Christians alike seem to

---

55. "En altra manera si mes de xviii deners haurien a costar [los
chrestians] volem que haiats xxv ballesters chrestians a aquell preu
que porets, guardant tota vegada lo profit de la Cort, e los romanents
de los ballesters a compliment de los l, sien de los moros del dit infant don Marti, los quales haurets per xviii deners lo dia ho per menis;
la qual salari los paguets en esta forma, ço es, que'ls donets vj deners per dia per lur provisio, e lo romanent los sia pres en compte del
die que deuen dar a senyor. Axi empero qu'els moros qui estaran en Cri-
villen meten per rehenes lu[r]s infants en lo loch de Eltx. E si muller
ne infants no ha, no sien meses en compte dels dits ballesters" C 1569:
29-30 (Nov.10, 1359).

56. C 1569:71 (Nov.6, 1360).

57. C 1569:92 (May 20, 1361).

58. C 687:105 (July 9, 1356).

have understood their duty as involving the actual furnishing of men and horses themselves (unlike the Jews--see above). The levy of 1359 makes pellucidly clear that the affected towns were responsible both for the knight and his salary, and in a letter to Elche and Crevillente there is clear indication that the practice was of employing locals first, then hiring others: "...this salary for the six cavalrymen may be paid or given to six armed horsemen from among the men of the said town of Elche if men competent and sufficiently experienced as horsemen and [?] are to be found there."[59]

At the time of the levy of 1363, the official salary for an armed cavalryman was 7s per diem, and all cavalrymen were paid exactly the same, at least in theory.[60]

Some aljamas were exempt from cavalry duties. Those of Monzón, Ripol and Podio in Aragon were all subject to the Hospitallers of Monzón and dispensed from the obligations of providing either cavalrymen or their salaries.[61] Local officals, through greed or need, often attempted to ignore or violate such concessions, as in Monzón, where a local official had to be restrained from holding Muslims captive

---

59. "...dictum solidum dictorum sex equitum exsolvatur et detur sex equitibus ex hominibus dicti loci de Eltx, dum tamen suficientes et bene periti in equis et [?] reperiantur in eodem" C 983:85 (Jan.20, 1359). Crevillente was included in this letter.

60. C 985:115. An armed soldier ("alforrado") was entitled to 5 sueldos per day. Most military designations of the day were of Arabic provenance, e.g., "alforrado," "geneta," etc. This in itself would seem to imply Muslim participation in the Crown's military corps on a fairly extensive scale, since most Arabic words entered Romance in areas of greatest Muslim participation, e.g., architecture, markets, commerce, irrigation, farming, etc.

61. C 695:82 (Apr.1, 1359).

to force them to contribute to the cavalry levy.

The aljamas, however, were not the only source of Muslim cavalry. Numerous outstanding individual Mudéjares furnished one or more cavalrymen at their own expense, either voluntarily or under obligation. Faraig de Belvis kept at least one knight "continually in the king's service on the borders of Aragon and Valencia" and was reimbursed for the horseman's salary by monies allotted the king at the Corts of Monzón (1365).[62] Mahoma Ayudemi Ballistarius[63] served personally as a cavalryman for the king from the outset of the war,[64] but was nonetheless compelled by suit of his aljama to contribute with them for the war effort, not only toward the upkeep of the walls and other similar works, but even toward the salaries of the aljama's other equites.[65]   Çaat Alcafaç, on the other hand, a prominent and wealthy Valencian, received compensation for his outlay in maintaining a cavalcadura for fifteen days in Játiva in 1362.[66]

---

62. In C 1207:4 (May 30, 1365) the king orders that Faraig be paid 533s "por sueldo de un cavallo armado que ha tenido continuament en el nostre servicio en las fronteras d'Aragon e de Valencia." I am assuming that the cavallo mentioned is a horse and rider, rather than simply a horse.

63. Ballistarius is a surname here, not a military designation.

64. "...ipsum Mahoma cum equo alforrato nobis continue deseruisse a die qua incepit dicta guerra...." The material for this and the following comments about Ballistarius is derived from three separate entries: C 688:91 (Dec.17, 1356), C 908:79 (Dec.20, 1362), and C 908:84 (Dec.20, 1362). For more on the Ballistarii, see p.43, n.38.

65. This must have doubly galled Ballistarius, who had been previously granted immunity from the aljama's debts: see pp.213-216.

66. RP 1708:18ss: "...lvi sol. qui...foren donats a Çaat Alcafaç per provisio de si e de i caualcadura ab la qual estech per la dita raho xv dies en Xativa." This amount is exactly half what Alcafaç should have received, but there may have been extenuating circumstances. The account was drawn up in Alcafaç's absence.

It is fairly clear that a certain number of Saracens were professional horsemen permanently in the king's service rather than ordinary subjects drafted in time of war. Such was undoubtedly the
case with the fourteen Saracens "de la geneta de casa del Senyor Rey"
paid 1,000s and sent to Valencia to fight in 1358.[67] A curious entry of the same year leads one to wonder whether the Aragonese king may
not have had some apprehensions about these professional warriors not
unlike the anxieties experienced by Byzantine emperors in regard to
the Catalan companies they hired to fight for them. When the company
of a hundred men who had been serving in Valencia under Matthew Mercer, the king's chamberlain, was disbanded on the latter's being sent
abroad, eight Saracen knights of the company came to Aragon, "seeking
to serve the king," and he immediately and emphatically ordered them
back to Valencia, reminding tham that he had already expressly forbidden their coming into Aragon.[68] Clearly these Muslims served in
ordinary companies, and were not segregated from their Christian counterparts.

In addition to the Mudéjar components of the king's forces, there
was a considerable number of foreign Muslims fighting for him during
the war with Castile. In the five years between 1355 and 1361 the king
issued at least six different edicts of safe-conduct to groups of for-
eign-born Muslims who had been in his service for various lengths of

---

67. RP 2468:101. For "geneta" see note 70, below. It was not unknown
for Jews to be professional soldiers, but not cavalrymen: see Baer, History, I, p.204.

68. C 1381:160 (Sept.12, 1358). There are two copies of the document;
the king apparently took no chances about missing them.

time and now wished to leave the country.[69] Most of these were subjects of the King of Granada, but a few came from Tunis and some from
Tlemcen. It seems reasonable to assume that most such knights eventually left the country, and that their Spanish sojourn was principally
a mercenary concern. They were paid considerably less than native
horsemen. A group of eight "moros de Granada" with their retinue "a
la geneta" on the very frontier were paid by the king as little as
5s a day in 1358.[70] Nonetheless, Peter IV was on sufficiently good
terms with them that he could send Granadan cavalrymen to the King of
France in 1356.[71]

As the war with Castile became less and less decisive and more
and more difficult and costly, the orderly and "legal" use of Moorish
troops increasingly gave way to rash, almost indiscriminate demands
on the already hard-pressed Muslim communities, and finally to forced
wholesale impressment. The illegal seizure and "confiscation" of Muslim properties is discussed elsewhere in this study, as is the taking
of Mudéjar hostages to ensure Saracen loyalty. There are few better
examples of the utility of a subject population with no real personal
rights than that offered by the desperate campaign of the spring of

---

69. These entries are C 703:25 (May 28, 1360)—seven Muslims from
Granada returning home from the king's service; C 898:51 (Nov.7, 1355)—
a Granadan noble and his family of five returning home from the king's
service; C 901:252 (Jan.24, 1358)—one Muslim of Tunis leaving the
king's service to go to Granada; C 903:142 (Nov.12, 1359)—four Muslims
leaving for Granada; C 906:63 (Oct.25, 1361)—five subjects of Tlemcen
leaving Aragon to serve the king in Valencia; C 1403:62 (May 19, 1357)—
three Muslims formerly serving against Castile now departing to North
Africa.

70. RP 2468:79. For standard pay, see p.235. "Geneta" is of Arabic origin
and denotes a style of riding and armament; cf. French "génétaire."

71. C 688:18 (Aug.2, 1356).

1365. As the winds of war blew through Valencia, every Mudéjar who did not enjoy the unassailable protection of a Christian magnate was swept into the army of one side or the other.   In March of that year the king wrote to the qadi of Artana demanding that he send 80 men from the aljama to the king immediately to serve in the army.[72] This number probably represented the entire male population of the aljama, though it is impossible to know for certain.   In that same month, however, in an order to the qadi of Eslida, the monarch specifically commanded that the entire population of the aljama of Eslida be brought with their amin to join the army at the castle of Castro, and that the amin be given whatever armaments he might need to outfit these new troops.[73]   As in many such levies, the traditional division of one-half archers and one-half lancers was specified.[74]

On the very same day the king sent the letter to the aljama of Almonazir he wrote to the nearby Mudéjar community of Espada requesting

---

72. C 1211:11 (Mar.16).   To be sure, large irregular drafts were sometimes made on Christian communities as well, but never on the same scale or with the same frequency as those on the aljamas.   Moreover, Christian co-operation was nearly always obtained only at the price of generous concessions by the monarchy, usually under the form of Capitula, e.g., C 1381:232.

73. C 1211:31 (Mar.25, 1365).   The amin appears to have been the usual military commander for such impressed "companies": in April the king ordered 100 Muslims from the aljama of Almonazir to join the army under the leadership of some suitable person, "either the amin or someone else," to help in the siege of Murviedro.

74. C 1211:37 (Apr.1, 1365) (two separate entries). See above, p.172, for this common division of Mudéjar troops.

that they send 200 men to assist in the taking of the castle of Almonazir.[75] Another 100 Saracens were drafted from the same small aljama to guard the castle once it was taken,[76] and yet another demand
was made--this time for "all men capable of bearing arms"[77]--only little more than a month later.

Needless to say, compliance with such stiff demands posed considerable hardships for the aljamas, and duplicate letters and repeated
demands bear witness to the king's difficulty in enforcing this type
of levy.[78] By the end of May, stern threats of punishment for non-
compliance began to appear appended to such documents, and during the
final weeks of the month a hailstorm of such comminations issued
from the Court as the king tried to commandeer the services of the
communities of Muslims in Serra, Eslida, Artana, Almonazir, Espada,
Guayell, Bencanduç, Xenguer, Mosquera, Atzuena, Chona, and Castro, to
assist in the burning of the crops around Segorbe.[79] In addition to

---

75. C 1204:55 (Apr.1, 1365).

76. C 1204:56 (Apr.1, 1365).

77. C 1204:127 (May 4, 1365); identical copy at C 1209:87 (May 4,
1365).

78. C 1211:31 (Mar.25, 1365) and C 1204:69 (Apr.12, 1365), for instance; cf. C 1209:87 (May 4, 1365), C 1205:99 (may 28, 1365), C 1210:
101 (May 27, 1365).

79. C 1205:99 (May 29). There is an interesting parallel, in this
instance, of demands on the Christian communities in some--though not
all--of the same towns in a document of the same register, f.111. Following are the relative numbers of men demanded:

Town	Muslims	Christians
Serra	200	200
Eslida	150	300
Artana	100	300
Espada	100	300
Almonazir	100	---

threats, the monarch was apparently reduced to deception to fill out his armies; in the original letters to the Muslim communities above, the levy is described as being specifically to facilitate the burning of crops. In another letter, however, Peter made clear to the Count of Ampurias his intention to forward these men to him once the job was done.[80]

It requires little imagination to picture the devastation wrought on the aljamas of Valencia by having all the able-bodied men away fighting during the crucial months of spring. Just how many of the men returned and when is impossible to say, but whether due to lack of co-operation, royal compassion, or simple depopulation, the demands on the Mudéjares declined sharply in the beginning of June.[81] By August formal impressment of specific Saracens had, at least for the time being, all but ceased, and the exhausted communities were ordered, albeit firmly, merely to "co-operate" with whoever had been put in charge of military operations in their area.[82]

Ironically, the long-range effects of the war with Castile and the exploitation of the Muslims attendant on it may actually have been beneficial for them. Especially in the last years of the war, numerous questions about the exact nature of Mudéjar military duties arose,

---

Guayell, Benicanduç, Xenguer, etc., each provided 20 Muslims, but no Christians were demanded from them. For fifteenth-century levies on some of these same towns, see Piles Ros, Estudio, p.214.

80. C 1210:101 (May 27, 1365).

81. The highest drafts on Muslims in that month were for thirty "well armed men" from Artana, Espada, Eslida, and Uxó: C 1210:121 (June 21, 1365).

82. Viz., C 986:20, in Appendix.

partly as a consequence of excesses such as those noted above, and
the Court was called upon to define precisely what sort of demands
could and could not be made on Muslim subjects. Such definitions were
almost inevitably helpful to the latter, since almost any specific
obligation was preferable to the previous condition of nearly all-in-
clusive liability. In 1365 the question arose, especially in the
southern realm, of whether the many Muslims who took refuge in the
cities from the war-ravaged countryside were liable to drafts on the
city. The king decided that since such Saracens were at least technically bound to serve in the localities whence they came, the city
of Játiva could not require them to fill out its muster, whether they
were actually residing in it or not.

> ...when the city raises its troops and the number of men
> in the aforesaid morería is determined, money should only be paid
> by or demanded of those who are actually members of the said mor-
> ería, since other Saracens who have recently come to this morería
> on account of such things mentioned previously [i.e., the war] are
> already obligated in the places they used to inhabit to pay tithes
> and to make troop contributions such as have been described.[83]

In a decision the following year the Crown made clear once and for all
that all such military drafts were to be made on the basis of the actual number of Saracens residing in the aljama at the time of the levy,
a measure designed to force officials to correct census figures rendered
extremely inaccurate by the plagues of 1348-50.[84]

---

83. "...cum universitas antedicta facit oscem [=hostem] et numerus
hominum predicte morarie recognoscitur, tantum solvuntur et demandan-
tur illi qui proprie sunt de dicta moraria, cum alii sarraceni qui ad
dictam noviter premissorum occasione morariam venerunt, sint jam scrip-
ti in locis in quibus habitare consueverunt per deçenas, et faciant oscem ut est dictum" C 1206:151 (Oct.15, 1365).

84. C 910:118 (Sept.16, 1366): "...aljama iuxta dictum compensatum

Undoubtedly the most important decisions to result from the war and its confusion were the two decrees establishing "separate but equal" military duties for Muslims and Christians in Játiva. It cannot be proven that either of these edicts was subsequently applied to all the king's lands, or even to all of Valencia, but both the enormous influence of the aljama of Játiva and the wording of the documents themselves in the very best Chancery Latin militate towards such an interpretation of their importance. The first is a grant to the aljama of the right to make its army with the city ("de faciendo exercitum cum universitate"),[85] a landmark concession in view of the previous status of Muslim soldiers, and, indeed, civilians, as subject to the royal beck and call regardless of the draft status of their Christian compatriots. By this linking of the military liabilities of the two peoples the Mudéjar communities gained enormous political leverage and protection from the caprice of the throne (in theory, at least), since the subjects of the Aragonese Crown in the fourteenth century were certainly among the most jealous of their personal liberties of all medieval Europeans, and little apt to be conscripted lightly.

The second edict established the separateness of the Mudéjar troops, while safeguarding the valuable link between the relative liability of the two peoples: "...therefore, each and every time the whole army

---

numerum domorum seu focorum suorum tamen et non in pluri habeat sive mittere in predictis." Although efforts had been made in this direction before (see pp. 198ss), this measure was sorely needed.

85. C 913:34 (Sept. 16, 1366).

of the said city [Játiva] shall have to go out of the city, for
whatever need, reason, or cause, the whole army of the [city's]
aljama shall do likewise."[86]

Two separate armies, with separate but equal duties: a method of
coping with the tensions of ethnic and racial plurality as old as
Rome's barbarian military units and as modern as separate units for
blacks in the armed forces of the United States in World War I. It
is, indeed, a tribute to the openness of the Crown of Aragon and the
peoples under it that this expedient was not adopted until hundreds
of years after the political amalgamation of the peoples concerned,
that even then it was employed in favor of the minority rather than
the majority, and that, insofar as is known, it was not a nation-
wide rule, but merely a practical measure applied to largest and most
influential minority community.

---

86. "Quia si quando et quotienscumque totus exercitus universitatis
predicte Xative habuerit aliqua quavis necessitate ratione seu causa
predictam civitatem exire, habeat ipsius aljame sarracenorum totus exercitus pari modo" C 910:118 (Sept.16, 1366).

Chapter V

Mudéjar Taxes and Aljama Finances

Jews, Christians and Muslims all paid regular annual taxes:
the peyta (=tributum, trahut, tallia, questia), the cena, and
the censal (or censualia). The cena and peyta averaged about
100s per aljama for the Muslims, with very large communities paying more. The cena had originally been a feudal duty for the provisioning of the king when he visited a town (cena de presencia)
or traveled elsewhere (cena de absencia), but by the mid-fourteenth
century it was merely a standard tax. The censualia, often referred
to in the documents as exaccions, were an aggregate of annual taxes
on property and business operations such as ovens, baths, shops,
mules, etc.[1]

Although the morabetín was originally a specific tax (see below),
it had become merely another general imposition by the mid-fourteenth
century. The word was applied to annual taxes as well as to irregular demands for the replacement of officials.[2] That it was not collected at regular seven-year intervals, as is commonly supposed, is
clear from the annual appointment of officials to collect it.[3]

Subsidies were officially irregular offerings made to the Crown
to meet special expenses, but by the period in question they had
become standard exactions. The precise amount of the subsidy collected from each aljama varied slightly more than that of other
taxes, but so little that it is possible to describe it fairly as

---

1. Macho y Ortega incorrectly assumed the censal to have been the
debt incurred to pay off royal exactions: "Condición," p.186.

2. E.g., C 1068:111 (May 4, 1356).

3. For the standard opinion: Macho y Ortega, "Condición," p.203;
for the annual appointments: RP 2402:23 (1355).

a regular tax. Occasionally subsidies in the original sense were
collected in much larger amounts than the annual subsidies, but
this was rare.[4]

There were a number of minor annual taxes as well, such as the
lezda, imposed on meat, the cabecagium (head tax) for the walls of
the city, etc. These varied widely from city to city and can best
be appreciated by examination of the records of the individual
aljama. Cavallerías were collected in most towns during war time
on a regular basis; the amount of one cavallería varied from 1,500s
to 365s.[5] Some aljamas were liable for cavallerías in peace as
well as war, and under such circumstances they were simply additional
taxes.[6] Royal Mudéjares paid a small property tax called the besant.[7]

Heavily agricultural areas, such as southern Valencia, paid
taxes somewhat more agricultural in orientation: Aspe, for instance,
paid, in addition to those mentioned above, a head tax on livestock
("atzaque"), a tax on hens, a head tax of one almut of barley for
every person of whatever age or sex, "tithes" on such crops as grain
and olives, and special monetary taxes on grain (the "canaxir").[8]
The standard head tax ("peyta") in such communities was often known

---

4. E.g., that of 20,000s demanded of the Jews of Barcelona in
1352: C 1473:115 (Mar.13, 1352).

5. C 1382:67 (Borja, 1348): 1,500s; RP 1694:2 (Daroca, 1364): 635s.

6. E.g., C 980:4 (1355).

7. C 1209:44 (Mar.14, 1365).

8. RP 1711:12ss (1366). Elda, Novelda, Alicante, and most other
towns in this area paid similar taxes, and were subject to a special bailiwick ("bajulia regni Valentie ultra Sexonam").

under some other name, but was levied in amounts comparable to
those collected in northern communities. It is likely, in fact,
that the rate of taxation in the South did not exceed that of
the North by much, although in absolute terms the income from the
richer and more populous communities of Valencia was much greater.
The large number of agricultural taxes collected is deceptive:
the amounts were often quite small. "Tithes," for instance, were
usually only one-third of one-tenth of the quantity of the grain
stored by the aljama.

General taxes were always assessed on the basis of real population figures; it was the responsibility of the tax collectors
themselves to assess communities fairly. During the late 1350's
and early 1360's a number of aljamas complained that they were
being taxed unfairly, since their populations had declined drastically due to plague and war, and they were being taxed for many
persons no longer alive or inhabiting their aljamas.[9] In Teruel
such complaints led to the king's establishing tax assessors in
pairs, one from the aljama and one from the Court, so that any
population figures would represent the view of both sides.[10] In
Borja he instructed the collectors to recount the population--Chris-
tian and Jewish as well as Muslim--after the entire city complained

---

9. Actually such complaints had been voiced as early as 1271,
when the Crown conceded to the aljama of Aranda that they should
no longer pay taxes for Saracens who left or were baptized; C 862:
127 (1337) is a fourteenth-century confirmation of this. Property
abandoned was, of course, taxable as before.

10. C 982:188 (Feb.5, 1359).

of an unfair levy.[11]   In some cases the Muslims may have taken
advantage of the Crown's attempts at fairness in this regard;
Peter thought so, at least, in regard to the aljama of Teruel,
which he accused of duplicity in a dispute over its actual population for the purposes of a levy of 1360.[12]   But the principle
stood that taxes should be levied on the basis of current, accurate population figures.[13]

Individual taxes, such as property taxes, were assessed by
individual. All subjects of the Crown paid property taxes, and
those involving Muslims seem to have been consonant with the general practice. The rate of taxation for Muslim property was probably
higher: although there is no direct evidence of this, it is suggested
by the great concern exhibited by the Crown to keep Muslim property
from being sold or willed into the hands of non-Muslim subjects.[14]
The original morabetí was a property tax of 7s for every household
owning property of 15 morabetíns or more,[15] and was collected every
seven years, but by the mid-fourteenth century property taxes were

---

11. C 1383:233 (Nov.22, 1360) and C 1384:22 (May 30, 1361).

12. C 1383:239 (Jan.2, 1361), but see note 150, below.

13. C 910:118 (Sept.16, 1366).

14. On the universality of the property tax, see C 903:290 (May
7, 1360); on a typical (?) assessment, see C 904:73 (May 10, 1360),
where 800s worth of Muslim property is taxed 12d annually. Of course,
sales tax was also paid when Muslims were sold themselves: this jus
quinti might be considered a contribution of the Mudéjar community.
See C 1207:145 (Oct.3, 1365), for one of many examples. For more
on the sales tax and property taxes in general, cf. López de Meneses,
Documentos, p.92 (document of 1350 [= C 890:165]).

15. Hamilton, Money, p.9.

either annual or in the form of inheritance or sales taxes.

Inheritance taxes ranged from one-twelfth to one-third the
amount of the estate, and were paid directly to the Crown. They
included other taxes such as the loisne, cens, sisa, peyta, besant,
etc.[16] There were also individual taxes paid by users of "royal
possessions," such as wood.[17]

The question of tithes is as perplexing to the historian as
it apparently was to the Muslims. In the twelfth century it was
thought that Muslims should be liable to tithes only on Christian
property which they worked or inherited.[18] But the Fueros of
Aragon tried to make Muslims subject to tithes generally, regardless
of Christian ownership:

> All Jews and Muslims are liable to pay tithes and first-
> fruits directly for whatever real property they have..., and
> not merely for that which belonged to Christians at some
> point which can be remembered.[19]

During the late 1350's the Bishop of Tortosa made it his special
mission to see that Muslims began paying tithes, at least in lands
under his control.

> Although it is stated in canon law that Jews and Saracens
> must pay tithes and first-fruits on lands which they cultivate,
> as well as for their animals, nevertheless...they scheme to
> avert these tithes and first-fruits with evil designs. We

---

16. See RP 1708:18ss, and other RP registers.

17. E.g., a Muslim of Lérida paid one morabetí annually for wood
for his oven. The wood tax was commonly called the çofra. (RP 994:40).

18. See Macho y Ortega, "Condición," pp.205-6.

19. "Todos los iudíos e los moros son tenudos de dar décimas e
primicias entrega ment [sic] de quantas heredades an o oujeron lures
auolorios, si non sola ment d'aquellas que non foron de cristianos
an algún tiempo que omne se pueda acordar" I.5 (Tilander, p.11).

therefore...with the advice and consent of our aforementioned
chapter decree and ordain that if any Saracen shall decline
or refuse to pay tithe or first-fruits on the said property,
unless he show why he should be exempt from this sort of duty,
at our command (or that of our _officialis_) the laymen of the
parish in which such a Saracen lives or has residence (or in
which are located or pastured the land and animals for which
he is liable to tithe and first-fruits), should be warned that
within three days, which we allot the parish and its members
as canonical warning, they must cease to have commerce with
the said Saracen or Jew, and from then until he shall have
made adequate satisfaction they may not join with him in con-
versation, greeting, eating, drinking, buying, selling or any
other commerce. And if anyone refuses to desist, or does the
reverse, he should know that he will himself be excommunicate.[20]

Outside of the bishop's chapter considerable doubt persisted

about the liability of Muslims to tithes, and the king's majordomo,

who held Muslim-inhabited lands under the jurisdiction of the bishop,

resisted his edict and was threatened with excommunication. The

king's defense of his servant to the bishop strongly implies that

the Crown considered Muslims necessarily exempt from tithes:

> ...he [the majordomo] refused to yield tithes and first-
> fruits of the Vall d'Uxó, which you assert belong to you or
> to someone in your church, although it is certain that in the
> said valley, where only Muslims live, they do not pay tithes

---

20. "Licet in canonibus caveatur quod judaei, et sarraceni de
terris, quas colunt, et de animalibus suis decimas, et primitias
solvere teneantur..., ipsas tamen decimas et primitias perversis
machinationibus subtrahere moliuntur; nos igitur...de consilio
et assensu praedicti nostri capituli statuimus, et ordinamus
quod si aliquis sarracenorum contradixerit seu recusaverit solvere
decimam, et primitiam de praedictis, quod nisi ostenderit quare a
solutione hujusmodi sit immunis, ad mandatum nostrum, vel officialis nostri, layci illius parrochiae, in qua dictus sarracenus habi-
taverit, seu domiciliatus fuerit, et in qua terra et animalia de
quibus solvendae sunt decimae et primitiae sita fuerit, et ipsa
animalia pascentur, moneantur quod infra tres dies quos ei, et·
cuilibet ipsorum pro canonica admonitione assignamus, abstineant
participare cum dicto sarraceno vel judaeo, et ex tunc donec satis-
fecerint competenter, non participent cum eodem, in loquendo, salu-
tando, comedendo, et bibendo, emendo et vendendo, aut aliter parti-
cipando. Et si desistere noluerit, seu contrarium fecerit, excom-

or first-fruits, nor have they ever been accustomed to do so.[21]
In reply the bishop appealed not to a general principle of Muslim
liability, but to specific letters from earlier Aragonese monarchs
concerning the inhabitants of Uxó.

On the other hand, it is quite clear that numerous small Valencian aljamas did pay tithes and first-fruits, although some of
them obtained exemptions from them during the later years of the
war.[22]

There is no doubt about the fact that departing Muslims had to
pay a "tithe" of their personal property and cash at the point of
departure from Valencia. What such "tithes" reveal about the
economic condition of the émigrés is discussed below. In Barcelona
(and presumably other northern ports, such as Tortosa), a flat
rate of 15s (the "mostalaffia") was charged instead. Both port
"tithes" and the mostalaffia appear to have been charged of foreign
visitors returning home as well as subjects of the Crown of Aragon.[23]

When a Muslim slave or captive was freed the king received a

---

municationi eo ipso se noverit subjacere" Villanueva, Viage, V, pp.
352-3.

21. Emphasis mine. "...recusavit tradere decimam et primitiam vallis de Uxone, quam vobis vel quibusdam de ecclesia vostra dicitis
pertinere, quamquam certum existat quod in dicta valle, in qua tantum sarraceni inhabitant, non solvantur decima et primitia, nec unquam solvi consueti fuerint" C 711:161 (Feb.27, 1363). Cf. C 725:
12 (Feb.17, 1366), where the dispute is still unsettled. The king
appears to have upheld the majordomo in the end.

22. See C 1204:63 (1365), C 1205:45 (1365), C 1209:44, 54, 55 (1365
For tithes in the fifteenth century (when the issue was equally uncer
tain), see Macho y Ortega, "Documentos," p.151; "Condición," pp.231,
284-5.

23. On port tithes, see C 1072:161 (Aug.30, 1360), and RP 1708:9,

<u>dobla</u> (=15s 10d),[24] but it is not clear whether this was paid by
the lord or the slave. Since Muslims generally raised the sums
of money necessary for redemption themselves, it is not unlikely
that they could have paid a tax at the time of the "removing of
the irons," and it would therefore be properly considered a tax
on Muslims.

For the most part the registers of the Royal Patrimony do not
distinguish the source (i.e., Muslim, Jewish, Christian) of
incomes recorded as received,[25] and it seems likely that tax collectors were not usually appointed to specific religious groupings.
In the South, some accounts were kept in Arabic, and the collectors
of such accounts must therefore either have been Muslims themselves
or employed them.[26] The account books were held by the aljamas
themselves, though an aljama might be required to surrender them to
a new appointee in need of them for arranging accounts.[27] The money
collected by the aljama from taxes administered internally (such as
those on meat, etc.) was kept by the <u>amin</u> and likewise surrendered
upon request.[28] General taxes were collected by appointees delegated
in a variety of ways: election, royal choice, appointment by the city,

RP 1719:13, and <u>passim</u>. On the <u>mostalaffia</u>, see C 904:139 (Aug.13,
1360), RP 994:43 (1363), and <u>passim</u>.

24. RP 1711:11 (1366): "...per dret al senyor rey pertanyent de un
moro catiu qui's reeme e's atalla de aquell, e es acostumat que com se
atallen ells leuen los ferres donen una dobla al senyor Rey."

25. E.g., RP 338:18 (1356).

26. C 1569:75 (Dec.12, 1360).

27. RP 687:90 (May 4, 1359).

28. C 1208:78 (Sept.6, 1365).

etc. In some cases, such as the collection of the morabetí, they
received a percentage of the take,[29] but for the most part they
were paid a fixed sum by the aljama itself.[30] Tax collectors
were generally empowered to use any means at all--foreclosure,
sale of property, incarceration--to collect taxes under their
charge,[31] but the Crown kept a close watch on their activities
and frequently called them to answer for malfeasance in office.[32]

For general taxes on Mudéjares the governor, justice, local
justice, and local bailiff had ultimate authority after the king.[33]
The Curia could not intervene, and if it tried, the king disregarded
its dispositions.[34] The local bailiff was customarily responsible
for the lezda, subsidium, tributum or peyta, and cena.[35] In most
cases the collection of such taxes was farmed out, very often to
Muslims (even for collecting from non-Muslim residents),[36] and in
some cases private individuals were granted even the authority of
the bailiff over local taxes.[37] Taxation of the aljama as a whole,

---

29. RP 2402:23 (1355).

30. C 699:169 (Feb.15, 1360).

31. C 1380:78 (Nov.21, 1356).

32. RP 687:47 (July 7, 1357).

33. C 683:175 (Mar.25, 1356), C 1151:79 (Feb.19, 1357).

34. C 719:88 (Jan.31, 1365).

35. C 970:197 (Oct.31, 1364).

36. Macho y Ortega, "Condición," p.161; Piles Ros, "Situación,"
p.79.

37. C 983:59 (Jan.4, 1359); cf. C 968:5 (Apr.2, 1359).

however, was licit only in the presence of the bailiff, <u>adelantati</u>,
and the <u>amin</u>.[38] In Daroca the Muslims were by special exemption
immune to taxation from anyone but the bailiff, although the king
sometimes violated this;[39] only the <u>merinus</u> of Zaragoza could
collect or levy municipal taxes in that city after 1337.[40]

All Muslims were liable to royal taxes, even those living under
the jurisdiction of nobles or the Church. No matter who collected
them, or how much was skimmed off by prelates, cities, or nobles,
the proceeds from Mudéjar taxation ultimately belonged to the king.
Taxes such as those on livestock, or tolls, or special demands for
marriages or the upkeep of castles could be charged by nobles or
clerics and kept, but all the major taxes--<u>cena</u>, <u>peyta</u>, <u>subsidy</u>, etc.--
flowed back to the king, or from 1359 on, to the queen. Peter had
been obliged by his marriage contract to provide Eleanor with a certain minimum source of revenues, and during the war much of this income dried up, due either to the general economic decline occasioned
by the plague and the war, or to occupation by Castilian troops.
Peter therefore began granting her, in 1359, various aljamas which
had been under his control to supplement her dwindling incomes:

> Considering how, owing to the war with Castile, the said
> revenues and rights of your patrimony are so diminished and
> strained that they scarcely suffice for the maintenance of
> your household, since many of the more notable cities, towns,

---

38. C 684:233 (July 8, 1356).
39. C 699:220 (Apr.23, 1360).
40. C 862:130 (Jan.21, 1337).

and castles of your patrimony, both in Valencia and in Aragon,
have been captured and occupied and are even yet held by the
King of Castile, it is therefore fitting, according to the terms
of our [marriage] contract, and also proper for the pre-eminence
of your position, as well as for our mutual honor...that we give
you, the said queen, the subsidies, tribute, and cenas of the
Jewish and Saracen aljamas of the city in question[41], so that
you, the said queen, may from these aljamas request, demand, possess and impose subsidies and other exactions, just as you were
accustomed to do with other aljamas of places in your patrimony.[42]

In this way the queen came into the rights over the aljamas--Sara-
cen and Jewish--of Huesca, Calatayud, Murviedro (Sagunto), Alcira,
Morella (--1359), Montblanc, Tarrega, Villagrassa (--1360), Tarazona (1361), Tortosa, Torella, Borja, Burriana (--1364), Eslida (1365),
and the Jewish aljamas of Barcelona and Valencia.[43] In each of
these aljamas her jurisdiction became supreme, the king ceding all
rights, and she exercised direct control, though generally retaining
the royal officials previously employed by her husband. Eleanor
also received a share of the general taxes levied on the Mudéjares

---

41. Tortosa.

42. "...considerantes etiam qualiter propter guerram Castelle
dicti redditus atque jura camere vestre...in tantum sunt diminuti
et extenuati quod vix possunt sufficere provisioni domus vestre, cum
plura ex notabilioribus civitatibus, castris, et locis dicte camere
vestre, tam in Aragonie quam in Valentie regnis constitutis, fuerunt
capta et occupata et adhuc detinentur per regem Castelle. Ob quod
expedit sicuti ex conventione tenemur, et aliter prout sublimitati
status vestre ac honori nostro congruit...[ut demus] etiam vobis,
regine prefate, subsidia, tributa, et cenas aljamarum judeorum et
sarracenorum eiusdem civitatis, ita quod vos, dicta regina, possitis
a dictis aljamis petere, exigere, habere et imponere subsidia et
alias exactiones prout facere consuevistis aliis aljamis locorum
camere vestre..." C 1536:62 (July 31, 1364).

43. C 1534:137 (Oct.5, 1359); C 1536:45 (Feb.20, 1360), C 1536:62,
ut supra, C 1537:48 (June 15, 1361). Many of these grants were so
sudden that the king had to enjoin the former owners specifically
from collecting taxes which they previously handled under royal
privilege, e.g., in Tarazona (last named entry, above). Note that
the Muslims of Eslida asked to be given to the queen: "...hauem sabut

of the kingdoms specifically for the war with Castile.[44]

Liability for specific taxes was decided as the outcome of a constant tension between the needs of the ruling classes and a complex and intricate structure of exemptions and remissions. Jews did not pay _fogatge_, a periodic tax assessed by household, though Mudéjares did.[45] Both Jews and Muslims were obliged by law to contribute in all general levies on the Christian population, at the same rate,[46] but an effort by the Muslims of Nabal to obtain a similar ruling for Christians to contribute with levies on Muslims was rejected by the Court.[47] There was constant confusion about overlapping jurisdictions: should rural Muslim serfs be assessed as Muslims, for instance, or as vassals of their lord? Should the Muslim population of Barbastro pay _fogatge_ with the city or with the Count of Urgel, their lord?[48] If Mudéjares could not meet tax payments, who confiscated their property--the local lord, or the person to whom the taxes were owed?[49] How were free rural Mudéjares

---

que a vosaltres plau esser de la dita Reyna" C 1205:60 (Mar.31, 1365).

44. C 1537:58 (July 28, 1363).

45. C 1506:66 (Jan.22, 1364: _Corts_ of Tortòsa).

46. C 1505:167 (July 4, 1365). The base rate was that paid by the Jews of Barcelona.

47. "...homines loci prefati non teneantur contribuere et solvere in predictis demandis vel subsidiis cum sarracenis aljame jamdicte, ...[quinimo] sub solo nòmine separati a sarracenis iamdictis..." C 685:33 (originally Apr.14, 1355, reconfirmed Oct.12, 1355).

48. C 1206:20 (Aug.9, 1365).

49. The local lord: C 694:127 (May 8, 1358).

to be taxed--with the nearest large city or the nearest powerful lord?

There were no easy answers to these questions. In the case of free rural Mudéjares, for instance, the king adopted first one expedient, then another. For the Muslims living in the valley of Almonacir outside Segorbe he simply created a new tax district specially for them,[51] while for those living in the hinterlands of Borja he ordered taxation with the aljama.[51] Similarly, after receiving numerous complaints from nobles that their Muslim serfs had been compelled to contribute to levies both as Muslims and as vassals, often losing their property when they were unable to meet the same demand a second time,[52] the king first established that no Jew or Muslim be constrained to contribute to a local levy if his lord was also responsible for his taxes, but reversed himself two years later, declaring that Muslims must contribute with the aljama nearest them no matter who might be their lord.[53] The vagaries of the war itself severely exacerbated the confusion: the Muslim aljama of Daroca, for example, had a royal concession that all Mudéjares in its area should contribute through it, but the

---

50. C 1205:69 (Apr.7, 1365).

51. C 701:48 (June 5, 1360).

52. E.g., C 700:230 (Apr.24, 1360), C 714:23 (Mar.22, 1363).

53. "...si en algun lugar haura christianos, iudeos e moros, que sean vasallos de otro senyor, que aquellos pagan com su senyor e en aquell braço del qual sera el dito senyor e no com los del dito lugar" C 985:105 (1363). Lords paid a fee set by the Corts or the Crown for each vassal, depending on the number of vassals and the wealth of the lord. Thus in the assessment for the recovery of Tarazona the highest assessment was that for Prince Ferdinand, who paid

noblewoman Milia Roderic obtained an exception for her vassals in the area, who were allowed to contribute through her. When Castile occupied Daroca, her vassals (who apparently capitulated) ceased to be her vassals, and became liable to taxation through the aljama once more. The king had to intervene to restore her privilege.[54]

Although the tax base—i.e., the number of taxable persons— had to be assessed fairly, there were no limitations on the <u>rates</u> of taxation, and when the king found he could not get enough money from one aljama, he simply raised the taxes of others.

> It seems that there are some aljamas which are on the border[55] and which cannot be taxed without great difficulty and danger. Whence it will be necessary, once it is clear in which of these aljamas no collection can be made, to share [the tax burden] among the other ones which can afford it, so that from the aljamas of Valencia nothing is lacking of that which has been assigned to them. And we [wish] that in this way the aljamas support each other.[56]

There was, moreover, no compulsion for the king to use the taxes

---

4s 3d for each of 800 vassals (=12,016s 3d), and the lowest was that of the Count of Luna, who paid 3d for each of 4,000 vassals (=1,166s 8d): C 1382:119 (Apr.8, 1360). For the subsequent reversal of royal policy, see C 1207:162 (Sept.26, 1365).

54. C 1205:8 (Dec.28, 1365).

55. I.e., Aragonese aljamas on the border with Castile.

56. This document was written to the collectors for the Aragonese aljamas in great haste and contains errors of grammar, as well as the omission of several key words, such as "vullam" or its equivalent in the last sentence: "...es ver que y ha algunes aljames qui son en frontera, de que sens gran dificultat e dan no's poria hauer la tatxacio, per que sera mester, apres que sia vist que de aquelles aytals aljames res no pora esser haut, que sia carregat a les altres que suportar ho poran, per tal que a las aljames de Valencia res no falga de ço que'y es estat ordenat. E nos per semblant forma '[vullam] que les unes aljames suporten les altres" C 1188:174 (Sept.10, 1363). It is questionable whether the sense of the penultimate sentence is as I have given it above, or whether the meaning is rather that the money raised from Aragonese aljamas is used for the defense of the

for the purpose they were supposedly directed toward: in 1356 he
wrote to the aljama of Zaragoza that the 2,000s they had recently
contributed toward the marriage of his daughter was to be used
instead for construction on the royal palace.[57] Redirection of
this sort of funds raised from Christians would have put the king
in a severely awkward position, certainly limiting the funds he
could expect to raise in the future. The Mudéjares accepted it
without protest.

The Mudéjares did complain, on the other hand, about persons
who lived in the morería or enjoyed the privileges of the aljama and
did not pay taxes. As in other tax problems the king vacillated
between one expedient and another. In 1355 he ruled that joculatores
(wandering minstrels) must pay taxes with the aljama of Játiva along
with all others resident at the time of taxation.[58] But in the following year he limited the aljama to enrolling only Muslims actually
members of the aljama and resident in it, excluding thereby temporary visitors as well as members who happened to be away.[59] (By
contrast, the municipal authorities of the city of Valencia could

---

Valencian ones, and that this amount must not be diminished so
the war effort will not flag. In either case the fact remains
that when some aljamas cannot meet their tax demands the rates
are raised for those which can.

57. C 1473:181 (Apr.4, 1356).

58. "Ita quod in dicto dono seu collecta per vos inde fienda solvant aut contribuant joculatores sarraceni dicte aljame et quicumque alii singulares ipsius aljame tam mares quam femine eiuscumque
condicionis existant" C 1401:86 (June 2, 1355).

59. C 898:258 (Apr.12, 1356).

tax everyone within the confines of the city: Jews, Christians, Muslims, strangers, foreigners, et al.)[60] The king reacted favorably
to a petition by Christians and Muslims (n.b.) in 1359 to force the
higher ranks of society (clerics, nobles, knights) to contribute
to war levies on their communities,[61] and in 1362 he ordered
even those holding specific royal exemptions in Zaragoza to contribute their full share toward war taxes and at least one-half their
share in ordinary ones.[62] In the following year the aljama of
Daroca brought to the king's attention the fact that numerous Muslim subjects of lords and knights resided or worked in the city and
refused to pay taxes with the aljama. The king ordered them to pay.[63]

Then, in 1365, the king reversed completely his attitude of
nearly a decade, as well as a specific ruling of less than a month
earlier, and ruled that the aljama of Játiva could not tax Muslims
living in its morería unless they actually belonged to the aljama.
He adduced five reasons for his new policy:

> First, because those Saracens who have recently moved into
> the said morería on account of the present war with Castile or
> due to an order given by the captain, justice, and councilmen
> of the city maintain residences in places and towns belonging
> to wealthy men, knights, and burgers, which are in the juris-
> diction of the city of Játiva, and not in the morería.

---

60. C 692:35 (Jan.28, 1357).
61. C 700:34 (Nov.5, 1359).
62. C 1183:158 (Dec.1, 1362).
63. C 711:135 (Jan.24, 1363).

Second, because these Saracens who have recently come to the moreria pay and contribute with the other Saracens of the places and towns in which they usually reside, and are still bound and obliged [to do so].

Third, because these Saracens owe military service with the said city, and pay their share in levies for it.

Fourth, because when the said city levies troops and the number of men in the moreria is tallied, only those who are actually [members] of the moreria are counted, since other Saracens who have fled to the moreria for the reasons mentioned above are already enrolled in the places where they usually reside for tithes [n.b.] and owe military service there, as has been mentioned.

Fifth, because such Saracens pay and contribute with the city for the upkeep of the walls and for their share in other [municipal] duties, and not with the Saracens of the moreria.[64]

Feelings ran so high on this issue that it may well be one reason the king circumscribed the right of Mudéjares to change residence in the later years of the war.[65] But there was an even more vexing problem, which the monarchy brought on itself by granting franchitas, freedom from the aljama's obligations, to favored Muslim servants. These grants theoretically excused the recipient from all royal taxes on Muslims--lezda, peyta, questia, subsidium, demanda, etc.--both those imposed by the aljama and those by royal officials. The aljamas could not grant franchitas after 1336,[66] but the king continued to do so, and since most such grants were hereditary,[67] the number of Mudéjares enjoying freedom from taxa-

---

64. C 1206:151 (Oct.15, 1365). Cf. below, p.422. The edict this one reversed is C 1207:162 (Sept.26, 1365). Although these reasons are mentioned by the king, they may be merely the ones submitted to him by the city, which had protested the earlier decision.

65. E.g., C 1573:165 (Oct.4, 1365); cf. Macho y Ortega, "Documentos," pp.447-451. This problem is discussed at length in Chapter VI.

66. C 860:6 (Sept.21, 1336).

67. E.g., C 899:137 (Dec.1, 1356), which confirms the rights of living Muslims to a franchitas granted their ancestors in 1258.

tion, especially in northern cities, became considerable. During
the war years, when the aljamas were harder and harder pressed to
meet the rising demands of the king and municipal officials, the
fact that a significant number of the morería's more prosperous
citizens did not pay taxes caused intense bitterness and wrangling.
In 1356 the king ordered all franchi in Valencia to contribute with
the aljama in war demands and other special taxes (such as for the
wedding of his daughter),[68] and this seems to have been the end
of the issue in the South.

In the North, however, the problem became more exasperating
and complicated as the war wore on. Franchitas was always granted
for service to the Crown, and since Muslims were indispensable for
one of the projects dearest to Peter's heart, i.e., the reconstruction of the aljaferia in Zaragoza, that city had undoubtedly the
highest percentage of franchi among its Muslim population of any
city under the Crown. In 1356 a ruling similar to that for Valencia
instructed all of Zaragoza's franchi to contribute with the aljama
for the current war levy,[69] but was almost immediately rescinded
by another directive enjoining the aljama not to tax the franchi
after all.[70] Yet a third ruling, on the same day as the latter one,
ordered the mayor of Zaragoza to cease excusing the Muslim Jahiel
Aterrer from royal taxes on the aljama simply because he enjoyed

---

68. C 684:207 (Apr.16, 1356).
69. C 1380:95 (Dec.1, 1356).
70. C 1379:92 (Dec.21, 1356).

franchitas.[71] Two days later the right of Ali Almaligerat to
exemption from taxation on the grounds of his franchitas was
upheld by the king against all previous royal enactments.[72] Probably more to clear up this staggering confusion than to realize
monetary gain, the aljama sued in 1357 to force Mahoma Ballistarius
to pay taxes for the war even though he possessed franchitas. The
king ordered an investigation.[73]

The confusion not only persisted but grew worse. In 1357 the
king granted a new franchitas, despite the utter uncertainty of the
status of the franchi, and reconfirmed it in 1358 against the efforts of the aljama to force the recipient (Abdulaziz Aterrer, a
stonecutter in the service of the Archbishop of Zaragoza) to contribute with the aljama.[74] In February of 1361 the aljama again tried
to alter royal policy, or perhaps clarify it, by suing. This time
the suit was against the heirs of a Muslim originally given franchitas more than a century before.[75] The suit dragged on for months,
and the aljama eventually lost after attempting unsuccessfully to
prove the heirs illegitimate.[76] In the meantime, however, the king

---

71. C 687:7 (Dec.21, 1356).

72. C 1379:95 (Dec.23, 1356).

73. C 688:145 (Jan.31, 1357). Ballistarius was also called Mahoma Ayudemi, ballistarius. He was first granted franchitas for himself and his wife and children for 10 years, in 1352. In 1354 this
was extended to last his lifetime, but the edict of 1356 (above) effectively annulled this privilege. Cf. C 908:79 (Dec.20, 1362), and
below.

74. C 900:42 (Mar.7, 1358).

75. C 905:219 (Feb.16, 1361).

76. C 905:231 (July 6, 1361). The loss of the aljama may have been

did reverse himself, whether due to economic necessity or the importunings of the aljama, and declared that Zaragoza's _franchi_ must pay war taxes with the aljama, although their _franchitas_ should otherwise remain intact.[77] Further pressure from the aljama brought an even greater concession in the following year, requiring the _franchi_ to pay their full share of war levies and one-half their share of ordinary ones:

> ...each and every Saracen of the said aljama, as well as any residing within the aforesaid city, [albeit] privileged or exempt, shall pay and be held to pay and contribute henceforth in each and every _peyta_, _questia_, loan, demand or any other exaction which may be made to, imposed on, or demanded of the aljama by us or our officials on an extraordinary occasion by reason of the war we are currently waging with the king of Castile, or for any other reason; and also in half of the ordinary _peyta_ or _questia_ which is customarily charged or levied annually from the said aljama, absolutely regardless of any privileges, concessions, laws, or customs which have been conceded or granted to such Saracens by us or our predecessors or anyone else in our name....[78]

Ballistarius, however, had the last word. With no less a personage than Queen Eleanor interceding for him with the king, he obtained

---

due to the fact that the abbot of the monastery to which the heirs owed labor interceded for them.

77. C 905:172 (Mar.30, 1361); cf. C 908:79.

78. "...omnes et singuli sarraceni dicte aljame et infra civitatem predictam degentes, privilegiati seu exempti, solvant et solvere ac contribuere teneantur decetero in omnibus et singulis peytis, questiis, mutuis, demandis, et aliis quibuscumque exactionibus que per nos seu nostri occasione extraordinarie fient seu imponentur et petuntur ipsi aljame ratione guerre quam habemus cum rege Castil quecumque alia ratione necnon in medietate peyte seu questie ordinarie, que indici seu imponi est solita anno quolibet aliame predicte, quibusvis privilegiis, concessionibus, foris, aut usaticiis dictis sarracenis per nos aut predecessores nostros seu per quoscumque alios nostri nomine concessi seu indultis obsistentibus nullo modo..." C 908:79 and C 1183:158 (Dec.1, 1362).

a "clarification" of the preceding command which effectively
quashed the provision requiring him to pay one-half the ordinary
taxes incumbent on members of the aljama, but left him liable for
war levies and other "special taxes."[79] Whether this then applied
to other franchi in Zaragoza and Aragon is not clear. A minor
entry in a register of the Real Património indicates that an an-
nouncement was cried in the streets of Barcelona to the effect
that all Saracens living in the city in 1365 who wished to be
counted as franchi had to present themselves with their letters
of franchitas to the general bailiff within six days.[80] Since
the general bailiff had ultimate jurisdiction (after the king) over
Mudéjar taxation, it seems likely that such Muslims, upon proving
that they were in fact franchi, were to be excluded from taxation.
Some advantages must have remained for the franchi, at least, since
the king used the promise of franchitas during the later war years
to woo Castilian Mudéjares to his side.[81]

      There were, moreover, other ways of escaping taxation. Unchal-

---

79. C 908:79 (Dec.20, 1362): "...hoc tamen adiecto et nobis specialiter retento, quod tu, dictus Mahoma, tenearis solvere pertem te
solvere contingente in operibus murorum et vallorum, ac stipendio
equitum, et aliis missionibus et demandis quas dicta aliama et eius
singulares occasione guerre tam quam [sic] cum rege Castille et aliis inimicis habemus et habebimus solvere facere seu prestare habuerint quomodo..." Cf. executory order: C 904:84 (Dec.20, 1362).

80. RP 996:15 (1365): "E abatuts ii sol. que En Jacme ça Plana,
crida publich de Barchinona, hague per salari seu de una crida que
feu per certs lochs de la ciutat de Barchinona, que tots serrahins
franchs se haguessen a presentar al batle general ab lurs cartes
dins vi dies."

81. E.g., C 912:166 (May 27, 1366). For fifteenth-century franchitas, note the document published by Piles Ros, Estudio, pp.182-3.

lengeable immunity was regularly granted to Muslims who would
move to settle new territories, or to help repopulate the lands of
a royal favorite.[82] Such immunity, however, usually lasted only
for five or ten years, after which the immigrant would be liable to
the usual taxes. Others escaped by working on royal projects for
reduced pay, in return for which they received remissions or reductions of their personal taxes.[83] Some resorted to duplicity: numerous cases are reported of Muslims arranging with Christians to
hide their property on Christian lands or even in their homes, so
as to avoid being assessed for it. Even nobles co-operated in foil-
ing royal tax collectors in this way, and the king finally had to
enact very strict penalties against it.[84] Distorting population
figures was another popular ploy, although it was often detected and
punished.[85]

While individuals might escape taxation through one ploy or
another, the aljamas had no choice but to pay, and as time passed
they found themselves more and more in debt. Aljamas were not
allowed to impose special internal taxes to meet extraordinary tax
demands of the Crown unless they had specific royal permission.
They thus had little choice but to borrow the money. Even when they
did impose taxes, it took some time to raise the money, and it was

---

82. E.g., C 898:183 (Feb.22, 1356). Such grants were extremely
common in Valencia.

83. E.g., C 899:195 (Jan.25, 1357).

84. E.g., C 701:32 (May 14, 1360), C 705:178 (July 22, 1361).

85. E.g., C 1068:111 (May 4, 1356).

generally necessary to borrow the money initially to satisfy
the king's tax collector. Thus, although the aljama of Játiva,
the wealthiest in the kingdom, had been granted royal authority
as early as June of 1355 to levy a tax to meet an upcoming royal
demand of 6,000s, they still had to borrow money in April of
1356 when the tax was actually collected, and continued the tax for
a year thereafter to pay back the debt. The effect of this one debt
on a large and prosperous aljama is illustrative of the general
economic vulnerability of Mudéjar communities. The same year, the
king was obliged to extend the authority to tax even further, so
the aljama could get back on its feet,[86] and the same authority had
to be extended again in 1357.[87] By 1359 the aljama's condition
seemed worse than ever.

> Moved with compassion for the poverty and want to which
> you, the Muslim aljama of Játiva, are brought by virtue of the
> excessive burden of debt incurred and owed by you, on account
> of which without our favor, allowance and grace in regard to
> these and other debts you might easily come to utter ruin, we
> therefore, favorably responding to your entreaties to us, con-
> cede to you by authority of this document that for four years
> from the present date, in order to satisfy your debts more read-
> ily, you may impose and ordain all those taxes which the Chris-
> tian community of the same city has imposed and levied with
> our permission, or similar ones, in the same way, manner, and
> form. And you may sell or rent these taxes, if you wish, to
> anyone you can, and cause them to be exacted and levied during
> the time designated above, and you may use the money accruing
> therefrom or apply it to the satisfaction and payment of your
> debts.[88]

---

86. C 1401:86 (June 2, 1355), C 898:257 (Apr.19, 1356).

87. C 901:128 (Aug.5, 1357).

88. C 903:175 (Nov.27, 1359), in Appendix.

Such money was generally borrowed from Jews. A royal edict
provided that Christians could not be held accountable for any
debt owed to a Jew after six years had elapsed, but a ruling of 1357
specifically allowed Jews to collect from Muslims at any time after
the debt was incurred.[89] There was, moreover, no statute of limitations: unless relieved by the king, an aljama could be held responsible indefinitely for any debts incurred at any point in its history, even if the original signers of the loan were long since
dead.[90] Furthermore, the ability of officials to force aljamas to
take out loans gave rise to great abuses, and contributed considerably to the ruin of aljama finances. This practice was, however,
curtailed at some point between July of 1362, when the king specifically empowered Peter Boyl to raise money from the aljamas of Valencia in this way, and November of the same year, when the king sternly
rebuked Raymond de Vilanova for forcing loans on aljamas in violation
of "the chapters we have directed to you regarding such loans, according to which you may not [extract money] from aljamas of Jews or
Moors, but only wealthy individuals...."[91]

The burden of debt on the aljamas was already staggering by the
opening of the 1360's. As of May, 1361, the aljamas of Elche and

---

89. C 901:205 (Nov.15, 1357).

90. E.g., C 1206:96 (Sept.15, 1365); for an example of royal relief,
see C 1547:18 (Oct.27, 1358).

91. "...los capitols que nos vos hauem liurats per fer los dits
aempraments, segons los quals no deuets aliames de juheus ne de moros,
sino singulars que sien richs..." C 1183:104 (Nov.14, 1362). The
letter to Boyl is C 1183:27 (July 22, 1362). Some word has been
omitted in the passage above after "deuets," undoubtedly due to the
carelessness of the scribe. Many war documents were written hastily
and contain errors.

Crevillente jointly owed about 32,000s to various creditors, who insisted on foreclosure to get back their money.[92] In lieu of this, the queen directed that, if the figures were accurate, letters of debt should be drawn up and the debts paid back in installments at the rate of three per year for the largest creditors and one per year for smaller amounts.[93] Even so, the two aljamas were still hopelessly in debt five years later, and the Crown finally simply cancelled all the debts owed members of the royal family, leaving the aljamas to work out arrangements with any other individuals to whom they owed substantial sums.[94]

In Aragon-Catalonia, though the finances of the aljamas were equally desperate, the causes were different. Loans from Jews were rare, and in some places (e.g., Tarazona) forbidden.[95] Both Jews and Muslims, in fact, appear to have borrowed heavily from Christians to meet their tax loads.[96] More humane laws in Aragon protected all citizens, and Muslims and Jews in particular,

---

92. C 1569:91 (May 20, 1361) and C 1569:97 (June 15, 1361). Of this, 26,433s 6d was owed to Prince Ferdinand (8,000s by forty individuals, the rest by the aljama). G. Bosch was owed 5,160s (see C 1569:92, in Appendix).

93. C 1569:117 (Sept.10, 1361), and ibid. (Sept.16, 1361).

94. In the meantime the small amount the aljama had been able to pay the prince was misappropriated by his procurator: C 1572:15 (Apr.18, 1363). On the final arrangements: C 1572:63 (Oct.15, 1366).

95. C 1566:115 (Mar.4, 1357). This edict was obviously intended to protect Muslims.

96. E.g., a debt owed the king's chaplain by the Muslims of Lérida: C 983:5 (Dec.3, 1358), or that owed jointly by Muslims and Jews of las Torres de Galinda to a Christian (in the amount of 4,200s): C 691:109 (Sept.22, 1357).

from being seized or imprisoned for debts,[97] and the monarchy made
sure they were actually enforced. Nobles forced aljamas to contract
debts, sometimes for their own personal expenses, but the king was
much more apt to hear about such abuses in the North, and in at
least one case he forced the noble in question to repay the debt
himself.[98]

When the queen took over the major Aragonese aljamas, moreover,
she regulated their finances minutely, and prohibited the taking of
loans which were not in the best interests of the aljamas:

> We forbid you...or any members of the aljama...to attempt
> or allow the borrowing of money or the taking of a loan at
> interest or otherwise, or to sell rights to loans or tax-returns,
> or to receive any advance--even if the local bailiff or his
> lieutenant should approve--on any amount of money from any
> person. Rather, all those sums which it is incumbent on the
> aljama to raise you shall obtain and collect by means of levy-
> ing among yourselves a tax ("peyta"); or arranging payments
> and contributions among yourselves, as has been [previously]
> ordained in similar matters.[99]

---

97. E.g., Fueros of Aragon, II.75; the law of 1228, "De non tra-
dendis," in Villanueva, Viage, XVI, p.192; the laws of Valls (1299-
1325), in Carreras y Candi, "Ordinacions," XII, especially p.286.

98. Peter of Luna forced the aljama of Pincesch to borrow large
amounts of money, of which the king noted, "quantitates in dictis
obligationibus contente fuerunt converse in necessitatibus eiusdem
nobilis et non sarracenorum predictorum" C 703:124 (Sept.23, 1360).
The case came to light when an exchange was to be effected involving Pincesch and another noble's aljama. The other noble, the Lady
Violante d'Urrea, refused to accept Pincesch in return for Sariñena
when she learned of the debts of the former. What makes the incident particularly distasteful is that the Count of Luna·apparently
allowed the Muslims to be turned over to their creditors for his
debt, until the king ordered an end to the practice: C 699:204
(Apr.2, 1360).

99. "Inhibemus ne...vos seu aliqui singulares dicte aljame...
audeat vel permittat manulevare seu mutuo accipere, sub usuriis aut
aliter, vel violaria aut censualia vendere, seu baratam aliquam
recipere, etiam si bajuli dicte civitatis vel eius locumtenentis
consensus interveniat, a quacumque persona quasvis peccunie quan-

Indeed, the queen's zeal seems to have affected even the king, who began to defend the aljamas against the unscrupulous interference of his own officials. He harshly rebuked the Justice of Aragon in a letter of 1365 for having presumed to arrange some financial matters for a Jewish aljama:

> ...for well you know that you have no right to intervene in any matters regarding the Jews and Moors, who are our treasure and subject to our will. Wherefore we order and command you expressly to revoke at once the said agreement, and henceforth never to undertake to make such contracts with these or any other Jews or Moors....[100]

Despite more enlightened rule in the North, the Aragonese aljamas' financial state became more and more hopeless throughout the fourteenth century, and by the early fifteenth another queen had to point out to the creditors of her hard-pressed aljama in Zaragoza that "all of the goods of the aljama are not sufficient to pay its debts."[101]

The disastrous finances of the aljamas, of course, were not due wholly to taxation. In addition to royal demands, the aljama

---

titates, quinimo quantitates omnes et singulas dictam aljamam solvere contingentes per modum ordinationis peyte inter vos ordinare vel ordinande peytare et contribuere quilibet vestrum habeatis et teneamini prout in similibus est fieri ordinatum." C 1570:87 (Mar.6, 1361).

100. "Car ya sabedes que de judios y moros, qui son nostro tresoro, y estan a nuestro voler, en res no us deuedes entremeter. Por que nos dezimos y mandamos espressament que la dita firma revoquedes de feyto, e daqui adelant ellos ni otros judios ni moros por tal razon a firmar de dreyto no recibades..." C 1210:83 (Apr.24, 1365).

101. "...todos los bienes de la aljama no son capaces de pagar las deudas..." C 2422:60 (1413); cf. C 2423:273 (1414), where the queen warns the aljama's creditors that if the aljama perishes utterly, it will be their fault ("a culpa de vosotros"). Both documents are published by Macho y Ortega, "Documentos," pp.158-9.

was responsible for the salaries of various officials, such as
the qadi. Even small aljamas often paid qadis salaries between
2,000s and 4,000s,[102] and had to pay them pensions when they
retired (or even if they were removed for incompetence).[103] The
aljama could, moreover, be dunned for the outstanding fines of its
members: in 1355 the aljama of Játiva bought amnesty from all fines
owed by its members to the king or his officials for 3,000s, which
implies an actual aggregate of outstanding fines at least in excess
of that figure.[104] The king voluntarily extended this amnesty twice
subsequently, owing to "the great poverty of the aljama."[105] Aljamas often had special expenses parallel to the obligation of the
Jews to keep the royal menagerie: the aljama of Huesca was required
to support a law student named Dominic Egidius at the Studium Generale.[106]

Rents were a considerable drain on Mudéjar finances, both individually and collectively. Many landless Muslims rented royal or
ecclesiastical lands to farm "so they could pay royal taxes."[107]
This rendered them liable to financial exploitation of various kinds,

---

102. E.g., C 971:124 (May 25, 1366): salary of 2,000s in peacetime
and 4,000s in war for the alcayde (Christian) of Costant to be paid
by the Jews and Muslims of the area.

103. E.g., C 966:89 (Apr.16, 1356): pension of 200s annually for
qadi removed for malfeasance in office.

104. C 901:135 (Aug.9, 1357).

105. Ibid., C 910:120 (Sept.16, 1366).

106. C 697:17 (May 21, 1359).

107. C 686:218 (May 10, 1356).

which are discussed elsewhere. Royal remissions did not apply

to rents.[108] Many aljamas rented lands collectively,[109] possibly

for greater security, and all paid "rents" to the Crown for various

positions or buildings which were licensed, such as baths, meat

markets, glove-making, barbering, etc.[110]

Aside from periodic cash gifts from sympathetic nobles,[111]

aljamas had little alternative to borrowing except to sell off

property or taxes. The sale of property was, as will be discussed

elsewhere in this study, complicated. Each town or morería had its

own intricate laws and customs about the legitimate sale of Muslim

properties and the collection of taxes thereto appertaining. Some-

times the Crown would intervene to override local statutes when the

sale of property was crucial to the aljama's well-being, and the

ueen, conscientious in the extreme about the state of her aljamas,

frequently remitted her share of the revenues from such sales so

as to facilitate economic recovery for the morería.[112] Still, the

hard-pressed Mudéjares reached further and further to meet their

demands: the officials of the aljama of Borja cold-bloodedly sold

off the patrimony of two orphans to meet the aljama's obligations,[113]

and the Muslims of St Stephen Litarie sold to a domestic of the

108. C 1210:130 (July 3, 1365).

109. C 1210:146 (July 6, 1365), RP 1711:passim.

110. E.g., RP 1711:passim; cf. Chapter II, p.69, and note 24.

111. E.g., for construction of houses: C 1567:124 (Sept.10, 1359).

112. E.g., C 1571:159 (Sept.1, 1363).

113. C 704:68 (Aug.19, 1360).

king one-fourth of the possessions and houses they actually occupied.[114]
More commonly, aljamas sold off the rights to their revenues to the
highest bidder, or farmed their taxes;[115] in a curious twist on
this ancient practice, the Muslims of Seta "rented" from the queen
their own revenues: i.e., they paid her a flat sum in return for
keeping what was actually collected.[116]

The Crown's voracity was not untempered, however, and this
gloomy account of the sad state of aljama finances leaves out--
as do most other studies, such as that of Küchler--a crucial element
of Aragonese tax structure: the remission. Both the king and the
queen were well aware of the disastrous fiscal state of Mudéjar
communities in the mid-fourteenth century, and--whether for humanitarian reasons or self-interest or both--tried hard to alleviate
their plight, while still maintaining a level of taxation sufficient
for their own needs. It would be grossly unfair to characterize
the Aragonese Crown as rapaciously milking the Muslims for all it
could get, or as keeping them as economic chattel. There is
ample reason to believe that individually many Muslims flourished
and grew wealthy even while the aljamas sank deeper into debt. It
is extremely likely, moreover, that Muslims paid a smaller percentage of the total tax burden than their numbers alone would have

---

114. C 702:163 (May 4, 1361).

115. E.g., C 1569:92 (May 20, 1361), in Appendix. On the bidding,
see C 2338:30 (1402), in Macho y Ortega, "Documentos," p.154.

116. C 1573:148 (June 28, 1365); the transaction is described as
a "rental" in the document. Part of the fee had to be remitted due
to the aljama's poverty.

dictated.

In 1315 royal revenues from taxation amounted to 150,000s.[117]
Allowing for inflation and increased needs of the monarchy, a
conservative estimate of the total revenues from taxes in the decade 1355-1365 would be about 200,000s annually.[118] The figures
in tables A and B appended to this chapter suggest an annual
Muslim tax burden of from 7,000s to 54,500s per year, with an
annual mean of 19,552s   This would mean that at the absolute
most the Muslims paid slightly more than 25% of the total taxes of
the kingdom, and that more likely their contribution ranged from
3% to 10% of the total. Since 25% represents an extremely modest
estimate of the proportion of Muslim population to the general
one,[119] and since no stre⁺∽h of the imagination could put this
percentage as low as 3%, one is forced to conclude that in all
likelihood the Mudéjares under the Crown of Aragon paid far less
in taxes than their demographic proportions would have warranted.[120]

Part of the reason for this was the extremely common practice

---

117. Küchler, "Besteuerung," p.234.

118. The cenas alone increased by 300% between 1327 and 1357: see
table F at the end of this chapter. Note also that in 1363 the Muslims of the kingdoms were taxed 400,000s for a single war levy.

119. A widely accepted figure (of Vicens Vives) for Aragon alone
is 35%. Cf. introductory remarks, pp.7ss .

120. Batlle Prats and Millás Vallicrosa estimated that the combined Jewish and Muslim populations of the kingdoms under the Crown
of Aragon paid only 22% of the total royal income from taxes ("Noticias sobre la aljama de Gerona a fines del siglo xiv," Sefarad,
V [1945], p.132). Küchler estimated ("Besteuerung," p.236) that
the Jews alone paid more than half this amount throughout the thirteenth and fourteenth centuries. This would put the Muslim contribution at well below 11%.

of granting whole or partial relief from the taxes levied on Muslims
and Muslim communities. The terminology varies in the documents;
in this study "remission" will apply to a complete amnesty from any
particular tax, i.e., no part of it to be demanded at any time;
"partial remission" means that part of the demand is completely
excused, the rest to be demanded now or later; "elongamentum"
refers to the practice of proroguing the debt for a specified
time, after which it would be due as originally levied. Since
elongamenta were--theoretically, at least--eventually collected,
they have been excluded from the following computations. It is
important to recognize, nonetheless, the role they played in re-
lieving the financial distress of the aljamas: very often the immediate exaction of a tax would have resulted in the ruin of an aljama or the imprisonment or loss of property of its members. Under
such circumstances the Crown, by granting an elongamentum, was
able both to show its creditors some evidence of ability to pay
in the future and to spare the aljama utter ruin. In view of the
severe financial embarrassment of the Crown itself during the latter
half of the fourteenth century, the frequency of such grants is
certainly testimony to the restraint, if not the benevolence, of
royal fiscal policy.

Even more impressive were the remissions, which represented
a complete loss of revenue for a royal house struggling to keep.
ahead of its creditors. It is impossible to compute the exact sums
of remissions to the aljamas, even for one year, because they are

most often phrased as "all of the peyta," or "one-third of the
subsidium," and since the peyta or subsidium for that year would
then not be recorded (even if only a percentage of it were remitted),
there is no way to be certain exactly how much revenue the Crown
lost.   It is possible, however, to provide an estimate of the
proportion of Muslim revenues remitted, by figuring what percentage of communities paying regular taxes received remissions of
those taxes.

Twenty-two aljamas paid regular taxes during the period 1355-
1366.[121] Of these, an annual average of 44% received whole or partial remissions of their regular tax payments during the years in
question. This means that the Crown was receiving, throughout the
difficult war years, only slightly more than half the revenues it
customarily received from the Muslim communities under its authority. During three of these years--1361, 1362, 1363--the Crown received income from considerably less than half of those communities
usually liable: 37%, 33%, and 36%, respectively. In the vast majority of cases--83%--the remissions were total, and in all but one
they were for one-half the tax or more. These figures, moreover,
refer only to regular taxes, i.e., cena, peyta, subsidium, etc.
They do not include extraordinary war demands, of which the number

---

121. Alcira, Alagón, Ariza, Aspe, Barbastro, Borja, Brea, Calatayud, Daroca, Elche, Huesca, Játiva, Lérida, Magallón, Nabal, Orihuela, Sta Cruce, Tarazona, Teruel, Tortosa, Valencia, and Zaragoza.
The information in this paragraph and those following is all derived
from the tax tables at the end of this chapter, q.v.

of remissions is undeterminable, since the data are not adequate,
nor miscellaneous taxes, of which at least 10% were remitted annually, although figures are inadequate for these as well.

These statistics do not begin to show the gap between the
theoretical tax liability of the Mudéjares and their actual payments.
The figures given above, for instance, are based on recorded remissions, i.e., cases where a document survives excusing a particular
aljama from a particular tax. But a great many aljamas for which
no such record of remission survives did not pay taxes during one
or more years in the eleven-year period under discussion. If, for
instance, each of the twenty-two aljamas which paid regular taxes
at some point during the years 1355-1366 had paid regular taxes
every ye r, the revenues from such taxes would have been 59,418s
annually.[122] This figure exceeds only slightly the estimate of
total regular income from all Muslim communities for 1294 as given
in table E. Yet the total of all incomes, including irregular
demands, during the period 1355-66 only equals this figure in one
year, 1363, and this is due to an enormous war levy of over 400,000s.
Excluding this peak year, only three years even approach the theoretical tax burden (1356, 1357, 1365). The actual mean annual intake
from all Muslim taxes for the years 1355-66, exclusive of the 400,000s,
is only 33% of the theoretical annual intake from regular taxes alone.

If an estimate is made of the theoretical tax liability of all

122. N.B. that this figure excludes all irregular taxes, such as
war levies.

the aljamas which at any time paid taxes, i.e., if, as was officially the case, the cena, peyta, subsidium, and censualia were collected from every aljama under the Crown which had no specific exemption, the annual total would have been approximately 105,000s. The
mean annual income from all Muslim sources during 1355-66 (again ex-
lusive of the 400,000s in 1363) is only 19% of this figure.

What does this mean? First, it supports the suggestion made
earlier that fourteenth-century Muslim tax contributions to the
Crown in reality fell far below what should be expected from official theory. Second, it shows that no matter how difficult the theoretical burden on any aljama may have been, there was great latitude
for avoidance of payment, and that in fact only an average of about
60% of the aljamas paid all their annual taxes, with the figure
dropping in some years to as little as 33%. Third, it shows that
the Crown was collecting in any given year less than a third of the
total sum it was supposedly entitled to demand from the aljamas.

If the aljamas were actually taxed at less than one-third of
their official liability, how is it that royal taxation brought
them to such financial straits? Were the official tax rates so
far   out of line with economic reality that demanding only a third
of them drove the Mudéjar communities into debt? One clue may lie
in the tremendous increase in some tax rates between 1330 and 1360.
Information is scanty, but judging from the figures in table F, it
would seem that the average rate for the cena in 1356 was about 300%
of the rate in 1327. If this increase was uniform for all taxes,

Muslims paying only one-third of their official liability in 1360

would simply be paying the same taxes they had paid in 1330, and

the Crown would have accomplished nothing but making itself appear

generous in remitting an increase which could not be collected.

This explanation does not seem altogether convincing. There

is no evidence that tax rates increased uniformly; the cena under-

went more change than other taxes because its very nature demanded

revision by the mid-fourteenth century, when it was no longer prac-

tical to view it as a feudal duty of hospitality, and it became

merely an annual tax. Most likely at this juncture its amount

was appraised at figures which were more in line with the inflated

monetary values of the day than were the former levels.

Moreover, even if the tax rates had been increased substantially,

this would not necessarily represent exorbitant royal taxation.

Despite royal efforts to control them, prices had risen astronomically

following the plague years, and salaries were at least two to three

hundred percent higher than before the pestilence struck. A tax in-

crease across the board of several hundred percent would probably

have barely offset the Crown's expenses under inflated prices and

salaries.

On the other hand, general taxes were almost certainly higher--or

at least collected in greater amounts--in the late thirteenth and

early fourteenth centuries than during the period of this study, as

table E demonstrates. Moreover, during the decade in question, reg-

ular taxation of Mudéjares was on the same terms and at the same

rate as that for Christians, and roughly the same can be said of
extraordinary demands. There was no major tax imposed on the Muslim
communities which was not also levied on the Christian ones at roughly the same rate. Yet there is no hue and cry about the Christian
municipalities being "ruined and utterly devastated" by royal taxation and debts. There are complaints, to be sure, and hardship,
but no gloomy predictions of ultimate disaster, no desperate measures
taken to ward off depopulation due to emigration of debt-ridden citizens, no wholesale remissions of tax burdens.

What then? There were probably more excesses in the taxation
of Mudéjares, certainly more forced loans and abuses of that nature,
but these alone could scarcely account for so dramatic a phenomenon.
Were the Mudéjares so much poorer than the Christians that they
could not pay equal taxes? Verlinden concluded that in most Mudéjar
communities there were no well-to-do individuals ("gens aisés").[123]
Although the nature of documentation for the period provides little
direct evidence to support or contradict this assertion, a good many
indirect indices of Mudéjar wealth can be extracted from Chancery
materials. Such data point not only to the existence of a wealthy
class of Mudéjares, but to the general prosperity of the Muslim
community in toto. Individual Mudéjares regularly took out loans
from Christians and Jews in amounts of 1,000s or 2,000s,[124] and
rented buildings (such as silos) from Christians at rates like

---

123. L'Esclavage, I, p.534.
124. C 687:6 (1356), C 700:4 (1360), C 708:168 (1362), C 1205:69
(1365).

3,000s annually.[125] Fines paid by them are often surprisingly high,
and never very different from those charged of or paid by Christians.[126]
Numerous Mudéjares were prosperous enough to travel to the Holy Land
and back with their families and servants.[127] Many Muslims owned
considerable property, real and moveable: flocks of 150 to 250
sheep (worth about 875s),[128] real property valued at from 500s to
2,500s.[129] A Saracen from Zaragoza was reimbursed for goods seized
from him on a business trip in the amount of 3,000s;[130] the emigrating Muslims captured by Arnald de Caneto were awarded 30,000s as restitution for their lost personal property;[131] Mahomat del Rey, at
the time of his murder, was carrying 1,200s cash;[132] a Muslim
friend of the king owned a horse worth 750s.[133] Maymo Xehep left
an estate in excess of 36,000s,[134] and Maymo Fuster's estate paid
as one of numerous fines 23,000s for tax fraud.[135] Between them
Maymo and Neixma Fuster left behind when they emigrated personal
valuables auctioned for 4,000s--and these were the ones they had

---

125. E.g., C 1571:93 (Feb.11, 1363 [two entries]).
126. E.g., 500s, 900s, 1,000s: RP 1704:23 (1357); RP 1709:19 (1364).
127. C 901:113 (1357), C 905:220 (1361), C 980:70 (1363).
128. C 720:39 and 88 (1365).
129. C 1570:66 (1360), C 723:158 (1365).
130. C 1205:68 (Apr.2, 1365).
131. C 906:133 (Dec.15, 1361): but they only got 4,000s.
132. C 688:180, in Appendix.
133. C 1211:66 (May 27, 1365).
134. RP 1708:18 (1362).
135. RP 1706:19ss (1360). Abraham Abenxoa left an estate of 2,000s:
RP 1719:25 (1363).

abandoned.[136]

Middle-class Saracens commonly owned real estate ranging from
50s in value to 300s,[137] and an ordinary Muslim grain store (for
personal use) was worth about 190s.[138] Emigrants taxed at the
port of Valencia--mostly freed captives and therefore hardly well-
to-do--wore clothing worth on the average 30s, and most had at
least 25s in cash on them.[139] Aside from a few notable exceptions,[140]
moreover, Mudéjares were paid as well as Christians for their services,[141] and were in great demand as skilled laborers. Although
skilled craftsmen were prohibited by a law of 1349 from asking more
than 70s annually as salaries,[142] Mudéjar carpenters in Zaragoza
customarily received more than 18s per day in 1357,[143] and a master
was paid well in excess of 200s annually.[144] A Muslim juglar on the
king's ships was paid wages at the rate of 900s annually, plus 80s
for clothing and 1s per day as food ration.[145] On the same ship a

---

136. RP 1708:18ss (1362). The taxes alone on the goods of Çaat
Fuster's personal goods were 289s 2d (ibid.).

137. C 1573:127, 128 (1365); C 904:73 (1360).

138. C 1569:75 (Dec.12, 1360).

139. RP 1708:9 (1362); RP 1719:13 (1363).

140. E.g., C 700:144 (1360), where Muslims of Calatayud are forced
to work free for the war effort; cf. C 1569:29 (1359), and in Chapter
IV, pp.182ss.

141. C 1069:73 (1357).

142. Tilander, "Fueros aragoneses," p.24.

143. C 899:195 (Jan.25, 1357).

144. C 1170:7 (Jan.21, 1360).

145. C 1402:153-4 (1359).

Mudéjar cableman earned 360s per year, plus 20s to eat on for

four months.[146] (By contrast, a minor Muslim public official in

Játiva, the fiscalis, made only 100s annually.)[147] In the army

Muslims made considerably more, and there is every indication that

(with the exceptions noted above) they were paid at exactly the

same rate as the Christians.[148]

If, then, the Muslim communities included wealthy men and a

prosperous middle class, what is the reason for their relatively

small tax contribution, and the extreme generosity of the Crown

in excusing them from their tax duties? The answers are not easy.

One reason may be the inequity of distribution of taxes, both

among communities and individuals. Although twenty-two aljamas

paid regular taxes of some sort during the period 1355-66, 75% of

the entire tax burden was met by seven of these aljamas. These were,

in order of percentages, Játiva, Valencia, Zaragoza, Borja, Elche,

Huesca, and Calatayud. Játiva alone paid 35% of all taxes received

during the eleven years of the war. (See table C.) It is easy to

imagine how, in a time of stress, the drain on the resources of

---

146. C 1402:153-4 (1359).

147. C 1209:125 (May 29, 1365).

148. According to the capitula regulating military salaries as
of 1363 (C 985:115), cavalrymen were to be paid 7s per day regardless of religion, and infantrymen with armor 5s per day, likewise
regardless of religious preference. Numerous documents (e.g., RP
2468:79 [1358]) indicate that this was the practice as well as the
theory. Fourteen Granadan knights were granted a lump sum of 1,000s
as payment in 1358: perhaps payments were irregular (RP 2468:101).
Muslim arms-makers were paid just under 2s per day in Zaragoza in
1363 (C 1075:91), which is rather low.

these seven aljamas might become virtually insupportable, and this
is precisely what is suggested by the table of remissions: the
names of the seven occur more frequently than any others.

Another part of the answer may be provided by the *franchi*: there is
reason to believe that the wealthier a Mudéjar was, the less apt
he was to be compelled to pay taxes (cf. the tax-fraud case of Maymo Fuster, above). If in the seven aljamas paying three-fourths of
Mudéjar taxes, the most prosperous members avoided taxation through
royal exemption, influence, or fraud, the tax burden would then
fall on the shoulders of those less able to pay, and while wealthy
individuals would continue to prosper, the poorer classes in the
aljamas would be gradually ruined by the weight of taxation.

On the other hand, the Crown did respond to the demands of the
aljamas in regard to the *franchi*, and inequality in taxation cannot
wholly answer the question. Nor is it likely that the kings and
queens of Aragon were simply "soft touches." When it came down to
their survival or the aljamas', they were not inclined to be too
altruistic.[149]

Two other factors seem to be primarily responsible for this
phenomenon. It is apparent that the Muslim population of Aragon-
Catalonia-Valencia was declining markedly in the latter half of
the fourteenth century. Though there are few statistics even vaguely

---

149. In October of 1359 the aljama of Elche begged the queen to
remit their annual taxes, since they were utterly destitute, but the
queen refused to do so, explaining that she was receiving no rents
from them and absolutely required the tax money to maintain herself.
She would, she said, honor their request as soon as her own finances
were in better shape: C 1569:20.

approaching reliability, the enormous number of Chancery documents
which describe the "utter ruin" and "devastation" of the aljamas,
the constant complaints by the aljamas themselves that they were
being taxed for numbers which far exceeded their real membership,
the severe measures taken to check Muslim emigration, and the lengths
to which the Crown and nobles would go to win back or attract Muslim
serfs and vassals all testify to the dwindling number of Mudéjar
subjects. The few figures extant bear out this conclusion: the
aljama of Teruel, customarily paying war taxes for 92 "persons," in
1362 contained only 42 "persons," a drop in population of more than
fifty-percent.[150] The population of the once thriving aljama of
Ariza had been depopulated by 95% in 1361, and the king painted a
gloomy picture of its condition in writing to Peter Jordan:

> ...more than twô hundred Saracens used to have residence in
> the city, and now only about ten live there; all of the proper-
> ty which once belonged to the other Saracens of the town has
> devolved upon these ten, who must sell some of this property
> to pay their debts, but cannot get a fair price for the proper-
> ty because they must find among these same ten both buyers and
> sellers....[151]

The largest aljamas suffered less: Huesca had been reduced by 1361

---

150. C 701:140 (Sept.20, 1360), and ibid. (Sept.21, 1360). "Person"
presumably refers to the head of a household: see introductory remarks
for possible ratios to the general population. These figures were
subsequently challenged by the king, but the challenge is suspect,
since he did not order a new tally, as was customary in such cases, but
rather that they be taxed according to the old number: C 1383:239
(Jan.2, 1361).

151. "...cum in dicta villa solerent commorari ducenti sarraceni,
domos foventes, et ultra, et nunc non inhabitent in eadem nisi decem
vel circa, et ad ipsos decem omnes hereditates aliorum sarracenorum
ipsius ville pervenerint, et cum eos opportet vendere ex ipsis hereditatibus pro solvendis suis debitis, non reperiantur pro ipsis hereditatibus pretia condecentia, cum ex ipsis decem habeant esse vendi-

from its former 540 persons to 410, a drop of only about 20%.[152]

Fewer statistics are available for Valencia,[153] but in view
of the extreme anxiety displayed by Christians there to prevent
Mudéjar emigration or even relocation, and considering that in
years when passage to other lands was permitted Valencian Mudéjares
emigrated from the country in numbers exceeding 200 persons annually, the situation cannot have been much better there.[154]

It is, in fact, generally accepted that the entire population
of the lands under the Crown of Aragon declined throughout the
latter half of the fourteenth century; possibly the Muslim decline
was not appreciably greater than that of the population as a whole,
but what little evidence there is suggests otherwise. In 1294 the
Muslims of Aragon paid about 90% of their theoretical tax liability.
In 1315 this had been reduced to only about 60%, and by 1360 it
was down to nearly 30%.[155] By the beginning of the fifteenth century
the Muslim aljamas were very nearly destitute, their populations
even lower than in the mid-fourteenth,[156] and by the middle of that
century the Crown abolished nearly all taxes on the major Muslim aljames because they could no longer pay even a part of them.[157]

---

tores et emptores..." C 702:91 (Jan.18, 1361).

152. C 1384:40 (Jan.3, 1362).

153. But see figures for Orihuela, Alicante, and Aspe, on p.9, above.

154. See below, pp.310ss.

155. See tables A and E.

156. Macho y Ortega, "Documentos," p.157.

157. Küchler ("Besteuerung," pp.242ss) states that the cena, peyta,
and censualia were no longer collected in Valencia after 1455 due to

The reasons for this population decline are not properly under-stood. There is not even scholarly agreement about its extent.
But in the case of the Mudéjares part of the explanation undoubtedly
lies in the regular attrition which resulted from the emigration
of dissatisfied Muslims to other countries. There is abundant evi-dence that many Mudéjares were actually leaving the lands of the
Crown throughout the fourteenth century. This gradual decrease
was acutely aggravated by the great plagues which swept Europe in
1348 and thereafter, and which affected Iberian Muslims no less
than Christians. A third factor exacerbated the situation: the
extreme disruptions of Mudéjar life and prosperity occasioned by
the war with Castile. The exact nature of the effects of the war
will be discussed elsewhere; suffice it to observe here that the
Mudéjares appear to have been affected in particularly disastrous
ways by the mid-century war, and the consequent abrupt and dramatic
decline in their economic stability and well-being must account in
very large measure for the inability or unwillingness of the Crown
to extract from them the full complement of taxes officially owed.[158]

---

the inability of the aljamas to pay. For the abolition of such taxes
in Aragon, see Macho y Ortega, "Condición," p.171. For the question
of taxes in the fifteenth century generally, see, in addition to Küch-ler, Macho y Ortega, "Condición," pp.184, 188-90, 201ss, and 232; cf.
idem, "Documentos," pp.147, 444-5. Macho y Ortega is mistaken about
the novelty of Muslims' hiding their property on Christian lands in
the fifteenth century to avoid assessment ("Condición," pp.181ss):
as has been pointed out, this was common in the fourteenth century.
He also (ibid.) misinterprets the significance of the struggle over
Muslim serfs between king and nobles as being primarily a tax ques-tion, when it was in fact symptomatic of more deep-seated demographic
problems.

158. Note that, for instance, in 1359 the king harshly rebuked

Excluding the single levy in 1363 of 400,000s from all three kingdoms (200,000s from Aragon-Catalonia and 200,000s from Valencia), the total revenue from Muslim sources during the war years was 234,626s. The mathematical mean annual income from all Muslim sources to the Crown is thus 19,552s. The mean annual income for the years 1351, 1352, 1353, and 1368 (the years immediately preceding and following the war for which figures are available) is 6,825s. This figure closely approximates the average (or most common, as opposed to the statistical mean) annual amount of Muslim taxes received during the entire period 1351 to 1368, which was approximately 7,000s. This indicates an annual increase of about 12,727s in the amount of taxes received during the war. In view of the fact that seven aljamas paid almost exactly 75% of the total Muslim tax revenue, the burden on these seven communities during the war years must have been enormous.

The amounts of revenue received from the Muslim aljamas show clearly the rapid exhaustion of the communities' finances. Taking 7,000s as the average annual payment to the Crown after the plague years, the tax burden during the war divides itself almost neatly in half on either side of the year 1360. In every year up to and including 1360 the Muslim revenues collected exceeded the average

---

his treasurer, Berengar de Codinachs, for trying to raise the amount of the peyta collected from the aljama of Valencia from 250s to 1,000s. The king had himself previously allowed such a raise "if need should arise," but apprised subsequently of the plight of the aljama, he changed his mind and threatened officials with loss of their own property up to the amount they extracted from the aljama beyond the allowable maximum of 250s: C 1473:230 (Nov.20, 1359).

annual revenues for peace time. (In four of these years they
exceeded the average by more than 1,000s) Four years fell below
the standard rate--all four in the last half of the war (1361,
1362, 1364, and 1366). Moreover, excluding the great levy of
400,000s (much of which was remitted), and the unusual contribution of Seta to the queen in 1365,[159] the rate of taxation during
1361-1366 was only a little better than half the rate in the period 1355-1360:

     total taxes 1355-60 = 134,053s: annual rate = 22,342s

     total taxes 1361-66 = 84,065s: annual rate = 14,011s

It is clear that the aljamas were becoming increasingly unable to
pay taxes throughout the war years: in 1362 they could pay only
4,400s, and in 1364 only 2,525s. In 1361, 1362, and 1363, the Crown
was obliged to remit approximately two-thirds of the taxes owed
it because of the desperate plight of the aljamas. In 1367 so little tax money was received that statistics cannot be compiled for
the year. (There was a slight recovery in 1368.)

     Inequities in the tax structure sanctioned by custom and
difficult to alter, a severe decline in the Mudéjar population of
most areas, and acute fiscal crisis of the aljamas due largely to
the war with Castile convinced the Aragonese monarchy that to force
full payment of taxes would be to risk losing their Muslim subjects
altogether. Efforts were made both to lure new Muslims to lands under
royal control and to limit the departure of those already there, but

---

159. The 16,000s recorded for Seta in 1365 are the sole recorded
tax for the aljama during the war, and can scarcely be considered
regular taxation; but cf. table A, note (p.244).

along with this the Crown adopted the wise expedient, of foregoing
immediate cash to foment economic recovery of the aljamas.

Many aljamas regained some solvency eventually, and at the
beginning of the fifteenth century there apparently was a period
of short-lived prosperity when the aljamas, although still depopulated, were able to pay more of the taxes they owed the king and
queen. The tax policy of the Aragonese rulers regarding the Muslims was vindicated as well as it could have been under the severe
stress of the age. It was a policy of restraint, sympathy, and
realism, balancing as well as it could the needs of the Muslims
and those of the Crown.

TAX TABLES

Unless otherwise specified all figures represent sueldos, either Valencian or jaccenses.

All data for the period 1355-1366 were derived from the registers of the Archive of the Crown of Aragon, both those of the Chancery and of the Royal Patrimony. Earlier material is either also from the Crown registers or, where so indicated, from the material published by Manuel de Bofarull y de Sartorio in Rentas de la antigua Corona de Aragón (Barcelona, 1871), XXXIX, in Colección de documentos inéditos de la Corona de Aragón.

N.B. that during the entire period under consideration (i.e., 1355-1366) the aljamas of Elda, Novelda, and other nearby towns were under the control of the King of Castile, and that all subsequent figures ignore the income from these aljamas, which were ordinarily liable to the Crown of Aragon.

TABLE A: TAXES ACTUALLY RECEIVED BY THE CROWN, 1351-1368

YEAR	By the king alone: Aragon-Cat.	Valencia	By the queen alone: Aragon-Cat.	Valencia	TOTAL
1351					7,000
1352					7,500
1353					4,000
1354					-----
1355	1,985	6,000			7,985
1356	19,150	19,345			40,000
1357	11,778	34,830	800	7,100	54,508
1358	1,635	2,740	800	1,500	7,235
1359	368	4,550	400		7,913
1360	2,545	500	1,875	12,000	16,920
1361	250	4,413	1,000		6,613
1362		3,300	1,100		4,400
1363	15,425*	25,600*	*	*	41,025*
1364	145	500	1,000		2,525
1365	5,187	10,080		16,000†	39,267
1366	4,185	1,000	1,500		6,685
1367					-----
1368					8,800
	62,653	112,858	8,475	36,600	262,376

* The 400,000s collected in this year from all three kingdoms as a special war demand was in large measure remitted subsequently, but it is impossible to know how much was forgiven. It has been deleted from all calculations except where otherwise noted.

† Although this figure represents a rather unusual tax contribu-

TABLE A, continued

Observations:

The mean annual income to the Crown is 19,552s during the years 1355-66; 16,370s during the years 1351-1368. The real average for both periods, i.e., the approximate figure which occurs most frequently, is about 7,000s per year.

During the years 1355-66 the Valencian aljamas paid 64% of the total tax burden, the Aragonese and Catalan aljamas 31%, and individuals about 5%. Twenty percent (20%) of the income during this period was paid to the queen, the remainder either going to the king specifically or to "the Crown."

For percentages by aljama, see table C.

---

tion from so small an aljama (Seta), was recorded only for this year, and may have been partly remitted, I have included it here and elsewhere in my calculations, except where expressly excluded, because such periodic levies may have been one of the ways in which the Crown offset the generally low return from Muslim taxes, and thus represent a real and standard--if erratic--part of the royal tax system.

TABLE B: THEORETICAL ANNUAL TAXES, 1355-1366

Figures in parentheses represent estimates based on available data; for details of these estimates, see "Observations," below. Place names in parentheses are those of aljamas for which no regular taxes are recorded during 1355-1366. Their liability to taxation has been inferred from other types of taxation levied on them or from non-fiscal records. (A) before a number indicates an average has been derived from three or more years in which the tax amount varied.

Aljama	Cena	Peyta	Subsidium	Censualia
Alagón	100	(100)	300	(300)
Alcira	(100)	100	(400)	(400)
Alicante	(100)	(100)	(400)	(400)
(Aranda)	(100)	(100)	(500)	(500)
Ariza	100	(100)	500	(500)
(Artana)	(100)	(100)	(400)	(400)
Aspe	(100)	(A) 3,000	(A) 3,000	(A) 3,000
Barbastro	(100)	(100)	750	(750)
Borja	100	(100)	2,000	3,000
Brea	60	(60)	(240)	(240)
Calatayud	(100)	(100)	(A) 750	(750)
(Crevillente)	(200)	(200)	(800)	(12,000)
Daroca	200	(200)	(A) 750	710
Elche	(200)	(200)	(800)	12,000
(Eslida)	(100)	(100)	(400)	(400)
(Espada)	(100)	(100)	(400)	(400)
Huesca	100	(100)	1,000	(1,000)
(Fanzara)	(100)	(100)	(400)	(400)
Játiva	600	1,500	8,000	5,000
Lérida	100	100	100	(1000)
Magallón	(50)	(50)	200	(200)
(Montalbán)	(50)	(50)	(200)	(200)
(Muntroy)	(50)	(50)	(200)	(200)
Nabal	(50)	(50)	1,000	(1,000)

TABLE B, continued

(Onda)	(100)	(100)	(400)	(400)
Orihuela	(100)	(100)	(400)	1,000
(Perpunxen)	(50)	(50)	(200)	(200)
Sta Cruce	50	(50)	(200)	(200)
(Seta)	(50)	(50)	(200)	(200)
Tarazona	100	(100)	400	(400)
Teruel	200	(200)	(A) 450	(450)
Tortosa	(100)	(100)	500	(500)
Uxó	(100)	(100)	(400)	(400)
Valencia	100	250	4,000	(4,000)
(Vilamalur)	(50)	(50)	(200)	(200)
Zaragoza	150	3,000	(A) 3,000	2,000
Totals (1):	1,960	7,950	23,700	23,710
Totals (2):	(4,110)	(10,910)	(33,840)	(54,400)

Grand total 1: 59,418s
Grand total 2: 105,358s } these totals include taxes not appearing in the table, but described below, and totalling 5,798s

Observations:

Total 1 is the total of all numbers without parentheses, i.e., the total sum of the tax monies actually received in one given year from all the aljamas listed. It is theoretical in the sense that in no one year did all the aljamas pay all their taxes, but it does represent a likely estimate of the standard tax burden before the great remissions of the post-plague years. If certain Valencian taxes such as the morabetí and the tithe are included for the areas in which they were collected (chiefly Muntroy, Onda, Perpunxen, Valencia, Játiva, and Teruel), the over-all sum of the total 1   figures is 59,418s.

TABLE B, continued.

Total 2 represents the total which would have been collected
had all the aljamas subject to royal taxes paid all royal taxes,
i.e., were there no dispensations, privileges, remissions, exemptions, etc., and were the royal tax collectors absolutely effi-
cient. The grand total of these figures would be 105,358s--a
wholly theoretical figure which was never attained in practice.

Total 1 is approximately 56% of Total 2. That is, under ideal
conditions it appears that the Crown collected just over half of
the taxes it could have legally demanded. Under less than ideal
conditions enormously less was collected: viz., table A.

The estimates were arrived at in several ways. In some cases
there was indirect evidence; e.g., it was known that the aljamas of
Elche and Crevillente were closely allied in fiscal matters and
generally shared tax burdens equally. Information for Crevillente
can thus be inferred from that for Elche. In other cases figures
had to be derived from other data.

Where there was no other means of estimation, Sta Cruce was
assumed to represent the minimum level of taxation for the cena for
a small aljama, Lérida the minimum for a medium aljama, and Daroca
the minimum for a large one. The peyta is nearly always the same
figure as the cena, and was assumed to be when other information was
lacking. In rough terms, the subsidium demanded of most aljamas was
at least four times the amount of the cena, and this figure has been
adopted when there is no other clue. The censualia actually recorded,
except in one case, never differ by more than one-third either way

from the amount of the _subsidium_. Wanting better guidelines,
unknown _censualia_ have thus been assumed to equal the _subsidium_.

The error in estimation is almost certainly in a downward
direction, and the estimates are conservative. Magallón, for
instance, is assumed to have paid a _peyta_ of 50s, although it s
is known that in 1294 it paid an annual _peyta_ of 200s.*

---

*Bofarull, _Rentas_, p.233.

TABLE C: TOTAL CONTRIBUTIONS BY ALJAMA FOR THE PERIOD 1355-1366

Aljama	Total contribution
Alagón	800
Alcira	200
Ariza	1,300
Barbastro	500
Borja	13,200
Calatayud	6,850
Crevillente	200
Daroca	2,830
Elche	13,200
Fanzara	2,000
Huesca	8,675
Játiva	82,500
Lérida	465
Muntroy	98
Nabal	1,500
Perpunxen	98
Onda	413
Orihuela	1,000
Seta	(16,000)*
Tarazona	400
Teruel	3,100

* Excluded here as atypical; cf. Table A, note.

TABLE C, continued

Tortosa	500
Uxó	6,000
Valencia	29,545
Zaragoza	18,700

Seven aljamas paid 75% of the total tax burden:

Játiva	35%
Valencia	13%
Zaragoza	8%
Borja	6%
Elche	6%
Huesca	4%
Calatayud	3%

TABLE D: REMISSIONS, 1355-1366

The percentage figures represent the percentage of towns ordinarily paying taxes (=22) which did not pay the tax recorded in that column; e.g., in 1356 nine percent of towns liable to it did not pay the peyta.

YEAR	CENA	PEYTA	SUBSIDIUM	CENSUALIA	DEMANDA	TOTAL	MISCELLANEOUS: FOR
1355							Calatayud: walls 4%
1356		Ariza Uxó 9%	Ariza Huesca 14%	Uxó 9%		22%	Calatayud: walls 4%
1357		Ariza 4%	Alagón Borja Ariza 14%	Ariza Borja 9%		27%	Calatayud: walls 4%
1358		Uxó Valencia Játiva 14%	Játiva 4%	Ariza Borja Uxó Valencia Játiva 23%		41%	Calatayud: walls Borja: cavallerías 9%
1359	Játiva 4%	Játiva 4%	Játiva 4%	Ariza Borja Valencia Játiva 18%	Valencia 4%	30%	Calatayud: walls Borja: cavallerías Crevillente: alfarda Elche: alfarda Valencia: quintes 23%

TABLE D, continued

YEAR	CENA	PEYTA	SUBSIDIUM	CENSUALIA	DEMANDA	TOTAL	MISCELLANEOUS: FOR
1360		Játiva Zaragoza	Játiva Zaragoza	Ariza Borja Elche Valencia Játiva Zaragoza 27%		45%	Aranda: cavallerías Borja: cavallerías Calatayud: walls 14%
		9%	9%				
1361	Aranda	las Fayas Játiva Zaragoza	Játiva Zaragoza	Aranda Ariza Borja las Fayas Elche Valencia Játiva Zaragoza 36%		63%	Aranda: cavallerías Calatayud: walls 9%
	4%	14%	9%				
1362	Aranda	Elche las Fayas	Játiva Zaragoza	Aranda Ariza Borja Elche las Fayas Valencia Játiva Zaragoza (Crevillente) 36%		67%	Calatayud: walls 4%
	4%	18%	9%				

TABLE D, continued

YEAR	CENA	PEYTA	SUBSIDIUM	CENSUALIA	DEMANDA	TOTAL	MISCELLANEOUS: FOR
1363	Aranda	Elche las Fayas Zaragoza	Valencia Zaragoza aljamas of Valencia	Aranda Ariza Borja las Fayas Elche Fanzara Zaragoza	Nabal Zaragoza		aljamas of Catalonia: fogatge Calatayud: walls 9%
	4%	14%	14%*	32%	9%	64%	
1364		las Fayas Elche Zaragoza	Zaragoza	Borja Elche las Fayas Ariza Zaragoza			Calatayud:walls 4%
		14%	4%	23%		41%	
1365		las Fayas Travadell	Fanzara Vilamalur	Borja las Fayas Espada Travadell	Muntanejos		Artana: cavallerías Artana: lezda Calatayud: walls Vilamalur: cavallerías 18%
		9%	9%	18%	4%	36%	

*.Since "aljamas of Valencia" is too vague to compute statistically, and since the aljama of Valencia itself was already exempt, I have included this as if it were a remission to the aljama of Játiva. This is undoubtedly a slight distortion downward.

TABLE D, continued

YEAR	CENA	PEYTA	SUBSIDIUM	CENSUALIA	DEMANDA	TOTAL	MISCELLANEOUS: FOR
1366	Játiva	Aspe Játiva	Vilamalur Játiva	Borja las Fayas Espada Nabal Játiva			Artana: cavallerías Artana: lezda 18%
	4%	9%	9%	23%		45%	
	4%	10%	8.5%	23%	6%	44%	10%

The bottom figures are averages for the eleven years.

TABLE E: TAXES RECEIVED FROM ARAGONESE ALJAMAS IN 1294 AND 1315*

Aljama	1294	1315
Almonacir	3,000	----
Alagón	300	300
Aranda	800	1,500
Ariza	500	500
Borja	3,000	3,000
Daroca	730	730
Huesca	---	1,000
Huesa	300	300
Magallón	200	---
Nabal	100	100
Nuelia	500	---
Ricla	2,000†	---
Rueda	210	---
Tarazona	924	600
Teruel	---	˙450
Zaragoza	4,000	3,000
Total	16,464s	11,480s

Observations:

During the years 1355-1366 the percentage of the total Muslim revenues contributed by the Aragonese-Catalan aljamas was 31%.

---

* From Bofarull, Rentas, pp.129ss and 214ss.

† This figure includes both Christians and Muslims. I have retained it because there is no way to determine the percentage paid by the Muslims alone, and to delete it altogether would have distorted the overall total more severely than to include it.

TABLE E, continued

Assuming this to have been the case earlier as well, the total
taxes from all kingdoms in 1294 would have been approximately
53,110s. In 1315, they would have been about 36,386s. For the
significance of this, see above, pp. 229ss.

These figures do not correspond exactly to those for the later
periods in other tables, since the tax structure underwent considerable change during the fourteenth century. They are interesting as
points of comparison, but probably represent far less than the Crown
was actually receiving from each community, since taxes in kind were
also collected from nearly all the aljamas on the list. Numerous
small fees and taxes were also collected and listed sporadically;
most of these were systematically recorded during the decade 1355-
1366, and this makes the disparity in amount even greater.

Note that neither Barbastro nor Calatayud appears on the list,
although they became rather important in the mid-fourteenth century
(cf. table C).

TABLE F: INCREASE IN RATES OF CENA, 1327 - 1357*

Figures for 1327 apply also to 1328, 1329, 1330. Some 1357 figures
are averaged from more than one year during the period 1355-1366.

Aljama	1327	1357
Alagón	33s 4d	100s
Ariza	33s 4d	100s
Borja	33s 4d	100s
Brea	100s	60s
Calatayud	33s 4d	(100s)†
Daroca	83s 4d	200s
Huesca	100s	100s
Játiva	200s	600s
Lérida	33s 4d	100s
S. Creus	50s	50s
Tarazona	33s 4d	100s
Teruel	66s 8d	200s
Uxó	100s	(100s)
Valencia	33s 4d	100s
Zaragoza	50s	150s§

Observations:

In about thirty years the cenas owed by the aljamas increased
by about three times.

---

* Data for 1327 are all derived from Bofarull, Rentas, pp.375ss.

† Figures in parentheses are estimates based on table B.

§ Five aljamas which paid cena in 1327 do not appear in records for
1357: Nuelia, Ose, Turilles, Beniopa, and Gallinera.

Chapter VI

Rights of Mudéjares

In a modern frame of reference the over-all well-being or "status" of a minority group in relation to the larger society tends almost inevitably to be viewed in terms of those historical intangibles ambiguously known as "rights." Whether or not such a concept has much validity in the twentieth century, it certainly has little, if any, relevance to the fourteenth. Nonetheless, this chapter will attempt to deal with what will probably strike the contemporary reader as the "rights" of the Mudéjares under the Crown of Aragon.[1] In one sense, and one sense only, such a conceptualization is valuable: in other chapters taxes, duties, and problems particularly, if not exclusively, applicable to Muslims are discussed. If one groups these generically under the idea of Mudéjar "obligations" to the society, then the contents of the present chapter may be viewed as a discussion of Mudéjar "rights" in that society, in the sense of political benefits or promises of personal liberty. It is essential to bear in mind, in this context, that despite treaties of capitulation between Muslims and Christians, and despite numerous sections of various local and national law

---

1. It should not be necessary to point out that all those liberties one could call "rights" neither have been nor could be discussed in this chapter. In general the aim has been to clarify areas of confusion or uncertainty in the literature existing on the subject, or to raise questions which might readily occur to historians. Certain human prerogatives which have at one time or another been denied oppressed groups--such as the right to marry legally--but which were never a source of controversy in the case of the Mudéjares, either in their own or in subsequent literature, have been consciously omitted. Others, such as the right to play certain games denied to Christians (above, Chapter II), the right to regulate their own sexual mores (see Chapter VII), the right to defend their homes and neighborhoods against unlawful search (above, p.66), their special rights in trials (Chapter III), etc., are discussed elsewhere in this study.

codes, all of the Muslims living under the Crown of Aragon were
directly or indirectly the personal dependents of the monarchs
bearing that crown, and were neither subject to nor protected
by any higher law. What this chapter really treats is "concessions": an unending series of royal grants designed to alleviate,
foster, or control the condition of the Muslims and Jews of Aragòn--
the "royal treasure." To the extent that each king respected the
privileges granted by his predecessors (or by himself previously),
these concessions constituted the "rights" of the Muslim communities, but as will become apparent, neither the recognition by each
acceding ruler of the grants of his predecessor nor the most fer-
vent royal oaths guaranteeing the perpetuity of a king's own grants
sufficed to ensure the observance or protections of such "rights"
as the Aragonese Mudéjares enjoyed.

RELIGION

Probably the most obvious--though not necessarily the most pres-
sing--concern of the Muslims themselves was their right to practice
their own religion. The tolerance--or the canniness--of the conquerors themselves in regard to this was extraordinary, and throughout
the thirteenth century the Mudéjares, at least in the newly conquered
realms, were able to preserve their mosques and cemeteries, their
schools and religious customs, just as before the Reconquista. The
rents of the mosques were used for the mosques themselves,[2] ˙and,

---

2. "E que sien les rendes de les mezquites a ops de les dites mezquites axi com era antigament " ARV, Enajenaciones, 1:229, quoted in

most important of all, Saracens were allowed to chant the çala

publicly.[3] The çala is one of the primary duties of Muslims, en-

joined upon them by the Prophet himself: "O ye who believe! When

the call is heard for the prayer of the day of congregation, haste

unto the remembrance of Allah and leave your trading "(Koran LXII:9).

Many Christians, however, found the practice objectionable,

among them the pope:

> In 1311, Clement V, at the Council of Vienna, addressed
> himself to all the princes of Christendom, advising them that
> the freedom currently enjoyed by their Saracen subjects con-
> stituted an offense against the Christian faith; at the same
> time he forbade absolutely the public invoking of the name
> of Muhammad to call Muslims to prayer, as well as pilgrimages
> to visit the tombs of their saints.[4]

To the extent that it was possible, Spanish monarchs appear to have

resisted these papal edicts of oppression. Half a century after

Clement prohibited them, Peter came to the aid of Saracen pilgrims

trying to visit the shrine of Muslim saints in mosque at Godalesc,

not only allowing such pilgrimages within his kingdom, but absolutely

---

Roca Traver, "Un Siglo," p.10, n.15. Cf. ibid., p.18, n.29: "Concedentes vobis quod habeatis mezquitas vestras et cimiteria. et çaba-
çallanos qui doceant filios et pueros vestros et possint preconizare
in mezquitis vestris prout est consuetum inter sarracenos " (ARV,
Real, 658:15).

3. The çala is the public prayer ritual of Muslims. The word çala,
derived from the Arabic salât, is used in contemporary documents to
refer both to congregational worship and the public call to prayer
which preceded it. It is unlikely that the worship itself was ever
prohibited under the Crown of Aragon, but, as will be seen, strenuous
efforts, bitterly resisted by the Muslims, were made to prevent the
public call to prayer.

4. Roca Traver, "Un Siglo," p.27. See the Corpus Iuris Canonici,
Clementinarum, V, I.1.26.

forbidding the growing practice of charging the pilgrims six diners apiece to enter the mosque and pray.[5]   It is clear from the
document that the king's Muslim subjects were free to come from
anywhere in his kingdoms on this type of pilgrimage: "...many
Saracens both in former times and in the present used to come
and do still come from the said kingdom of Valencia as well as
from other areas...." As late as 1360, moreover, the Aragonese
ruler granted to some of his Muslim subjects the right to construct a mosque and a graveyard near the castrum of Benavento,
free of all financial obligations,[6] and even in the fifteenth
century Aragonese Mudéjares were granted lands for the support of
their mosques.[7]

Nonetheless, it was not very practical to resist the popes
in these matters, since the Spanish clergy and the king's Christian
subjects were not nearly as concerned with religious toleration
as they were with the triumph of the Christian faith. In 1311
James II prohibited, under pain of death, the public crying of the
name of Muhammad.[8] Roca Traver, using the text of this prohibition
to prove that the previous custom involved the invoking of Muhammad
so loudly that even the Christians could hear it,[9] tries to cite

---

5. This document, dated 1337, is published in the Appendix: C 862:121.

6. C 905:62, text in Appendix.

7. Document from Alfajarín, dated 1446, and published by Macho y Ortega, "Condición," p.246.

8. Roca Traver, "Un Siglo," p.27.   This action, or a similar contemporary one, evoked a protest from at least one foreign Muslim sovereign:
see M. Alarcón Santón, Los documentos árabes diplomáticos de la Corona
de Aragón (Madrid-Granada , 1940), p.150.

9. "Un Siglo," p.27.

this as proof of the "extreme tolerance" of the Christians, but
overlooks the fact that the custom was being not merely checked,
but outlawed under pain of death. Despite the wording of the
privilege, moreover, it is certain that the call to prayer was
chanted only in the morerías of Aragonese cities, and not in the
Christian quarters.

This was not, however, the end of the issue, and the question
of the çala provided the focal point of the whole controversy of
Mudéjar religious liberties in succeeding decades. Displaying a
cunning mixture of compassion and realism, Peter the Ceremonious
had worked out by 1357 a completely unofficial compromise presumably satisfactory to all parties. Under this agreement the aljamas
paid a certain sum of money each year into the royal treasury, in
return for which they could chant the çala "in a low voice and in
a low place":

> ...received, from the aljama of Saracens of the raval
> of the morería of the city of Játiva, 500 sueldos, by way of
> an agreement made with me, in regard to which the king issued
> the following command by word of mouth: to wit, that the çabi-
> çala or the faqi of the said aljama may in a low voice and in
> an inconspicuous place chant the çala, as is customarily done
> in the morerías of Valencia and in other royal places of the
> kingdom, and that this [agreement] should last until the king
> provide otherwise.[10]

(Játiva being the largest of all the aljamas, 500 sueldos was probably an unusually large amount to be paid for the agreement.) It
is notable that this agreement was made verbally, and intended to

---

10. "...reebi de la aljama dels sarrahins de raval de la moreria
de la ciutat de Xativa per avinença que feren ab mi al qual per lo
senyor [Rey] de peraule fou comanat lo negoti deus scrit, ço es qu'el

last only as long as the king wished; whether this was due to fear of protest from the clergy, the papacy, or the general population is not clear. Indeed, it may only have been intended to keep the price involved flexible rather than fixed. Whatever the intention, the results of its being clandestine were mixed indeed for the Muslims.

In 1359 the Bishop of Tortosa held a synod to discuss, among other things, the "deplorable, detestable, and execrable calling and proclaiming of the name of Muhammad," the net result of which was an absolute prohibition of the practice. The bishop was apparently very aware of the reluctance of secular authorities to enforce such measures, and made provision to deal with any diffidence on their part in the enforcement of his edict:

> And if any of the temporal lords exercising dominion
> over the Saracens within their parishes shall not forbid the
> said proclamation [of the name of Muhammad] to be made, as is
> specified in the said constitution, or shall not prohibit
> to Saracens living among Christians the public performance of
> manual or servile labor on Sundays and holydays, as is pre-
> scribed in the same constitution, they [the clergy] shall be
> responsible for notifying either us or our vicar or _officialis_
> within eight days...."[11]

çabaçala [sic] o alfaqui de la dita aljama, submissa voçe en loch baix, pogues cridar la çela [sic] segons que's fa e es acostumat fer en les mories [sic] de Valencia e altres dels lochs reyals del regne, e que aço duras tro qu'el senyor Rey en altre manera hi pro vehis, 500 sol,...." RP 1704:23 (1357). The "me" is the bailiff.

11. "Et si quis dominorum temporalium sarracenorum dominium obtinentium, infra ipsorum parrochiam constitutus dictam proclamationem fieri non prohibuerit, ut in dicta constitutione continetur, aut non prohibuerit dictos sarracenos simul cum christianis degentibus in diebus dominicis, et festivis servilia, se mecanica opera coram christianis publice operari, ut in eadem constitutione expressatur, nobis aut vicario nostro, vel officiali infra octo dies notificare teneatur...." Villanueva, _Viage literario_, pp.351-2.

It is difficult to estimate how far-reaching the effects of
this Catalan synod might be, but it is abundantly clear that in succeeding years Mudéjares as far away as southern Valencia felt severely threatened, for some reason, about their right to chant the çala.
Of the four sets of demands made on the king in 1365 as conditions
for aljamas returning to the service of the Crown of Aragon, three
required that they have the right to chant the çala,[12] and although
all three indicated that the communities involved had at some time
previously enjoyed this right ("segons que han acostumat"), it is
nevertheless obvious that they were very worried about the matter.
In 1366 the monarch granted the aljama of Aspethe right to chant
the çala and even to sound the trumpet as they entered the mosque,[13]
rights which, according to him, the aljamas of Valencia and Játiva
currently enjoyed.[14]

It is possible that the smaller aljamas of the kingdom, not
being able to raise sums of money comparable to those paid by
Játiva and Valencia for çala privileges, did not therefore normally
enjoy them. This could explain why some of those aljamas returning
to the king's service demanded these rights and others did not. It
seems slightly more probable, however, that Peter was willing to en-

---

12. Atzuena, Castro and Alfandequiella, and Eslida, in C 1209:55,
1204:63, and 1205:45, respectively. For complete summaries of these
demands see Chapter VII. Only Espada did not mention the çala.

13. Appendix, C 913:91.

14. "...prout sarraceni civitatum Valentie et Xative cantare dictam
çala [sic] et sonare dictum nafil utuntur in mezquitam eorundem "
(ibid.). Note that there is no mention of money.

ter into an informal financial agreement with any aljama, for
whatever sum it could afford, and that these demands represent
efforts by the Muslim communities, now temporarily in positions
to dicker, to wrest from the king written guarantees that these
agreements would not be abridged. The futility of their efforts
is attested to by the fact that even in Játiva the privilege was
short-lived: Ramos y Loscertales quotes a late fourteenth-century
document concerning the imprisonment of a Saracen for invoking
aloud the name of Muhammad "against the royal ordinances."[15]

ALMSBEGGING

Lo! Those who give alms, both men and women, and lend unto
Allah a goodly loan, it will be doubled for them, and theirs will
be a rich reward.
The alms are only for the poor and needy, and those who
collect them, and those whose hearts are to be reconciled, and
to free the captives and the debtors, and for the cause of Allah,
and for the wayfarers; a duty imposed by Allah. Allah is Knower,
Wise (Koran, LVII:18 and IX:60. Cf. II:215, XXIV:56, and LVIII:12).

There are few organized religions which do not require, in some
form or other, charitable gifts to the poor. In Islam the giving and
asking of alms is particularly sacred. The Prophet himself became
increasingly insistent on the care of the poor and the necessity of
almsgiving as he grew older, and a large part of the opposition to
him was based on the apprehensions of the wealthy classes about his
concern for the poor. Unlike Christians, therefore, who have often
been able to gloss over the social concerns of early Christianity,

---

15. *Cautiverio*, p.142, n.5: "Abdala Abenxando...captus detinetur
in Xativa pro eo quia contra [sic] inhibitionem et ordinationem nostram alta voce nomen Maffometi clamavit quod ipse confessus fuit "
(C 247:139).

Muslims have enjoined upon them as a cardinal duty of their faith
the giving of alms to those who ask them, and there has traditionally
been much less stigma attached to mendicancy in Muslim countries
than in Christian ones. As a consequence, it is necessary to view
the right of asking alms as one of the fundamental rights of a
Muslim community, though it is a matter which would scarcely merit
much attention among most Christians.

Alms were begged and gathered in a Muslim society, as seen
on the preceding page, not only for the poor and the needy, but
also for captives, debtors, and wayfarers. The right of captives
to beg was particularly pertinent to fourteenth-century Mudéjares,
many of whom were captives either as prisoners of war, through the
commission of some crime, or as the booty of some pirate enterprise.[16] As early as 1333 Valencian Mudéjares were requesting--
and obtaining--from the Aragonese monarchy guarantees of the right
to seek alms for redemption from captivity.[17] Prior to 1337, however,
a Muslim was required to obtain from the General Bailiff of Valencia
an albaranum, or certificate of poverty with license to beg: "...any
Muslim, male or female, free or captive, may beg alms so long as he
bears with him a letter testifying to his poverty...."[18] In 1337,
however, the Muslims of Valencia complained to the king that this ordinance worked undue hardship on those living far away from the city

---

16. On the question of captives, see Chapter I.

17. See the document of Feb.10, 1333, granting this right to six
Muslims, in Ramos y Loscertales, Cautiverio, p.148, n.1.

18. "...quicumque sarraceni et sarracene tam liberi quam captivi,
dum tamen secum ferent [sic] litteras testimoniales de eorum pauper-
tate possint elemosinas quererere" C 694:30 (Sept.10, 1347); cf.n.23.

of Valencia, where the bailiff lived, as it required them to make

a long, expensive journey when they were obviously ill able to do

so. In response, the king altered the ordinance, allowing hence-

forth the local bailiff or qadi to grant the albaranum to "the poor,

the old, the weak, the ill, the wards and the orphans," all of whom

might then beg alms in their own morerías.[19] There is no doubt

that the government actually attempted to prevent unlicensed mendi-

cancy, at least outside the morería: in 1358, for instance, three

Saracens were prosecuted by the general bailiff, because "they

were wandering through the kingdom seeking alms to aid in their

redemption, which was forbidden in the kingdom of Valencia."[20]

Similar stipulations were in effect in Aragon as well, with the

added difficulty that Muslims had to have their master's permission

to beg.[21]

Despite the apparently frequent practice of imprisoning Mudé-

jares guilty of infractions of the alms regulations (see note 21),

the only legal penalty for such violations was a fine (originally

fairly high, but reduced in 1358 to 10 aceti).[22] Perhaps to avoid

such extra-legal incercerations, the king removed any jurisdiction

over mendicants from the hands of the General Bailiff of Valencia

---

19. C 862:124 (Jan.28, 1337).

20. C 901:276 (Feb.11, 1358). The sentence against them was commuted by the king on condition that they pay court expenses.

21. The king released from a Zaragoza prison in 1356 three Muslims
who were being held on charges of begging unlawfully when he determined that the men (one free Muslim and two slaves) did have their
master's permission to seek elemosinas (C 688:97 [Dec.17, 1356]).

22. C 694:30 (Feb.1, 1358).

altogether in 1357, decreeing that only those local officials
mentioned in the edict of 1337 could issue the albaranum.[23]
But within six years the Crown reversed itself, put the enforcement
of such matters back into the hands of the general bailiff, and
forbade even more stringently the practice of begging outside the
morería. The suzerain did this, he said, because he had heard
that a great many Muslims "who were poor or pretending to be so"
were wandering throughout the kingdom begging, and experience
had taught him that such activities were dangerous to the realm as
being conducive to "the spreading of rumors and the making of con-
spiracies." The penalty for Saracens found seeking alms outside the
locale they were supposed to be inhabiting during the war was to
be confiscation to the Curia of their persons, and/or imprisonment
by the general bailiff.[24] For obvious reasons, this ordinance was
intensely unpopular with the Muslim population, in desperate financial straits due to the war and without other means to redeem the
many members of their communities being held for ransom as prisoners of war by the Castilians (as well as royal officials: see
Chapter VII.). The monarch was therefore constrained to alter his
provisions three months later, ordering that only foreign ("extranei")
Saracens be restrained from begging outside the morerías in which
they were residing (under pain of imprisonment), since these were
the ones, he wrote, who fomented conspiracy and spread "sinister

---

23. C 692:154 (July 21, 1357).
24. C 1075:71 (Jan. 28, 1363).

rumors."[25]

In spite of the financial disasters of the war, a fair number of Muslims were wealthy enough to make sizeable gifts to such poor members of their community. In 1362, for example, a wealthy Valencian Muslim, Çaat Fuster, donated twenty-five _sueldos_ to a captive _sarracena_ for the redemption of her person and that of her daughter.[26]

ARMSBEARING

It seems curious that a minority group called upon to perform military service with the general population could at the same time not enjoy the right to bear arms, but such was, in practice at least, the case under the Crown of Aragon in the mid-fourteenth century. As in many other cases, the Muslim populations had generally been granted this right under their original charters of capitulation,[27] but the privilege had been gradually eroded through succeeding centuries by wave after wave of local and royal oppression.[28] It is true that during various periods of the war Chris-

---

25. C 1075:111 (Apr.3, 1363).

26. RP 1708:18ss (1362). If Küchler ("Besteuerung," p.246) is correct, it was much more expensive to obtain an _albaranum_ (which he oddly calls a "carta de acaptar de moros") in the fifteenth century: the initial fee was 110s, with a 10s supplement for renewal.

27. Viz., that of Tudela (1115): "Et non devetet nullus homo ad illos moros lures armas" (Muñoz y Romero, _Colección_, p.417).

28. The _Usatges_ of Barcelona had forbidden selling arms to Muslims without the express consent of the prince, or of divulging to them any military plans of the _señor_, as early as the twelfth century (_Usatges de Barcelona i Commemoracions de Pere Albert_, ed. Josep Rovira i Ermengo [Barcelona, 1933], Appendix [="Official text"], s.123, "Christiani..."). Cf. the letter from Bishop William of Moncada (1257-82) condemning Christians who sell arms to Muslims (Villanueva, _Viage_, XVI, p.314). In both these cases the aim was clearly

tians, at least in Valencia, were prohibited as well from bearing arms, but the fine for the same offense was at least six times higher for a Muslim,[29] and sometimes simply astronomical.[30] In Aragon, the zeal of officials in preventing Muslim armsbearing grew so excessive that the Mayor of Zaragoza had to be restrained by the king from confiscating weapons carried by the king's own Muslim troops going to and from the border near Mediani. In this case the king (reacting to the complaint against the mayor lodged by the Saracens' lord, the Count of Luna) ordained that these particular Muslims, while fighting for him against Castile, were not to be denied the right to bear their own weapons (n.b.), but he made no broader declaration of Muslim rights in this area.[31] In Huesca, violating one of the oldest and most fundamental rights of the aljamas, officials illegally entered the morería to seize arms from the homes of Saracens. Again without in any way guaranteeing the right of Muslims to bear arms, the monarch severely forbade

---

to prevent arms falling into the hands of enemy Muslims, but such proscriptions could, according to their literal tenor, be applied to any Muslims, and apparently were (see below).

29. RP 2911:1 (1355). Christians paid 10s; Muslims 60s.

30. RP 1706:18 (1360). In this document a Mudéjar is fined 800s for the combined crimes of theft and taking arms out of the city. Even if the penalty for illegal posssession of arms is a small percentage of this total it is a staggering figure. It is more likely, in view of the legitimate purview of Christian justice over Mudéjar crimes, that the 800s represents the fine for the arms violation alone, since crimes of theft were ordinarily handled by the aljama, even if they involved Christians.

31. C 695:140 (June 15, 1359).

such "excursions into the morería" under fine of 100 morabetíns
for each offense, and sternly ordered the officials to observe to
the letter the privileges of territorial inviolability granted
the aljamas by James in 1273.[32]

PROPERTY: SALE

The official intention of the Crown at the time of the
reconquest of Aragon-Catalonia was that Jews, Christians and Muslims should all be treated equally in regard to such basic rights
as property and inheritance. Hence, Alfonso I promised the Saracens of Tudela in 1115, "And if anyone shall wish to sell or mort-
gage his property let no one oppose or gainsay this,"[33] and those
of Calatayud in 1131, "And Christians and Muslims and Jews may buy
from each other wherever they may wish and are able."[34] The Crown,
nevertheless, soon discovered unforeseen advantages to altering its
policy. As things developed, the royal rights over property belonging to Muslims were somewhat more lucrative than the ordinary jura
attendant on the property of Christians. For this reason, it was

---

32. C 1570:23 (June 22, 1360). Christian officials could enter
the morería only if accompanied by both the amin and the adelantati
of the aljama, and then only under certain conditions, rigorously
controlled. This was one of the best preserved "rights" of the aljamas until the pogroms of the late fourteenth century.

33. "Et qui voluerit vendere de sua hereditate aut impignorare,
quod nullus homo non contrastet, nec contradicat" Muñoz y Romero,
Colección, p.416.

34. "Et christianos et mauros et iudeos comprent unus de alio
ubi voluerint et potuerint" Ramos y Loscertales, "Fuero concedido,"
p.412.   Cf. the Costums of Tortosa, where Jews and Muslims were
guaranteed equal property rights with Christians, to own, buy, and
sell immovable property to or from whomever they wish (I.1a.19-20).
Cf. also José Ma. Ramos y Loscertales, "Recopilación de fueros de

obviously in any particular king's best interest to prevent the passing of property, real or movable from the hands of Mudéjar subjects to those of Christian ones. In the thirteenth-century Fueros of Aragon this right of free property transfer had already ceased to apply to transactions between Mudéjares and Christians, though such dealings between Jews and Muslims were free of royal control:

> ...And if perchance they should be under royal or ecclesiastical jurisdiction, they may not alienate [their property] to a Christian in any way, although Jews may sell to Muslims their possessions without the consent of the king or his bailiff, so long as they do not hold such possessions under stipulations of tribute or a certain portion of their fruits.[35]

Mudéjares under royal jurisdictions could sell their property to Christians with the king's permission, but a third of the sale price reverted to the royal treasury, presumably to offset the loss to the king by the transfer from one "law" to another (ibid., VII, 278).

In the fourteenth century, the rights of Mudéjares in this matter varied widely according to place. In Borja, although it was violated, a royal ordinance expressly forbade the selling of proper-

---

Aragon," AHDE, II (1925), pp.241ss, sections 150 ("Moro potest vendere...") and 153 ("Infançon non debet comprare..."). This "Recopilación" dates from the first third of the thirteenth century, and is based on the Fueros of Jaca, but represents an older text than the extant lemosin text of the latter.

35. "E si por auentura fuessen del rey o de sennor dios cuyo sennorio son, no las pueden allenar a cristiano en nenguna manera, mas los iudios bien pueden uender a moros lures possessiones sin consentimiento del rey o de so bayle, maguer que non tiengan aquellas possessiones por nenguna conueniença a treudo o a cierta part de fruitos" Fueros de Aragón, VII:274. ("Maguer"=licet; "treudo"=tributum.)

ty held by Mudéjares to Christians under any conditions:

> ...in accordance with and by virtue of royal privilege
> granted the said aljama for the preservation of our revenues,
> estates which belonged to Saracens may not be alienated or
> transferred to Christians through sale or any other means....[36]

When the property of Castilian Saracens of Tudela held in Borja

was confiscated in 1363, the king wrote to the General Bailiff of

Aragon, instructing him specifically about the sale of this pro-

perty: "...we ordain that no real property held by any Saracens

of Tudela in the said city of Borja may be sold to anyone but

Saracens of the same city."[37] Other sales, he added, would not

be honored, since this measure was essential to preserve, "and if

possible augment" the revenues from the aljama of Borja.

In Ariza, on the other hand, the thirteenth-century rule was

observed, and property could pass from Jews or Muslims to Chris-

tians so long as the king received one-third the sale price.[38] In

1360 even this was relaxed, owing to the tremendous debts owed

by the Muslims to the Jews and the generally abysmal state of the

aljama's finances. Under the new dispositions, property of Muslims

could be freely sold to any person of any faith, so long as the spe-

cial tax for the upkeep of the castle (to which Mudéjar property was

uniquely liable) was transferred with the property and paid by the

---

36. "...iuxta et per priuilegium regium dicte aljame concessum
pro conservatione peytarum nostrarum hereditates que fuerint sarracenorum non possunt in christianos causa venditionis vel aliter
alienari vel etiam transportari...." C 684:196 (Apr.2, 1356).

37. "...providerimus ne aliqua bona immobilium que aliqui sarraceni ville Tutele habebant in dicta villa Burgie aliis preter-
que sarracenis eiusdem ville vendantur...." C 712:117 (Feb.18, 1363).

38. C 700:238-9 (Apr.28, 1360).

new owner. The king had been worried that it might be difficult
to prove, after several transfers, which property was liable to
this special tax and which was not, but when he ascertained that
the Mudéjar property was all quite separate from the Jewish and
Christian parts of the city he decided to relax the ordinance.[39]

In Huesca the situation seems to have been somewhat different.
It appears that the royal one-third was exacted from all sales of
Saracen property, regardless of the buyer's faith. In 1363, at any
rate, the queen granted a relaxation from such a rule, stipulating
that henceforth the royal third would not be collected from sales
to Muslims, as long as they were vassals of the Court:

> Nor will you be required to pay us the royal third or
> any other royal portion of the price of such homes or pro-
> perties, provided that you make such sales only to Saracen
> vassals of ours and to no one else....[40]

The exemption, however, was applicable only to Muslim buyers who
actually lived or paid taxes in the city ("vassallis sarracenis
in dicta civitate commorantibus seu peytantibus").

---

39. C 700:238, ut supra (Chapter II). This relaxation, though
no mention of time was made in it, must have been temporary, since
in the following year the monarch granted the same relaxation for
different reasons. This time it was due to the extreme reduction
of the population of the aljama that the king relaxed the requirement
of the royal third. If the Muslims had continued having to sell only
to other Muslims, the king observed, it would be the same ten people
continually buying and selling the same property, and the debts of
the aljama could not be paid off; hence the royal third was not to be
exacted as "long as the king should wish," subject to the same limitations as before (C 702:91, text in Appendix).

40. "Et de pretio dictarum domorum vel possessionum tertium aut
aliud quodlibet jus regale nobis exsolvere minime teneamini dum de
predictis possessionibus sarracenis vassallis nostris et non aliis
personis venditiones ipsas feceritis... " C 1571:159 (Sept.1, 1363).

There is, unfortunately, insufficient evidence to draw inferences about the question in the most important city in Aragòn, Zaragoza. A bill of sale of 1360 (reprinted in the Appendix, C 904:
73/85) involved the sale of property to a Muslim by a Christian;
while this is not in itself indicative, the fact that the property
was located in the morería might indicate that the Christian owners
had previously purchased it from Mudéjares. It is clear that Jews
could receive property from Muslims and vice versa (Appendix, C 903:
290), though the circumstances of the grant cited are unlikely to
be typical.

One of the demands made of the king by the returning Muslims
of Valencia in 1365 was the right to sell their goods to anyone they
chose: "Item, that any Saracen may sell his lands and goods to whomever he wishes, paying what is owed the Lord King." The king rejected this demand--one of the very few he would not accept--and granted instead that they could sell to any Muslim ("It pleases the king
that they be able to sell to any Muslim...").[41] Probably this is
indicative of the law in Valencia in general, but it is impossible
to be sure of this on such scanty evidence.

Over the long run the thirteenth-century custom seems to have
prevailed, at least in Aragon. Macho y Ortega quotes a fifteenth-
century Fuero which is almost a verbatim repeat of the corresponding
disposition of two centuries previously,[42] and the king himself was

---

41. "Item que cascun sarrahi puxe vendre ses terres e sos bens a
qui's volia, donant son dret al senyor Rey.... Plau al senyor Rey
qu'els pusque[n] vendre a moro" C 1209:44 (Mar.14, 1365).

42. "Nullus judaeus, aut sarracenus haereditatem potest vendere

of the opinion that all the Muslims dwelling in his lands could
dispose of their property with complete freedom, or at least he
did not hesitate to assure Muslim sovereigns of other nations that
such was the case.[43]

PROPERTY: INHERITANCE

Obviously, the same concern which prompted the king's efforts to
limit the sale or alienation of Muslim property would have considerable effect on legislation relating to wills and inheritance. Royal decrees on inheritance were, in fact, a clear case of the Crown's
violating Koranic codes in decisions regarding the internal affairs
of the aljamas. According to the Koran (and the almost universal
practice of Islamic law), the property of a Muslim who died childless and intestate was divided among his near relatives, beginning
with his siblings (Koran IV:7ss, 11ss, 177; cf. II:180ss, 240).
These provisions notwithstanding, James the Conqueror established

---

christiano nisi Baiulo regis assensum praestante, et instrumentum
etiam confirmante. Si vero judaei, aut sarraceni venditiones inter
se fecerint, Baiulus domini regis non debet se intromittere....
Baiulus regis debet recipere pretii tertiam partem cum fit venditio
christiano" Macho y Ortega, "Condición," p.177, n.7.

43. See C 985:152 (Dec.26, 1363), addressed to the "Sultan of Ba-
bylon," where the king requests that Christian clerics residing in
the Sultan's lands be accorded the same treatment: "...[ut] possint
de bonis suis libere disponere sicut faciunt omnes sarraceni in
nostro dominio commorantes." Naturally, Muslims could purchase
property from whomever they wished, since this would not in any way
effect a diminution of the royal income. Nevertheless, some doubt
about this must have arisen in the fifteenth century, since in 1441
the queen issued a document affirming this right: "...dando eis [=
sarracenis] licentiam posse emere a quibuslibet xrianis [sic], campos,
vineas, domos, ortos, et alias quamlibet possessiones" Macho y Ortega,
"Documentos," p.446 (= C 3138:107).

in 1248 a law by which the property of Aragonese Mudéjares who died <u>sine prole</u> was divided equally between the aljama and the Crown, a practice which, though directly contrary to Islamic law, remained in effect till the mid-fourteenth century.[44] Peter the Ceremonious, at the time of the Black Death, added to this legislation an edict rendering null the wills of childless Muslims, claiming that "according to Islamic law neither males nor females dying without legitimate offspring may dispose of their goods by legacy, nor otherwise effect their wishes...."[45]

All of this changed abruptly, if temporarily, following the devastations wrought on the aljamas by the plague. In 1349 the king granted the aljama of Borja, at its request, the right to follow the usage prescribed by the Koran, though he did not identify it as such:

> ...we concede to the aforementioned aljama and to its residents present and to come that if it should chance hereafter that any Saracen, male or female, should die without legitimate offspring, he may make a will concerning his goods and arrange his wishes, any provision to the contrary hereby being voided. And if any should die without a legitimate heir or successor, we desire and direct that those most closely related to him may succeed to his goods freely and with impunity. And we wish and command this to have effect regarding all goods, past and present.[46]

---

44. C 908:233 (Sept.1, 1363); C 903:252 (Jan.30, 1360).

45. "...iuxta çunyam sarracenorum, sarraceni et sarracene absque filiis legitimis decedentes, de bonis eorum nequeunt testare seu aliter eorum voluntates omnimodas ordinare." C 888:154 (1349), published in Lopez de Meneses, <u>Documentos</u>, p.51. Note that this edict is falsely attributed to Islamic law.

46. "...concedimus memorate aljama et singularibus eiusdem presentibus pariter et futuris quod si forte de cetero aliquis sarracenus uel sarracena obierat absque filiis legitimis, de bonis eorum omnibus testari [sic] valeant et eorum voluntates omnimodas ordinare,

Possibly this was an act of pure magnanimity on the part of the king, but it seems more likely that it represented an effort to restore the finances of the badly depopulated aljama, and in this context constitutes a corollary to the remissions of the royal third granted Aragonese aljamas for the same reasons during the war with Castile (see above).[47]

During the decade of the war entirely new distinctions were introduced into the legal niceties of Muslim inheritance. In 1356 the king confirmed to the Saracens of Ricla a sort of "bill of rights" issued eight years previously to most of the aljamas of northern Aragon, which included several provisions relating to inheritance rights, to wit: that the property of Muslims who died sine prole and intestate be given to their near relatives; that the wills of deceased members of the aljama be respected only if the designated heirs were royal vassals; that if a Muslim die without heirs or a will three men of the village should pay for his burial from his goods and distribute the rest to those who would make the same use of it as the deceased did while he lived.[48]

---

impedimento quocumque cessante. Et siqui eorum absque herede seu successore legitimo decesserit, volumus et decernimus sic quod in ipsorum bonis propinquiores sui succedere possint libere atque tute. Et hoc locum habere volumus et jubemus in bonis omnibus tam temporis quam futuri" C 888:154, quoted ut supra.

47. Only eight days later, for example, to alleviate the poverty into which the aljama had fallen, the king granted the Muslims of Huesca 500s worth of goods "de bonis vaccatibus...que fuerunt illorum sarracenorum que decesserunt sine prole legitima carnali et naturali," and stipulated that such goods could not be sold to Jews or Christians, but must be used solely for the good of Muslim members of the community. (C 1315:228 [1349], in Lopez de Meneses, Documentos, p.57).

48. C 898:222, in Appendix. Note that the property of a Muslim

The question of royal vs. nobles' Muslims proved to be quite a thorny issue. The aljama of Huesca complained to the king in 1357 that non-royal Muslims were removing from the city property which they inherited from local Muslims:

> ...other Saracens who are not royal [vassals] are coming to the city and, as heirs of the deceased, are receiving and carrying away with them out of the city the property of the deceased, and--it is claimed--transporting it to places not under royal [jurisdiction].[49]

If they tried, on the other hand, to recover property left to them by their relatives living in places belonging to nobles, knights, or clergy, they were refused the right to do so. In response, the king ordered that henceforth the property of local Saracens was not to be removed from the city by Muslims of other places, unless they were either royal or specifically mentioned in the will of the deceased.[50]

In Zaragoza the older disposition whereby one-half the goods of intestate Muslims devolved to the Court and the other half reverted to the aljama was not abrogated until 1360, when the more generous Koranic provisions previously granted to Huesca were put into effect. Zaragoza was the last major Aragonese aljama to enjoy this

---

who left the aljama was to be treated the same way as that of the dead. The last clause of the edict presumably represented an attempt to encourage continuity in the use of land and buildings, thereby fomenting prosperity in the aljama.

49. "...veniunt ad dictam civitatem alii sarraceni qui non sunt de realencho et ut heredes illius sarraceni defuncti recipiunt et secum deferunt et extrahunt a civitate predicta bona defuncti ipsius, ea ad loca non regia ut asseritur transportando..." C 688:122 (Jan. 14, 1357).

50. _Ibid._

privilege, which applied to those living in the environs as well as the city itself.[51] Three years later, with the devastation worsening under the strain of the war, the king declared all relatives eligible to inherit, apparently abandoning the distinction between royal and non-royal.[52] In the same year, moreover, the king ordered an immediate halt to an inquisition in progress against the Jews and Saracens of Huesca, undertaken

> because of certain properties, goods, and rights which are now in their possession and formerly belonged to Jews and Saracens who died without heirs within the diocese of Huesca from the year forty-four on....[53]

No further action was to be taken against the aljama of Huesca until such suits were also brought against every other episcopal city in Aragon, and all goods so far confiscated under the nineteen-year-old commission to investigate were to be turned back at once to the Muslims.[54]

The king also intervened in individual cases, again in violation of the çuna. In 1363 he granted to a Muslim bridge-worker of Zara-

---

51. C 903:252, ut supra.

52. C 908:233 (Sept.1, 1363). Note the reasons given: "Quia tamen fidedignorum relatu comperimus aljamam sarracenorum predictam tam temporum sterelitatibus quam mortalitatum cladibus et aliis fortunis plurimis et diversis quasi ad desolationis interitum [sic] devenisse.... This letter is addressed to Huesca.

53. "...ratione quorumvis bonorum, rerum et jurium que existant in posse eorum que fuerunt judeorum et sarracenorum defunctorum filios non habentium ab anno xliiii citra intra diocesam Oscensam degentium..." C 712:164 (Apr.9, 1363). The year must be 1344.

54. "...vobis dicimus et mandamus quatenus contra judeos vel sarracenos quoscumque dicte civitatis Osce minime procedatis occasione contentarum in vostra commissione predicta donec omnino processeritis in omnibus aliis episcopaliensibus civitatibus et villis Aragonie predictis" C 712:164, ut supra (addressed to a Christian jurist of Huesca).

goza with no male heirs the right to leave his property to his

daughters, "and otherwise to dispose of [his] goods as he should

wish, despite the fact that it was not allowed [him] by the çuna

to leave more than a third of [his] goods to [his] daughters...."[55]

In Valencia there seems to have been wide variation in the

regulation of this matter. The general rule for the kingdom is

quoted during a dispute between the relatives of the Saracens of

Algar and the monastery of Arguinis. When certain Muslims living

in Algar and subject to the monastery died childless and intestate,

the monastery appropriated their goods, asserting that

> according to the general custom of the kingdom of Valencia
> the property of such Saracens belongs to the lord of the place,
> regardless of any blood relatives or relations of equivalent
> degree the deceased Saracens may have in other places within
> the kingdom aforesaid.[56]

The Mudéjares, on the other hand, maintained that by virtue of a

royal privilege granted them they were entitled to succeed to any

property left them in royal jurisdictions, and that Algar fell under

royal jurisdiction since it was subject to rule from Murviedro (Sa-

gunto). The accuracy of the Muslim claim was not challenged by the

monastery, whose comendator merely objected that although Algar lay

geographically within the royal jurisdiction, it had merum imperium

---

55. C 908:140 (Mar.15, 1363). Cf. Koran IV:11.

56. "...secundum consu[et]udinem genera[lem] Reg[ni] Valentie
talium sarracenorum bona ad dominum pertinent dicti loci [non] ob-
sta[nte] quod in aliis locis Reg[ni] predicti sarraceni mortui jam-
[dicti] parentes seu in gradu parentele habeant [pro]ximiores" C
713: 182 (Mar.6, 1363). The text is very badly damaged.

and was therefore not actually subject to royal jurisdiction in such matters, a contention the king seems to have upheld.[57]

Within the city of Valencia itself the rule was that no one living outside the city, royal or not, could succeed to property left by Mudéjares living inside it. Just what percentage of property left without legitimate heirs reverted to the Crown, however, seems to have been highly flexible. Only one-twelfth of the goods of Maymo Xehep fell to the king, though he died sine prole,[58] but the same year Peter laid claim to two-thirds the estate of one Hamet, "sarrahi lixador," since he had bequeathed it to two nephews who lived outside the city.[59] When Neixma Fuster went to Bougie, the portions of her will respecting her two sisters and her niece were honored by the bailiff, and 1,040s was allotted to the sisters together and to the niece (i.e., one-third of the estate for the niece and one-third for the sisters, in accord with the çuna), but because they had moved to Játiva, the remaining one-third which was to have gone to her father and uncle was sold and remitted to the Court.[60] In the following year, when Abraham Abenxoa died leaving two wives, one in Onda and one in Valencia, only the Valencian wife was entitled to inherit, and the king succeeded to the other half of Abraham's

---

57. C 713:182, ut supra. He ordered Garsia de Loriz to deal with the comendator as he ordinarily handled such disputes in cases involving prelates, richshomes, and knights and their vassals.

58. RP 1708:18 (1362).

59. Ibid.

60. RP 1708:19 (1362).

estate of 2,000 <u>sueldos</u>.[61]

In the final analysis the determining factor in the tension between the Crown and the aljamas on the subject of inheritance seems to have been the relative strength of either at any given moment, and the extent to which the Saracens involved were aware of alternative possibilities. Of the sets of demands made on the king as conditions for returning to his service, two mention inheritance rights. The Muslims of Espada demanded in 1365 that relatives of deceased Saracens who did not live in the same jurisdiction be allowed to inherit property so long as they resided within the señorío of the king, to which the king acceded "com se fa en la vall d'Uxo."[62] At almost the exact same time, however, the Muslims of Castro and Alfandequiella were demanding from the monarch that they be able to inherit property from Muslims anywhere in the "kingdom of Aragon," regardless of the issue of being royal vassals or not, and he granted this demand,[63] too, leaving the entire question of inheritance as vague and erratic as before the war, though some-

---

61. RP 1719:25 (1363). It must be observed in fairness that in general the king and his officials observed scrupulously the bequests of Valencian Muslims, so long as they conformed to the law of the kingdom. The bailiff of the city of Valencia, for instance, very conscientiously carried out the provisions of the will of Çaat Fuster stipulating that 25s of his estate be used to free two <u>serracenas</u> from captivity. (RP 1708:19 [1362]).

62. C 1209:44, <u>ut supra</u>.

63. C 1204:63 (Apr.8, 1365). For fifteenth-century inheritance practice, see Piles Ros, <u>Estudio</u>, p.211, n.378, and p.218, n.411. In some areas Muslims could pay a duty and then legally designate a "stranger" as heir (Küchler, "Besteuerung," p.245). Küchler considers "stranger" to apply to foreigners, but it seems more likely, in view of the controversies described above, that it simply re-

what more favorable to the Muslims.

TRAVEL

> Perform the pilgrimage and the visit to Mecca for Allah....
> And pilgrimage to the House is a duty unto Allah for mankind,
> for him who can find a way thither.....
> And proclaim unto mankind the pilgrimage. They will come
> unto thee on foot and on every lean camel; they will come from
> every deep ravine (Koran II:196; III:97; XII:27).

One of the five basic duties incumbent on every Muslim is the

pilgrimage to Mecca. As a consequence, the right to travel to

other lands must be viewed as one of the most fundamental rights

required by the subject Muslim population of Aragon, a right which,

in theory, they enjoyed from the very beginning of the Christian

re-occupation.

> ...and whoever may wish to leave and pass from Tudela
> to Muslim lands or any others shall be given leave, and may
> go with impunity along with his wife and children and all his
> possessions, by land or sea, whenever he may wish, by day
> or night.[64]

It should be clear, however, that given the generally subservient

position of most of the Muslim population, such freedom of movement

could prove something of an inconvenience to Christian lords and

masters of Mudéjar serfs and slaves. By the thirteenth century

penalties were already in effect, not only for the Muslims who went,

but also for the Christians who carried them out of the country with-

---

fers to Muslims who were not royal vassals or natives of the testa
tor's town or village.

64. "...et qui voluerit exire, vel ire de Tudela ad terram de moros vel ad aliam terram, quod sit solto, et vadat securamente cum
mulieribus et cum filiis et cum toto suo aver per aquam et per terram qua hora voluerit, die ac nocte" (from the agreement with Tudela, in Muñoz y Romero, Colección, p.416). This also applies to the
right to emigrate, discussed below, pp.289ss.

out permission from their masters.

> Any man found transporting Muslims to Muslim domains
> without the consent of their lords shall be despoiled of
> all his goods, both the man transporting and the Muslim he
> transports, so that whoever encounters them is entitled to
> them. But their persons, that is, those of the transporter
> and of the Muslims, should be surrendered to the king or to
> the mayor of the place where this occurs.[65]

Still--apart from the issue of the master's consent--the basic

right to travel outside the country had not been abridged before

the middle of the fourteenth century, and had been explicitly up-

held on several occasions by Peter the Ceremonious.[66] Perhaps

more than anything else it was the great plague of 1348-9 that

sounded the death knell for free travel of Mudéjares, both because

it increased the necessity of their presence, having decimated the

serf classes of Aragon, and because it gave rise to an era of sus-

picion and distrust of transients in general and of heterodox tra-

vellers in particular. Charges against travellers of poisoning

wells and causing the massive deaths that so terrified Europe in

the years of the plague created a climate of opinion so hostile

to travellers that even Portuguese Christians had to obtain special

guidatica to pass through Aragon on pilgrimages.[67] It is scarcely

---

65. "Tot omne qui fore trobado leuando moros a tierra de moros sin
uoluntat de lures sennores, deue seer espullado de todos sos bienes,
tan bien el qui los lieua como el moro a qui lieua, d'aquel qui los
trueba qui quier sea, sea deue seer suyo. Enpero los cuerpos d'ellos,
ço es del qui los lieua é de los moros, deuen seer rendidos al rey o
al merino del logar o aqueste achaeciere" Fueros de Aragon, VII:276.

66. E.g., "Preterea quicumque sarracenus vel sarracena ad terram
sarracenorum, causa mercandi aut romerie, tempore pacis, pergere voluerit, possit ire salve pariter et secure'," quoted in Roca Traver,
"Un Siglo," p.55, n.148.

67. C 887:42, published in Lopez de Meneses, Documentos, pp.11-12.

surprising that such paranoia should have particularly affected
the Muslim community, already suspect for its obstinacy in refusing
the Christian faith. In 1356 the king took steps for the first time
to end an annual assembly of Valencian Mudéjares, which had taken
on a sinister aspect in the eyes of the beleaguered monarch. Not
anxious to offend his Muslim subjects by outright oppression, the
king asked Garsia de Loriz to "devise a means whereby the meeting
might be suppressed":

> ...as regards the assembly which the Saracens hold each
> year in the kingdom of Valencia, during which they discuss
> matters injurious to the kingdom, we desire that you devise
> a means whereby this sort of assembly may be done away with.[68]

There were, indeed, various subtle means of checking the travels
of Muslims within the kingdom of Aragon. The city of Játiva,
for instance, attempted to prohibit non-resident Muslims from
buying or eating meat in the morería--a measure which would force
them to go without, since they could not eat any meat slaughtered
by a Christian butcher.

> ...by order of the community of Christians of the city...
> a public announcement was made through the city that no foreign-
> born Saracen might presume or dare to buy meat in the market
> of the morería, either to eat it within the city or transport
> it outside....
> ...by virtue of this edict [these Saracens] were constrained
> to fast, since according to their law they dared not eat any
> meat except that butchered and prepared at the hands of a
> Saracen butcher.[69]

---

68. "Quo ad congregationem quam sarraceni faciunt annis singulis
in certo loco regni Valentie super quo tractant aliqua contraria
dicto regno, volumus quod vos cogitetis modum per quem talis congre-
gatio telli possit" C 1068:134 (June 16, 1356). I have no other
references to this meeting or to its intended suppression.

69. "...per universitatem christianorum dicte civitatis...facta

In this particular case, where the commercial activities of the aljama--and therefore its prosperity--were endangered by such an effort, the king intervened immediately to put a stop to it and to guarantee the right of free travel, at least to Muslim merchants.

> Each and every non-resident Saracen of the morería who presently or in the future comes to the city of Játiva to sell his merchandise or for whatever reason, should and must be allowed without incurring any penalty to buy meat in the morería...and to eat it there or export it to his own home town safely and securely, just as [such persons] used to purchase it and eat it and export it to their residences before this edict.[70]

Nonetheless, there were great difficulties in travelling, not the least of which were the varying codes of different localities in such matters as the distinctive dress required--in theory--of all Muslims (see Chapter VII). A Muslim of Bétera complained to the king in 1360 that he had been unjustly enslaved in Valencia for having been found without the garceta, or tonsure, although he was, in fact, immune to such penalties by virtue of a grant to the Muslims of his home town.[71] The mere fear of being sold as a slave

---

fuit preconizatio in dicta civitate quod nullus sarracenus alieni-genus audeat seu presumat emere carnes in macello morarie ipsius nec ipsas in dicta civitate comedere seu extra aliunde deportare....
...vigore preconizationis iamdicte oportet eos jejunare, cum secun-dum eorum legem non audeant comedere carnes nisi per manus carnifi-cis sarraceni fuerint parate et excoriate" C 683:181 (Apr.19, 1356).

70. "Omnes et singuli sarraceni alienigeni dicte mararie qui ven-iunt seu venient ad dictam civitatem Xative causa vendendi eorum mercimonia seu alia de causa possint et debeant absque alicuius pene incursu emere carnes in morarie...et ea ibi comedere seu portare extra ad eorum loca salve pariter et secure quemadmodum emebant et comedebant et deportabant ad eorum loca ante preconizationem iam-dictam" ibid.

71. An investigation revealed that the Saracens of Bétera had been granted the privilege, in return for serving under their lord (Pe-dro de Exerica) in the king's forces against the Union, of paying

or confiscated to the Curia must have been enough to deter a great many Mudéjares from running the risk of violating unfamiliar ordinances in strange locales, and hence convince them to remain safely at home.

Although being enslaved probably represented the greatest single dissuading factor in the minds of Mudéjares contemplating a journey, it was not always legal confiscation they feared. The trade in Muslim slaves and captives was so brisk that the Queen felt constrained in 1360 to issue a blanket _guidaticum_ to all her Muslims in Huesca to protect them from such hazards on journeys.[72] And although the king made efforts to protect Mudéjares in general, it can scarcely be claimed that there was no conflict of interest in such matters. Muslim slaves, both native and foreign, made up a substantial body of the work force, and the Crown received a percentage of the purchase price of every new one sold. The king's ambivalence is typified in the case of some Aragonese Muslims illegally seized, along with their goods, by Aragonese pirates in 1357. Though Peter ordered their immediate release, and commanded the Bailiff of Aragon to make good all their losses out of his own

---

the same Pedro 20 deners and subsequently being liable only to a fine of one gold _duplum_ if caught without the _garceta_ by royal officials, rather than being sold into slavery, which was the prescribed penalty for such an offense. Peter therefore dictated that if it could be established that the said Mudéjar was actually comprised under the privilege and had, in fact, paid the 20 deners, he should not be sold into slavery ("...vobis dicimus et expresse mandamus quatenus constituto vobis dictum suplicantem viginti diners soluisse nobili jamdicto et dictam gratiam ipsum comprendisse, eo casu ad confiscationem et venditionem dicti suplicantis non procedatis...") C 703:55 (June 20, 1360).

72. C 1567:173 (Feb.10, 1360).

pocket if necessary, he enjoined no penalty whatever on the corsarii
who committed the crime.[73] When a group of emissaries from Granada
were attacked in Figueras returning from an audience with the king,
Peter demanded in outrage that the guilty be severely punished:
not only was a kinsman of the King of Granada "atrociously wounded"
in the attack, but the group bore with it the king's own safe-conduct, making the assault especially heinous.[74] Nevertheless, only
a month later the king surreptitiously absolved two men of Figueras
for their part in the crime--hardly the type of toughness apt to
deter such events in the future.[75]

Cautious Muslims would not, indeed, hazard a journey at all
without some guarantee of royal protection. The aljama of Torrelles
petitioned the king specifically to guarantee the personal safety
of Mahoma Dayhu, whose testimony they needed regarding some ransom
money, since he refused to travel the distance from Agreda to Tor-
elles without such an assurance from the king himself:

> Since we understand from supplication made to us on behalf
> of the aljama of Torrelles that they have need of your account
> regarding the case of the hostages which they placed in your
> care, under certain conditions, at the instigation of Gomeç Car-
> riello, and since you do not dare come to the said accounting
> without assurance from us, we hereby guarantee your safety in
> coming, staying, and returning.[76]

---

73. C 901:134 (Aug.10, 1357).

74. C 688:18 (Aug.2, 1356).

75. C 1149:8 (Sept.30, 1356).

76. "Como nos hayamos entendido por supplicacio a nos feta por
part de la aljama de Torrelles que haurian menester de vuestra
faula sobre'l feyto de las rehenas que ellos a instancia de Gomeç
Carriello vos comendaron con ciertas condiciones, e que menos de
nuestra segurança non osavades venir a la dita faula, por aquesto

Despite the manifold hazards of such travel, quite a number
of Mudéjares continued to move about both within and without the
kingdom as long as it was legal. Mahomat del Rey, for instance,
a Huescan merchant, transported goods from Exea to Huesca on a
regular basis throughout the decade following the plague years,[77]
and numerous prosperous Muslim families obtained the king's permission to make the pilgrimage to Mecca. In 1357 the king acceded to the request of the King of Navarre and granted safe-
passage through his realms to two Navarrese Saracens making the
pilgrimage;[78] he granted three Aragonese Mudéjar families and their
six servants safe-conduct for the pilgrimage in 1361;[79] and in
1363 he granted a license for such a trip to three Saracen families
"libere et impune," so long as they travelled on a ship authorized
by the Holy Father.[80] The penalty for making trips to "partes sarracenorum" without royal license was a stiff fine. A Valencian
Muslim and his wife were fined 200s in 1364 "because, it is said,
they went to Saracen realms without permission, for fear of the war

---

vos seguramos de venida, estada, e tornada" C 1170:62 (Mar.11, 1360).
A similar safe-conduct had to be issued to two Muslims on royal business in 1365: C 1211:44 (Apr.6). Cf., on the subject of freedom to
travel, the king's prohibition to certain Saracen knights, under
Chapter IV.

77. C 688:160 (Feb.16, 1357).

78. C 901:113 (July 18, 1357).

79. C 905:220 (June 26, 1361).

80. C 908:70 (Jan.12, 1363). As is well known, sailing to Muslim-
controlled lands was prohibited by the papacy, and special dispensation had to be obtained to avoid the risk of excommunication for the
ship's owner, captain, crew, and passengers.

with Castile, and then returned without permission to the kingdom of Valencia."[81]

EMIGRATION

Important as the right to travel was to the Muslim communities
under the Crown of Aragon, it was subsidiary both in operation and
in importance to another, more basic right, one which probably
constitutes the ultimate determinant of the well-being of any
minority group or subject population in any age: the right to
emigrate.   The extent to which Aragonese Mudéjares enjoyed this
right is not readily determinable, and will be considered here
in some detail under two categories, the right to change places
of residence within the kingdoms under the Crown of Aragon, and
the right to leave for Muslim-controlled lands.

The Fuero conceded to Calatayud in 1131 provided that any Muslim
who fled the jurisdiction of the city forfeited his property, which
was to be given to a Christian.[82]   This was, of course, during a
period in the history of the area when very large numbers of Muslims
would have been leaving the newly reconquered land and taking re-

---

81. "...sobre ço que's deya aquells por temor de la guerra de Castella sens licencia esser anats a part de sarrahins e tornats sens
licencia a les parts de regne de Valencia" RP 1709:19. In the fifteenth century Valencian Mudéjares enjoyed the right of travelling
freely within the country, but could leave for Castile or Muslim
lands only with the express permission of the king or the general
bailiff: see Piles Ros, Estudio, p.225 (#441), and pp.149 (#120),
257 (#580bis), 259 (#586).

82. "Et toto mauro qui est in termino de Calataiub, et fugerit
ad escuso, donet concilio sua hereditate ad christiano, et de ju-
deo similiter fiat" Ramos y Loscertales, "Fuero concedido," p.412.

fuge in the South, where Arab hegemony was still intact, if shaky.
A century later the _Fueros_ of Aragòn dealt more specifically with
the problem of Muslims changing residence within the kingdom,
and attempted to provide a compromise between the competing desires
of king and noble by allowing the lord of a Muslim who changed
residence to confiscate his goods, real or movable, so long as he
was still on his original lord's lands, but not after he had
reached those of the new lord, be it king or noble.[83]   No other
penalty was prescribed, so that if a Muslim was dissatisfied and
willing to risk the loss of his property, he could abandon his
estate and freely move to someone else's lands.

There are abundant indications in the documents of the period
that the king's Muslim subjects exercised this liberty of movement
to a considerable degree; e.g., Abderramin, the _amin_ of Plasencia,
was the son of Mahomet Amiadre of Coglor;[84]   Juceffus Dalmura was
described as "once of the village of Fraga, but now a resident of
Alcolegia";[85] Mahomet de Bendeziembre, a prominent Muslim of Zaragoza, was the son of Muce Aben Deziembre of Borja;[86]   En Juci, a
Muslim of Castile, owned an oven in Lérida and paid taxes to the
Crown of Aragon.[87] Moreover, as late as 1360, when this right

---

83. VII, 277 (in Tilander's edition, pp.164-5).

84. C 858:57 (May 10, 1336).

85. C 1379:93 (Dec.24, 1356).

86. C 699:131 (Jan.13, 1360).

87. RP 994:40 (1363). This is one of the rare instances of the
application of the honorific "En" to the name of a Muslim: "Item lo
dit dia [Dec.6] reebe lo dit Batle General d'En Juci, sarrahi castella, a qui havien enderrocat un forn per lo mur de la ciutat de
Leyda...."

had already been considerably abridged, the Muslims of Teruel used abandonment of their homes as a threat against the king in response to what they considered an excessive military levy, and did so apparently to good effect, since the monarch capitulated.

A license was required for a transfer of domicile, and failure to obtain it rendered one liable to prosecution. Peter Jordan, the Governor of Aragon, was ordered by the king to investigate personally the accusations brought against Fatima of Aranda and her sons, against whom it was charged that "without obtaining permission from any of our officials, she left Aranda and travelled to the said place of Deça with the intention of changing her residence." The king ordered the governor in his investigation to take into account both the motive for the move and the question of the license:

> If, indeed, you find this information concerning these previously mentioned matters [to be true], and that this Fatima went to the said place to recover her property rather

---

88. "...si eadem super ea servaretur predictis gravati opporteret eosdem eorum lares desere et aliunde eorum domicilia transportare" C 701:140 (Sept.20).

89. "...non obtenta licentia ab aliquo nostro officiali dictum locum d'Aranda exiebat et ad dictum locum de Deça se transferebat causa mutandi inibi suum domicilium" C 691:95 (Sept.7, 1357). Fatima herself had appealed to the king, claiming that the charges against her arose "more from malice than love for the king's laws," and that she had only returned to Deça temporarily after the truce of 1357 (Deça is in Castile) so that she could sell the property her husband had held there before he was killed in the war and get money for herself and her two sons. She had, furthermore, obtained license from the bailiff and qadi of Aranda to return to Castile on the errand, she asserted, and could not therefore be prosecuted for failure to obtain a license.

than to change her place of residence, and that [she did so] with the permission of the said [officials], then you are to release her from the custody in which you hold her and allow her to remain in Aranda and to move about freely there just as she could before the charge [was made].[90]

It would be naïve to imagine that in a time of greatly diminished servile classes the lords of Aragòn would quietly watch their serfs traipse off to òther places, royal license or no, and there is, indeed, evidence that they did not. In 1359 Peter addressed a royal edict to "all and sundry prelates, barons, gentlemen, knights, burghers, and any others who have or will have lands inhabited by Muslims." The Mudéjares of Aragon had, he reminded them, "for as long as anyone can remember," enjoyed the right to move freely from one place to another within the kingdom:

> ...any one of them who resides either in our jurisdiction or yours may, as often as he wishes, change his residence from one place to another, so long as he does not leave the lands of our kingdoms, and may no less [freely] sell his goods, movable and real, without any objection from anyone, provided he pays whatever [is owed] the lord and other residents of the place where he had been living, and provided he was not bound by some agreement to remain or to establish his residence in some one of these places.[91]

---

90. "Si vero predictam informationem ipsam de predictis inserentem reperritis et causa recuperandi suum ad dictum locum iret, et non causa transferandi domicilium suum, et obtenta licencia a predictis,Ffatimam ipsam a captione qua detinetis liberetis, et ipsam stare in dicto loco d'Aranda et per ipsum libere ire permittatis sicut poterat ante diffamationem predictam" C 691:95, ut supra.

91. "...quod quilibet ipsorum sive in locis nostris sive in locis vestris predictis populatus existat, potest de uno loco ad alium totiens quotiens voluerit suum mutare domicilium, dumtamen non exeat a terra regnorum nostrorum potest, nec minus vendere bona sua mobilia et immobilia absque impedimento cuiusque [sic], ipso tamen solvente quidquid domino et vicinis loci in quo fuerat populatus, nisi tamen fuerit per pactum astrictus de stando vel suum domicilium in aliquo ex dictis locis fovendi" C 700:106 (Dec.9, 1359).

Such explicit guarantees notwithstanding, the king went on, it often happened that when a Muslim wished to move from some noble's lands either to those of another noble or the king's, and to sell his goods, either to pay off debts there or to be able to move what was left to another place,

> you or your men prevent such Saracens from departing places under your jurisdiction, and if they sell their goods you force them to sell them for much less money than they are worth, and, what is worse, under the guise of some inquiry you seize them and hold them either in captivity or under arrest until they redeem themselves from you, either yielding all their possessions to you or selling them to someone else for practically nothing.[92]

All of these abuses were to stop immediately, the king enjoined; Muslims could not be detained and forced to redeem themselves or part with their belongings for less than their real value, but must be allowed to change residence freely as permitted them under the law.

Ironically, it was only a year later that the Crown specifically prohibited such movement for the duration of the war with Castile, at least in Valencia: see below. Whether or not this injunction applied to Aragon-Catalonia is not clear. A document of 1365 in which the queen grants a Muslim from Huesca permission to sell his Huescan property and move to Tortosa implies that this would not be allowed without special dispensation from the Crown, but it may be merely the formula for granting the license mentioned

---

92. "...vos seu vestrum aliqui impeditis tales sarracenos ne a vestris locis exeant, et si eorum bona vendunt facitis quod pro multo minori peccunie quam valeant ea vendant, et quod deterius est, aliqua questio [?] ipsos capitis et captos vel sub manuleutis detinetis quousque a vobis se redimunt aut vobis dimittunt vel vobis aut

above.[93]

If the Valencian edict did apply to the northern kingdoms, it did so only temporarily: there is evidence that in the fifteenth century Aragonese Mudéjares enjoyed the full benefits of the laws quoted above ensuring their right to move freely from place to place within the kingdom.[94]

Although Aragonese Mudéjares enjoyed extraordinary--by medieval standards--freedom of movement, it is difficult to agree with Roca Traver that the same was true of their Valencian brethren.[95] Officially the king upheld the right of Valencian Muslims to settle where they wished at least through February of 1356, when he ordered the release of a group of free Saracens who had been taken captive by Johannes Emmanuel when they tried to take up residence in

---

aliis quasi pro nichilo vendunt omnia bona sua...." C 700:106, ut supra.

93. "...pensantes quod in translatione sui domicilii nullum nostrum cernitur interesse nam et dictam civitatem Dertuse sicuti civitatem Osce tenemus jure nostre Camera assignata, et nichilominus hostendente [sic] coram vobis litteram bajuli dicte civitatis Dertuse per quam appareat quod ipse Abrayme mutavit in ipsa civitate domicilium suum, queque peytat cum aljama sarracenorum eiusdem civitatis, permittatis ipsum vendere dictas possessiones quas in dicta civitate Osce et eius terminis possidet"C 1573:165 (Oct.4, 1365).

94. According to Macho y Ortega ("Condición," p.194), Muslims could even demand repayment in cash from their señor for lands thus abandoned. The process was called desvallamiento. This seems to me dubious, but there was enormous freedom of movement throughout the century, apparently actively encouraged by the monarchy; cf. "Condición," p.171; "Documentos," pp.150 (C 2336:124), 157 (C 2340: 76), and 448 (doc. of 1458). Cf. also Tilander, Los Fueros, p.197, note on additional fifteenth-century rubric for section 277 ("Moros o moras que's camian d'un sennorio a otro").

95. "Los mudéjares valencianos disfrutaron en todo momento de una libertad de movimiento que difícilmente encontrará en ninguna comarca de la península   "Un Siglo," p.25.

a place called Carcelen, under his jurisdiction. Such enslavement was, in the king's own words, "contrary to justice, law, and
reason," and he therefore directed that they be permitted to settle
wherever they wished.[96] Unofficially, however, the royal attitude
must have been markedly different; three months later, in a letter
to the same official, Garsia de Loriz, the king upheld the right
of Sanctius Emmanuel to sell the captured Muslims--who had never
been released--to Valencian Christians, despite the vehement protests of Peter de Exerica, their would-be señor and general champion of the Mudéjar cause.[97]

It requires no special perspicacity to discern a pattern of
royal behavior favorable to the ruling Christian class in Valencia,
as opposed to the king's sincere efforts to protect the rights of
Aragonese Mudéjares from the usurpations of their señores. Possible
explanations of this are legion: the greater numbers of Valencian
Mudéjares, and their more recent amalgamation into the Crown of
Aragon, both of which might make the king apprehensive about keep-

---

96. C 683:114 (Feb.24, 1356).

97. C 1154:56 (Apr.16, 1356). The pretext for this enslavement
was that the Muslims in question had sheltered in their homes runaways and kidnappers from Granada: "...reperimus manifeste et satis
clare ipsos sarracenos et sarracenas esse veros captivos et capti-
vas eo quia quare? recollegerant in eorum dommibus [sic] acoller-
atos et alios sarracenos regni Granate, qui regnum jamdictum intra-
verant pro capiendo et captivando christianos et alios subditos nostros et regis Castelle illustris." That this is a bogus charge is
patent, since the Muslims never even had homes in the jurisdiction
where the charges were brought. What remains uncertain is whether
the king supported this travesty of justice in an effort to discourage relocation by Valencian Mudéjares or from some other motive,
such as friendship with the seller (or purchaser) of the enslaved
Muslims. On Peter de Exerica's being a champion of the Muslims, cf.
above, p.173.

ing them "under control"; the fact that much less of the royal income was derived from Muslims bound to the Court by direct feudal ties in Valencia than in Aragon, where a large percentage were serfs of the king; the fact that most of the land in Valencia held by Christians had been given to particular favorites of the royal family as rewards for services rendered in the reconquista (or elsewhere); the imagined threat of the proximity of Muslim-ruled Granada, etc.

Whatever the causes, the results were unmistakable. When the Muslims living on the lands of Arnald of Scriba, a domestic of the king, migrated en masse to Sirach, the king falsely asserted their action to be a violation both of the çuna and of Valencian law, and not only commanded that any Christians who found them detain them for prosecution, but also directed that they be severely punished, "so their action will not set a bad example."[98]

Arnald's erstwhile serfs had not, in fact, violated any law in Valencia, the king's assertion to the contrary notwithstanding, but steps were promptly taken to remedy this situation. By 1362 it had been publicly announced in every city in Valencia that no Muslim might henceforth "move or transport either his dwelling or his goods to another locale under pain of confiscation."[99] In some places the

---

98. What made this behavior particularly annoying, apparently, was that the Mudéjares had clandestinely returned and carried off their movable goods and even harvested their crops. The king's suggestion that the Muslims were "persuaded" to do so by "enviers and enemies" of Arnald is more than a little suspect. Arnald was an absentee landlord, living in Borja and receiving the rents from his benefice in Valencia. The episode occurs in C 693:40.(Oct.18, 1357).

99. "...un manament feyt de part del dit Senyor Rey ab crida feta

edict was promulgated as early as 1360, but there is reason to
doubt its success under the general confusion induced by the war
raging in Valencia during these years. Elche and Crevillente, for
instance, received the new law in 1360,[100] but in 1362 the queen
granted the Mudéjares living there a full remission of all sums--
including rent--owed the Court through October 1, on condition that
they remain in residence there for not less than six full years
from the date of the grant.[101] Anyone who violated this agreement,
i.e., moved away before the six-year term ended, would be liable
for the full amount previously owed, executable on his goods and
person. What makes this grant particularly significant is that
the queen offered it, by her own admission, in imitation of other
similar ones being made in the area by "gentlemen and knights to
their Muslims," strongly implying that such measures were widely
needed to stabilize the Muslim population in war-torn regions of
Valencia despite the new laws and the elaborate measures taken to
promulgate them.

---

en Valencia que algun sserahi o sserahina del raual de la moreria
de la dita ciutat de Valencia no mudats ne transportats sa habitacio
ne sos bens a altre loch sots pena de cors..." RP 1708:20. While
the phrase "sots pena de cors" would normally imply confiscation of
the person of the guilty party (i.e., enslavement), in practice the
penalty seems to have been merely confiscation of the goods left behind, as in the case of Çaat Fuster: RP 1708:18 (1362).

  100. C 1569:40 (Jan.18, 1360).

  101. "Axi empero que vos tots e sengles moros habitants en la
dita aljama siats tenguts e forçats necessariament de estar e habi-
tar continuament e fer residencia personal ab vostres mulleres e
infants segons tro ara hauets acostumat en lo dit loch de Eltxe e
son terme, e non mudar en altre loch o lochs vostre domicili" C
1569:134-5 (Mar.28, 1362).

In marked contrast to any difficulty the Crown may have experienced in enforcing laws against migration within the peninsula, the only difficulty presented by the laws about leaving Spain lay in protecting the liberty of Mudéjares exercising their legal right to so emigrate. This right had been clearly enunciated by the monarch as late as 1357 in a letter to all the Muslims of his kingdom:[102]

> We concede to every and all Saracens of our dominion, and we grant them the absolute right, regardless of any contrary edict, provision, or prohibition of ours past or present, legally and with impunity, without any fear or incurring any penalty whatever, to leave for foreign lands whenever they wish with their wives, sons and daughters, providing they pay to our general bailiffs or others thereto appointed the tax which has been hitherto paid in such cases.[103]

Since the king referred to a tax to be paid "as before," it seems likely that this decree constituted no more than a confirmation of a longstanding privilege.

It would seem that a fair number of the king's Muslim subjects exercised this privilege, despite a great deal of bureaucratic intervention in the process. A set of documents of 1360 yields a

---

102. "Concedimus omnibus et quibusvis sarracenis dominationis nostre et eis plenariam facultatem etiam [imperium] quia non obstante ordinatione, provisione ac inhibitione nostris in contrarium factis vel fiendis possint et valeant licite et impune absque metu et alicuius pene incursu quandocumque voluerint ad partes barbarie cum eorum uxoribus, filiis et filiabus se transferare [sic], ipsis tamen exsolventibus nostris baiulis generalibus vel illis quorum interest ius [per ipsos] in causa simili exsolvi hactenus assuerunt" C 901: 127 (Aug.7, 1357).

103. The words "by them" (per ipsos) have been scratched out with a thin line in the text, and I have not translated them. They do, however, seem to belong in the sentence where they occur, and I have accordingly placed them in brackets in the text above, note 102.

wealth of information about the details and complications of the
arrangements made for the emigration of Mudéjares. A merchant from
Lérida, Bernard Manresa, had in 1360 successfully petitioned the
king for permission to transport forty Muslims to Muslim lands.[104]
To do so he had first to collect the potential émigrés on the
beach of Barcelona, where they were to be examined by both the
General Bailiff of Catalonia (or his lieutenant) and the "comp-
troller of contraband." (The latter official's presence was probably occasioned by the fact of such transport's being regulated,
not prohibited.) The bailiff was then to note by name each of the
departing Muslims on the back of the privilege granted Bernard,
which was to be returned to the king so inscribed. Bernard was
himself required to obtain from each of his passengers fifteen suel-
dos--the standard tax for Saracen emigration, see below--in advance
of this examination, and present it at this time to the bailiff,
who returned it to the Court.

The red tape represented in this account apparently did eliminate
a considerable percentage of those aspiring to depart. Whether it
was the name checking--presumably to catch runaways or those still
in some indebtedness to a lord or the Crown--or the fifteen sueldos,
which must have been somewhat difficult to muster, since the Court
pointedly makes the ship's owner responsible for the sum rather
than the individual Muslims, only eighteen of the original forty
Mudéjares are recorded in the port records as having actually ob-

---

104. C 904:139, in Appendix.

tained license to leave the city for Alexandria in 1360.[105] Even
this number represents only those who paid (270s in all), as opposed
to those who actually left. A petition on the part of Bernard's
widow (n.b.) to send on the remaining Muslims three years later
reveals that only fourteen of those eighteen actually went, and
that the ship itself did not depart until October of 1361.[106] The
monarch granted the widow the right to send on the remaining Muslims,
who actually did leave Barcelona, after a three-year wait, in 1363.[107]

Although Muslim leaders of other lands seem to have concerned
themselves fairly frequently with the well-being and right to emigrate of Valencian Muslims (see below), only twice during the decade
1355-1365 did a foreign ruler intervene on behalf of Catalan followers of the Prophet. It is likely that outside Spain few Muslims
were aware of the Mudéjar populations north of Valencia, which certainly had the largest concentration. This was due in part to increasing acculturation of the Aragonese Mudéjares, who probably did
not even read Arabic in the fourteenth century (see concluding chapter). When King Bohanen protested the seizure of certain messengers

---

105. RP 1002:40.

106. C 908:164 (Mar.28, 1363). The document does not specify the
cause of Bernard's death, only commenting tersely of him: "...mari-
tus vester tempore quo vivebat...." His ship was called the Santa
Catalina, and was "patronitzat" by Jacob Coll of Barcelona.

107. RP 994:38. This time the port record indicates the number
was slightly swollen rather than diminished: 32 Muslims left rather
than the 26 mentioned in the grant to Sibil Manresa. This may be
due to the practice of several Christian parties contracting to
send Muslims on the same ship.

of his by Catalans in Majorca, the Aragonese king adopted a curiously literal attitude toward the guidaticum he had issued them,
decreeing that his officials should determine whether each of the
Muslim king's subjects in Majorca was there "of his own will, or
by force or chance," and in the case of the former to allow them
to go, paying the port tax of 15s, but to confiscate for the Crown
those there under duress, since the guarantee of safe conduct
covered only messengers coming of their own free will.[108]

In a somewhat more remarkable incident, the "Rey del Garp"
interceded for a particular family of Muslims living in Tortosa,
and Peter agreed to let Johia Abenaçen leave the kingdom free of
all duties--including the port tax--with his sister, wife, and
four children, specifically warning armatorii and corsarii not to
cause them any harm.[109]

Sometime around the year 1363--presumably after the concession
granted to Sibil Manresa--the Crown prohibited absolutely the emi-

---

108. "...havem deliberat que si'ls moros e los seus bens que son
venguts a Mallorquas [sic] hi son venguts de lur voler, que en
aquest cas los moros e lurs bens deuen esser absolts e licenciats,
pagant lo dret que es accostumat de pagar. E si los dits moros hi
son venguts per força del [?] o per fortuna, los dits moros e lurs
bens son consistats a nos, car per lo privilegi no son guiats sino
aquells moros que de lur voluntat vendran a Mallorqas" C 1068:96-97
(Mar.2, 1356). In a following letter the king commands that these
"confiscated" persons be forwarded to him: "Provets nos a man nostre
los persons e los bens lurs." C 1068:108 (Apr.30, 1356) provides
the mildly surprising detail that the seizure of the ship carrying
the persons and goods described was originally effected not by pirates, but by royal officials, and that the goods, consisting primarily of cloths and valued at 1,040 libri Mallorquini, had been
subsequently "misplaced" by the procurator responsible for them.

109. C 904:143 (Aug.21, 1360).

gration of Aragonese Saracens to Muslim lands. Although the exact
date and text of this injunction do not appear in any extant charter,
such a prohibition was clearly issued, probably consonant in details
both of wording and publication with that issued in Valencia in 1361.
In September of 1363 a group of Leridan merchants, claiming to derive
the inspiration for their act from "concessions made by the king,"
agreed to allow the Muslims working for them to leave for partes
ultramarinas, and asked the king to co-operate by releasing the Muslims from duties or processes pending against them. Peter reacted
sharply, declaring that in spite of any "concessions" granted by
him or others in his name, absolutely no Aragonese Mudéjares were
to be allowed to emigrate from Lérida or any other city in the
kingdom, and that any Saracens found leaving Aragon should be forcibly returned to their place of residence. Furthermore, all such
"concessions" issued by the Court were immediately and summarily
revoked.[110]

Dutifully obeying this edict, the qadi of the aljama of Lérida
arrested in October of the same year a Saracen woman of Fraga and
her husband, who were attempting to leave Lérida for partes ultramarinas. In an apparent reversal of the previous policy, the monarch
ordered their release, stating that the prohibition issued against
such emigration applied only to Mudéjares living under direct royal
jurisdiction, and that since Roquea and her husband were serfs of

---

110. C 1075:129 (Sept.16, 1363).

the Count of Luna they could not be prosecuted under its terms.[111]

Despite this clarification, the entire issue, at least in Aragon, was and is somewhat confusing, since the port tax continued to be collected from departing Muslims in the years following the revocation of the right to leave, and some of those leaving came from royal aljamas. As a final, ambiguous comment on the emigration of Aragonese Mudéjares, the port records are summarized on the following page in a chart, based on the collection of the 15s all Muslims had to pay on leaving Barcelona, as noted in the books of the Real Patrimonio.

---

111. C 715:50 (Oct.13, 1363).

Muslims paying the port tax on leaving Barcelona after the revocation
of the right to leave in 1357

Year	RP Register	Number	Provenance	Destination
1358	991:1	7	Zaragoza	Mecca
		1	?	Majorca*
		1 (female)	Barcelona†	"ubi voluerit"
1359	992:36	2 (couple)	?	Majorca
		4	Barcelona	Majorca
		2 (couple)	?	North Africa
1360	1002:40	1	Catalonia	North Africa
		18§	Catalonia	Alexandria
1361	993:41	1 (female)	Barcelona	Alexandria
		3	Barcelona	Majorca-North Afric
		9	Barcelona (?)	Granada
1362	no tax recorded			
1363	994:42	2	?	Majorca
		4	Barcelona	North Africa
		1	Almunya	North Africa
		32§	Aragon	Alexandria
1364	no tax recorded			
1365	996:42	3	Barcelona	Majorca
		3	?	Bogia
1366	997:68	1 (female)	?	North Africa
		3	Barcelona	?
		1	Barcelona	North Africa

---

* Majorca was listed in several places because it was the next port
of call. It is clear from the documents that the final destination
is some Muslim territory. Few if any of the Muslims actually were
headed for Majorca.

† In view of the tiny Muslim population of Barcelona, it is almost
certain that the Mudéjares listed as coming from Barcelona were only
residing in the city long enough to obtain passage to their final
destination. I have recorded it where given, nevertheless, since
it is interesting to know which persons arrived in the city immediately before leaving and which ones stayed long enough to be counted
as "living" there. As noted above, complications might keep prospective emigrants waiting up to three years for passage.

§ See above, pp. 303ss.

Muslims paying port taxes on leaving Valencia after the revocation
of the right to leave in 1361

Year	RP Register	Number	Provenance	Destination
1362	1708:9	1	Fez	Fez
		1	Eslida	North Africa
1363	1709:10	2 (females)	Chiva	Bogia
1364	1719:13	1	Valencia	North Africa
		3	Sot	Granada
		1	?	?
		1	Fez	Fez

For 1365, see below, p. 318.

N.B. that Küchler ("Besteurerung," pp.246-7) mistakenly considered
the dret de passatge to be variable in Aragon, a conclusion to which
he was falsely led by not separating fines for offenses from the
drets themselves.

In contradistinction to those of Aragon, Valencian Mudéjares
only briefly enjoyed the right to emigrate during the decade of the
war, and even the Muslims themselves, in requesting it of the king,
appear to have thought of it more as special concession than as
right.   In 1360 Peter granted a Moroccan Muslim the privilege of
taking with him out of the country all other Moroccan citizens who
wished to leave.   Since the monarch specified that such Muslims
must be "free and quit" of all obligations, these Moroccan "citizens"
were manifestly not just temporary visitors;   most likely they were
Muslims captured by Valencian pirates or sold to Valencians by
Aragonese ones, and had therefore been living in Valencia for
quite some time, perhaps even several generations.   It seems likely
that the Muslim to whom the grant was made, Jacob Ibn Musa Arran-
cani, was in fact a messenger of the King of Morocco, perhaps an
ambassador of sorts, since accompanying the grant to "lead out" the
said Mudéjares was a grant of personal safe-conduct implying
the possibility of his own subsequent return to Spain.[112]

During this same year, because "he had heard that quite a few
Saracens of the southern kingdom wished to pass to other lands,"
the king grandly declared that all who so wished might do so, so long
as they paid the Court one-tenth the value of all their possessions--
including clothing worn on their persons--and "other rights customarily paid us on such occasions."   To facilitate their rapid departure, the king even appointed two officials specifically to receive

---

112. C 904:144, in Appendix.

the monies thus collected (Johann Dolit and Fferarius Gilbertus)
and instructed all other Valencian officials to defer to their
authority in this matter.[113] Two facts are conspicuously wanting
in the information provided by the original grant, facts which are
supplied in secret letters of the king, and which make quite clear
the real motives behind this seeming generosity. In the first
place, Peter failed to mention that he was _obliged_ to make this
concession by diplomatic pressure from the King of Granada. In a
letter to the King of France Peter confided that

> according to the treaty recently concluded between
> us and the King of Granada we are constrained to send the
> said Muslims with their belongings to the homeland of the
> said king, free of our suzerainty and without any objections
> from anyone.[114]

Still, one might forbear to criticize the king for glossing
over this fact in his letter to the Muslims and allowing them to
infer the dispensation was an act of spontaneous kindness. But
there seems to have been very little kindness involved, either
with regard to the King of Granada or the Mudéjares. The grant was,
in fact, no more than a royal scheme to raise money for an embassy
to Granada, as is made perfectly clear in a private letter to the
two officials commissioned to expedite the departure of the Muslims:
their commission was to be valid, the king explained, only until
it produced the sum of money needed to arm one galley and guarantee the other expenses of Peter Boyl and his party on their trip.

---

113. C 1072:161 (Aug.30, 1360).

114. "...iuxta pacem inter nos et regem Granate noviter inita[m]
dictos sarracenos cum eorum bonis absque cuiuscumque contraveniente
a nostro liberatos iugo ad patriam dicti regis mittere tenebamur"

Beyond this, the grant to the Muslims was not to be honored, nor could the money thus raised be used for any other purpose.[115]

There is an implication in two letters written at about this same time that the king estimated about two months income from the money exacted from emigrating Muslims would suffice for the diplomatic mission of Peter Boyl.[116] The estimate was surprisingly accurate: by December of that year (three months later) Boyl was in Granada, and the following May the king summarily revoked the general emigration license he had granted the Valencian Muslims, for a reason "consciously not mentioned."

> Even though we have recently granted to all the Muslims resident in the kingdom [of Valencia] the right to leave this land and move to barbarian domains or to Granada, so long as they pay the tithe, nevertheless, since for a reason which we deliberately refrain from mentioning here, we wish you to yield [jurisdiction] over these matters until we shall be personally in the kingdom of Valencia,[and we forbid] all and every official, brigand, owner of a ship or of any marine vessel, and every one of our subjects to dare or presume to take out of the kingdom any one of these [Muslims] either by land or sea, or to transport [them] during the prescribed time [i.e., until the king should dispose.otherwise] to the said lands, under the pretext of any license or privilege gener-

---

C 1073:63 (June 3, 1361).

115. C 1072:162, reproduced in the Appendix. Those Muslims suspected of complicity in the "conspiracy of Cilim" (see concluding chapter), moreover, were not included in the permission to leave, and the addressees were to see that they did not try to make use of the privilege. To maximize the financial potential of such "suspects," nonetheless, the king disposed that all monies derived from the inquisition in progress against them should be used for Boyl's trip as well: "...quamcumque peccuniam que ad manus vestras et cuiuslibet vestrum pervenit seu perveniet tam ex inquisitionibus qui fiunt contra sarracenos regni Valentie qui in ipso regno pro facto illius perfidi sarraceni vocati Cilim seditionem ponere sategerunt seu ex compositionibus sique inde facte sunt aut fient..." C 1072:164 (Aug.30, 1360).

116. C 1072:164, 165 (Aug.30, 1360).

ally or specifically granted or conceded to the said Muslims, under pain of bodily and financial punishment.[117]

Even during the period of free emigration--about nine months-- the journey to other lands was by no means easy for those who undertook it. An entire shipload of such emigrants was seized by a pirate from Barcelona, Arnald de Caneto, and taken to France. There was, as Verlinden has demonstrated, a thriving slave trade in southern France, and presumably Arnald considered the chance of repercussions of royal intervention to be less in France (or perhaps slaves brought a higher price in the Midi?). In any event, Peter was constrained by his treaty with the King of Granada to request from John of France the return of the captured Muslims. Arnald, the king directed, was to be apprehended and tried for unlawful seizure, and his fidejussores (financial backers) were to be compelled to reimburse the Crown for any expenses incurred in making restitution to the Muslims. The Vicar of Barcelona was even ordered to have it publicly cried throughout the city that all those who had purchased any of the goods of the Muslims must bring them forward to be returned to their rightful owners.[118]

---

117. "Quamvis dudum licentiam dederimus omnibus sarracenis in dic- to regno collocatis exeundi ipsum regnum et ad partes barbarie seu Granate transfretandi, dumtamen jus decime exsoluissent, attamen quia in predictis ex causa quam hic scienter omitimus declarare vol- umus supersedere donec nos in civitate Valentie quam primo personal- iter fuerimus constituti. ...[mandantes] omnibus et singulis offici- alibus, cossariis, patronibus lemborum et aliorum vasorum marinorum aliisque subditis nostris ne aliquem ex eis a dicto regno per marem vel terram extrahere audeant vel presumant, ac ad dictas partes trans- ferre pretextu alicuius licentie seu gratie generaliter vel special- iter prefatis sarracenis indulte seu concesse, sub pena corporis et [?] durante tempore predistincto" C 1176:1 (May 14, 1361).

118. C 702:195 (July 4, 1361).

Arnald himself did return to Barcelona with the victims, but a question then arose as to whether all of the Muslims had actually paid the tithe. While an investigation was still under way about this, someone (unidentified) transported them to Granada, and after considerable angry correspondence between the Court and Valencia it was finally determined that all the Muslims were, in fact, legitimately quit and "soluts," a fact which was then relayed to the King of Granada. It seems fair to infer from this incident that the king's heart was never in the protection of the Valencians' right to emigrate, despite diplomatic gestures: as soon as the correspondence with the irate Granadan monarch was concluded, he promptly ordered an end to all processes in progress against Arnald or his guarantors, and even issued him a <u>guidaticum</u> specifically mentioning his offenses against the Mudéjares and guaranteeing his safety in spite of them.[119] Furthermore, once the right had been revoked, considerable vigilance was exercised in preventing illegal emigration. In August of 1361, twenty-seven Muslims were returned to their homes in the valley of Seta after an unsuccessful attempt to escape to Granada.(cited below).

That the king's interest, however, was directed merely toward maintaining a stable Muslim population, and not motivated by any authoritarian or vindictive concern, is patent from the handling of

119. "...non obstante quod citatus fueritis ac banniatus, eo quod sicut fertur nonnullos sarracenos cum eorum bonis qui de regno Valentie versus partes Granate navigabant solutis per eos iuribus assuetis indebito cum quadam galiota per vos armato more piratico occupastis" C 905:229 (July 4, 1361). Other documents relating to the incident are in C 1073:63, 64 (four separate entries), 65, 80.

such captured runaways, caught <u>flagrante delicto</u>: other than

their forced return to Seta, no penalty of any kind was inflicted

on the Muslims. The money they had contracted to pay the ships'

captains (12s 2d apiece) was disbursed to the owner of the two

ships by the royal treasurer, and even the other Muslims who lent

them money for food and their passage from Barcelona to Valencia

were reimbursed 150s from the royal treasury.[120]

The Christian population of Valencia seems not to have been

quite so disinterested. At the meeting of the General Corts held

in 1363, they complained bitterly about the frequent privileges

granted by the king or his bailiffs in Valencia to leave for other

lands, and pointed out that, especially during time of war, this

was a dangerous practice,

> ...since it often happens in the kingdom of Valencia that
> various and sundry Muslims of this kingdom either with our
> license or permission, or that of the general bailiff of the
> realm or his lieutenant, move with their belongings to North
> Africa, Granada, or some other foreign country in order to
> remain there and make it their residence, ...and since such
> Muslims are able to explain and point out the vulnerabilities
> and weaknesses of our kingdoms....[121]

---

120. "Et exsolvit etiam dictus thesarurarius eisdem sarracenis
quos eis mutuavit inter diversos vices ad opus alimentationis ipsorum et ad opus naulei eiusdem barche cum qua transfretarunt de
civitate Barchinone ad civitatem Valentie centum quinquaginta solidos barchinonenses" C 1570:122 (Aug.12, 1361). Cf. the cases of runaways from 1332 mentioned by Verlinden (L'Esclavage, pp.422-3),
some of whom were sold into slavery while others suffered no penalty whatever. It is probably significant that the fourteen not punished had fled the lands of two traditional friends of the Mudéjar
cause: the Archbishop of Zaragoza, and the Exerica family.

121. "...cum sepe contingat in regno Valentie jamdicto quod nonnulli et diversi sarraceni regni eiusdem tam ex nostri quam bajuli
generalis regni predicti vel eius locumtenentis licentia vel permis-
su cum eorum bonis ad partes barbarie, Granate, et alias terras ex-

Whether or not he sincerely agreed with the charges he related, the king very much needed the cooperation of the Valencian Curia, and agreed, at their request, to prohibit the issuing of any licenses to leave the country so long as the capitula under which the order was issued should be in effect. All previous grants, royal ones included, were revoked and annulled, and no one was to honor them. Most drastic of all, the monarch granted the demand that any Saracen caught leaving the country in defiance of this edict should become automatically the personal property of his captor.[122] While enslavement of Muslims was a part of Spanish life in the mid-fourteenth century, it seems unlikely that the monarch was pleased to grant this concession, potentially very damaging to the Crown's interest, both as protector of the Mudéjares and as feudal lord of many Muslim serfs; hence the limitation of time imposed by the king. There are no figures or documents on the number of Mudéjares who may have risked enslavement to escape; the case of Neixma Fuster, who suffered only the confiscation of the estate she left when she went to Bougie in 1362, has been mentioned above, and the number of Muslims who left Valencia legitimately is given in the chart on p.305.

---

traneas se transferunt pro stando et inibi moram suam faciendo, ...etiam quare dicti sarraceni necessitates et pericula dictorum regnorum nostrorum inimicis possent intimare ac etiam manifestare..." C 1506: 20 (Mar.22, 1363).

122. "...statuentes etiam vobis per hanc eandem concedentes quod si ex nostrum dominium [sic] aliquis sarracenus terre nostre inventus fuerit per mare aut per terram, illum capere et vendere possitis tamquam proprium et captivum de bona guerra captum durante tamen proferta jamdicta" ibid.

That the Valencian aljamas bitterly resented this disposition
is patent. Two of the four sets of demands presented the king in
1365 list as a major prerequisite to their allegiance to the Crown
of Aragon the granting of their right to emigrate to Muslim lands
when they wished; in each of the other two the demand that the
king "reconfirm all privileges previously granted the aljama" would
probably entail the respecting of this right (granted in 1361, albeit
briefly). The king acceded in all cases, stipulating only in the
case of Castro-Alfandequiella that he receive the tithe of the
emigrant's goods, as before, and in the case of the Serra d'Espada
that real property sold by prospective emigrants be sold only to
other Mudéjares.[123]

Indeed, conscious of how prized this right was, the monarch
granted it voluntarily as a reward to a number of prominent Mudéjares
in 1365 in gratitude for their part in bringing recalcitrant aljamas back into his service. Thus the "teniente" of Atzuena, the amin
of Eslida, and others were all granted the right to sell their goods
and move to North Africa ("barberia"), without even paying the reemço
usually required,[124] and the faqi of Eslida (and others) received both
the alcadia of the aljama and the right to emigrate with his family
and retinue to Muslim lands whenever he might wish.[125]

---

123. C 1204:63 and C 1209:44, respectively, ut supra.
124. C 1209:56 (Mar.20, 1365); two separate entries.
125. C 1209:64 (Mar.12, 1365).

What emerges most clearly from all this is that, in direct contrast to the case in Aragon-Catalonia, where the Muslim communities regularly enjoyed the right to emigrate but rarely exercised it, in Valencia a great many Mudéjares would have liked to leave but could not, because it was seldom allowed them under the law. In 1357 the tithe collected from departing Muslims was 3,789s 3d.[126] The number of persons departing is not given, but using an average figure derived from the statistics given for the period 1362-64, when the individual taxes are listed,[127] one could arrive at a conservative estimate of 250 Muslims leaving Valencia for Muslim lands. In the years 1358-59 no Muslims legally departed Valencia. In 1360, as noted above, two simultaneous relaxations were granted, and an estimated total of 105 Mudéjares exited, paying an aggregate tax of 1,575s 10d.[128] (The minuscule, albeit well-documented totals from 1362 to 1364 are summarized in the chart on p. 309.) In 1365 the floodgates opened again, due to individual grants from the Crown and the generic privileges conceded to returning aljamas at the close of the war, and the sum received from "various Muslim men and women who during the present year, wishing to pass to Muslim lands, tithed their goods...and paid the duties of the besant and mija dobla" amounted to 3,180s, or about 212 persons.[129]

---

126. RP 1704:13.

127. The tithe was based on an assessment of the emigrant's personal worth at the point of departure: see under Chapter V. The average figure for the years 1362-64 is slightly less than 15s.

128. RP 1706:10.

129. "...diverses sarrahins e sarrahines qui en l'any present, com

The reasons for this phenomenon should be obvious. The Muslim communities of Aragon-Catalonia, having been conquered as much as 250 years previously, and having enjoyed a more or less constant right to depart since that time, were already reduced to those Muslim families thoroughly acclimatized to Christian rule and an Iberian life-style, whereas the Valencian communities, more recently conquered and much nearer to the more Arabic culture of Granada and North Africa, still chafed, to a certain extent, under Christian domination and felt the pull of cultures more favorable to their religion. Perhaps even more important, all of the Mudéjar communities of the northern kingdoms, even those technically under the jurisdiction of nobles or ecclesiastics, were regarded by the king as his special concern, and as such received much more solicitous attention (particularly considering their small numbers) than the masses of Valencian Muslims, who often spoke no Romance, had few contacts with Christians, and felt little kinship to the Crown of Aragon. It was for the latter that the Crown's attitude toward the right to leave constituted the greatest hardship and for whom such trickery as that described above (p.311) was cruellest. In fairness to Peter, it deserves to be reiterated that his concern was almost always demonstrably directed toward the good of the kingdom of Valencia, and never exhibited racial or ethnic bias, and that he re-

---

se'n volguessen passar a les partes de Barberia, delmaren lurs bens... e pagaren lo dret de besant e mija dobla..." RP 1710:12. N.B. that Piles Ros quotes a document (Estudio, p.138) suggesting that the right to leave was generally not enjoyed in the fifteenth century.

sisted strongly the efforts of the Valencian Christians to end utterly the right of the Muslims to leave. That he was not above exploiting a subject minority thoroughly mistrusted and even execrated by popes and princes throughout Europe seems a small charge to lay against his character.

On balance, the rights of the Mudéjares seem to be like other human phenomena: complex, equivocal, relative. A certain degree of freedom was allowed in the practice of their religion, but this freedom was circumscribed by various factors such as fear of the fanaticism of the lower classes of Christians, intervention by the popes, etc. When possible the king protected the aljamas, for a price, and when it no longer seemed practical he desisted. The right to beg alms was regulated, sometimes in ways offensive or harmful to poor Muslims, but never terminated. Muslims could bear arms when in the service of the king, and possibly otherwise, depending on local authority. The right to inherit property freely within and without the aljama and the royal señorío was not widely or freely enjoyed, but there was considerable latitude in the application and enforcement of the royal edicts on the matter, and the position of the Crown was clearly flexible. In this case, indeed, the exigencies of the war seem to have worked in favor of the Muslims, allowing them enough political leverage to wrest favorable concessions from the king.

Likewise, the right to sell property varied within the kingdom but was never wholly abridged, despite the advantage that would have accrued to the monarchy under such a disposition. And though

the freedom of the Mudéjares to move about within the kingdom or to
exit from it altogether was strictly regulated, and sometimes--as
in Valencia--absolutely proscribed, most areas under the Crown
allowed them as much freedom, if not more, as was enjoyed by the
average Christian serf in France. There was, moreover, extensive
mobility both in and out of the realm throughout the period, in
spite of legislation or in accord with it, depending on the time
and place. Withal, the Muslims were not, as regards "rights," very
much worse off than the Christian peasantry of any European country
of the time, including Spain.[130] The most justifiable criticism of
the Aragonese Crown could be that those elements of the Mudéjar population who might have lived better than the ordinary peasant were
"kept down" solely because of their religion. That such was the
case, however, is not certain: Muslim nobles, if there were any under the Crown of Aragon in the fourteenth century, may indeed have
enjoyed special privileges which simply do not survive in the royal
records. Further, and finally, it is questionable whether such
rights as can be sketched in studies of this nature are true indications of the quality of life. The following chapter on "oppression"
is probably a much better index of the real status of the Muslims
of Aragon in the fourteenth century.

---

130. Note, for example, the case of a Christian woman Bella, who
was tried in 1359 for illegally leaving the country and travelling
in pagan lands. Though an isolated case, it would imply that Christians were sometimes prosecuted for the offense as well as Muslims
(C 1071:76 [Oct.24, 1359]).

Chapter VII

Oppression of Mudéjares

The subject of this chapter is probably the most difficult and elusive of all those presented in this study, and it seems desirable to preface it with a few general remarks. The subject in question is the oppression of the Mudéjares: the aggregate of problems in living experienced by Aragonese Muslims as a consequence of their religious and/or ethnic differences from the dominant Christian society. Such problems might be economic or legal, religious or moral, major or minor, physical or psychological, individual or generic. Any problem which is not considered in another chapter and which relates to Muslim distinctiveness has been dealt with here.

It is extremely important, therefore, to make clear at the outset what sort of assumptions underlie the observations in this chapter, and what types of implicit comparisons have and have not been made. A great many of the problems discussed here in reference to the Mudéjares were also encountered by Christians. There has been no effort to show that Muslims were, on the whole, uniquely oppressed or persecuted. The writer has, in fact, for the most part deliberately refrained from drawing explicit parallels between Muslims and Christians. Such analogies would be misleading, both for the lack of parallel documentary evidence and for the great diversity of undeterminable variables involved. Nor is there any comparison drawn or intended between the Jewish communities of Aragon and the Muslim ones. Where it has seemed worthwhile, comments have been made on problems Jews may have encountered which were similar to the problems of Muslims, but this has not been done consistently or thoroughly, and the aim has been merely to shed further light on Muslims rather than to make any general comparisons.

The most misleading parallels are temporal ones. It is almost fatally tempting for the modern historian, living in an egalitarian society and highly sensitive to the interests of minority groups, to draw invidious comparisons between the treatment or status of minorities in his own society and those in the societies he studies. Such comparisons are necessarily extremely risky. It must be remembered that medieval Spain was not and did not pretend to be an egalitarian society. Nobody--including the Mudéjares--would have claimed that all were equal under the law, or that religious or ethnic minorities had a "right" to equal treatment or status. Neither Christians nor Jews had been "equal" under the law in Muslim Spain, and all Christians were certainly not equal under the Crown of Aragon. Fourteenth-century Iberian society was quintessentially hierarchical, and the hierarchy was a Christian one. Muslims could not have expected (and would not have demanded) any lofty rung in a Christian hierarchy.

On the other hand, certain parallels with modern pluralistic societies inevitably present themselves to anyone studying the Spanish Middle Ages, and these parallels cannot be lightly dismissed. Despite the lack of theoretical equality under the law, there was, as has been shown elsewhere in this study, overwhelming de facto equality in many areas of Christian-Muslim co-existence, an equality which might justly evoke the envy of modern minorities.

Such practical equality prompts in the historian's mind today, as it did in the Muslim mind then, the expectation of generally equal footing in the quotidian affairs of Aragonese citizens. It is abundantly clear from protests to the king that when such equal footing was denied Muslims they took it very ill.

Parallels with modern societies, moreover, may be very useful for the purposes of contemporary scholarship. Questions about rights of citizenship or of holding offices ordinarily held by Christians may never have occurred to fourteenth-century Mudé- jares, but they will inevitably occur to the modern scholar, and they deserve to be dealt with. One might argue that it is mislead- ing to class mere discrepancies between Christian and Muslim status as "problems," when the Muslims themselves did not perceive them as such, but such objections stem from a confusion of "problems" with "issues." Inflation was as much a problem in fourteenth-cen- tury localities where it was not recognized or discussed as it was in those where its nature was clearly perceived. (Air pollu- tion was a real problem in nineteenth-century London before it became an issue in the twentieth century.) Even if the Mudéjares did not perceive their exclusion from municipal government as oppressive, it was clearly to their disadvantage not to participate in the making of decisions which vitally affected them. It was a problem in their lives directly related to their distinctiveness.

It will be clear to the reader at this point that the general co-existence of Muslims and Christians under the Crown of Aragon was remarkably successful, considering the energies that had been and were even then being poured into "holy wars" by both Muslims and Christians within and without the Iberian peninsula. One might even take the view that, given this militant fanaticism on both sides, and the rigidly hierarchical structure of nearly all medieval societies, it is ridiculuous to speak of the oppression of the Mudéjares at all, since their mere existence within the bosom of Christendom constituted an astounding concession on the part of Iberian Christians.

To argue thus, however, severely distorts the facts. The Muslims of Spain were not simply a tolerated minority. In the South they were not a minority at all, but an enormous majority, and while the evidence is less clear for the North, it seems that in Aragon-Catalonia they comprised only a little less than a third of the rural population, and possibly even more of the urban population of the major centers such as Zaragoza, Huesca, Borja, Lérida, Tortosa, and others. To think of them, in fact, as a tolerated minority is somewhat like thinking of American Indians as a tolerated minority in North America in the seventeenth century. The Muslim population had not been imported, or admitted as immigrants, or incorporated through centuries of co-existence (like the Iberian Jews): they had been admitted to the Crown of Aragon by treaty and capitulation during a long series of wars between peoples with rival claims to the same soil, struggling as equal adversaries. In return for submission to the Crown of Aragón, nearly every Muslim city in the kingdom had been guaranteed its basic liberties in absolute perpetuity, on the honor of the conquering monarch. Such guarantees resulted not from

Christian largesse, but from the fact that the conquests were not absolute or even decisive: the enormous Muslim populations left in the wake of military conquest by Christians had to be dealt with fairly because they were, in many cases, the major part of the king's subjects in a given area.

It is, for this reason, grossly inaccurate to draw comparisons, implicitly or explicitly, between the oppression of Muslim communities and oppression of contemporary Jewish or Christian ones. Their provenance, numbers, and relation to the monarchy were dramatically different. It is, of course, equally misleading to attempt to gauge the extent of their oppression by measuring their living conditions against those of citizens of modern democratic nations, whose ideals and practices are utterly different from those of medieval Spain. Parallels with other minorities in other ages may be suggestive and enlightening, but they cannot be pushed: the likenesses, no matter how fascinating, are generally superficial and will not bear close scrutiny.

One issue which to a modern mind might seem to be of fundamental importance for the well-being of any human, does not seem to have exercised the Muslims at all, though there is some reason to believe they were severely discriminated against in this regard: this is the question of citizenship. It is not at all clear that Muslims were considered citizens of the cities they inhabited in any of the kingdoms under the Aragonese Crown. No municipal codes or cartas de población take up this question. The Costums of Tortosa, which deal with urban Muslims more thoroughly than any contemporary

municipal code, do not comment explicitly on this, but define as

a citizen anyone born a free Christian, who has lived in the city

for ten years, who marries a citizen, or who receives a grant of

citizenship.[1] Whether the last three qualifications presuppose the

first is moot.

Muslims could not, it is clear, practice law or hold any office

over Christians.[2] Though a fourteenth-century ordinance of Valls

implies that Muslims could become pahers (town councilmen),[3] there

is no evidence that any Mudéjar ever actually did hold such a post,

and a good deal to indicate that everywhere else in the kingdom

they were prohibited by law from doing so. In Tortosa Muslims could

attend meetings of the town council, but had to sit at the feet of

---

1. Costums, I.9.14. N.B. the opinion of Küchler ("Besteruerung," p.1) that "die in den Ländern der Krone Aragons ansässigen Juden und Mauren galten landrechtlich als Fremde."

2. Costums, II.7.3. A possible exception to this--the only one I have seen--was the Muslim Procurator of Mizlata: see C 706:176 (Aug. 12, 1361).

3. The ordinance prohibits a Muslim's holding the office only if he has given aid to runaway slaves: "Encara ordonaren que no sia nuyl saray paher, ne sarrayne, que acula dins sa casa negun catiu, de qual- que condició ne stament que sia, et aquel o aquela qui u hará, x sol. li costará, que ya amor non trobará, los quals, si pagar nos pot, pendrá x açots a la quartera, sens que amor non trobará" (Carreras y Candi, "Ordinacions," XII, p.370; I have altered the punctuation, which was incorrectly inserted). The Diccionari Català Baleari uses this passage as an example of the other meaning of paher, i.e., "friend- ly, peaceful," (from paciarius), but it is obvious that this is not the meaning of the word in this instance. There were no hostile Muslims in the area of Valls at the date of these ordinances (1299- 1325), and legislation concerning them would have been quite super- fluous. Even if the edict dated from an earlier time, and was merely incorporated into a later code, the meaning "friendly" simply would not work: the punishment for the infraction under discussion was to

the prohomens, and did not actively participate in the delibera-
tions.[4] They could not be veguers or hold any other office in the
Christian civil administration.[5]   The Furs of Valencia likewise
prohibited Muslims from holding an office over Christians.[6]

It is unlikely, nonetheless, that their legal status was
perceived as oppressive by urban Muslims, whose aljama enjoyed
many of the same legislative privileges and limitations the Christian universitates did. It is true that the Christian community
could legislate for the aljama in some matters, whereas the Muslims
certainly could not impose any laws on the Christian "university,"
but Christian municipal authority over Muslim communities was limited.   Real oppression of Muslims was either royal--by the Crown
itself or its officials--or individual--by nobles or knights who
abused their Muslim vassals.

Some forms of oppression were designed to be obvious. The IV
Lateran Council of 1215 had demanded that all Christian monarchs
force Muslims and Jews within their dominions to wear distinctive
clothing, so they could be easily identified, and these demands were
repeated by Honorius III and Gregory IX.[7] Spanish monarchs acceded

---

be a fine, and a fine could scarcely be collected from enemy Muslims.
Paher is, to my knowledge, never used of Muslim officials, and must
apply to the Christian town council.

4. Costums, T.9.5.

5. Ibid., IX.8.1.

6. Furs, 83.1 ("Sarrahi no pot ser Batlle...").

7. See Corpus Iuris Canonici, II, Decretales, V.6.15. Cf. Roca
Traver, "Un Siglo," p.46, nn.117-118.

to these without protest, and even added to them.[8]   Between the

early thirteenth century, when the laws were enacted, and the mid-

fourteenth, there were certain modifications in the efforts to make

the Muslims distinctive. Originally Muslims and Jews had had to

wear a distinctive outer garment like a cleric's cape, round and

gathered, with a hood, and not striped, green, or bright red. They

could not wear rings of gold or precious stones, and had to grow

their beards long and cut their hair round rather than in Christian

fashion.[9] In the documents of the reign of Peter the Ceremonious

there is no reference to distinctive clothing, though the allusions

to the laws regarding hair and beard styles are numerous and varied.

It appears, indeed, that either the laws were no longer enforced

or that the wearing of the specified clothing had become so custo-

mary that infractions did not occur. At least two considerations

give greater weight to the former possibility: (1) there is no rea-

son to suppose the clothing would have become a part of Mudéjar life

when the hair styles did not, and the many violations of the rules

about the latter make it quite clear that they were not an accepted

part of Muslim life; (2) of the Muslims emigrating from Valencia whose

clothing was assessed as part of their departure fee, only a few are

---

8. Fernández y González, Estado Social, p.369; Tercera compilación
general. Constitutions y altres drets de Cathalunya (Barcelona, 1704),
I.12.

9. "...omnes et singuli sarraceni cuiuscumque dominationis existant
debeant incedere thonsis capillis in rotundo supra fronte et absque
garceta..." C 1071:192 (July 7, 1360); cf. C 981:22 (1355): "...suos
pilos in circuitu capitis scindi rotunde facere...." On the dress
codes, see also Costums, I.9.3-4.

described as wearing either of the two articles of clothing supposedly required of Mudéjares.[10]

The penalty for being found abroad in violation of the distinctive appearance code varied extravagantly. From 1347 on, all Muslims from royal jurisdictions could only be fined--a maximum of one gold doublet--for such infractions, while other Muslims found guilty of the same offense were sold into slavery.[11] Conscientious nobles-- or those simply afraid of defecting vassals--often applied to the king to have the privilege enjoyed by royal Mudéjares extended to their vassals. Sometimes the privilege was granted as a favor to the noble; others the Saracens themselves paid for it.[12]

Being sold into slavery was, of course, an ever-present threat for a Mudéjar, and the occasions of its occurrence manifold and capricious. The issue is discussed at more length elsewhere in this study.[13] Although it is somewhat misleading to speak of "degrees" of slavery, there were, in fact, ways in which a Muslim's

---

10. I.e., the aljuba or almeixa: RP 1708:9 (1362), RP 1709:10 (1364). N.B. that Christians were forbidden to wear such articles of apparel, at least in Catalonia: see the letter of James II to the school at Lérida (1300), published in Villanueva, Viage literario, XVI, p.231.

11. For royal Saracens and this privilege, see C 694:30 (Feb.1, 1358), and C 901:226 (Jan.12, 1358); for non-royal Muslims, C 703: 55 (June 20, 1360).

12. As a favor: C 903:144 (Nov.12, 1359): the king granted his cousin Alfonso, "quod in casu quo sarraceni locorum vestrorum que habetis in regno Valentie reperientur absque garceta sive ropeto rotundo in aliquibus locis regnis, seu aliis dicti regni, in quibus aliqua pena eiusdem sic repertis existeret infligenda, solum teneantur ad solvendum unam duplam auri, prout sarraceni locorum regiorum tenentur." The Muslims of Peter de Exerica paid 20d apiece for this privilege in Bétera: C 703:55, ut supra.

13. See pp.50 ss.

person might pass out of his control without his being either sold into slavery or imprisoned by a royal official. It was extremely common throughout the fourteenth century for Muslims to be seized and held for ransom, either by officials or civilians, and for any of a hundred reasons (or for virtually no reason at all). During an inquisition in Atzuena royal officials began seizing Muslims at random and forcing them to redeem themselves at terrific expense; they were forced to desist by the Crown only when the lord of the community complained that Mudéjares were beginning to emigrate in droves out of fear of being held for ransom.[14] The alcayde of Aranda seized the daughters of local Mudéjares and forced their fathers to ransom them until ordered to stop by the king, who professed to be "astounded" at the practice, but imposed no penalty on the alcayde.[15] Saracens were frequently held for ransom to raise money for military levies.[16]

During the war Christians often made "citizens' arrests" of Moors, whom they then held for ransom. The pretext for such arrests was usually that the Muslim involved was a "rebel," but the real motive was transparent: rather than shady or unknown Muslims who might indeed have been in the service of Castile, those arrested were nearly always prominent, well-to-do Mudéjares, of unquestioned loy-

---

14. C 695:190 (Sept.24, 1359).

15. "...si assi es, mutxo nos maravellamos..." C 1176:29 (Apr.24, 1361). The king merely ordered him "to refrain from such activities in the future."

16. C 695:82 (Apr.1, 1359): "...vos tamen multotiens eosdem [sarracenos] ad predicta compellitis et compellere nitimini faciendo eos redimi...."

alty but great ransom potential. Personal retainers of the king
were twice detained thus and held for ransom, and each time the
king came to their rescue. Far from punishing the Christian captors, however, he actually allowed them to keep the portion of the
ransom already paid (500s in one case; 600s in the other),[17] even
though he admitted that in each case the Muslim had been falsely
accused.

The redeeming of prisoners of war was, of course, standard
practice in the Middle Ages, and Muslim soldiers of the king ran
no greater risk of being captured than any others. It is not at
all surprising that some Muslims needed to be "redeemed" from Castile by Christians, or that the Christians should then have held
them to make good the outlay. Strict rules governed the ransom-
ing of Christians from captivity, however: rules requiring that
the ransomed man's family not be held liable for his debt, and that
he himself be free when he returned, no matter how great the debt
he might owe.[18] In the case of Mudéjares these customs either had
no force or were customarily violated. Redeemed Muslims were regularly recruited as vassals by their redeemers by being forced to
dwell in a certain place as a condition of their ransom;[19] if
they failed to meet conditions or payments they were sold into
slavery;[20] if they fled, their wives and children were sold as

---

17. C 1205:69 (Apr.3, 1365); C 1210:95 (May 23, 1365).
18. E.g., Costums, VIII.10.1-3.
19. C 693:75 (Jan.4, 1358).
20. C 901:260 (Jan.11, 1358).

slaves.[21] The amounts of the ransoms were, in view of the cash

disposed of by Mudéjares, staggering: they ranged from about 300s,

to be paid at 100s a year for three years,[22] to 1,000s,to be paid

in two installments of 500s each.[23] Except in cases of royal favor-

ites, an extension of time was the most that could be hoped for

from the clemency of the Crown.[24]

During the war with Castile the Mudéjares were subject to

seizure for an altogether different purpose.   In 1359, when the

Valencian town of Crevillente was threatened, Saracens were forced

to co-operate in its defense at a lower salary than Christians

performing the same tasks (see Chapter IV), and to ensure

their loyalty, their wives and children were taken and held as hos-

tages.[25] The taking of Muslim hostages became increasingly common

as the war went on. The queen's procurator was ordered to seize

the sons and daughters of the same Mudéjares at the mere threat of

an enemy approach in 1362, and to keep them in Alcoy, a considerable

---

21. C 1206:80 (Sept.9, 1365).

22. C 700:4 (Apr.8, 1360).

23. C 1210:95 (May 23, 1365).

24. Even a Granadan soldier in the king's service could obtain no
more than an extension of his ransom payments of 900s: C 700:4 (Feb.
2, 1360). For an account of a fifteenth-century ransom, see C 2338:
172 (1403), published in Macho y Ortega, "Documentos," p.155. Jews
were also seized and held for ransom, but the king seems to have been
more willing to intervene in their behalf: "Manam vos que encontinent
nos trametats aquellos juheus et juhies, los quals foren preses per
los almogavers prop de Sogorbe, com nos vullam declarar la questio
que es per raho dels dits juheus en nostre consell" C 1205:130 (July
4, 1365).

25. For text and references, see pp.182ss .

distance away.[26] The Saracens of Seta were forced to place all
their movable goods in the castle of Seta at the approach of the
enemy in the same year:[27] apparently the monarch's faith in the
loyalty of the Muslims had already reached rather a low point.

At the peak of the war in 1365 hostages were being held in
Segorbe, Eslida, and Elche, from the aljamas of Aspe, Artana, Espada,
Atzuena, Eslida, Elche, Crevillente, and Segorbe.[28] Two _amins_ of
Segorbe were among those being held by the Bishop of Valencia in
his jail: they escaped, but only to fight for the king; their
escape was pardoned.[29] In general the attitude of the Crown toward
the plight of the hostages seems to have been callous in the extreme:
acceding to repeated requests from the aljama of Artana, the king
finally allowed them to send messengers to Segorbe to negotiate
the feeding and care of the hostages there, and promised, in April
of 1365, that they would soon be home.[30] Only a month later, with
no mention of the hostages' returning at any time in the near future,
the king forbade the aljama to feed its people in Segorbe, alleging
that the food they provided for the hostages was falling into enemy

---

26. C 1569:145 (Aug.17, 1362).

27. C 1571:47 (Sept.15, 1362).

28. C 720:77 (1365); C 1205:45 (1365); C 1209:44, 55 (1365); C 1210:
76 (1365); C 1211:44 (1365); C 1547:72 (1365).

29. C 720:77 (Aug.30, 1365), in Appendix.

30. C 1211:44 (Apr.6, 1365); several separate entries.

hands.[31]

Indeed, the monarch may be justly accused of outright duplicity as well as callousness in the treatment of hostages. The aljamas of Espada, Eslida, and Atzuena all demanded, as a precondition of their returning to the king's service, the free return of the hostages from their communities, and the king solemnly promised, on March 15, that they would be returned absolutely free of any expense.[32] Yet when these hostages were actually released from the castle of Eslida, the official in charge demanded a ransom of 1,600s, which was guaranteed, but not paid, by a Christian (Miguel Blasco) and the *amin* of Eslida.[33] When the official demanded payment from these *fiancers*, and they turned to the hostages themselves, the outraged Mudéjares complained to the king, who refused to honor his promise and ruled that the official was entitled to collect whatever expenses he had incurred in the process of holding the hostages (though no more).[34]

The taking of hostages was limited neither to the Crown of Aragon nor to the kingdom of Valencia. A great many hostages were

---

31. C 1205:74 (May 6, 1365)..

32. C 1205:45 (1365).

33. Persons who acted as guarantors for the ransom demanded of hostages were known as *fiancers*; according to the Fueros of Aragon, anyone could act as a *fiancer*, regardless of his religion, as long as he had twelve sheep and five pigs and one mule (IV.197).

34. C 1210:76 (Apr.16, 1365). The king was even more deceitful in his dealings with the aljama of Artana. They had written him in the spring of 1365, worried about a rumor they had heard that he was going to grant the castle of Artana to Rodrigo Diaç. In April the king wrote back (C 1211:44), assuring them very specifically that he was not considering such a move, and that there was no need for

seized by both sides in Aragon, and Peter was constrained in 1366

to write the King of Castile requesting that the Muslims taken

hostage by him not be abused:

> ...we understand that many Moors from the village of Borja
> and other places within our kingdom of Aragon have been seized
> as hostages during the war with Castile, and their friends and
> relatives believe them to be ill treated. We therefore earnest-
> ly implore you to see that the said Moors are not badly treated,
> but rather that you order that they be cared for so that they
> may later return free and unharmed to their homes.[35]

Even after their release, moreover, hostages were not necessarily

"home free": about twenty-one hostages taken to Elche from Aspe

were finally released in 1366--only to be remanded to the queen's

procurator for an indefinite custody.[36]

Even if a Saracen's person was not confiscated on dubious charges

of disloyalty, his goods might be. Beginning in the 1360's an enor-

mous number of false accusations involving the seizure of Muslim

property were set aside by the king. The property of the Mudéjares

of Bechí was confiscated and sold before their case even came to

---

them to fear his doing so. In September he granted the castle to
Rodrigo Diaç (C 986:43).

35. "Entendido hauemos que de la villa de Borgia et de otros
lugares del regno nostro d'Aragon ha muytos moros que fueron levados
por manera de rehenas en tempo de la guerra a Castilla, et sus parentes e amigos dubden se que sean mal tratados. Por que vos affet-
uosament rogamos que providades que los ditos moros no sian mal tratados, ante aquellos mandedes guiar de manera que liberament luego
puedan a sus casas et sin danio alguno tornar" C 725:76 (Apr.12,
1366).

36. C 1547:72 (July 11, 1366). It is only fair to point out that,
at least in Aragon, Muslim hostages were sometimes kept under the
surveillance of other Muslims (e.g., C 1170:62 [Mar.11, 1360]), and
that it was not unknown for Muslims to offer themselves or their families under certain circumstances (e.g., C 1206:80 [1365]). Cf. Piles
Ros, Estudio, p.254, #571.

court,[37] but most of their coreligionaries did not have a trial
at all: the "rebellious" Muslims of Buruaguena, Teruel, Tarazona,
Calatayud, Murviedro (Sagunto), and a host of other towns lost their
property by royal decree, without benefit of any legal process at
all.[38]

Loss of property was probably the single greatest problem of
Aragonese Mudéjares. They provided a ready source of plunder for
any official or private citizen who was in dire need of food, animals, cash, or even a slave. The Muslim thus pillaged could always
appeal to the king, who might, if the supplicant was sufficiently
important, grant some sort of restitution, but it was extremely unlikely
that the Christian would suffer anything greater than a reprimand.
Even if he was forced to pay back the Muslim himself, which very
rarely happened, he could consider it an interest-free temporary
loan. Severe laws and certain retribution made physical resistance
by Muslims unheard of.

Thus the documents record cases of monks seizing vineyards
from their Muslim owners and selling them to Christians,[39] of wealthy
nobles robbing the aljama of Borja of its mules and food,[40] of the
officials of Calatayud selling and pawning the goods of Muslims in
the city to help fund the rebuilding of the walls (leaving the Mus-

37. C 714:137 (Sept.14, 1363). The vicar of the Archbishop of
Zaragoza interceded for them with the king. Cf. C 1385:148 (1363).
38. C 723:158 (1365); C 1206:44 (1365); C 1573:130 (1365).
39. C 684:196 (Apr.2, 1356), in Lopez de Meneses, Documentos, p.134.
40. C 983:68 (Jan.9, 1359).

lims destitute),[41] of groups of nobles despoiling Mudéjar salt-
carriers of their mules,[42] of mercenary soldiers seizing beds
and other goods from the very homes of Saracens of Elche,[43] of
ordinary soldiers in Huesca appropriating mules and other animals
from the Mudéjares and taking them with them when they left,[44] of
Saracens in the king's cavalry being despoiled of horses, arms,
and other goods by Christian nobles, and sold into slavery when
they tried to prosecute.[45] Sometimes excuses were offered: when
the mules of the Muslims of Bitorp were appropriated, it was claimed
that they were selling grain in defiance of a royal decree;[46] other
times there was no pretense whatever: the portarii confiscated the
mules of the Muslims of Játiva simply because they needed them.[47]
For some time the king turned his back on these confiscations by
his officials, and when complaints about them reached him he passed
the buck to the aljamas: "We also command the said aljamas and their
members that if through forgetfulness or some other reason some
such demand should be made of them for any cause, either by us or
our officials, that they should not be held to obey it."[48]

---

41. C 983:156 (Jan.21, 1359).
42. C 1402:147 (Feb.1, 1359).
43. C 1569:26 (Oct.17, 1359).
44. C 699:161 (Feb.11, 1360).
45. C 703:241 (Dec.24, 1360).
46. C 714:165 (Nov.14, 1363).
47. C 1207:159 (Sept.26, 1365).
48. "Mandamus etiam dictis aljamis et cuilibet earum quod si forsan
pro [sic] oblivionem aut aliter per nos seu dictos officiales nostros
aliqua demanda ex quacumque causa eis facta fuerit, eamdem observare

This was obviously useless advice: there was no way an aljama

could resist a royal official, who had unquestionable authority over

Muslims in any way he might choose to exercise it.   Only when such

authority was utilized to the manifest detriment of the Crown's

interest was the aljama likely to be relieved by the monarch himself.

In 1365, for instance, the Count of Ampurias became so engrossed in

his depredations on the wealthy Muslim communities in and around

Segorbe that the king had to remind him that he had been delegated

authority as a military commander, and that his duty lay in defend-

ing the city, not sacking it:

> ...greetings to the Count of Ampurias, our dear cousin,
> the Captain of Segorbe. We recall that we have, in other letters
> of ours, strictly charged you not to interfere with the populace
> of Segorbe or their property, but only with the war itself and
> the recovery of the castle. Yet we understand that you and your
> officials there persist in seizing Moors and Jews and their goods,
> whereof we are much astonished. We therefore direct and decree ex-
> pressly and unequivocally that you take no action against the said
> population of Segorbe, Christian, Jew, or Muslim, or their goods,
> but [that you concern yourself] exclusively with the affairs of
> the war....[49]

War was not the only--or even the major--occasion of exploitation

of Muslims, nor were the victims always aljamas or communities.   It

was pathetically easy for Christians in positions of power to plun-

der and abuse Muslims subject to them or simply unable to resist.

A procurator of Elche confiscated and sold the mules of a local Mudé-

jar to pay off his own debts;[50]   an alcayde of Aranda took a mule

from a Muslim to use in the castle;[51]   a sarracena was tortured by

---

minime teneantur" C 1534:137 (Oct.5, 1359).

49. C 986:28, in Appendix. Cf. C 1569:26-7 (1359).

50. C 1569:76 (Dec.12, 1360).

51. C 702:167 (June 2, 1361). Cf. a similar document, addressed

the Vice-governor of Valencia until she yielded 300s to him;[52]   Hamet

Abuçali was despoiled of 3,000s worth of animals and merchandise by

the king's commissarius;[53] two Muslims of Valencia lost 250 sheep

to two private citizens of Valencia, who simply confiscated them.[54]

Even Muslim officials suffered such depredations: the Saracen

bailiff left in charge of the estate of Laurence Taxo while he was

in Rome was unable to prevent the Christian officials of Calp from

seizing his master's grain as part of an unfair tax, and when Taxo

returned and complained, the officials avenged themselves on the

bailiff by confiscating all the animals of the local aljama, which

were in the bailiff's care.[55]   When the Bishop of Tortosa was act-

ing as military commander of Gandia, he seized and tortured the amin

of the aljama to extract from him the revenues of the community,

which were in his keeping.   The Christian lord of the town, the right-

ful possessor of the money, complained to the king, and Peter ordered

the sum restored, but took no punitive action against the bishop.

The return of the money, in fact, was to be under the supervision

of the same Vice-governor of Valencia who had committed a similar

---

to all nobles of the area around Uxó, where the monarch attempts to
forestall nobles' seizing goods brought to castles for provisioning
of Muslims taking refuge in them: C 718:87 (Nov.30, 1364).

52. C 1211:63 (May 26, 1365).

53. C 1205:68 (Apr.2, 1365).

54. C 730:39 (Sept.1, 1365) and C 720:88 (Oct.2, 1365); note that
the figures about the animals differ in the two entries.

55. C 702:59 (Dec.22, 1360).

offense against a Saracen the same year.[56]   In Teruel poor Muslims
with no land of their own rented land from orders or secular clergy
to make enough money to pay royal taxes.[57]   It often happened, apparently, that new procurators appointed to collect the rent would refuse to honor the terms of the rentals effected by former procurators, "especially when the land or property had been improved."[58]
In such cases "it was common for these [new] procurators either to
confiscate from the renters the lands and possessions improved by
them, or to force them to pay higher rent, in violation of the agreements signed."[59]

Mudéjares were also oppressed in many areas of their private
lives, most notably in regard to sexual mores.   If a male Muslim

---

56. C 1208:78 (Sept.6, 1365); on the vice-governor, see above, and
note 52.   It should be noted in the context of confiscation that Muslims sometimes were the property confiscated, as in the case of the
allegedly rebellious commendator of the Order of Calatrava , whose
two Saracen slaves were seized along with the rest of his property:
C 725:82 (1366).   It is also worthy of note that on one occasion
the king empowered the aljama to reap the benefits of "citizens' ar-
rest" and property confiscation: he allowed the aljama of Fanzara in
1363 to confiscate the property of all "rebellious" Muslims in the
city in order to meet the tax he had imposed on them for the repair
of the castle: "Tenore presentis damus et concedimus vobis, dicte
aljame et singularibus vestris, omnia et singula bona mobilia et sedentia omnium sarracenorum in termino dicti loci de Fanzara et eius
tenentia habitantium nobis rebellium adhuc nostro dominio non devol-
utorum. ...possitis exigere, petere, et habere et ipsa in reparationem operis dicti castelli et aliis vestris necessitatibus convertere et applicare..." C 909:74 (Dec.11).

57. C 686:218 (May 10, 1356).

58. "...potissime cum ipse terre seu possessiones melioramentum
susceperint..." C 686:218 (May 10, 1356).

59. "...sepe contingit que ipsi procuratores aut afferunt ipsis
conductoribus dictas terras et possessiones per eos melioratas aut
ipsi conductores habent augere precium arrendamenti dictarum terrarum instrumentis inde confectis obstantibus nullo modo..." ibid.

slept with a Christian woman, she was theoretically liable to be burned, and he could be put to death either by being drawn and quartered or burned.[60]   A Christian man who slept with a Muslim woman was liable to no penalty at all, but the Muslim woman was invariably sold into slavery (unless she was already licensed as a prostitute).   In short, those members of the society with no power, i.e., Muslims and women, were penalized for unions which were permissible for the members with power, i.e., Christian men.   That Muslim women seem to incur a lighter penalty than Christian ones is probably an indication that Christian men did not want to erect barriers to their own recreation (see below).[61]   (On the other hand, a Jewess of the period found to have had relations with Christian men [as well as Muslims] was ordered by the king to be exiled or

---

60. A rather striking parallel between the oppression of the fourteenth-century Aragonese Mudéjares and the black population of the United States in the nineteenth and early twentieth centuries is discernible in the attitudes of the dominant majority in each case toward sexual relations between the two groups. No southern gentleman ever protected his daughter's purity with more righteous fervor than medieval Catalans defended Christian maidenhood. Nor was there much difference in the inequity of laws or process. "Si jueus o sarrains seran trobats jaen ab crestiana lo jueu o el sarrai deuen esser tiraçats e rocegats, e la crestiana deu esser cremada: en manera que muyren. E aquesta acussacio pot fer tot hom de poble senes pena de talio ne daltra" _Costums_, IX.2.7. Cf. _Furs_, IX.2.8-9, where both parties are condemned to be burned. At the time of the _Costums_ the testimony of Christians had the weight of full proof in cases of sexual union between Christian women and Jewish or Muslim males, but this was subsequently modified at the insistence of the Muslims: see below.

61. Their outrage at the idea of a Christian woman's committing such an act no doubt also played a role. A Christian woman tried in Valencia in 1359 for carnal relations with Muslims so appalled her accusers that they refused to call her "Christian": C 1071:76 (Oct. 24, 1359).

dismembered.)[62]

That these penalties were really inflicted, at least on Muslim males, is patent: in February of 1357, for instance, a Catalan Muslim was actually condemned to be burned to death by the Curia of Lérida.[63] The king generally reserved to himself the right to try such cases, since they were capital,[64] and sometimes pardoned those accused of the crime before the trial, in return for a substantial contribution.[65] The crime was considered so heinous by the population in general that once a Muslim had been convicted the king had to declare the whole trial invalid to pardon him, rather than merely reversing the decision, as he was wont to do in other cases.[66] It was common for Jews accused of the same crime to get off with a fine, even when charged under the same inquisition as Muslims who did not get off.[67] Anyone could bring charges against a Muslim for this crime, including a Christian prostitute who had voluntarily slept with him,[68] and such accusers enjoyed complete immunity. Abuses of this and the dire consequences for the Mudéjares eventually prompted them to demand that a Muslim be convicted of sleeping with a Christiana only on the testimony of two or three witnesses,

---

62. C 691:127 (Oct.23, 1357).

63. C 692:36 (Feb.7, 1357).

64. C 1380:108 (Dec.19, 1356).

65. C 905:238 (July 14, 1361); cf. C 903:263, ut infra, where the two Muslims involved pay more than 1,800s.

66. C 903:263 (Jan.13, 1360), in Appendix.

67. Viz., the several documents at C 1071:192 (July 17, 1360).

68. C 1239:73 (July 21, 1376).

one of them a Muslim.[69]

Although Christian males incurred no penalty whatever for sleeping with Saracen women,[70] the women violated not just one but two laws by doing so. Under Muslim law they could be stoned or given 100 blows, depending on the leniency of the qadi, and under Christian law they were liable to confiscation and enslavement.[71]

---

69. Macho y Ortega, "Condición," pp.193, 241. The penalty may well have been mitigated in the later fourteenth century, when the demand for manpower was great and the supply of Muslim slaves low: the document quoted in n.68, above, implies that the general penalty in Aragon at the time was confiscation to the Crown as a slave: "...com lo dit moro encontinent confessa lo dit crim desius dit, et fur d'Arago diu generalment que los corsos de los moros son nostres propris...."

70. The law in Valencia which required that a Christian male and Saracen female caught sleeping together be forced to run naked though the streets (Furs, IX.2.8-9) was clearly a dead letter by the mid-fourteenth century. This law is particularly illustrative, however, of the varying standards of sexual morality in vogue at the time of its drafting: Christian males sleeping with Jewesses are to be burned with them, as are Jewish or Saracen males found to have lain with a Christian woman. The penalty for Christian males caught with Saracens seems ludicrously mild compared to these. Cf. Roca Traver, "Un Siglo," p.162, and notes 123-125.

71. In the early fourteenth century the blows seem to have been more frequently assigned by qadis: see C 861:107 (1337), C 862:40 (1337); by mid-entury, however, stoning seems to have prevailed: see RP 1710:22, 23ss (1365). Perhaps increased frequency inspired the greater severity. Cases of confiscation for this crime are legion, e.g., C 691:84 (1357), C 1209:114 (1365), C 1071:96 (1360), C 1075: 130 (1363). Legislation on the subject dated at least to James II: see Verlinden, L'Esclavage, p.420. Christian males could apparently be liable to some action if their liaisons with Muslims were notorious or scandalous: "Et qui cum judaea vel sarracena, vel quae cum judaeo vel sarraceno vel bruto animali coire ausu temerario, et nephario presumpserit, si sit publicum, vel fama..." Villanueva, Viage literario, V, p.362 ("Synod of Tortosa" of 1359). Both Verlinden and Ramos y Loscertales quote this text misleadingly: it does not refer to captives, but to Jews and Muslims in general, and only to notorious cases. The extreme frequency of this type of liaison is attested not only by such documents as those mentioned above, but also by numerous legal enactments about the proper treatment of the offspring of such intercourse: see especially Costums, VI.1.12, 16-8; VIII.8.2.

All of the women who appear in the documents of the fourteenth century opted for slavery, and the trade in sarracenas thus enslaved was very brisk. In fact, so many women became the property of the Crown in this way that there was lively competition among royal favorites to receive the "rights" over Saracen women caught sleeping with Christian men. The women were either sold, with the proceeds going to the king, queen, or the lord of the scene of the crime, or were granted as rewards to favorites.[72] The Crown seems to have preferred the cash to the person, and since the enslaved women would naturally tend to be young, the profits were considerable, averaging about 700s per Muslim.[73] Pardons were extremely rare, and granted only at the insistence of a prominent Christian.[74] Even conversion to Christianity did not guarantee pardon unless accompanied by help from a powerful Christian: a Muslim woman of Teruel who had committed such offenses not only became a Christian, but apparently married the bailiff of the city, yet the townspeople still demanded she be punished.[75]

---

72. E.g., Garsia de Loriz: C 575:132 (1332); Jacob de Oblitis: C 862:40 (1337); the Abbot of Mons Aragonie: C 1209:114 (1365).

73. See RP 1710:23 (1365). Both the accuser and auctioneer received a small percentage of the profits.

74. The Bishop of Valencia saved a Muslim who had been converted to Christianity (see below) after being condemned to be sold into slavery (Verlinden, L'Esclavage, p.420). Garsia de Vera (who judged the case between the aljama of Aranda and the city mentioned in C 699:202 (Mar.25, 1360), obtained pardon for his own Muslim mistress, Axa, on condition that she no longer engage in relations with Christians (C 576:125 [1335]; published by Verlinden, L'Esclavage, pp.866-7; cf. p.423). I have seen only one apparently spontaneous remission for this offense in all the documentation I consulted--C 905:251 (1362)--but Verlinden refers to at least one other case (p.866).

75. The material is in C 1566:48, 75, 157 (May, 1356, to November,

Rape of Mudéjar women was not uncommon,[76] but the cruellest aspect of the situation was the potential for abuse in the law of enslavement. A gentleman of the king's Court was granted as a slave a Muslim woman whom he had himself induced to violate the law,[77] and this double exploitation occurred to others as well: in 1356 Peter granted the monastery of Roda the "rights" over all Saracen women under its jurisdiction caught sleeping with Christians; i.e., they were to have them as slaves, either for their personal use or to sell, and the monarch instructed the General Bailiff of Aragon to honor this.[78] In the following year, however, he had to alter his original grant, and specify that the monks could not have as slaves those women who had been convicted of sleeping with the monks themselves.[79]

This sexual exploitation of Mudéjar women, with its horrible consequences for them, seems even more deplorable in view of the fact

---

1357). It is possible that the bailiff became her godfather rather than her husband. In the grant of remission she is styled Francesca de Marziella; the name of the bailiff of Teruel was Franciscus Garcesius de Marziella. It was common for Muslims to adopt the names of their godparents, but one would have expected her to take the name of her godmother. She had been married before she was accused of the crime with Christians. The final settlement required her to pay 250s--a modest sum, indicating the queen's reluctance to trouble her further. Apparently the Crown did not question the sincerity of her conversion, which further strengthens the idea that she had married the bailiff. Cf. C 211:269 (1314).

76. E.g., C 705:68 (1361).

77. C 861:107 (1337), mentioned in Verlinden, L'Esclavage, p.862.

78. C 1149:23 (Nov.12, 1356).

79. "Sane cum intentionis nostre non fuerit nec existat concessisse prelibato abbati et eius monasterio sarracenas illas quas cum monachis dicti monasterii repertum fuerit contubernium comisisse..." C 1070:23 (Sept.2, 1357). Such Muslims were to be sold, with the profits accruing to the Crown.

that the lands under the Crown of Aragon abounded in prostitutes,
both Muslim and Christian. Fourteenth-century Aragonese monarchs
licensed prostitutes throughout Aragon-Catalonia-Valencia, assigned
them neighborhoods or specific houses for their practice,[80] and considered them such a natural part of life that they provided in considerable detail for the quartering of prostitutes kept by mercenaries during the war.[81] Although such women were generally quartered in Muslim homes, there is good reason to believe that Muslims
were not allowed to resort to Christian prostitutes;[82] there is no
indication that Christians could not employ Muslim ones.

---

80. There were fines for taking _meretrices_ outside the areas assigned to them: C 686:14 (1355), but they were granted houses in
which they could practice with impunity: see the document in the
Archivo Municipal de Barcelona, Sección Judicial, Cartas Reales,
Oct.18, 1362 (published in López de Meneses, Documentos, no. 152, pp.
138-141), and C 702:194 (1361), which describe the building thus
employed as a "bordellum." (It appears to have been constructed
by the prostitutes themselves.) It was close to the monastery of
St Eulalia, and, upon complaint of the monks, the king ordered it
moved elsewhere. The attitude of the Aragonese monarchs was by no
means unusual: the English Crown had in its employ at one time a
Marshall of Prostitutes (see John Bellamy, Crime and Public Order
in England in the Later Middle Ages [London, 1973], p.60). The
precise attitude of the Aragonese populace toward the prostitutes is
difficult to ascertain. In Solsona in the fifteenth century they
were barred (along with Jews) from practicing agriculture or hus-
bandry, and were required to wear special clothing (Carreras y Candi,
"Ordinacions," XI, p.328), but there seems to have been no stigma
attached to the men who had recourse to them, provided that
they were not married. The king himself refers to their occupation
as a "malum propositum," and they are often styled "males fembres"
in the documents, but there is little sign of real antipathy or
opprobrium.

81. C 701:50 (1360). If the mercenaries were away, and the
prostitutes were Christian, they were to be moved out to another
place.

82. E.g., the documents above (note 81), and the efforts of James
I to prevent Muslims from associating with Christian prostitutes in
taverns: C 38:72 (quoted in Roca Traver, "Un Siglo," p.49, n.127).

Indeed, of the prostitutes officially registered with the
Maestre Racional of Valencia, the "majority were Muslim."[83]   Such
women had to register themselves to practice in a specific place,
designating it as either royal or noble, and could be captured and
sold as slaves for plying their trade in a locale for which they
were not registered.   This provision was apparently seen as burdensome by the women, since those of Peter Boyl (the General Bailiff
of Valencia) managed to obtain from the king a dispensation from
it:

> ...we therefore concede to you and your heirs, the
> lords [of Picasent], by way of special privilege, that des-
> pite any custom,practice, or law of the kingdom of Valencia or
> the law of the Saracens, any female Saracen inhabitants of the
> said place, or visitors to it, even if they have not been or
> caused themselves to be registered as prostitutes in royal pla-
> ces, may not be seized or confiscated for the royal treasury by
> us or our officials, even if they are found operating within
> [such officials'] districts, so long as they have had themselves
> registered as prostitutes in the said place of Picasent, regard-
> less of where they come from....[84]

Oddly, the penalty for operating as a prostitute without being
registered at all seems to have been only a fine--and a modest one
at that.[85]   There were also fines for plying the trade after the
curfew established for it.[86]   Owners of Muslims could not put them

---

Cf. the Christian prostitute who accused a Muslim of sleeping with
her, above, note 68.

83. See Roca Traver, "Un Siglo," p.47; cf. Piles Ros, Estudio, documents 9,10,12, and passim (all fifteenth-century documents).

84. C 905:176 (May 28, 1361), text in Appendix.

85. It was 50s: see RP 1706:18ss (1360), where it was collected from
Huceyt Ribaroja, "per ço com se deia aquella hauer comes crim de adulteri sens que no sera scrita per fembra publica."   On adulteri in this
context, see note 88, below.

86. RP 2911:35 (1355).

out as prostitutes or use them thus themselves, according to the laws of Valencia.[87] The extent to which such laws were honored is undeterminable.

Probably the most galling intervention of the Crown into the sexual mores of the Muslim population was its pretense to jurisdiction over cases of fornication and adultery between Muslims, which clearly lay under the jurisdiction of the qadi.[88] In only one recorded case of such activities during the decade 1355-65 was the qadi allowed to judge (and in this case only on appeal). In all others it was either the king himself who heard the case, or the lord of the place where it occurred.[89] Jurisdiction over cases of sexual liaisons between Muslims and Jews was also usurped by the Crown, and farmed out to favorites, who were encouraged to realize as much profit as possible from them:

> ...we hereby grant and concede to you, the said Martius, all rights which we do hold or might or should hold over Maria, a Jewess who had been a Muslim, both for her having recently

---

87. Furs, I.8.2: "Encara fem fur nou, que ningu qui haura serrahina no la tinga per putana sabuda, ne'n prengue soldada, e si ho fara, que la perda e sia a nos confiscada."

88. This was supposed to be so even in cases of adultery between Muslim women and Jewish or Christian males: "...sarracenis dicti regni concedimus cum presenti, quod si aliqua sarracena, habens coniugem seu maritum, cum aliquo chirstiano sive iudeo crimen commiserit adulterii, puniatur iuxta eorum çuna et pena inde sibi debita in peccunia nullatenus convertatur..." Aureum Opus, priv.8 of Peter IV, published in Roca Traver, "Un Siglo," p.67, n.205. In the fifteenth century the General Bailiff of Valencia specifically claimed the right to try cases of adultery between Muslims (Piles Ros, Estudio, p.145), and sometimes imposed stoning as the penalty, from which the Muslim could save him(her)self by paying an enormous fine, although this violated the provision quoted above. There is no distinction in the legal terminology of the day between adultery and fornication, and the researcher must be wary of this.

89. C 1070:74 (Nov.12, 1357).

abandoned the religion of perfidious Muhammad and embraced
the law of the Hebrews, and for the crime of adultery which
she is alleged to have committed with Jews while she was
still a Muslim, as well as for other crimes which she is said
to have committed. And we accord and allot you, the said Mar-
tius, full power and authority to settle with the said Muslim
on that sum of money which you shall best be able to agree
upon with her, and of keeping and using for your own purposes
everything which you shall be able to get from the said settlement..., as well as absolving and sentencing this Jewess for
the aforesaid and whatever other crimes may have been committed by her, just as if such absolution were accorded her by
us in writing....[90]

Pardon for adultery with another Saracen was common--for a sum--
even though the penalty for the act was confiscation.[91] Possibly
the king realized that actually enforcing the penalty of enslavement in a matter where he ought not to have exercised jurisdiction
at all would cause grave resentment among the Mudéjares. The only
penalty for Christians caught in adultery was a fine of about 100s.[92]

A similar disparity obtained in regard to fornication, for
which both Muslims might be fined, whereas Christians incurred no
penalty at all unless an injured party insisted.[93] The monarchy
seems to have displayed, moreover, a cavalier disregard for Muslim

---

90. C 899:60 (Aug.22, 1356), text in Appendix. Her conversion
was probably of little concern (note that she is called a "Jewess";
cf. concluding chapter). The real issue was the charge of adultery.
Note that this concession directly violates the one given by Peter
to the Muslims (note 88, above) in two ways: (1) the sarracena is
clearly not going to be judged according to the çuna, which required
the qadi to handle such cases, and (2) the penalty is to be a monetary one. Cf. the curious case cited by Verlinden, L'Esclavage, p.
535, where a Jewish father and son compete for the favors of a Muslim captive with apparent impunity.

91. For the penalty: C 1569:26 (1359), RP 1710:22 (1365); for pardons: C 1207:124 (1365), and possibly C 899:60, ut supra.

92. Fueros, VIII.306 (Tilander, p.179).

93. The fine was about 15s, depending on the evidence: C 898:222

marriage and morality in general: a Muslim woman who bought pardon for adultery was given permission to remarry, though her first husband was known to be living,[94] and the children of illegitimate u unions between Muslims were ordered to be hung--a startling provision from a Catholic monarchy.[95]

There were thousands of ways in which Christian officials could, if they wished, harass those Mudéjares under their jurisdiction. A few examples should suffice to demonstrate the sort of oppression Muslims suffered at their hands. In Valencia officials regularly fined Muslims for "offenses" which Christians could commit with impunity, or imposed enormously larger fines on Muslims than on Christians for the same crime.[96] In Aranda officials harassed and detained a widow trying to settle her husband's estate in Castile. Though their actions were technically within the law, the king himself admitted that they acted "more from malice than love for the king's laws."[97] In Calatayud, Seta, and Bartaxell Muslims were impressed into municipal service, without pay, and even forced to

---

(Apr.1, 1356). Cf. for Christians, Costums, IX.2a.5.

94. C 1207:124 (1365).

95. C 898:222 (1356): "...et filius sit horco..."; text in Appendix. But note that the king did honor Muslim polygamy, even in regard to the settling of estates: RP 1719:25 (1363).

96. RP 2911:9 (1355); cf. Chapter IV, above. Jews and Muslims were also more apt to be dunned for debts than Christians. In 1363 the king ordered Bernard Arlouin to cease prosecuting them for non-payment of a recent demanda which few citizens of any type were able to meet, but allowed him to retain all goods confiscated so far: C 1188: 65 (July 7).

97. C 691:95 (1357).

provide weapons and materials at their own expense--all in violation of existing law and custom in those locales.[98]   In Crevillente they were illegally forced to keep watch at night without pay, and forced by the Crown itself to work as archers at considerably less than standard pay, a large percentage of which was to be withheld "on account."   In fact, it was all withheld for many months, until the Muslims protested.[99]   The same Muslims of Crevillente had been storing their own grain in a building in their town, hoping to save enough to pay back a debt they owed the king's brother John, when Prince Ferdinand attempted to seize the grain for himself, offering the aljama a recompense much less than the market value of the grain (by the estimation of the Crown itself).[100]   This threat having been dealt with, the Muslims found the grain confiscated by the queen's procurator in the same year, on the grounds of its being needed for provisioning the castle.   There had been a plague of locusts in Valencia in 1358-9, and a period of general sterility, due possibly to drought, had preceded this plague for a period of three or four years.[101]   It was no doubt at great sacrifice that the aljama had managed to store its grain to repay their debt, and they were severely pressed when it was confiscated.   The queen offered to allow them to buy grain elsewhere, in defiance of war-time non-exportation laws, but, of course, they had no money to make such purchases.   Af-

---

98. C 983:150 (1359); C 1567:124 (1359).

99. C 1569:26, 29, 71 (1359-60); cf. Chapter IV.

100. "...minus pretio quam hodie valet vel de cetero valebit..." C 983:85 (Jan.21, 1359).

101. C 1567:124 (1359).

ter some hesitation, the queen decided to allow them to withdraw a certain amount of grain from the store, but specified that a sufficient supply be retained for the castle. This still could not meet the needs of the aljama, and when a number of Muslims, driven to desperation, broke in and stole the grain they needed, the queen relented and allowed a period of grace before the final confiscation, during which the Muslims holding grain in the silo could come and withdraw what they needed.[102]

Despite the general goodwill between the Muslim and Christian populations, private citizens as well as officials abused Mudéjares. Sometimes such abuses were obscene: in 1363 Peter had to order the Christians of Huesca to stop pasturing their swine in the Muslim graveyard of the city, since the pigs were exhuming the bodies; the Christians themselves, moreover, were to cease at once their practice of stealing gravestones from the cemetery at night.[103] In Calatayud, as has been noted, Christians simply occupied the homes of Muslims when theirs were destroyed, to the manifest detriment of the Mudéjares.[104] A group of Christians in Barbastro collaborated in robbing an inn where Faraig de Belvis was staying by actually boring

---

102. The account of this is in C 1569:26, 27, 70, 72. In 1361 the queen had to order the bailiff to release more of the grain, since the aljama had nothing to plant: C 1569:100.

103. "...continue de die faciunt esse et morari porchos suos intus ciminterium sive fossar que dicta aljama jure suo obtinet juxta dictam civitatem, quiquidem porchi multotiens circumfodiunt et dissepeliunt cadavera inibi cumulata..." C 1188:50 (Oct.7, 1363). Note that, curiously, the Christian officials of Zaragoza had been specifically instructed to prevent violence being done the Muslim cemetery of the city fifty years before by James II: C 860:6 (1314).

104. C 983:149 (1359).

through its walls.[105] An employee of the king in Borja took
possession of the kiln of a Muslim and made his living using it,
without compensating the Muslim in any way.[106]

A Muslim official of Crevillente was severely oppressed by
the queen's procurator, Domingo Lull, who tried to force him to
provide translations "en crestianesch" of all the account books
the Mudéjar was keeping (in Arabic) as tax collector of Elche
and Crevillente; he refused to give the Muslim receipts for amounts
remitted towards the taxes owed the queen; he extorted "advances"
from the collector on the sums to be paid the queen and then
refused to reimburse him or credit the aljama with the amounts;
and he seized 228 bushels of the aljama's grain for his own personal
use.[107]

Sometimes prominent Christians terrorized whole communities
of Muslims with acts of wanton violence and cruelty. The knight
En Francesch d'Alos and his sons wreaked such havoc on the aljama
of Jabút that the local Hospitallers finally felt constrained to
intercede with the king on behalf of the Mudéjares. They had in-

---

105. "...perforarunt quendam parietem qui est inter hospicium
Mahome Barbastri, ubi hospitabantur dicti Nicholaus et Guillelmus,et
[domum] Brahe de Mogen, sarraceni [ms. has "sarracenorum"] Montis-
soni, ubi hospitabatur Ffaraig de Bellvis, menescalcus [sic] domus
nostre, et per foramen quod fecerunt in dicto pariete intrarunt intus
domum dicti Brahe de Mogen, et ab ipso furtive abstraxerunt quasdam
vestes novas dicti Ffaraig panni lane de propre [sic], et cas secum
duxerunt..." C 711:194 (Mar.4, 1363).

106. C 692:205 (Sept.16, 1357). The kiln was located in a field
near the morería.

107. C 1569:75 (Dec.12, 1360). The king ordered restitution, but
no punishment for the procurator.

sulted Muslims viciously, struck them if they replied, beaten them without provocation, punished them for grooming their animals on holydays (while they did precisely the same themselves), beat and crippled a Muslim for pasturing animals on their lands, and one son even broke into the home of a female Muslim and raped her, causing her to move to another town.[108]

Many things of this kind probably happened to Christians as well, and most serfs in most European countries in the Middle Ages could have made the same complaints, or similar ones. But this is not the point. Many of the complaints that southern American blacks have made, or American Indians, or gay people, or women, could have been made as well by members of the very groups oppressing them. It is the cause of oppression which makes it intolerable. It is the fact that one is maltreated because of what one is, not because injustices randomly occur; it is the fact that one's oppressor does not feel responsible, considers he is committing no crime, perpetrating no outrage. In the case of fourteenth-century Aragonese Mudéjares nothing could make this clearer than the fact that in every single instance given in the preceding pages the Christian oppressor was let off absolutely free, paid no penalty whatever except--in a few cases--making restitution to the Muslims thus injured or maltreated. Any of these same crimes or excesses might have been committed against Christians, or by Muslims against other Muslims,[109] but in

---

108. C 705:68 (1361), text in Appendix.

109. Such things did, in fact, occur frequently, and always met with summary justice; e.g., C 683:126 (1356), where Muslims co-operate

either case justice would have been swift and certain by the time the case had reached the point necessary for it to appear in documents of the royal Chancery. Yet, as has been shown, not only did the monarch not punish the Christians guilty in these instances, but he often allowed them to keep the profits and proceeds of their crimes, reimbursing the Muslims out of the royal incomes to prevent their dissatisfaction from getting out of hand. Such a policy was hardly apt to be much of a deterrent to oppression of Mudéjares; in fact, such oppression appears to have grown steadily throughout the fourteenth century, requiring greater and greater royal efforts to contol it, and culminating in great pogroms in the 1390's. Already in 1366 the king found it necessary to issue a strong command to the Christian populace of Játiva to cease persecuting the aljama there. This document is particularly interesting, both for the royal attitudes it reveals and for the fact that it addresses itself to a problem which is recognized to be general rather than specific:

...since it pertains to the power of a prince[110] to fore-

---

with Christians in defrauding other Muslims; C 683:153 (1356), where Muslims harass other Muslims by bringing false charges against them which they must appear in court to refute; C 688:160 (1357), where a wealthy Muslim is murdered in an elaborate plot involving numerous other Mudéjares (text in Appendix); C 1569:73 (1360), where officials of the aljama of Crevillente defraud it. In each of these cases the guilty party is fined or otherwise severely punished. For injustices of Muslims to Jews, see C 687:189 (1356). There is one case of an injustice of a financial nature perpetrated against the aljama of Borja which elicited from the king a threat to imprison the "capitaneus Burgie" if he did not reimburse the aljama for certain goods he had seized, but again, this is not intended to be a punishment, or even retribution, but simple restitution: C 983:68 (1359).

110. Ms. has "princes" which I have altered to make the grammar of the rest of the sentence more comprehensible. I have felt obliged

stall future dangers to subjects and to defend the weak and
helpless from the powers of antagonists, so that through the
conscientiousness of his care he restrains from his crime the
potential evildoer, and rescues the oppressed from evil, and
since it behooves us to defend...the Saracens dwelling in our
cities, towns, and villages more than others residing within the
borders of our dominion..., partly because the yoke of an inferior[111] law burdens them, and more because they constitute a special royal treasure, we therefore, by virtue of this letter, re-
solutely and for all time establish, receive, and place under
our protection, care, security, and special safekeeping you,
the said aljama of the city of Játiva, and its members....

[We do so] for your greater safety, even though you...are
already under our general protection and safekeeping, because
we have determined with certainty that the Saracens of the Raval,
or morería, of the city of Játiva are very frequently ill-treated
by Christians, in regard to their persons as well as their goods,
and generally have greater cause to fear measures which are
specifically invoked or generally imposed.[112] Henceforth, no
one enjoying our grace or favor shall dare or presume...to attack,
seize, injure, detain, damage, pawn, confiscate, or otherwise
cause any harm, misfortune, injury or inconvenience or offense
to you or [your goods], either openly or secretly, in any way

---

to take many liberties in the translation of this document. The text
is unusually tortured, even by Chancery standards, with extremely
long periods and constant repetition of long, stock phrases, which
severely strain the reader's comprehension, even in English. I have
rearranged some of the clauses, to make their relationship clearer,
and have left out some of the repetitions of phrases, such as "you
the said aljama of the Saracens of the city of Játiva and its members, both those dwelling and residing within the Raval, or morería,
of the said city, and those who contribute in the taxes, tributes
and other duties of the said aljama, wherever they may be or dwell,
that is, all generally and each one singly, just as if they were
herein mentioned or designated by name, whether living or to come,
of whatever sex, rank, estate, or condition they may be, along with
their servants, male and female, and any other dependents, and all
and sundry of their goods, movable and real and living, goods and
merchandize either of their own or of their servants, etc., etc."
This phrase, which continues for another four or five clauses, has
been deleted from the sentence beginning "[We do so] for your...,"
the deletion here (as elsewhere) being indicated by ellipses.

111. The manuscript has "humilioris"; "humbler" is clearly inadequate. "More modest" is possible, but seems to jar with the much
more pejorative sense of "conditio gravat...."

112. I.e., laws aimed at the general populace are applied with
greater stringency to Muslims; see above, pp.174, 272, etc.

whatsoever or for whatever cause, fault, or crime committed
against or owed to others, unless such things have been settled
between you and them personally, or unless you or they are obli-
gated in such matters as principals or co-signers, and not even
in these cases except insofar as law, justice, and reason shall
permit....

Let him who would rashly presume to act in violation of this
protection, safeguard, and command know that he incurs [thereby]
our wrath and indignation, and a fine of fifty morabetíns of gold,
to be collected by our treasurer, without any appeal, plus full
and complete restitution for the injury caused.

...And lest anyone should be able to plead ignorance of this
our protection, safeguard, and order, we expressly enjoin upon
our officials and their subordinates that, at your request, or
that of your agent, they shall cause, if requested, our safe-
keeping, protection, and security...to be made known by public
crier according to the manner and form expressed above, which
is to be strictly adhered to....[113]

Fifty morabetíns (about 350s) was a steep fine, and the king appears

to have meant to see it enforced. Certainly the provisions of the

decree are as detailed as the Muslims could have wished them to

be without diminishing their applicability.

But this edict and others like it were doomed to fall very short

of their lofty aims. The tide had turned against the Mudéjares even

before Peter ascended the throne. The very nature, in fact, of the

Iberian symbiosis made oppression inevitable, because it was not

merely a convivencia of Muslims, Jews, and Christians, but of upper

and lower classes of each, of religious fanatics and cynical merce-

naries, of thieves and ascetics, of "public women" and cloistered

nuns. The Crown of Aragon itself was a tense union of disparate po-

litical elements, of peoples who spoke at least four different lan-

guages. Its power base was weak--never weaker than in the decades

following the revolt of the Union and the Black Plague, though con-

---

113. C 913:33 (Sept.16, 1366), text in Appendix.

temporaries did not recognize this--and it was threatened by enemies within and without the Iberian peninsula. Even if Peter had wished to restrain the oppression of the Mudéjares he could not have. But his own attitude was far from single-minded. The very reasons he adduced for the grant of safe-keeping to Játiva manifest this: a monarch, he realized, must watch over the well-being of all his subjects, but the Muslims especially required attention, not because they were a subject people mistrusted by the masses, not because they occupied a political position which rendered them peculiarly vulnerable to exploitation, not even because their unique contributions to Aragonese society deserved to be protected; the reasons were bald-faced and simple, and pregnant with unfortunate consequences for the Mudéjares: they were simply that they suffered under an "inferior" religion, and constituted a major source of revenue for the Crown ("a special royal treasure").

The conjunction of these two factors would in any society render a minority group's oppression inevitable. The mere conviction that a minority is in some way inferior constitutes oppression when it is held by a majority superior in numbers as well as power.[114] It is impossible--as modern minorities have discovered--to maintain psychological equilibrium in a society which affirms the wrongness of some aspect of one's being.

One might suppose that the great economic exploitability of the

---

114. At least as regards the kingdoms as a whole; in Aragon and Catalonia Muslims were a numerical minority; in Valencia a numerical majority, but a subject group. For population figures see the introduction.

Mudéjares would either increase or mitigate their suffering directly, but in fact this was not the case. The economic needs of the majority contributed to and directed certain forms of exploitation and abuse, but at the same time tempered and dampened the extent of oppression in general. In the long run, the extreme tension created by conflicting desires on the one hand to expel or forcibly convert the "infidels," and on the other to maintain them in an exploitable position, backfired on all concerned, with disastrous political, physical, and psychological consequences. Possibly the oppression of the Mudéjares would have been greater if they had not been economically indispensable, but the subtler, inexorable exploitation brought upon them by the ambivalent needs and desires of the Iberian Christians may well have caused more exquisite suffering than grosser forms of oppression could possibly have wrought.

On the other hand, the temptation to over-dramatize the plight of the Mudéjares is great, especially in an age of much social breast-beating, and when the religious beliefs underlying the intolerance of Iberian Christians are held in low esteem in many countries outside of Spain. It is particularly fortunate, therefore, that in the case of the Mudéjares a sort of "control" is available against the excesses of conscience of modern historiography. During the final years of the war with Castile, when the Castilians had overrun much of the kingdom of Valencia and undermined--through force or persuasion--the tenuous loyalty of many Muslim communities, the King of Aragon was forced to grant to these aljamas a great many concessions in order to win them back to his service. Some of these agreements, containing the demands, or "grievances" of the Mudéjares (and the responses of the monarchy), survive in the Chancery documents, and provide a fascinating glimpse into what the Muslims themselves saw as the major forms of oppression they suffered from king and nobles. Four such sets of demands by the Muslim aljamas are reproduced on the following pages (along with a comparable settlement from the fifteenth century as a point of comparison). It is worth remembering that, enlightening as these documents are, they are not necessarily any more accurate than the judgements of historians centuries removed from the reality: it would be naïve to imagine that the victims of persecution were the most objective judges of its nature, or that the members of a minority group were in the best position to assess their welfare as compared to that of the society as a whole. The comments of the Muslims are appropriate as the final comment on the subject in this chapter: they are not necessarily the last word on the subject.[115]

---

115. In addition to those settlements on the following pages, similar agreements were reached between the king and the aljamas of Vilamalur (sometime before March, 1365; no text survives, but see C 1209: 25); Fanzara (Dec., 1363), which regained "more privileges" not specified in extant documents (see C 909:75); Aranda (June, 1366), which regained its old privileges (C 912:191); Uxó (March, 1365), which obtained "favorable treatment" (C 1210:53); Almonacir and Almodexir (March, 1365), which got "favorable treatment" as well as absolution of war crimes (C 1211:32); Dues Aygues (March, 1365), which only obtained absolution from war crimes (C 1211:35); and Artana (March, 1365), which wrested from the king absolution for war crimes, a guarantee of the rights of çuna and xara, and a two-year remission of royal taxes and all military demands for the war (C 1205:34, 36, 37). Some of these agreements undoubtedly represent more than a return to the king's service: quite likely many of the aljamas are coming under direct royal jurisdiction for the first time, having been previously under noble control. This is implied in several of them, but stated in none, so I have avoided unwarranted inferences.

Demands of Muslim aljamas made as pre-conditions for their returning to the king's service. Responses of the king are indicated by the sign ¶; where no response is indicated it is to be understood that the king agreed to the condition. The numbering and divisions are the author's.

Eslida   March of 1365   C 1205:45

1. that the king reconfirm their royal charter

2. that he grant forgiveness and immunity from prosecution for all crimes committed to date, and remission of monetary fines thereunto appertaining

3. that hostages given to the King of Castile and now held in the castle of Eslida be returned without any charge

4. that they be allowed to chant the çala as before

5. that they be free of all debts to the king for three years, including the sisa (war tax)

6. that he reconfirm all previous privileges

7. that they not pay tithes or first-fruits
   ¶ so long as there is no debt outstanding

8. that they be given a copy of this document free of charge

9. that the absolution for war crimes comprise the Muslims of Bechí, Vall de Sego, Alfara, Altura, and Guayell, if they also return to the king's service

10. that the Muslims of Laurent be counted under the jurisdiction of Eslida and its qadi by virtue of this settlement

11. that they may not be separated from the Crown for any reason

12. that they may not be compelled to take water to the castle

N.B.: the Muslims of Xona were comprised under all the provisions of this document by virtue of an agreement between them and the king signed in the same month: C 1209:55.

Serra d'Espada, Vall d'Enveyo, Benicandut, Alcudia, Xenguer, Ayhi

March of 1365   C 1209:44

1. that they receive absolution for all war crimes

2. that their hostages held in the castle at Eslida be returned to them free and quit

3. that they be judged in all cases according to çuna and xara, and not by Fur or any other law

4. that all previous rights and privileges be granted them

5. that for four years they be excused from all exactions, and have free use of the ovens and mills, and not have to pay rent for their rented lands
   ¶ that they be excused for three years, like the Muslims of Eslida

6. that they be excused from all tax or tribute for four years
   ¶ they should be required to pay tax and tribute to none but the king for four years

7. that relatives outside their lands may inherit goods of deceased Mudéjares so long as they are subjects of the king, just as in the valley of Uxó

8. that they tithe their crops as before, under Peter de Exerica, and that the amin and jurats collect this along with the qadi, if there is one

9. that they not have to pay çofra to Eslida, nor service the castle there, nor be subject in any way to the qadi of Eslida, but that they be accounted as separate and independent of Eslida

10. that if the king wishes to construct a castle in the Serra d'Espada, they will contribute to that (rather than the one in Eslida)
    ¶ they must contribute to the repair of the castle of Eslida, since they take refuge in it, unless one should be built at Espada, in which case they would maintain that one

11. that any Muslim be able to sell his lands to whomever he wishes and depart to Muslim lands or wherever he might wish to go
    ¶ he must sell to a Muslim, and may leave if he pays what he owes the king

12. that the king remit debts owed by Veyo, Ayhi, Benicandut, Alfara, and Xenguer

13. that they have a copy of this document at no cost to them

Atzuena   March of 1365   C 1209:54

1. that the king pardon all war crimes to date, including the
looting of the castles of the Count of Prades and other nobles

2. that all outstanding debts to the Crown be forgiven

3. that the hostages given to the King of Castile be returned
from Segorbe and the castle (of Eslida?) without charge

4. that they be able to chant the çala as before

5. that they be excused from all royal exactions and the sisa
for three years

6. that the king reconfirm all rights and privileges previously
enjoyed by them

7. that they not pay the tithe or first-fruits

8. that they have copies of this document free of charge

9. that they not be required to provide water for the castle

Castro and Alfandequiella   April of 1365   C 1204:63*

1. that they be free of all exactions for five years
    ¶ they may be excused for three years

2. that they have all the privileges they formerly enjoyed under
Peter de Exerica

3. that they be free to follow the çuna

4. that no Christian be able to bear witness against a Muslim
    ¶ this may be as before

5. that no official be able to enter their lands, and that they
retain their merimperium

6. that they pay no more tithe or first-fruits than they did before

7. that they be able to chant the çala as they did before

8. that they not be held liable for more than ten barcelles† of wheat,
nor be constrained to pay agricultural taxes such as raims, garafes,
ortantes, etc.

9. that they may legally inherit property anywhere in the kingdom
of Aragon§ just as they did before the Castilian occupation

10. that any Muslim wishing to sell all he owns and emigrate to
Muslim countries shall owe the Crown only one-tenth the value of
the goods sold

11. that a Muslim who wishes to move elsewhere within the king's
dominion may do so without paying anything

12. that Muslims may collect all debts owed them from sales or
purchases anywhere in the kingdom, or from agreements signed with
persons who have since been seized or passed to Aragon (proper)

13. that pastures and land-holdings be as they were before

14. that all captives who changed sides be free, and that all
crimes committed under the rule of Castile be forgiven

---

* Text in Appendix.

† A barcella was a unit of dry measure equal to about 17 liters.

§ What is meant by this phrase is unclear: probably any land under
Peter's dominion is intended. Castro ·and Alfandequiella are in Valencia. Cf. number 12.

15. that neither Christians nor Jews be permitted to settle with them

16. that they not be required to pay a çofra to the castle or lord, and that the custom of Eslida be followed in the matter

17. that they not be required to make payments with hens or the like, but only in currency

18. that a public document of this agreement be executed at no charge to them

19. that they never be required to pay the sisa or cavallería
    ¶ they may be exempt for three years

20. that pasturage and public lands belong to the aljama, and that ovens and mills be free for five years

21. that no captive coming from other parts be questioned by anyone outside the domains of their lord, so long as he is not a subject of the lord (i.e., that they be able to offer sanctuary to runaways from other places)

22. that no one be taken captive without the testimony of a Muslim witness

23. that they be permitted to elect their amin

24. ¶ that they pay for the upkeep of the castle there

Alfajarín   March of 1446

1. (that they not pay, or that adjustments be made in, a series of agricultural taxes, most of them unknown to the Muslims of Valencia making the previous demands)

2. that they not pay any greater _çofra_ than one cord of wood per year

3. (further agricultural adjustments relating to vineyards and grain)

4. that they not be tortured when accused of crimes

5. that they not be convicted of sleeping with a Christian woman except on the testimony of at least two witnesses, one of whom must be a Muslim

6. that the estates of Muslims deceased without heirs and intestate revert to the aljama, with no part of them belonging to the lord

7. that the lord may constrain one or two Muslims to work for him anytime but June or July at the rate of 3s and two loaves of bread (for both) each day, or 16d and two loaves for one man

8. that the lord grant two plots of land free and quit of all dues to be used for the support of the mosque

9. that Muslims may sell or otherwise dispose of their lands as they wish to other vassals of their lord

Published in Macho y Ortega, "Condición Social," pp.241ss.

Note that this agreement was not made with the king, but with the lord of Alfajarín, Don Juan de la Mur.

Chapter VIII

Acculturation, Loyalty, and the War with Castile

> We must not admit, even for a moment, that intolerance and lack of understanding toward the conquered people which we have so often read about in some monographs (Roca Traver, "Un Siglo," p.12).

There can be little doubt, as the preceding chapters have demonstrated, that the general level of tolerance and co-operation among the disparate elements of Aragonese society in the fourteenth century was surprisingly high in view of the hostile religious attitudes of the era, and of the events which had resulted in the propinquity of the various Iberian ethnic groups. Muslims and Christians worked together, formed companies together, lived in close proximity with each other, had recourse to the same low life, even committed crimes together.[1] They operated joint "vigilante" groups to protect their cities and villages.[2] Christian nobles, farmers, and clergy allowed Mudéjares to use their lands and their homes to hide property subject to royal taxation.[3] Runaway Muslim slaves were protected and helped by Christians.[4] Christian religious orders interceded with the king for the well-being of Muslims mistreated by their lords and masters.[5] Christians regularly had recourse to Jewish and Muslim doctors and surgeons.[6] Members of all three religious groups borrowed and lent money to each other, and prominent Jews and Muslims advanced large

---

1. C 683:126 (Feb.24, 1356).
2. RP 2911:1 (1354-5).
3. C 701:32 (May 14, 1360); C 705:178 (July 22, 1361).
4. C 720:45 (Sept.4, 1365).
5. C 705:68 (January, 1361).
6. C 909:154 (July 11, 1364).

sums of cash to the Crown itself.[7]

The monarchy used Muslims as its most trusted servants, and showered them with favors. Muslims not personally in the king's employ also obtained his favors, and letters of commendation to Christian officials.[8]   Peter entered into treaties with Muslim rulers guaranteeing the safety and well being of his Mudéjar subjects,[9]   exempted Jews by royal decree from general inquisitions,[10] and tried (unsuccessfully) to get special tax relief for non-Christian subjects during the war levies of 1362.[11] At times, in fact, the Aragonese symbiosis seems almost utopian, as when the Christian king sends his personal Jewish physician to attend a favorite Muslim who has been wounded fighting in the king's service.[12] The uniqueness of this co-existence struck the Aragonese themselves: when French troops were passing through Lérida in 1365, the king ordered very special precautions   taken by local authorities so that the French, not used to the tolerance taken for granted by the Catalan populace, would not harm the large Jewish community there.[13]

It is, nonetheless, easy to exaggerate this rosy and appealing

---

7. E.g., C 986:48 (Sept.5, 1365), C 1210:84 (Apr.25, 1365).

8. An example of such a letter for a member of the royal household, Faraig de Belvis, is translated on p.46.   For others, see C 1149: 54 (Jan.12, 1357), and C 1573:29 (May 1, 1364).

9. C 1401:130 (Aug.20, 1355).

10. C 1494:21 (Nov.12, 1360).

11. C 907:204 (Sept.26, 1362).

12. C 683:240 (Aug.8, 1356).

13. C 1387:182 (Dec.18-19, 1365).

picture, to draw it a little larger than life, to omit certain
unsightly details which seem to mar its harmonious contours. Significant progress was made in Iberian human relations between the
time of the reconquista and the war between Aragon and Castile, as
a glance at the development of law in the country will show. In
the first redaction, for example, of what was to become the Fueros
of Aragon, Christians were forbidden to stand as witnesses for Muslims, because Muslims were "enemies of the Cross," "plotting day
and night to bring harm to Christians."[14] The final version of this
same law simply suggested that Jews and Muslims have at least one
witness of their own faith, since Christian witnesses would be unlikely to undergo an ordeal for a Muslim or Jewish defendant.[15]

The fact remains, however, that Iberian law codes consistently
referred to Islam as "paganismo," and frequently classed Muslims in
the category of "slaves, horses, mules, donkeys, cows, or other
animals";[16] that Muslims were excluded from any official position
in Christian government and severely disadvantaged before the law;
that Muslims and Christians both in city and country were officially

---

14. Ramos y Loscertales, "Recopilación," s.121: "...et certe numquam debet aliquis christianus testari pro mauro vel iudeo, tum quia
sunt inimici crucis Christi, per quam totus mundus saluatur et vite
salus reparatur, tum quia sunt proditores et die et noste cogitant
christianis fraudes multimodas laqueare, et contra quod maius est
numquam sompniant eis bonum."

15. Tilander, Fueros, s.107.

16. Ibid., p.160, and passim; Furs of Valencia, IX.17.9.

segregated both for the Muslims' protection and because they themselves did not wish Christians or Jews to live among them.[17]   In
fact, there was frequent and bitter acrimony between Muslims and
Jews as well as between both groups and Christians, so great in
some cases that the king had to intervene to protect one group
from general harassment by the other two.

> ...we have learned that numerous inhabitants of the city
> of Borja, Christian as well as Saracen, despise the Jews of
> [the city's] aljama, and seek to injure them, severally and
> singly, confiscating their property and committing other injust-
> ices against them with no justification for their actions....
> Wherefore we commend the said aljama and its members to your
> protection, guardianship, and defense....[18]

The Christian populace of Valencia was notably mistrustful of its
Mudéjar compatriots, and not only falsely accused them of selling
Christians to Granada, but induced the monarchy to curtail their
right to emigrate for fear of their betraying secrets to "the enemy."[19]

The king himself, moreover, exhibited considerable suspicion
of Valencian Mudéjares, and "fearing an uprising," asked the Governor
of Valencia to terminate subtly both their annual meetings and their
right to wander freely about seeking alms.[20]   Any unusual gathering

---

17. See Chapter II, pp.64ss; Chapter VII, p.368, n.15.

18. "...perpendimus [ut] aliqui habitatores ville Burgie tam Christiani quam sarraceni odio habentes judeos aljama ipsius ipsos et eorum singulares vilipendere conantur, pignorando et alias injusticias
nulla de causa pereuntes, ut fertur, eis faciendo.... Idcirco nos
in tuitione, presidio ac defensione vestra commendamus aljamam jam-
dictam et singulares de eadem..." C 691:166 (Jan.31, 1358). Cf. C
1566:106 (Jan.12, 1357).

19. C 1209:128 (June 3, 1365); C 1506:20 (Mar.22, 1363).

20. C 1068:134 (June 16, 1365); C 1075:71 (June 28, 1363); cf.
p.288.

of Mudéjares apparently aroused the suspicions of both the king and the populace: in 1362, during the war with Castile, a number of Muslims of Elche gathered their wives and children together in one place, and the monarch immediately dispatched an official to see "if there were too many Moors, and if so, to have as many as [he] should see fit forcibly removed."[21]

Peter, in fact, considered that Muslims "could not discern right from wrong," and that they were "burdened by the yoke of an inferior law"; he publicly addressed even the exalted Belvis family as "tu" rather than "vos," the customary form of address for adults with status.[22] Indeed, in the entire documentation for the period only one Mudéjar is addressed as "vos," and one has the impression this was due to the carelessness of the scribe.[23]

The picture seems even less rosy when one considers that these suspicions of the king and populace were not unfounded. Sometime prior to June of 1360 a Muslim named Cilim organized an uprising in València, inducing a "very large number of Mudéjares to commit... sedition and rebellion in the kingdom of Valencia against [his] royal majesty, and murder, rape, theft, assaults on towns..., highway robbery, and various other horrible crimes...."[24] An inquisition was

---

21. "Pregam que vos sapiats si en lo dit loch ha massa moros, e si ni ha massa, qu'en façats traure aquells que us sera semblant" C 1074: 130 (June 25, 1362). Cf. C 1075:71 (Jan.28, 1363), C 1075:111 (Apr.3, 1363).

22. "...malum a bono discernere nesciunt..." C 1071:173 (Jan.14, 1360); "...illos humilioris legis gravat condicio..." C 913:33 (Sept.16, 1366).

23. C 692:182 (Aug.18, 1357).

24. "...seditionem et rebellionem in regno Valentie contra nostram

begun in June on a small scale, with the principal aim apparently to make money for a proposed embassy to Granada,[25] but it gathered momentum throughout the summer months as local lords sought and received the right to try their own Mudéjares for complicity and to inflict such bodily punishment "that from it a horrifying example should remain forever."[26]   Once the needed money for the expedition had been collected, however, the king began to put a damper on the process against the Muslims, and in July and October effectively quashed it by reserving to himself personally jurisdiction in all royal areas (that is, in most of Valencia, since those areas not controlled by the king were mostly in the hands of Eleanor or Prince Ferdinand).[27] In May of 1361 the first of a long series of pardons and amnesties was granted to various aljamas "whether or not they were involved in the conspiracy," on condition that they pay court expenses to date, and in April of 1362 the issue was more or less laid to rest along with its initiator, Cilim, who was burned at the stake with his chief collaborators.[28]   Revolt in Valencia was not new: there had

regiam magestatem, ac homicidia, rapinias, et furta ac expugnationes locorum committendo, vim publicam et alia nonnulla enormia crimina..." C 907:74 (Apr.10, 1362).

25. C 1071:173 (June 14, 1360), C 1072:164 (Aug.30, 1360), and ibid., bis.

26. "...ut ipsarum penarum exemplum terribilem perpetuo relinqueritur..." C 1494:12 (July 10, 1360) and C 704:51 (July 7, 1360); cf. C 1072:162 (Aug.30, 1360).

27. C 1072:83 (July 11, 1360), C 904:183 (Oct.7, 1360), C 904:185 (Oct.3, 1360).

28. C 905:175 (May 28, 1361); cf. C 905:177 (May 28, 1361), and ibid., bis, C 905:181 (May 28, 1361), C 708:213 (Apr.6, 1362), and C 1073: 197 (Apr.16, 1362).

been several before, and another one took place in 1364.[29] There
is no indication in any of the documents that that of Cilim related
in any way to the war with Castile, and one is led to infer that it
resulted rather from more permanent tensions.

Converts provide an interesting focus for discussions of acculturation. Ramos y Loscertales advanced the opinion that the very
small number of Muslim converts to Christianity during the period
of Christian rule was proof that Mudéjares did not feel any need to
escape their hard lot as a religious minority, especially when compared to the frequency of conversions among Christians in Muslim
lands.[30] This is questionable in the extreme. There were, it is
true, very few converts from Islam to Christianity in the fourteenth
century, but it is far more likely that this was due to the Muslim's
fear of worsening his lot than his satisfaction with the status quo.
Although legislation forbade that any convert to Christianity suffer
loss of his goods as a consequence of his conversion, the same legislation declared his estate confiscated to the Crown after his death,
so that any Mudéjar who became a Christian did so to the manifest
detriment of his descendants.[31] Moreover, frequent efforts on the
part of the monarchy to curtail the harassment of converts imply

---

29. C 986:13 (Aug.23, 1365). Cf. Piles Ros, Estudio, p.299, #819.

30. Cautiverio, p.142.

31. From the laws conceded to Játiva in 1252, quoted by Roca Traver
("Un Siglo," p.34, n.82) from the unpublished work of Miguel Gual Camarena, Cartas pueblas del Reino de Valencia. This was to prevent the
Crown's losing the special prerogatives it enjoyed over Muslim real
property, as is implied in the law itself: "...et possimus eas [=her-
editates sarracenorum] dare sarracenis et non christianis." It was,
on the other hand, clearly in the interest of Muslim slaves to con-

that Mudéjares actually lowered their status in the eyes of Christians by abandoning their faith. In Valencia "numerous persons" were in the habit of "shouting out loud various harsh and injurious words of insult, whenever they felt like it, against those who... converted to the Catholic faith, and of calling them names such as 'dogs,' 'sons of bitches,' 'renegades.'"[32]

There is, in fact, only one documented case of a conversion to Christianity during the decade 1355-65, and this under duress of a sort,[33] whereas numerous instances of conversions from Islam to Judaism occur. This is the more remarkable in view of the fact that such conversions were punishable with death:

> It has been humbly brought to our attention on behalf of
> the Muslim aljamas of the kingdom of Valencia that Muslims are
> permitted by their law to put to death any Muslim or Muslims
> converted[34] to the Jewish faith, yet when it happens that some
> Moor or Mooress is converted to the said Jewish faith, numerous
> Christians nonetheless endeavor to defend the said converted
> Jews and to prevent justice being done to them according to
> their law, to the detriment of the Muslims, and in flagrant

---

vert: Verlinden, L'Esclavage, pp.425, 534; Piles Ros, Estudio, p.256.

32. "...contra illos qui...ad fidem catholicam se convertunt diversa gravia et enormia injuriarum verba ad libitum prorumpe clamando, et dicendo hec verba vel similia: 'canes,' 'filios canum,' 'retallats'" C 1176:8 (May 19, 1361). This was prohibited under a fine of about 700s, of which one-third was the king's and one third belonged to the parish in which the incident took place: a clear incentive to report such doings, and an indication of the king's sincerity. Cf. Tilander, Fueros, pp.160-1, where Christians are forbidden to call converts "tornadiço ni renegado ni otra semblant palaura."

33. See Chapter VII, p.348. C 695:155 (July 20, 1357) mentions the trial of Berengar de Apilia, who is described as "conversus habitator civitatis Valentie, filius Açan Abenxa, sarraceni menescalli civitatis prefate." If Abenxa = Abenxoa, this is an interesting note on the Muslim civil service aristocracy (see pp.43ss).

34. The Latin has perversos rather than the usual conversos: a concession to Mudéjar sentiment?

violation of their law. We, therefore, in response to the humble
entreaty made to us on their behalf, direct and command you that
whenever it should happen that a Moor or Mooress is converted
to the Jewish faith, you shall permit them to be judged and
punished totally by Muslim qadis, according to their law, without
mercy, financial compromise, or any sort of remission or interference whatever.[35]

In Catalonia this provision was enacted into law by the general Corts

as well.[36] The fact that Christian monarchs would acquiesce in the

execution of converts from Islam to Judaism implies several interest-

ing things. There must have been a large number of such converts to

evoke the demands from Muslim communities in the first place, and

this could imply--among other things--that conditions were on the

whole better for Jews than for Muslims.[37] On the other hand, the

fact that the king would favor the Muslim cause, as it were, against

the Jewish one, implies a rather stronger bargaining position for the

Mudéjares.[38] At the very least, the situation bespeaks a close

co-existence between the Muslim and Jewish communities of Aragon,

since the conversions were on the whole apparently the result of

---

35. C 862:121 (Jan.12,1337), in Appendix. Instead of "without mercy, financial compromise...," the text may mean "without benefit of
financial compromise."

36. Described in 1358 as "recently enacted" (C 691:232 [May 18,
1358]): "...iuxta quamdam constitutionem generalem Cathalonie dudum
in civitate Tarraçone editam sive factam, nullus sarracenus nec nulla
sarracena valeat seu presumat quovismodo ad legem judaycam se trans-
ferre, et si contrarium per aliquem sarracenum vel sarracenam fit,
quod incurrat ille talis penam corporis et bonorum...."

37. C 691:232, as above, C 690:31 (Aug.12, 1356), C 899:60 (Aug.
22, 1356), C 905:68 (Jan.4, 1361). Cf. Verlinden, L'Esclavage, p.
459.

38. Nonetheless, in the case cited at C 905:68 (above), the Jewish
aljama of Barcelona was pardoned by the king for having "persuaded"
a Muslim to convert to Judaism.

dialógue and conviction rather than ulterior motive.[39]

Names provide, if not an index of acculturation, at least an interesting comment on the degree to which Mudéjares became part of the Christian culture in which they lived. Christian names became increasingly common for Muslims throughout the fourteenth century. The aim was not necessarily to "pass" as Christian: Mahomat Alfoll kept his obviously Muslim first name while adopting a clearly Catalan surname, as did Mahoma Ballistarius, and Mahoma Tintorer. Some Muslims maintained two names, both of which appear in Christian records: "quidam sarracenus vocatus Lopello de Serrha, mahometi modo cognominatus Abraham"; others simply adopted wholly Christian names: Jassia Ferris, Garcia Gomez, Mateu Mercer, Joan Tandero.[40]

Two reasons suggest themselves for this phenomenon. The first is quite obvious. Christians had a great deal of trouble with Arabic names, as is evidenced not only by the inaccurate transcriptions of them into Chancery documents, but also by the uneasiness of lawmakers before what they considered the indistinguishability of Mudéjar appellations.[41] The second is that the Muslims themselves, at least in the North, appear to have been rapidly losing what little Arabic they

---

39. See note above. Verlinden cites a case of a Jew converting to Islam: L'Esclavage, p.536; Christians who did so could move to Muslim land with impunity: Roca Traver, "Un Siglo," p.30, n.72 (= C 39:162).

40. C 905:68 (Jan.4, 1361). Christian names became more common in the fifteenth century: see Piles Ros, Estudio, #s 116, 332, 333, 548, etc., and Macho y Ortega, "Condición," pp.197ss.

41. See Costums, VI.9.5. Note that the description of the oath Muslims were required to swear by is regularly so garbled in Christian law codes that (if at all recognizable) it would violate the conscience of a Muslim to repeat it: e.g., "Et mauro qui voluerit iurare ad christiano ei dicat, 'Alamin canzano et talat teleta" (Ramos y Loscertales,

knew in the fourteenth century. Muslim learning and literature evaporated from the kingdoms under the Crown of Aragon with surprising celerity once their sustaining patrons among the aristocracy had fled to "partes Barbarie" in the thirteenth century, and it is quite likely that most northern Mudéjares read little if any Arabic in the middle of the fourteenth century. In 1363 the king sent to Lérida for a translator for some Arabic documents, since he had "been given to understand that here in Lérida there is a Moor who can read and translate written Arabic."[42]

Merely finding a Mudéjar who knew how to read Arabic, however, was not the end of the king's problem, as a note from the translator of a letter sent to Peter's predecessor, Alfonso IV, by the Sultan of Damascus eloquently demonstrates. This note is written on the back of a Romance translation of the letter, in the same hand, which strikingly resembles Arabic script. Although the writer professes to have had trouble with the Arabic of the letter, his Romance is difficult and uneducated, and the letter as translated would not seem to have presented any unusual difficulties. An approximate translation of the note follows:

> This is translated from a letter from the Sultan of Damascus which was sent to the very noble king, Don Alfonso, by the Grace of God King of Aragon, of Valencia, of Sardinia, of Corsica, and Count of Barcelona.

"Fuero," p.37). It often states, in fact, something on the order of "by God than whom there are other Gods." See Tilander, pp.266-9.

42. C 1075:66 (Jan.19, 1363): "E haiam entes que aqui a Leyda ha i moro que sap liger e esplanar letra morisca." On the decline of learning in the post-crusade era, see Burns, Islam, pp.413ss.

The person who translated this letter says that no one
who saw it was able to say what this Arabic meant, ...but that
it is executed with great skill, in verses of enormous subtlety
of the type which is effected with Arabic grammar.

In many places he was not able to translate words, because
such words do not exist in Romance, or he had to translate the
meaning.

This is the translation which follows.

The most difficult part is when he speaks in the third
person.[43]

Due either to the Crown's inability to locate bi-lingual Mudé-

jares or to their inability when found to cope with formal Arabic,

Peter the Ceremonious generally relied on interpreters from the Mus-

lim kings themselves to read him letters from their masters ("...Abd

ar-Rahman ibn al-'Adwi wa Mus'ud, the interpreter, brought you this

letter and translated it for you word for word..."),[44] or had the

letters sent to him with a Romance translation by his ambassadors in

the country of origin: "Two copies were made of this treaty: one in

Arabic and one in Romance, both of which have been brought to you by

your emissary, the aforesaid Francesch Sacosta, so that you may exam-

---

43. The letter is dated March 23, 1330. The text is as follows:
"Este es translado de una carta del Ssoldan de Damasco que fue enbi-
ada al muy noble Rey, Don Alfonsso, por la gracia de Dios Rey d'Aragon, de Valencia, de Çardena, de Corçego, Comte Barchilona. Dize el
que traslado esta carta, non sse cuyde niguno que viese esta carta
que es de entendeder este arauigu della segundo la lengua espeçial,
ante es fecha a gran maestria por viesos vesifagados de gran sotele-
za, del que la fizo en la gramateca del arauigo. En muchos logares
non se pudo trasladar los viervos, ca non auie tales viervos en el
romançe, o ve de tarasladar la entiçion. Este es el trasladu que sse
ssigue. Lo mas es como quan ffabla a terçera persona."

44. واب عبد الرحمن بن محمد العدوى ومسعود الترجمان اوصلاه اليك والقيا لك ما القى اليهما من الكلام.
وذكرت . M. Alarcón Santón and R. García Linares, Los documentos árabes
diplomáticos del Archivo de la Corona de Aragón (Madrid-Granada, 1940),
p.197. This document is incorrectly dated by Alarcón: the Arabic date,
the 29th of rajah, is the equivalent of Oct.2, not Sept.14, during the
Muslim year 751 (= A.D. 1350). Translators were often loaded with gifts
by the grateful suzerain: González Hurtebise, Libros, p.371 (1666-9).

ine and understand what is written in them."[45]

In the South the problem was the reverse: Mudéjares knew and wrote Arabic but did not know Romance, and official translators were required in each town to execute documents and interpret royal edicts. Christians, Muslims, and Jews were all employed in this capacity, and Muslim translators even accompanied tax officials.[46] The king occasionally relied on these minor officials for royal business, but does not seem to have had recourse to them for diplomatic documents.[47]

The Iberian symbiosis may have been beautifully woven of human tolerance and interdependence, but it was not one of those webs whose symmetrical patterns is readily visible, nor whose regular and harmonious spacing charms the eye. Incredibly complex, overlaid again and again with criss-crossed and tangled patterns, it was held in place more by the tension of its weaving than the genius of its arrangement. In the South the vast majority of the Mudéjares did not speak the language of the dominant culture. They were viewed with suspicion by their Christian neighbors, and not without justification, since they were given to revolts, and clamored for the privilege of

---

45. وكتب من هذا الصلح نسختان احداهم بالخط العربى والثانية بالخط العجمى وحملها اليك رسولك فرنسيس
سكوسطة المذكور لتقف عليهما وتعلم ما ارتسم فيهما. Alarcón Santón, *Documentos*, p.324. Alarcón has misread the date of this document as the twenty-ninth of Jumâda, although the Arabic clearly says the twenty-seventh. It should therefore be dated May 15, 1360, rather than March 18, as is given in the text.

46. See p.74, n.41, and pp.94-5, n.116. Cf. the case of the Fuster property in RP 1708:18ss (1362), where a Christian was paid 1s to translate Arabic wills into Romance.

47. But see C 1401:78 (May 19, 1355).

emigrating to Muslim lands. Yet they were the backbone of the society there, manufacturing its goods, constructing its buildings, producing its foodstuffs, even fighting its wars. In the North, the majority of Muslims spoke poor Romance but could not·read Arabic at all. They were far less disaffected, and emigrated in a slow, albeit steady trickle. Although less crucial in many areas, they were nonetheless visibly necessary to the Christian economy, and in great demand, especially as artisans and skilled laborers. Somewhat better trusted than their southern brethren, they were subject to the same exploitation and oppression, often denied basic civil rights, and viewed by the monarchy largely as children incapable of regulating their own lives.

Across this complex and tangled web cut, beginning in 1355, the broad, blunt sword of the war with Castile, a war fought mostly within the lands of the Crown of Aragon and at huge cost to the inhabitants of those lands. The remainder of this chapter will attempt to discover how much of the web remained after the sword had passed through it.

The economic effects of the war on the Crown's lands as a whole were devastating. The Aragonese florin, already devalued in 1352, was devalued again in 1362 and once more in 1365, only three years later.[48] Salaries rose drastically in Valencia from 1351 to 1370, owing to the extreme shortage of manpower occasioned by the combina-

---

48. Hamilton, Money, pp.13-14; cf. p.86.

tion of the plague and the war with Castile.[49] The price index for
Aragon, after falling steadily from 1326 to 1350, had approximately
doubled by the mid-point of the war, only ten years later, and continued to rise, doubling again in the following decade, after which it
began to drop.[50] The suffering of the citizens was staggering. Only
two years after the outbreak of hostilities the population of Borja
was practically destitute.[51] By the early sixties practically all
of Valencia west of Játiva was destitute and depopulated. Taxes
could not be collected, and lords and masters of formerly prosperous
lands were trying desperately to attract new serfs and farmers to
populate their empty property, abandoned by ruined peasants: "all of
their things were burned, and they were all totally undone by the
war, because they had to sell the land they lived on and take refuge
in the mountains...."[52] Countless individuals lost all they had,
and many had to flee when their farms, their villages, or even major
cities were occupied and destroyed.[53] Mudéjares fled in such numbers,
and those who remained were so ruined, that the aljama of Valencia,
once one of the major sources of wealth for the Crown, could not raise

---

49. Hamilton, Money, pp.68-9. Hamilton does not list either the
war or the plague as causes of this increase.

50. Ibid., p.190.

51. C 1381:33 (June 21, 1357).

52. "...totes les coses lurs son cremades, e ells tots deffcyto per
raho de la guerra, car hagueren a desemperar les alquaries on estauen
e pujar en la serra..." C 1209:44 (Mar.14, 1365). Cf. C 983:85 (Jan.
21, 1359), C 1569:102 (July 6, 1361), C 1569:134 (Mar.28, 1362).

53. E.g., C 1197:19 (Feb.26, 1364), C 715:50 (Oct.13, 1363). Both
of these incidents involved Mudéjar families.

100 sueldos in 1365 to pay the salary of its treasurer, and the
aljama of Játiva, the wealthiest under the Crown of Aragon, could
not pay any of its taxes in 1366, all of which had to be remitted
by the Crown.[54]

Far-reaching and almost inevitably disaffecting changes in
Mudéjar life-styles and economic position were occasioned by the
war. Numerous Muslims previously exempt from royal exactions
were made liable to royal taxes for the first time during the war
with Castile, even some of those personally serving in the king's
army.[55] Huge amounts of property passed out of Muslim hands, thus
reducing the tax base of the aljamas; new laws were passed by the
Crown limiting the sale of property by Mudéjares.[56] The financial
affairs of some aljamas, most notably that of Zaragoza, passed out
of their control altogether.[57] The export of grain from one town
to another was prohibited.[58] Muslims were forced to spend the small
amount of cash they had in fortifying sections of the aljama or city.[59]
In almost all of Valencia the crops were either burned or trampled,
and Muslims were sometimes forced to burn their own fields; they
were in any case prevented from planting in much of the realm by

---

54. C 1209:125 (May 29, 1365), C 910:120 (Sept.16, 1366).

55. E.g., C 688:91, 908:79 and 84, 1183:158, all discussed above,
in Chapter V.   Ballistarius was serving in the king's army
during the dispute discussed on p.214.

56. C 712:117 (Feb.18, 1363), C 723:158 (Dec.20, 1365), C 1206:44
(Aug.20, 1365), C 1573:127, 128 (May 6, 1365).

57. C 968:56 (Dec.10, 1362).

58. C 714:165 (Nov.15, 1363).

59. E.g., C 1566:115 (Mar.3, 1357).

open warfare.[60] Huge numbers of necessary facilities were bricked
up, burned, or razed, often leaving Muslims with no mills or granaries for years after the war.[61] Yet during this period most aljamas were forced to pay their officials' salaries at pre-war rates
or higher, and many did not receive exemptions or remissions of
royal taxes.[62]

Of course, as has been pointed out previously, the Crown was
on the whole indulgent about collecting taxes from impoverished Muslim communities, and it cannot be denied that some Mudéjares made
money out of the war. Many Valencian Muslims sold the Crown goods and
products needed for the war effort,[63] and in Aragon the much needed
laborers in war-related projects received double benefits: not only
were their salaries increased with the demand, but, to get them to
work, they were paid back wages which were owed them by the Crown:

> Since we have urgent need of the machine-makers Garcia,
> Mahoma, and Garcia Gómez, for making machines and other
> devices in Tarazona, we direct and expressly command you to
> pay them immediately, out of whatever fund of ours [are at
> hand], whatever is still owed them of the 500s which we
> ordered paid to them in another letter by way of salary....[64]

---

60. C 1204:127 (May 4, 1365), C 1209:87 (May 4, 1365), C 1209:68
(Apr.8, 1365), C 1573:148 (June 28, 1365), C 912:167 (June 5, 1366),
C 694:208 (Sept.20, 1358).

61. C 1569:118 (Sept.10, 1361), C 1569:145 (Aug.17, 1362).

62. C 966:96 (Feb.10, 1357) specifies that morería officials' salaries
should not be reduced because of the war. On taxes, see C 1569:20 (Oct.
1, 1359), where the queen declines to remit taxes owed by the desperate
aljama of Elche; but cf. C 1569:25 (Oct.17, 1359), where she remits
a different tax to the same aljama.

63. Especially cloth: RP 1710:47, 48 (1365).

64. "Quia Garciam et Mahomam et Garciam Gomecii, magistros machina-
rum, pro faciendis machinis et aliis artificibus in civitate Tirasone

Much of the property confiscated from Jews and Muslims suspected of collaborating with the enemy was returned to Muslim hands, and many Muslim communities co-operating in the war effort were given or lent supplies, animals, and even cash.[65]

The changes in Mudéjar lives were not, of course, wholly economic. As in any war, there were widows, orphans, wounded and maimed. Homes were destroyed, factories, livelihoods. Meat markets were torn down or burned, precipitating a moral crisis for Muslims with no access to approved meat.[66] Many officials were summarily relieved of their positions when military commanders were appointed to govern cities or countrysides.[67] The pace of enslavement of Mudéjares—both legal and illegal—quickened, and under the smoke-screen of the war went largely unchecked.[68] Muslims suffered a considerable decrease in their personal mobility: royal Mudéjares were prohibited from exercising their traditional right to move to other domains,[69] those who moved out of towns out of fear of the war were ordered to move back in,[70] and the right to wander about

---

festine necessarios habemus, ideo vobis dicimus et expresse mandamus quatenus incontinenti de quacumque peccunia nostra solvatis eis quicquid eis restet ad solvendum ex illis quingentis solidis barchinonensibus quos ipsis cum alia littera nostra dari providimus pro eorum salario..." C 1170:160 (May 9, 1360).

65. Property: C 903:290 (May 7, 1360), C 909:74 (Dec.11, 1363); animals: C 718:87 (Nov.30, 1364); cash: RP 1711:29 (1366).

66. E.g., C 1571:89 (Feb.4, 1363).

67. C 1569:108 (Aug.15, 1361).

68. See C 986:90 (Oct.4, 1365), in Appendix.

69. C 1569:40 (Jan.18, 1360).

70. C 905:234 (1361).

begging alms was effectively terminated.[71] Many ancient privileges
were abridged or ended, such as the right of the Muslims and Jews
of Daroca to be taxed only in the presence of the bailiff; towns
which surrendered to the King of Castile lost all their privileges,
including, of course, any which had been promised them by him.[72]
Many Mudéjares changed jurisdiction as a consequence of the war:
the Jews and Muslims of Ejea were removed from the jurisdiction of
the Vice-governor of Aragon and placed under the supervision of
Luppus de Gurrea, a knight; the Muslim aljama of Almonazir was
removed from the jurisdiction of Segorbe and made independent;
Mudéjares who moved into the city of Játiva out of fear of the war
in the countryside found themselves the object of long and bitter
jurisdictional disputes between the city and the aljama.[73] Some
of these changes represented the desire of the Mudéjares themselves:
of the many aljamas coming under the control of the queen as a result
of the war, at least one, Eslida, did so at the request of the Muslim
population itself.[74] Others, such as that of Vilafalig, were shuffled
around from lord to lord at the whim of the monarchy and the Christian
aristocracy.[75]

    There were, of course, gains as well, many of which have been

---

71. C 1075:71 (Jan.28, 1363).

72. C 699:220 (Apr.23, 1360); C 1536:80 (Sept.16, 1366); C 912:191
(June 18, 1366); C 1572:63 (Oct.15, 1366).

73. C 713:58 (Aug.25, 1362), C 1205:69 (Apr.7, 1365), C 1206:151
(Oct.15, 1365).

74. C 1205:60 (Mar.31, 1365).

75. C 1205:8 (Dec.28, 1365).

pointed out in preceding chapters. Many communities, especially
in Valencia, wrung from the desperate Crown concessions which they
could never have obtained under normal conditions: tax reductions,
changes in feudal duties, guarantees of religious rights, concessions
of merimperium, pardons for crimes, amnesties from fines, intervention
against noble abuse and exploitation.

The question is, were such concessions and favors necessary to
maintain the loyalty of the Mudéjar population, and if so, why?
Did they work? Unlike many questions involving Muslim-Christian
relations, the answers to these are relatively simple, albeit gener-
alized. The bare facts are eloquent, although they do not reveal
the whole story. In the North, only one aljama defected to Castile,
and rather few individuals. The aljama was that of Torellas, located
quite near Tarazona. It had been captured along with the city in
1357, when the Castilians overran the area. Peter had been so enraged
at the surrender of the city that he slew the messengers who brought
him the news. The aljama returned to the king's service even before
the Christian populace, and the Crown's anger does not appear directed
at all towards the Mudéjares, who could hardly have held out when the
well-fortified city could not.[76]

In Valencia, on the other hand, the case was quite different.
Beginning in 1363, defections by Mudéjar communities and individuals
snowballed into staggering proportions. Between that year and 1365

---

76. C 1175:186 (Feb.4, 1360) contains the king's offer to the Muslims; the Christians did not surrender till the twenty-third of the
month.

all or most of the Muslims either abandoned or surrendered to Castile
the aljamas of Bechí, Chelva, Fanzara, Muntroy, Dues Aygues, Serra,
Eslida, Artana, Castro, Valldigna, Alfandequiella, Benalguazir, Elche,
Segorbe, Ondara, Verger, Real, Beniharb, Eig, Miraflor, Pamies, Vinyals,
Espada, Enveyó, Benicandut, Alcudia, Xenguer, Ayhi, and Atzuena. Of
course, it would be rash to assume that mere disaffection was the
overriding factor in each of these cases. Both monarchs made constant
efforts to entice the other's vassals, Christian and Muslim, over
to their side. In many cases aljamas were simply conquered by superi-
or force, and in others they faced specific threats or vague fears
which inspired them with sufficient dread to surrender. In a few
cases, in fact, they may not have collaborated at all, but only annoyed
the Crown by not resisting "to the death," as he commanded the Mudéjares of Artana to do if Castilian forces should try to retake the
town after he regained it.[77] The fact that property which belonged
to Muslims or Jews merely "suspected" of disloyalty was regularly
granted away as if the case were definitely settled suggests a certain rashness of judgement on the part of the Crown in the matter.[78]

But such a massive scale of defection cannot be adequately
explained in this way. In the first place, the effect of enticement
worked both ways, and the Muslims attracted to Aragon came from Castile in groups of two or three individuals, not by the score of

---

77. "...mortem ultronei subeatis..." C 1205:35 (Mar.1, 1365).

78. "...in casu quo dictus iudeus nunc sit nobis rebellis et vasallus regis Castelle..." C 903:290 (May 7, 1360).

towns.[79] The element of fear also worked both ways: many aljamas

whose loyalty the Crown doubted were threatened with confiscation

and enslavement in the early years of the war (and the threat was

carried out),[80] and, when this failed of its effect, the Crown

began taking hostages from important aljamas to ensure their loyal-

ty.[81] Moreover, in the vast majority of cases the king was still

negotiating for the return of the Muslims to his service long after

the Castilians had left the area. In some instances the entire

aljama had even moved to Castile, and the king had to persuade them

to move back to Aragon.[82] Perhaps the most telling fact is that in

none of the cases recorded did the Christian population of Valencia

defect along with the Muslims; in one or two places the Christians

were occupied and surrendered, but no Christian population had to

be wooed back to the king's service as did the Mudéjar groups listed

on the previous page.[83]

What prompted so many communities to abandon the Crown of Aragon,

and why did they return to its service after doing so? To understand

this properly, it is essential to bear in mind the history of the

area, and the nature of its social structure. No doubt the lower

---

79. See C 912:166 (May 27, 1366), C 1189:224 (July 23, 1363).

80. C 1385:148 (Sept.5, 1363); cf. C 986:93 and C 1207:145, discussed
in Chapter I, p. 40.

81. See Chapter VII, pp.335ss.

82. E.g., the case of Benalguazir, C 1206:146 (Oct.7, 1365). Note
that the letter is addressed to the faqi, who had defected with the
rest of the aljama.

83. The king bitterly remarks on this in several places, e.g., in
C 986:93 (see note 80, above) and C 720:77 (Aug.30, 1365).

classes of Muslims living in Valencia under the Crown of Aragon were
disaffected and alienated. They doubtless felt little attachment
to the Crown itself, and probably even less to its "causes," especially
when these causes involved the destruction of their homes and crops.
They most likely entertained only little more affection for their
immediate rulers (except in a few cases), and viewed their Christian
compatriots with cool indifference, if not suppressed hostility.
Wholesale disloyalty under the circumstances was hardly surprising.
But what is crucial here is that wholesale disloyalty was a tradition in Muslim Spain. It was not a question of Muslim vs. Christian,
of Mudéjar vs. Conquistador, or even of Aragon vs. Castile. From the
time of the Muslim conquest of Spain in the eighth century there had
been massive disloyalty, wholesale defections, and self-interested
and shifting patterns of loyalty among both the Christian and Muslim
populations of the area. The ancestors of Peter's Mudéjar subjects
had shown no less alacrity in abandoning one Muslim lord for another
in the twelfth century, or a Muslim for a Christian in the thirteenth.
They were not assimilated, it is true, but they had never been assimilated, and there is no reason to believe that they resented unintelli-
gible, Romance-speaking overlords any more (or less) than unintelli-
gible Berber ones.

Nor, however, should their return to Peter's service be taken as
more than it really indicates. It is true that Peter offered the
rebellious Muslims new privileges, amnesties, pardons, tax advantages,
and various other royal favors to attract them back, but it is highly
unlikely that these achieved the desired end. What in fact brought

the majority of aljamas back under the Crown of Aragon was the extraordinary effort put forward to achieve this by Muslim leaders. Despite
the many privileges offered the Moors of Fanzara, for instance, as incentive to return to their previous loyalty--privileges which included
all those formerly enjoyed under Peter of Exerica, as well as "greater
and better ones"[84]--it was, in fact, the personal efforts of the _amin_
of Eslida which effected their return, and not the offers of the
Crown.[85] It was two _amins_ of Segorbe who effected the capitulation
of the city's Muslim population, the _amin_ of Millars who persuaded
the aljamas of Muntroy and Dues Aygues to surrender, two Mudéjares
of Cunyega and Artana who achieved the submission of Eslida, and the
amin of Eslida who got his Mudéjar brethren in Serra to give in to
the blandishments of the king.[86] The list could be expanded to cover
very nearly every rebellious aljama.

In most cases such Muslim notables were specifically deputed to
their roles as mediators for the king, and granted by him full power to
arrange any sort of settlement they might wish:

> We wish you to know that we are sending to you Ali Xarra,
> a Moor from Artana, regarding certain affairs of yours and ours,
> and that [he is] fully informed of our desires. We therefore
> implore you to accept whatever he may tell you on our behalf and
> to comply with it fully, because we promise you on our royal honor
> that everything the said Ali may promise you in our name we will

---

84. "...sed etiam aliis majoribus et melioribus..." C 909:75 (Dec.11,
1363).

85. C 1209:56 (Mar.20, 1365).

86. C 720:77 (Aug.30, 1365), C 1197:129 (May 6, 1364), C 1211:36 (Mar.
24, 1365), C 1209:57 (Mar.29, 1365), C 1205:37 (Mar.1, 1365), C 1211:
26 (Mar.21, 1365), and see note 87, below.

fulfill and be bound by without any exception.[87]

It is tempting to imagine a class of loyal servants of the king acting from pure devotion to bring back their recalcitrant and ungrateful compatriots from their treachery, and some of these emissaries may have been doing just that. The majority, however, were clearly following another Iberian tradition, one embodied in such heroes as the Cid and kept alive by the great Granadan and Catalan mercenary companies who served whichever king made them the most attractive offer: the tradition of self-interest. In return for their efforts, the amins and others who so persuasively enticed their Muslim brethren back into Peter's service were granted property, fields, houses, orchards, exemption from all royal taxes, rights over mills and granaries, and high positions in aljama governments.[88] Even this might not evoke too much cynicism about their own loyalty to the Crown, if it were not for the fact that the single most common reward granted to the Mudéjar negotiators was the right to emigrate to Muslim lands without royal interference of any kind. In fact, this privilege, granted to the recipient and his family, was frequently conceded along with a morería position, such as the alcadia of some

---

87. "Ffemos vos saber que nos enbiamos Ali Xarra, moro d'Artana, sobre algunos aferes nostros e vostros, de la nostra entencion plenament enformado. Por que us rogamos que lo creades de lo que us dira de part nostra, e aquello cumplades pro obra. Por que vos prometemos en nostra buena fe real que todo lo qu'el dito Ali vos prometra de part nostra, aquello cumpliremos e tendremos sin falta alguna" C 1210:52 (Mar.17, 1365).

88. E.g., C 720:77, C 1205:37, C 1205:41, C 1209:56, C 1211:36, C 1573:127, C 1573:128 (long series of such grants here). All are from 1365.

aljama, implying that the Moor would hold the position for a certain number of years and then retire, as it were, to an Islamic country[89]-- almost like British civil servants going home to England after years in India. (Most such British retirees, however, had not been born in India.)

Indeed, a certain cynicism seems to have pervaded the actions and attitudes of all sides during the period in question. After being promised "on the royal honor" that they would not be taxed for the war with Castile if they returned to the king's service, the Muslims of Fanzara quickly found themselves being dunned by royal tax collec- tors for 2,000s worth of back war taxes, and complained vehemently to the king. Although Peter acceded to their demands and instructed the officials not to force them to pay, his motivation was notably unrelated to any questions of justice or "royal honor": "This might be most disadvantageous to our interests," he observed coldly, "since the men in other places which the King of Castile has seized from us, and who have decided to return to our service, could draw an example from this, and it could be that we would lose such places."[90]

Of course, one must bear in mind that Christians, too, defected to Castile, albeit in vastly smaller numbers, that it was not uncommon

---

89. E.g., C 1209:56 (Mar.20, 1365), to a Muslim of Fanzara; C 1209: 64 (Mar.12, 1365), to the former faqi of Eslida, who became thereby its qadi, and received at the same time the right to emigrate.

90. "...de aço se puxa seguir gran dampnatge a nostres afers, car los homens dels altres lochs qu'el Rey de Castella nos ha occupats e han voluntat de tornar a la nostra senyoria ne porien pendre exempli e poria esser qu'en podriem [sic: sc. 'perdriem'] los dits lochs" C 1209:50 (Mar.18, 1365).

for medieval monarchs to find flagging loyalty among any type of
subject during long and costly wars, that in the North many individual Muslims and even some whole communities served the king with
loyalty and enthusiasm, and that the Crown itself, although not
single-minded about it, was probably sincerely grateful to those
Muslims to whom it granted rewards after the war was over.[91]
Indeed, that convivencia based on mutual acceptance and supra-
ethnic loyalty which so many Iberian scholars seem determined to find
in their medieval heritage may actually have existed--to a degree--
in Aragon and Catalonia, where Mudéjares were so acculturated that
they could not have survived in a more Islamic environment and
almost had to concern themselves with the welfare of the monarch
who protected them. Emigration for them was not a realistic alternative, since they probably knew a poor Arabic, if any at all, and
since they had become so thoroughly enmeshed in the Mudéjar culture
of Aragon that they could have left it only by abandoning all that
was familiar for new and alien surroundings and a culture almost
wholly unknown to them. Both the small number of émigrés from northern lands and the general loyalty of Aragonese and Catalan Mudéjares
during the severe crisis of the war with Castile are testimony to the
general success of Catalan-Aragonese convivencia, as are the superior
organization of Aragonese and Catalan aljamas, the generally fairer

---

91. Many Christians left royal territory during the war in Sardinia
to avoid military service, and Muslims and Jews took their places:
C 980:95 (1355). For an example of voluntary loyalty in Aragon, see
C 1379:93 (Dec.24, 1356). Even in Valencia, some Muslims returned
without royal promises or friendly persuasion, sometimes despite stiff
fines facing them on their return (for abandoning their homes in de-

attitude of the Crown to northern Muslims in such matters as honoring
agreements and safeguarding their (limited) independence within the
morería, and their slightly more advantaged position before the law
in regards to mobility, dress codes, etc.

In Valencia the word convivencia must be understood in a more
mechanical sense. Muslims, Jews, and Christians all lived in close
proximity and engaged in the same activities in all areas of life.
Mudéjares enjoyed many rights, grew prosperous, and were indispensable to the welfare of the realm. That real cultural interaction,
however, which smaller numbers, longer years, and a more stable social
matrix had made both possible and necessary for Aragonese Mudéjares,
was wanting in Valencia. Here Christians harbored deep suspicions
of Mudéjares, and the Muslims in turn resented the Christians who
ruled them. Muslims sought to leave the kingdom both legally and
illegally, and those with wealth or influence generally managed to
do so. Few, if any, prominent Valencian Muslims became part of the
civil service élite exemplified by Aragonese families such as the
Belvis. Instead, they found outlets for their energies either in
their own private lives and communities or in revolting against or
abandoning the dominant Christian society. They spoke little if any
Romance, and came into contact with the Crown which ruled them through
the office of translators, often Christian or Jewish. As a consequence

---

fiance of royal edict): see RP 1709:19 (1364), where two Muslims of
Alcocer pay 200s for such a fine. More frequently, however, such
fines were remitted, e.g., C 1205:69 (Apr.5, 1365), and C 1210:95
(May 23, 1365).

of all this, they had little or no loyalty to the society of which
they were part, or to the monarchy which ruled it, and when called
upon to support either one in a time of internal crisis either
refused or used the opportunity to wrest power and concessions from
those who needed their aid. Compared to the sort of co-operation
and cultural absorption visible among Mudéjares in Aragon, co-existence between the ethnic groups in Valencia was simply that: co-existence. It was characterized by the physical proximity of the groups,
and the absence of conflict, but little more. Perhaps this was
enough for a society used to internal strife and instability; perhaps the mere absence of conflict constituted a sort of miracle
on soil fertilized with blood shed over the names of prophets and
gods; perhaps Peter was not so dismayed as one might suppose by
the wholesale defection of his Muslim subjects. But if so, that
word so favored by writers on the subject--convivencia--must be
applied with extreme caution, for its implications, however vague,
go far beyond the tense stalemate which prevailed in the sunny
realm of Valencia.

Conclusions

In the preceding chapters an enormous quantity of material has been presented. Much of it may seem contradictory, some even internally inconsistent. It has been shown, for instance, that Muslim communities under the Crown of Aragon were well-structured, well-organized, and complex municipal bodies, with considerable independence and autonomy, but that they were in every way inferior and subordinate to the Christian universitas, and that the officials of the latter could intervene in all aspects of life in the morería if it interested them to do so. It has been argued that individual Mudéjares prospered during the   period of this study, that there was a wealthy class of Muslims high in the civil service who enjoyed exceptional royal favor, that Muslims not only took full part in but were indispensable to the economy of Aragon and Valencia; yet it has also been claimed that Muslims as a group were utterly ruined by the economic demands of the Crown during the war, and that they were preyed upon, robbed, and financially exploited by all levels of Aragonese society. One chapter demonstrated that Muslims were liable to the exact same military and feudal duties as their Christian counterparts, and another pointed out that they did not even enjoy the right to bear arms, and that they could be and were enslaved on a massive scale for any of a hundred reasons, or for no reason at all. The survival of the system of Muslim jurisprudence formed the content of one chapter, but the same chapter demonstrated that in well over half the cases involving Mudéjares their judicial rights were flagrantly violated by Christian officials. To make matters more confusing, the material

suggested that these usurpations frequently redounded to the benefit
of the Muslims, and often transpired at their request. That Mudéjares
enjoyed a number of "rights" consonant with those enjoyed by the
lower classes of medieval Christians in Europe generally was accepted
and elaborated, as was the fact that Muslims were basically non-per-
sons before Spanish law: such rights as they enjoyed could be terminated at will by monarchs, officials, clerics, or private landholders;
they had no claim to citizenship, could not hold public office except over Muslims, and had no part whatsoever in the making of decisions which vitally affected them (as Christians did through the
Corts).

   Chapter VII on oppression chronicled many and varied forms of
harassment, oppression, and abuse of Mudéjares by Christians, who
invariably escaped any punishment, and who seem to have felt absolutely
no compunctions about harming or exploiting their Muslim compatriots.
But the same pages showed many Christians taking up the causes of the
oppressed Mudéjares, speaking out against the abuses, demanding re-
dress from the king, trying fiercely to protect their Muslim vassals
or friends from injustices of this type. Indeed, with a slight shift
of emphasis, the chapter could be used to counter its own argument.
Taxes were shown to have wiped out the economy of many aljamas and
burdened others severely, and such abuses as forced loans, exorbitant
fines, and illegal exactions were recognized to have accounted for the
desperate plight of individual Muslims by the end of the war; but at
the same time, the remarkable leniency of the Crown in regard to pro-

roguing or remitting taxes was examined in great detail, and data presented established that the Aragonese monarchs remitted about half of all taxes owed them by Muslims throughout the entire period of this study. Muslims were not, a final chapter concluded, very well integrated into Valencian society, and defected to Castile in astounding numbers when presented with the opportunity. Yet the same documentation revealed that in Aragon Mudéjares were so thoroughly assimilated that almost none could read or write Arabic, and they acquitted themselves in the war as being among the most loyal of Peter's subjects.

Such contradictions may be difficult to comprehend. For those disposed to know whether Muslims were "well" or "ill" treated, or whether the Christians of Aragon-Catalonia-Valencia were "kind" or "cruel," "tolerant" or "intolerant," the presentation of these conflicting data may be frustrating. Such contradictions and uncertainties, however, were the reality of fourteenth-century Aragonese Mudéjar life, and the historian cannot alleviate the unpleasantness of confusion by covering it up or shunting it into convenient categories.

There are, moreover, sufficiently abundant, well-documented cases of the treatment of minority groups in recent times to make confusion on such matters unnecessary, and, indeed, culpable. It should be quite clear by now that one group is not "just" or "unjust" to another group, nor well or ill disposed, nor on either side of any other intellectual dichotomy. Attempts to class treatment of one group by another

as part of some deliberate, uniform policy on the part of the rulers
or a dominant class not only obfuscate, but distort. The condition
of Muslims in medieval Spain should be understood as the result of
a continuum of historical factors, some contingent upon human will,
others coincident with it, and still others wholly unrelated to
the actions or wishes of any humans or groups of humans.

It has been the purpose of this study to show the operation of
these historical factors on the situation called convivencia, and
their effects on the Mudéjares. A disastrous war, for instance,
straining severely the finances of the king and the ruling classes,
drove them to seek money from any source which was not securely protected by iron-clad guarantees inextricably bound into the fabric of
society. Muslims were the element of Christian society most exposed
and least protected by the rigorously traditional safeguards of medieval culture.

Likewise, in regard to law, Muslim rights to emigrate were terminated because they could be terminated. Most of the Christian population apparently did not enjoy this right at all, and yet the very system which denied the privilege to the majority protected absolutely
the same right for the few who did enjoy it. The king could not have
denied this right to the members of the Catalan Corts without severely
jeopardizing his own economic survival, nor could he have granted it
to the serfs of the Count of Luna without risking revolt and dethrone-
ment. But he could grant or deny it to Muslims without fear of any
repercussions stronger than protest and complaint, and without serious-

ly disrupting any other elements of the societies under his rule.

In regard to enslavement, intervention in sexual mores, limitations on property transfer, abridgement of legal process, even the practice of religion, the same factors explain--as far as any historical phenomenon can be explained--the quirks of the treatment of Mudéjares at the hands of the ruling Christian element of their society. Questions of tolerance, kindness, justice, intention, etc., are peripheral issues, affecting only a small percentage of the facts which have been considered here. The primary forces affecting the Mudéjares were the very same forces affecting the rest of the society in which they lived: war, inflation, depopulation, economic stagnation, political struggles, class tensions, long-term climatic and agricultural trends, and the thousand other factors one must figure into equations relating to a particular human condition.

But the effects of these forces were different for the Muslims than they were for the other members of the society in which the Mudéjares resided; not uniformly different, not always different, perhaps not even dramatically different, but they were different, as the preceding chapters have attempted to demonstrate. The reason is simple: the Mudéjares were an imperfectly assimilated element in a culture dedicated to stability, homogeneity, and tradition. Medieval society was designed to withstand the storms of a harsh and turbulent age by lashing each and every member and constituent part of its composition to another part; it was the fate of the Muslims of Spain to have been incorporated into this whole late, irregularly, and with considerable ambivalence on the part of the rest of the society. The position

they occupied in that society could be described in a number of ways.

In modern terms, the Muslims occupied the bottom rungs of a rigid,

paternalistic hierarchy. Pressure exerted on this hierarchy resulted

in efforts on the part of those at each level to alleviate their own

distress at the expense of those below them: since the Muslims occupied

the bottommost rungs, and since access to the higher levels was for the

most part denied them, they suffered the most from this pressure and its

side-effects. In those areas where Muslims were in a competitive rela-

tion to Christians--among the lower classes in Valencia, for instance,

or the civil service in Aragon--they fared well or ill depending on the

particular circumstances of their position, and their ability to make

their political or economic power work for them. In no case could it

be argued that the general situation of Muslims, whether desirable or

undesirable, was due to the bigotry or tolerance of particular Christians,

or to the enlightenment or fanaticism of the ruling classes, or to the

justice or injustice of Christian authorities. The situation of the

Muslims and their relation to the Christian society around them was

created and maintained by organizational and structural forces which

operate on most pluralistic societies, which respond to stress by exag-

erating social distinctions and cleavages regardless of the desires or

wishes of individuals involved, and which are better analyzed in terms

of their effects than their moral desirability.

As for the attitude of the Christians toward the Mudéjares, canons of scholarship, decency, and common sense unanimously enjoin upon the researcher total abstinence from conscious moral judgements regarding his findings. Few modern minds would find the benevolent paternalism of Aragonese monarchs toward "the royal treasure" a praiseworthy attitude, but it would be grossly unfair to judge the behavior of medieval Spaniards by the standards of cultures which have largely rejected the ideals most dearly cherished in fourteenth-century Spain. It is not, moreover, the province of the historian to praise or blame, but merely to understand. If the present study has given rise to greater understanding, however limited, it has more than fulfilled the expectations of its writer.

Appendix of Documents

Since the aim in publishing these documents is not to edit them for other scholars, but simply to provide illustration for materials quoted in the body of the study, they have not been substantially annotated. The modern forms of medieval place names can be located by having reference to the table of equivalencies following. Other material relating to or clarifying them--and translations for many-- will be found in the text preceding.

Because the Chancery registers are merely records of documents issued, they omit the salutation which the original letter carried. "Nos Petrus, etc.," is exactly what begins the documents in the regis- ters. I have, however, abridged the conclusions in most cases. Com- plete perorations are printed for C 898:222, C 903:203, and a few others. These are typical.

I have transcribed the documents as they stand, including errors of grammar, orthography, and syntax, except where these actually ob- scure the meaning. Thus, in C 1206:138 "alcadius elegi non debere" was allowed to stand without emendation or a note, since the meaning is clear and the scribe may have understood this to be the correct form. _Sic_ has been used sparingly, since errors are rife and diver- gences from standard grammar and orthography so numerous that putting _sic_ after every one would clutter the page beyond legibility. Only where the reader would imagine an error to be one of transcription or typing has _sic_ been used to verify the accuracy of the text.

The conjunctions "e" and "i" are used interchangeably and errati- cally in the Catalan and Aragonese documents; there is generally no

way to be certain which word an ampersand represents, and the transcription here is perforce somewhat arbitrary.

Orthographical variants have been allowed to stand for all nouns
and verbs, including proper names, except where the form of a geographical location is distorted beyond recognition, or where a spelling alter-
ation within the same document might confuse the reader.

I am of the opinion that adding accent marks or correcting
the spelling of medieval Catalan and Aragonese words is no more justifiable than printing Provençal with modern French orthography and
accentuation. Accents were not a part of fourteenth-century Catalan.
My only concession to the modern eye has been the addition of apostro-
phes in cases of ellision, without which many words would be unintel-
ligible or easily misread for others. "Non," for instance, might be
"non," "n'on" (= ne on), or "no'n" (= no en). This expedient distorts
some words, and results in such unsightly hybrids as "e'l" (= e el)
and "d'aqu'en" (= de aqui en), but it seems in the long run the most
satisfactory alternative in presenting documents to a public largely
unfamiliar with the niceties of medieval Catalan.

Note, in this connection, that in the originals the "d" before
place names is capitalized rather than the first letter of the place;
this has been altered for the sake of clarity, so that for Deslida
I have put d'Eslida; for Daragon, d'Aragon, etc.

TABLE OF PLACE NAMES

Because the Latin or Catalan equivalents of place names which appear on modern Spanish maps will be unrecognizable to some readers, a table of equivalencies is here provided as a convenience for those wishing to locate places mentioned in the documents following. A case could be made for the retention of the Catalan spelling even in the English text of this study, since most of Catalonia still uses Catalan as its language, but few English speakers would have the means of locating such names as Lleida or Oriola.

Only those names which occur frequently or in contexts of considerable importance, and whose Latin or Catalan forms differ significantly from the modern Castilian are listed. It is assumed that slight deviations, such as Arcana for Artana, or Azp for Aspe, will not present real difficulty for the average reader. Forms in parentheses are variants. The Latin is always given in its most characteristic form rather than in purest Latin.

Latin	Catalan	Castilian
Alaguant	Alacant	Alicante
Alfandeguella	Alfandech	Alfandequiella
Algeciras	Alzira (Alciras)	Alcira
Aqualeta	Aqualet	Igualada
Barchinona	Barcelona	Barcelona
Burgia	Borja	Borja
Calataiuba	Calataiu	Calatayud
Çaraniena	Çaranyena	Sariñena

Latin	Catalan	Castilian
Cesaraugusta	Çaragoça*	Zaragoza
Crivilliens	Crivillen	Crevillente
Dertusa	Tortosa	Tortosa
Exea	Eig	Ejea
Ella	Etla	Elda
Faransa	Fansara	Fanzara
Fariçia	Farissa	Ariza
Ilerda	Lleida	Lérida
Montissalbani	Montalban	Montalbán
Montissoni	Montçon (Montso)	Monzón
Muraveteris	Morvedre	Murviedro†
Oriola	Oriola	Orihuela
Osca	Osca	Huesca
Sogorbes (Sogorbia)	Segorb	Segorbe
Sirach	Sirat	Cirat
Turol	Terol	Teruel
Tirasona	Taraçona	Tarazona
Vitient	Vicent	Vicién
Xativa	Xativa	Játiva
Xelva§	Xelva	Chelva

---

* Modern Catalan is Saragossa.

† Modern Castilian is Sagunto.

§ The Catalan letter "x" enters Castilian as either "j" or "ch," depending on the Arabic spelling of the original word. Most Catalan place names can thus be located on Castilian maps by substituting one or the other letter, e.g., for Xiva, read Chiva; for Xixona, Jijona, etc.

Note: for ease of reference the documents are
arranged serially by register numbers rather
than chronologically by dates

C 685:44   (October 14, 1355)   (Secret Seal)

[Faraig de Belvis seeks to effect the return of a slave stolen from his brother, Jahia de Belvis.]

See pp.43ss, 55.

Petrus Rex, etc. Ffideli suo, baiulo civitatis Barchinone vel eius locumtenenti, salutem et gratiam. Ex parte Jahie de Beluis, sarraceni ville de Medine Celi, regni Castelle, fuit querelose propositum coram nobis quod queque ipse emisset in villa Daroce quendam sarracenum nomine Juce de Malega ab Egidio Alvari, scutiffero, habitatore loci de Luçon, regni eiusdem, pro pretie septingentorum morabetinorum Castelle, cum publico instrumento confecto per Franciscum Martini de Portu, notarium publicum auctoritate regia per totum regnum Aragonie, idemque exponens mississet prenominatum eius sarracenum ad regnum Valentie cum litteris suis pro quibusdam negociis eiusdem, nonnulli tamen homines Assixini, itinerum violatores, ceperunt ipsum (ut fertur) in itinere regio, eumque secum, manibus retro vinctis et ore eius obstructo, comittendo vim publicam apportarunt, ipsumque Petro Ballaro, civi Barchinone, minus debite (ut asseritur) vendiderunt in dicti exponentis evidens perjudicium et jacturam. Cum autem Farachius de Belluis, meneschallus domus nostre, nomine procuratorio prelibati Jahie, fratris sui, dictum sarracenum per vicarium civitatis jamdicte fecerit emperari, eumque jure suo seu illius cuius procurator existit, recuperare intendat, et propterea nobis duxerit humiliter suplicatum per nos sibi in hac parte de oportuno remedio provideri, ideo inspecta suplicatione ipsa, benigne vobis dicimus et mandamus quatenus, facta robis fide de instrumento emptionis, predicte faciatis dictum

sarracenum eidem suplicanti restitui et tornari, nisi rationes legi-

time in contrarium opposite fuerint que obsistant; super quibus,

si opponantur, vocatis evocandis faciatis breviter, summarie, et de

plano, et sine lite, quod justicia sua debit, proculsis malitiis et

difugiis quibuscumque.

Datis Perpiniani, sub sigillo nostro secreto, xiiii die Octobris,

anno a nativitate Domini m ccc l v.

C 688:160   (February 15, 1357)

[A prosperous Mudéjar merchant is murdered by other Muslims
while on a business trip. The guardian of his orphaned
sons describes the murder and seeks justice from the king,
who commends the matter to a Huescan jurist.]

See pp.75, 152, 233.

Petrus, etc. Ffideli nostro Bartholomeo de Senes, jurisperito

civitatis Osce, salutem et gratiam. Exhibita nobis per Muça

d'Almuçea, tutorem Mahomadelli et Loppelli de Rey, filiorum pu-

pillorum Mahometi de Rey, sarraceni sutoris quondam dicte civi-

tatis, querelosa petitio continebat quia cum nuper quadam die

jovis, mensis Januarii proxime preteriti, idem Mahometus, qui,

quamquam sutor esset, arte mercandi (ut asseritur) utebatur, pro-

posuisset accedere apud locum de Exea, ut inibi emeret coria pro eis

deferendis seu deferri faciendis ad dictam civitatem Osce, causa

ea inibi vendendi in suo videlicet operatorio sive tenda, venit ad

eum Mahoma de Cani, habitator loci de Vicent, dicens ei quod si

ipse debebat accedere ad locum de Exea et emeret ibi merces aliquos,

idem Mahoma del Canii iret secum et cum suis animalibus defferet

carricas mercium quas in ipsa villa de Exea emeret ad dictam civita-

tem Osce. Et facta conventione inter eos super illis predictis,

Mahoma de Canii dixit sibi quod si idem Mahoma del Rey vellet rece-

dere a dicta civitate die sequenti, reperiret eum in dicto loco de

Vicent* in domo sua, et daret sibi ad cenandum. Qua die sequenti

dictus Mahoma del Rey fuit in loco predicto de Vicent* in domo

dicti Mahometi del Canii, et cum sumpta cena posuisset se in quodam

---

*Manuscript has <u>Vitient</u>.

lecto et jam dormiret, dictus Mahoma de Canii ingressus fuit
dictam cameram cum quodam dogali sive resca in manu, et dum eam
poneret in collo dicti Mahoma del Rey, qui dormiebat (ut premiti-
tur), ipse se excitavit et dixit ei, "O Mahoma*, et talia [   ]
contra me perpetrare!" et vellet se defendere et vociferare, subi-
to intrarunt Habrahime del Galo, Abulcati Garlandello, et Moffrer
de Meel, complices sui, et tunc omnes cum dicta resca tranuolarunt
seu sufucarunt eum. Quo sufucato, immiserunt eum in quendam sacum,
eumque absconderunt in quadam domo ubi pales existebant; et post
quatuor dies de nocte tulerunt ipsum ad quendam torrentem seu bara-
neum termini loci de Tabernes, et inibi, abstracto de dicto sacco,
sauciarunt illum sic mortuum, jam fetentem existentem, terdeciens
ictibus, a quibus sanguis minime emanabat. Et eo quia cogitabant,
ut creditur, quod sanguis ab huiusmodi ictibus defluere vero debebat,
attulerunt secum edulum, et occiderunt eum super peremtum sepedic-
tum, ponendo de sa[n]guine dicti eduli in ictibus ipsius interfecti;
et quod de dicta nesse perpetrata, dicti homeside diviserunt inter
se peccuniam quam secum predictus Mahoma del Rey defferebat pro emen-
dis mercibus supradictis, qui summam mille ducentorum solidorum jaccensium (ut fertur) attingebat. Quapropter per dictum Muça, tutorem
predictum, fuit nobis humiliter supplicatum ut super premissis vel
ut exemplo pernitiosis dignaremur de justicia remedio providere.

Nos itaque, eius supplicatione benigne admissa, attendentes quod
predicta tanquam perperius et inhumaniter perpetrata sunt acriter
punienda, vobis dicimus, comissimus, et mandamus, quatenus de predic-

---

*Manuscript has <u>Mahona.</u>

tis inquiratis diligentissime veritatem, et quos culpabiles
repereritis in predictis taliter puniatis quod eis cedat ad
penam, et ceteris similia attemptare volentibus [ ]eat in exemplum. Et si vobis visum fuerit, ipsos reos ponatis questionibus
et tormentis, et aliis procedatis prout de justicia fuerit faciendum. Nos enim vobis super premissis comittimus per presentes
plenarias vices nostras.

Datis Ceserauguste, xvi die Ffebruoarii, anno a nativitate Domini
m ccc l vii.*

---

*Cf. C 690:232 (May 8, 1357), where the king censures de Senes for
his laxity in prosecuting this affair and orders immediate action.

C 701:50   (June 6, 1360)

[The king instructs the Justice of Borja to see that
the concubines of mercenaries not resident in the
city are moved out of the homes of Muslims and lodged
with Christians.]

See p.169.

...Intelleximus pro parte aljame sarracenorum dicte ville

quod aliqui frontalarii qui tempore preterito erant in dicta

villa dimiserunt concubinas sive focarias suas in domibus

aliquorum sarracenorum dicte aljame, que concubine sive focarie

a domibus vel hospiciis dictorum sarracenorum exire differunt,

in ipsorum sarracenorum periculum non modicum, ut dicitur, atque

dampnum.

   Quocirca volentes super hiis debite providere vobis dici-

mus et mandamus expresse quatenus visis presentibus compellatis

mulieres quascumque christianas quarum viri sive amasii* absen-

tes a dicta villa existant per impositiones penarum et aliter,

prout vobis visum fuerit expedire, ad exeundum a domibus et

hospiciis sarracenorum predictorum, assignando eis et tribuendo

alia hospicia christianorum dicte ville, ubi absentibus viris

sive amasiis* earundem hospi[ciar]e valeant mulieres prenotate.

---

* Each time this word occurs it has been written above a form of
focarius, which has been scratched through by the scribe.

C 702:91   (January 18, 1361)

[Because the Muslim aljama of Ariza has been reduced
from two hundred families to ten, the king relaxes
certain laws regarding the sale of property to Christians.]

See pp.8-9, 276.

...Pro parte juratorum et proborum hominum universitatis ville

de Ffarisia fuit nobis humiliter supplicatum ut, cum in dicta

villa solerent comorari ducenti sarraceni, domos foventes, et

ultra, et nunc non inhabitent in eadem nisi decem vel circa,

et ad ipsos decem omnes hereditates aliorum sarracenorum ipsius

ville pervenerint, et cum eos opportet vendere ex ipsis here-

ditatibus pro solvendis suis debitis, non reperiantur pro ipsis

hereditatibus pretia condecentia, cum ex ipsis decem habeant

esse venditores et emptores (pro eo quare ex statuto seu ordina-

tione super hiis facta: Si aliquis christianus emit aliquam

hereditatem ab aliquo sarraceno, tertia partis pretii quod ex

ipsa hereditate habet nobis noscitur pertinere), dignaremur

ad hoc ut ex dictis hereditatibus pretia decentia habeantur, ex

quibus possit satisfieri creditoribus dictorum sarracenorum,

licencia[m] concedere prefatis sarracenis quod suas hereditates

possint vendere christianis maiora precia pro eisdem dare of-

ferentibus, absque solutione dicte tertie partis preciorum que

ex eis habentur, dictis cum christianis solventibus annis singu-

lis illud jus seu ea jura ad que hereditates quas emerint ten-

entur seu sint obligate castro dicte ville pro retinentia eiusdem,

cum qua obligatione seu onere et non aliter dicte hereditates

vendantur. ...

C 704:129   (November 12, 1360)

[The king orders his lieutenant, the Count of Cervara to revoke edicts which he has lately promulgated forbidding Muslims who are not residents of the morería of Valencia to buy or sell taxable foodstuffs there.]

Cf. pp.287-289.

...ordinaveritis et imposueritis certas impositiones in dicta

civitate super pane, vino, carnibus, et aliis mercimoniis, cum

certis capitulis et conditionibus, et inter alia publice preconi-

zare feceritis quod nulla persona, cuiuscumque legis vel condi-

tionis fuerit, que non habitet infra clausuras juderie et morerie

dicte civitatis, non audeat vel presumat palam vel oculte emere

seu emi facere intus dictas clausuras panes, carnes, vina, pannos

nec aliqua alia de quibus debeat solvi impositio dicte civitati,

sub certa pena.   Et (ut asseritur) predicta fuerunt facta in pre-

judicium regaliarum nostrarum, cum inibitiones tantum possint fieri

per principem, et non per aliquas alias personas.

Propterea ffuerit nobis humiliter supplicatum pro parte dic-

tarum aljamarum quod predicta faceremus ilico revocari, necnon quod

deberemus tradere in mandatis justicie dicte civitatis quod voce

preconia licenciam tribueret universis predicta in dicta inhibitione

vestra contenta palam et publice faciendi, cum ipsi supplicantes

asserunt se fore peratas exsolvere in dictis vestris impositionibus

in omnibus hiis que contractabunt, vendent, vel ement cum christi-

anis, vel christiani cum ipsis, dumtamer impositiones quas exsolvere

habebunt de hiis que judei vel sarraceni privati vel extranei ad

invicem inter se ipsos contractabunt possint convertere licite

in eorum proprios usus, et eorum debita exsoluenda, et dumtamen
non compellantur in solutione illius tatxationis vocate "scala,"
que per vos et ipsos fieri solebat pro solutione solidi quingentorum equitum dicto primogenito nostro nomine nostro concessorum
ad opus guerre Castelle per generale* regni Valentie, cum predicte
impositiones per nos imposite, ut asseritur, solum fuerint ordinate
pro solutione predicti solidi equitum predictorum, et non ad alium
finem.

Idcirco eorum supplicationi utpote juste favorabiliter
annuentes, vobis dicimus et mandamus firmiter et expresse quod
quatenus [sic] predicta concernant seu concernunt prejudicium regaliarum nostrarum, ipsa ilico revocetis, et ad statum debitum re-
ducatis, mora qualibet quiescente, nichil innovando in predictis in
prejudicium dictarum aljamarum. Aliter si facere recusaveritis,
quod minime oppinamur, per presentes gerenti vices Gubernatoris
Generalis in dicto regno Valentie, seu eius locumtenenti, tradimus
firmiter in mandatis quod vos ad predictum facienda et compellenda
forciet et compellat remediis fori quibus decet....

---

*Sic; possibly = Curiam Generalem

C 705:68   (Undated; occurs between entry of January 4,
            1361, and February 11, 1361.)

[Hospitallers complain to the king on behalf of the Muslim
community of Jabut about atrocities committed against Mudéjares by the Alos family.]

See p.357.

Item...que N'Arnaldo d'Alos, fill del dit Francesch, sens tota

raho feri Maymonet, moro, servidor del dit Comenador [dels Hospital-

lers.]

Item...un altre jorn N'Arnaldo d'Alos, fill del Ffrancesch, viu un

dia de festa moro del loch, a qui die Alboquis, que perarie canes a

la porta de son alberch, et per ço cor a die de festa ho fahie en

casa sua, ma s[ ]a bon fart, e si aquell [= N'Arnaldo] peraue o fahie

contra la festa, no venia a ell la punitio, ni li ere comenade cura

danpnos[a].

Item...un altre jorn En Bort d'Alos, desus dit, per ço com un moro

a qui die Fama Poprell li contesta a peraules desonestes que ell

dehie, un dia que aquest moro ana a mercat a Leyda lo dit Bort se

fo mans en eguayt en lo cami e hach gran fart del dit moro.

Item...per anant un altre jorn N'Arnaldo d'Alos, fill del dit

Ffrancesch, per ço cor una mora del dit loch no volch fer sos

volentats, denits ab una scala muntasse per una finestra de la casa

on la dita mora stave, e entra dins, e aqui jach ab ella forçadament,

per que se'n es exida e ha pres marit en altre loch....

Item...enguany en quaresma lo dit Arnaldo, anant se deportar per la

orta, troba lo guardia del loch, que sembrava linos, e fora lo cami

en una costa bisties de la uila pexien o pasturauen en aquella costa, e lo dit Arnaldo dix, per que les hi tenien; que sua ere aquella

costa; se stiguessen d'aemprar.   E per ço cor lo moro li [ni]

allegua ni contesta a sa raho, li dona ab l'espasa un colp per la

ma de que es afollat, e altre per lo coll de que es cuydat morir,

e per un injrui [sic] que li caya tendra tots temps lo coll de

cort e romara affollat.

C 711:131   (January 20, 1363)

[The king upholds the immunity from taxation enjoyed by the wife and sons of Abdulaziz Aterrer, a stonecutter in the service of the Archbishop of Zaragoza, in accord with the provisions of his grant of 1357, quoted herein. Doubt had been cast on this immunity by C 899:230, q.v., but the king resolves the issue, demanding only 18s per annum from the said Mudéjares.]

See pp.212-216, 444-445.

...Mandantes per presentem Iusticie Aragone, merino Cesarauguste, ac universis et singulis aliis officialibus, portariis, comissariis, et subditis nostris quatenus dictam gratiam tibi [Abdulaziz Aterrer], uxori, et filiis tuis predictis observent inviolabiliter et faciant observari, teque, uxorem, et filios tuos predictos tractent ut sarracenos quitios atque franchos. Nos enim mandamus per presentem merino Cesarauguste presenti et illis qui pro tempore preerunt dicto officio merinato quatenus partem te, uxorem, et dictos filios tuos solvere contingentem in peytis, subsidiis, et aliis exactionibus supradictis in nostro compoto recipiant et admittant. In cuius rei testimonium presentem fieri nostroque pendenti sigillo iussimus communiri. Datis Calataiubi, xxiiii die Aprilis, anno a nativitate Domini millesimo trecento quinquagesimo septimo, nostrique regni vicesimo secundo. ...Verumtamen ut pro parte uxoris et filiorum prefati Abdalazir percepimus vos compellitis et distringitis eos ad solvendum in predicta ordinaria dicte aljame, contra tenorem gratie ipsius, cuius pretextu dicti, uxoris, et filii sunt a dictis peyta et tributis liberi et exempti quamdiu vitam duxerint in humanis; unde supplicato nobis super hiis de opportuno remedio providi, cum beneficia principum firma existere debeant et mansura, vobis et cui-

libet vestrum dicimus et mandamus de certa scientia et expresse
quatenus preinsertam gratiam eisdem uxori et filiis observetis et
observari faciatis inviolabiliter iuxta ipsius seriem et tenorem,
quibusvis concessionibus seu provisionibus per nos ante predictam
gratiam et post dicte aljame factis quomodolibet, seu concessis,
quas presentis serie revocamus et pro revocatis haberi volumus, quo
ad hec obsistentibus nullo modo. Hoc tamen proviso, quod de dicta
peyta ordinaria per dictam aljamam solvendam nobis deducatur decem
et octo solidos,ad quos solvendos taxati fuerunt prefati uxor et
filii pro facultatibus quas nunc habent, prout inde a merino dicte
civitatis informationem habuimus; quosquidem decem et octo solidos
annuatim in nostro compoto recipi volumus et admitti, sic quod ex
inde pro dictis decem et octo solidis nulla compulsa contra predictam aljamam queat fieri seu districtus. Nos enim expressius vobis
et cuilibet vestrum iniungimus quod aljama predicta solvente anno
quolibet in terminis assuetis peytam ordinariam supradictam, eidem
de dicta peyta ac decem et octo solidis antedictis faciatis apocham
de soluto. Mandantes magistro rationali curie nostre seu alii [sic]
cuicumque a nobis de predictis compotum audituro, quod in nostro recipiat compoto decem octo solidos predictos, cum nos ipsos haberi
velimus penitus pro solutis; cavendo tamen attentius ut a tempore
guerre predicte citra formam supradictam servetis nec presumatis
eosdem super hiis in aliquo molestari....

C 720:8   (August 18, 1365)   (Secret Seal)

[The king orders the General Bailiff of Valencia to find lodging for a foreign Muslim dignitary in the morería of Valencia.]

See pp.186-187.

...Manam vos que a Alabeç Abennafi, sarrahi de Berbaria, lo qual

a nos per certes rahons era vengut, e qui de licencia nostra

se'n torna a sa terra, donets poscida en la moreria de Valencia.

E no remenys la lexets traure i portar ab si de la dita ciutat

draps i robes i totes altres coses que mester haura, saluu [sic]

armes e altres coses vedades.

C 720:77   (August 31, 1365)

[In gratitude for their inducing the Muslim population of Segorbe to return to the king's service, the monarch pardons two amins of the city for having escaped from the jail of the Bishop of Valencia, where they were being held as hostages.]

See p.336.

Nos Don Pedro: Por la buena obra que vos, Abdalla Albardero e

Abrafim Razin, alamins de la aljama de los moros de la ciudat de

Sogorb, habitadores de la cita ciudat, a nos e a la cosa publica

fiziestes en converter e a la nostra part de coraçon e de volentat

retornar los moros de la dita aljama de la grant error en la qual

eran puestos, manteniendo al Rey de Castiella dins senyoria del

qual estavan, e guerra contra nos e nostras gentes por todo lur

poder faziendo;   por la qual razon se seguio que los christianos,

qui ya eran del nostre coraçon, ensemble con los ditos moros se

alçaron con la dita ciudat de Sogorb por al nostro servitio, e a

nos e al Arcebispe de Çaragoça, tudor de la Comtessa de Luna,

Senyora de la dita ciudat, se rendieron; e por tal como ante qu'el

rendimiento se fiziesse de la dita ciudat huviemos jurado de fazer

a vos el perdon siguient:

Por aquesto, mouidos por las razones sobreditas,

con tenor de la present carta nostra, perdonamos, defenetemos,

remetemos, e relaxamos a vos, ditos Abdalla Albaredo e Abrafim

Razin, tota accion, question, peticion, e demanda, e toda pena

civil e criminal e otra qualquiere, la qual contra vos e vestros

bienes podriamos mover o fazer por tal como vos con otro pressoners

trebantastes la preson del Bisbe de Valentia en do estavades
presos por catiuos nostros, e de alli vos fuesstes e vos andastes
per a la dita ciudat de Sogorbe, en do tractastes e fiziestes
luego la dita obra, or por qualquiere razon, assi empero que
d'aqui adelant por nos o los nostros officiales quales se quiere*
no podades seyer ponidos† o condempnados civilment o criminal§
por las cosas sobreditas, o en alguna manera seyer presos, ni mal
tractados; antes seades d'aqui adelant con todos los bienes vestros liures, quitos, e perdonados, e perdurablement absueltos.
Mandantes....
Dada en el sitio de Murviedre, postramero dia d'Agosto, en el
anyo de la Nativitad de nostro Senyor m ccc lx v; del nostro
reynado, trenta.

---

* Sic: three words. Cf. Catalan qualssevol.
† Sic: sc.: punidos.
§ Sic: sc.: criminalment

C 721:88   (December 3, 1364)

[Peter orders the resumption of a suspended trial
involving the murder of three Jews by two Christians
and eight Muslims. The trial is commended to the supervision of a jurist of Lérida.]

Cf. Chapter III, and p.375.

Petrus, etc. Ffideli nostro Raymundo de Cumbis, jurisperito

Ilerde, salutem et gratiam. Cum processus pacis et treuge [sic]

factus vel incohatus per vicarium Ilerde vel eius locum tenentem

ad instantiam seu querelam quarundam judearum aut judeorum, ratione

seu occasione mortis perpetrate in personas trium judeorum, in

termino loci de Ajabut, contra Bernardum Cubero, bajulum loci de

Ajabut, et Dominicum Culvera, habitatorem loci eiusdem, necnon

sarracenos subscriptos, habitatores ipsius loci, viz., Macadur Juniç,

Almariori Jornet, Brahim Almaiori (aliter vocatum Rossell Çoleyma),

Amargos Farayg, Popiell Amado, Alfahuell Aycuch, Maçada Badoç, et

Faragium Morola, dicatur esse nullus, certis de causis, et ob hoc

fuerit nobis humiliter suplicatum tam pro parte commendatoris dicti

loci quam dictorum hominum, ut de et super eis dignaremur superius

nominatos, contra quos proceditur, in eorum jure audire, ne contra

justiciam molestantur, propterea vobis dicimus, comittimus, et

mandamus quatenus, vocatis qui fuerint evocandi et resumpto processu

inde habito, quem vobis tradi jubemus, de similitate dicti processus

qui allegatur, cum dependentibus et connexis cognoscatis, et super

eis faciatis et decernatis quod de jure et ratione fuerit faciendum.

Nos enim vobis super hiis comittimus cum presenti plenarias vices

nostras.

Datis Ilerde, tertie die Decembris, anno a nativitate Domini m ccc lx iv.

C 721:135   (January 2, 1365)

[The king orders the Bailiff of Lérida to honor a previous
edict {of 1351, quoted herein} commanding certain Muslim
landowners of Benifallet to exchange their property with
a Jew for other property of equal value elsewhere, and
suggesting a system of arbitration.]

See p.69.

Petrus, etc. Ffideli nostro baiulo Dertuse vel eius locumtenenti,

salutem et gratiam. A vestri non credimus memoria dicessisse [sic]

qualiter dudum per Infantem Fferdinandum scriptum fuit vobis sub

hac forma: Infans Fferdinandus, serenissimi Domini Alfonsi, recol-

ende memorie, Regis Aragonie filius dei gratia, Ma[r]chio Dertuse

et Dominus de Albarrazino, ffideli nostro baiulo Dertuse vel eius

locum tenenti, Salutem et gratiam. Exponente coram nobis fidele

nostro Astrugo de Almenario, cive Dertuse, percepimus quod ipse ha-

bet quasdam domos in loco de Benifalleto, termini Dertuse, et ex

utraque parte dictarum domorum eisdem terrarum pecie alique sive

terre trotia contigue sunt et etiam confrontantur, quorum unum

trocium est quorundem sarracenorum dicti loci de Benifalleto, quod-

quidem trocium nunc de presenti detinet et possidet Mogehit del

Alsaig, ssaracenus dicti loci, habens partem etiam in dicto terre

trocio seu dictus Mogeit, nomino suo proprio sive nomine cuiuslibet

aliorum; aliudque etiam trocium terre cum quibusdam arboribus detinet

et possidet Haceyna sarracena, uxor Mochomat Alfarra quondam, et

heredes eiusdem Mahomi et heredes Maymo Alfarra, fratrum quondam,

seu dicta uxor dicti Mahometi, in nomine proprio sive nomine dic-

torum heredum aut cuiuslibet alterius. Et supplicavit nobis idem

Astrugus ut, ipso dante dictis sarracenis pecias terre similes

in valore in alio loco infra terminum dicti loci de Benifalleto
sive de Aldouesca, vobis mandare litteratorie dignaremur quod
predictos sarracenos jamdictas pecias sive terre trocios habentes juxta domum dicti Astrugui [sic] pro parte nostra rogare et
requirere deberetis ad faciendum concambium cum eodem de peciis
seu trociis supradictis pro peciis seu possessionibus aliis valoris similis,infra terminum dictis loci de Benifalleto aut de
Aldouesca, quas obtulerit, se daturum ad arbitrium duorum viro-
rum, scilicet unius eligendi per dictum Astrugum et pro parte
sua, et alterius sarraceni pro parte dictorum sarracenorum vel
possidentium nunc terras predictas, vel partem habentium in
eisdem, eligendi; quorum declarationi fiende per dictos eligendos
tam idem Astrugus quam jamdicti sarraceni vel habentes aut possidentes nunc terras ipsas et partes habentes in eisdem stare et
adqui[e]scere tenerentur. Quare supplicationi predicti Astrugui
favorabiliter annuentes, vobis dicimus et expresse mandamus quatenus, visis presentibus, dictos sarracenos aut tenentes et possidentes nunc ipsas pecias sive terras(vel partem in eisdem habentes)
requirere debeatis quia iuxta modum et formam superius expressatam
unum sarracenum pro parte sua eligere debeant, qui una cum alio viro
per dictum Astrugum eligendo, visis et subiectis ad occulum peciis
supradictis, earundemque valore et loci distantia equanimiter pen-
satis ac etiam ponderatis, tam hiis peciis sive trociis terre, videlicet qui dictorum sarracenorum sunt, quam hiis qui predictus sup-
licans in concambium dare et offere voluerit, et eis ad equitatem

juste requirens, predictos sarracenos compellatis ad standum et
adquiescendum declarationi fiende per predictos eligendos per
partes superius nominatas. Verum si predicti sarraceni aut habentes et possidentes nunc ipsas pecias seu trocia terre, vel in eisdem partem habentes, requisitioni obsecundare neclexerint, et sarracenum pro parte sua eligere noluerint ullo modo, volumus ac vobis
mandamus quatenus vos eligatis dictum sarracenum, partibus non sus-
pectum, qui una cum illo probo homine eligendo per jamdictum Astrugum predicta facere teneantur sub modo et forma* superius expres-
satis. Et facta declaratione per predictos eligendos fienda, eam
per partes ipsas faciatis teneri et servari etiam inconcusse. Et
hoc aliquatenus non mutetis, cum sic fieri de certa scientia providerimus et velimus; volumus tamen quia terre quas predicti sarraceni
pro dicto cambio et in emenda peciarum predictarum habuerint ad
ipsam honera qui sustinere nunc habent pro antedictis peciis teneantur, iure nostro in omnibus illeso ac etiam semper salvo.
Datis apud optam, pridie idus Martii; anno a nativitate Domini millesimo ccc l primo. Pere Gonuide.
Nunc autem per dictum Astruch fuit nostro culmini humiliter supplicatum quod, cum premissa in littera supradicta contenta non fuit
debito effectu mancipata, dignaremur de benignitate nostra regia
ipsa per vos exsequi mandare et ad debitum perduci effectum. Nos
itaque dicte suplicationi condescendentes benigne vobis dicimus et
mandamus quatenus, cum per dictum Astruch seu eius procuratorem inde
fueritis requisitus, litteram preinsertam et contenta in ea exequi-

---

*Manuscript has <u>morma</u>.

mini et compleatis et exequi et compleri faciatis per sarracenos
superius nominatos iuxta sui seriem pleniorem, omni dilatione et
excusatione remotis.* Et hoc aliquatenus non mutetis, cum sic nos
de certa scientia fieri providerimus et velimus.

Datis Dertuse, vicesima secunda die Januarii, anno a nativitate
Domini m ccc lx quinto.

---

* Ms. has <u>semotis.</u>

C 862:121   (January 12, 1337)

[The king instructs all officials to honor the right
of Muslim communities to put to death Muslims who are
converted to Judaism.]

Translated on pp.378-379.

Nos Petrus, etc. Universis officialibus nostris et eorum loca

tenentibus, salutem, etc. Pro parte aljamarum sarracenorum reg-

ni Valentie fuerit* nobis humiliter suplicatum quod, cum per

çunam eorum sit eis licitum condempnare ad mortem quoscumque

sarracenum vel sarracenos ad ritum judeorum perversos†, et

contingat interdum aliquem sarracenum vel sarracenam ad dictum

ritum judeorum perverti; tamen nonnulli christiani conantur

deffendere dictos judeos perversos, ac etiam impedire ne secun-

dum dictam çunam fiat justicia ex eisdem, in dictorum sarracen-

orum prejudicium et eorum çune non modicum lesionem.

    Quare ad supplicationem pro parte ipsorum humilem nobis

factam, vobis dicimus et mandamus quatenus cum sarracenum aut

sarracenam ad ritum perverti contigerit judeorum, eosdem per

alcadios sarracenos juxta eorum çunam, absque mercede, compositionem

peccuniariam§, vel remissione aliqua, et impedimento quocumque, ju-

---

* This error, like several subsequent ones, is due to the carelessness of the scribe. Rather than making the line dot for the "i" as
elsewhere in the folio, he accidentally made the sign for "er" (ᶜ).
Since he did not correct it, I have transcribed the error, as below
(§), and in the following entry from the same register.

† N.B. in loco de conversos: a concession to Mudéjar sentiment?

§ Scribal error for either compositionum peccuniariarum or compositione peccuniaria. Note that following remissione was written remis-
sionem, but emended. This whole register is rife with careless
errors.

dicari et puniri totaliter permitatis.

Datis Valentie, pridie idus Januarii, anno Domini millesimo ccc

xxx septimo.

C 862:121 bis (January 12, 1337)

[The king prohibits charging Mudéjares for the privilege of making pilgrimage to the Muslim shrine at Godalesc, previous royal grants notwithstanding.]

See pp.262-263.

Petrus, etc. Universis et singulis officialibus nostris et eorum

loca tenentibus presentibus et qui pro tempore fuerint, ad quos

presentes pervenerunt, salutem et gratiam. Ex parte aljamarum

sarracenorum regni Valentie fuit expositum coram nobis expositum*

conquerendo quia, licet in termino loci de Godalesc, tempore quo

regnum Valentie erat sarracenorum, in loco nostro vocato Zaneta, sit

quedam mezquita in qua fuit sepultus quidam sarracenus qui tunc

tempus per sarracenos iuxta credentiam eorum vocabatur et reputabatur

sanctus, et nunc etiam reputatur, cuius devocione sarracenica non-

nulli sarraceni preteriti temporis et presentis, tam de dicto regno

Valentie quam de aliis partibus, veniebant et nunc veniunt ad mezqui-

tam predictam, causa inibi faciendo orationem, prout hactenus est

fieri usitatum; tamen, ex concessione per nos facta Bartholomeo Car-

tasquiri, vicino dicti loci de Godalesc, ipse Bartholomeus ab uno

quoque sarraceno vel sarracena veniente ad dictam mezquitam sex dén-

arios regalium extorquere conatur etiam et habere, in dictorum sar-

racenorum--qui hucusque ad ipsam mezquitam franchi et absque extor-

---

* Sic: bis.

sione aliqua consueverunt venire--prejudicium, ut asseritur,
atque dampnum.

Quocirca, nostro [   ] premissis pro parte sarracenorum
jamdictorum debito remedio humiliter implorato, vobis et singulis
vestrum dicimus et mandamus quatenus omnes et singulos sarracenos
et sarracenas ad dictam mezquitam venire et inibi orationem per
eos fieri quotiescumque voluerint, absque redemptione vel servitute aliquo, prout consueverunt hactenus, permitatis, concessione
dicto Bartholomeo (ut premittitur) per nos facta de extorquendo
sex denarios pro quolibet sarraceno vel sarracena ad dictam mezquitam veniente, quam presentibus revocamus [nullo modo obsis-
tente]....

C 898:222   (April 1, 1356)

[The king confirms the civil and criminal code previously issued the royal Muslims of Ricla, Ariza,. and other towns, and the feudal duties owed by them to the Crown.]

See pp.166, 280.

Nos Petrus, etc. Viso quodam priuilegio serenissimi domini Petri, Dei gratia Regis Aragonie et Comitis Barchinone, concesso sarracen- is habitantibus in villa de Ricla, bulla plumbea sigillato, cuius tenor sequitur in hec verba: Cum leges et iura et vigore iudicorum in medio sint statuta, ut per ea cuiuscumque condicionis gentes et populi gubernentur, et unicuique vis sibi debitum tribuatur, non tantum bonis et modestis set [sic] etiam discolis, idcirco nos Petrus, Dei gratia Rex Aragonie et Comes Barchinonensis, per nos et omnes successores nostros damus, concedimus et laudamus vobis universis mauris, presentibus et futuris, et successoribus vestris in perpetuum, qui habitatis et habitaturi estis in Rota, in Lumpiach, in Calatorau, in Ricla, in Morata, in Arandega, in Corna, in Nullia, in Masones, in Vierga, in Illoca, in Xiarch, in Aranda, in Mors, in Sanuingen, in Paracolls, in Ermich, in Santos, in Terrer, in Ffariza, in villa Felich, hos scilicet foros et has consuetudines habendas inter vos perpetuo et tenendas:

Si aliquis maurus vel maura obierit sine infante, propinquior parens eius habeat* hereditatem et res ipsius. Si vero fecerit testamentum et de suo lexaverit alicui qui sit realencus, passet suum testamen- tum sicut factum fuerit; set non liceat ei aliquid admittere nisi homini realenco.

---

* Manuscript has habebat.

Si aliquis vel aliqua morte subitania moriatur ita quod non possit facere testamentum, tres mauri de mellioribus illius ville
vel loci unde fuerit emperent omnes res mortui, et facta tota
sepultura ipsius, totum residuum dividant aliis qui faciant inde
servitium quod ille dum viveret faciebat.

Et si aliquis maurus transtulerit se ad aliud regnum et lexaverit hereditatem, mandamus algemiam [sic] illius ville quod
donent hereditatem ipsius alicui de propinquioribus ipsius, vel
etiam alteri secundum suum çuniam, qui faciat inde solitum servitium.

Si vero aliquis maurus dehone[s]taverit alium verbis, uel ceperit
eum per capillos, et peterit inde comprobari secundum suam çuniam,
peytet quinque solidos. Et si cum fuste vel petra percusserit eum,
si sanguis inde non exierit, peytet similiter quinque solidos; et
si sanguis inde exierit, peytet x solidos. Et si affolauerit aliquid membrum, faciat quidquid et quantum mandaverit çunia maurorum.
Si aliquis maurus abstraxerit alteri culcellum, et non percusserit
cum eo, peytet quinque solidos; et si percussisset cum culcello,
peytet sexaginta solidos. Et si aliquis interfecerit alium, peyte[t]
integre homicidium.

Si aliqua maura apparuerit pregnata furnicatione [sic], peytet quinque solidos; et si ipsa imposuerit alicui mauro, quod ipse eam im-
pregnaverit, et ipse confessus fuèrit hoc esse verum, peytet uter-
que quinque solidos, et filius sit horco [n.b.]. Set si ille nega-
verit se eam impre[g]nasse, iuret ille secundum legem suam, et sit
inde solutus, et maura peytet quinque solidos.

Item statuimus firmiter et mandamus quod nullus sit ausus capere

uel agrauare seu perturbare, pro aliqua culpa uel pro aliquo

f[ ]ffacto aut causa, aliquem maurum vel maura[m] (vel res suas)

qui passit vel vellit dare fidantiam de directo.

Item si aliqua maura dehonestaverit aliam verbis, peytet tantum

duos solidos; et si verberaverit eam, peytet quinque solidos.

Si tamen de hiis peterit comprobari per çuniam sin aut [sic],

iuret secundum legem suam et sit inde soluta.

Item vos omnes mauri nostri predictarum villarum et locorum possitis

venari et piscari per montes et aquas libere et sine omni metu, ita

quod nichil inde dare vel facere teneamini nobis vel alicui alii

persone unquam.

Item de mauris de Ricla qui sunt villani nostri: qui habet unum

jugum bovum, serviat nobis sex diebus tantum in anno cum ipso iugo;

et qui habet bestiam traginetiam*, similiter serviat nobis cum illa

sex diebus tantum in anno; et qui non habet boues vel bestiam, ser-

viat nobis sicut pedo sex diebus in anno tantum. Et nos et succes-

sores nostri demus ad comedendum istis omnibus hiis sex diebus qui-

bus servierint nobis, et eadem die qua servierint redeant ad domos

suas.

Datis Cesarauguste, xvii kalendis Nouembris, per manum Fferracii,

notarii nostri, era m ccc xl octava.

Quicumque autem contra hanc cartam veniret iram nostram incur-

reret, et insuper nobis pro toto et pena peytaret mille morabeti-

nos. ...

---

* A goat? Cf. Greek, τράγος.

Idcirco ad supplicationem humilem pro parte dictorum sarracenorum ville de Ricla nobis factam, laudamus, approbamus, ac
etiam confirmamus dictis sarracenis habitantibus et habitaturis
in dicta villa de Ricla totum privilegium supradictum et omnia
et singula in eo contenta, prout melius actenus* usi sunt. Mandantes per presentem universis et singulis officialibus nostris
et loca tenentibus eorundem, presentibus et futuris, quod confirmationem nostram huiusmodi observent et observari faciant iuxta
ipsius oontinentiam [sic] et tenorem. In cuius rei testimonium
presentem cartam nostram inde fieri et sigillo nostro appendicio
iussimus sigillari.

Datis Cesarauguste, prima die Aprilis, anno a nativitate Domini
m ccc l sexto, nostrique regiminis xx primo.

Signum † Petri, Dei gratia Regis Aragonie, etc.

Testes sunt Lup[p]us, Comes de Luna, etc.

            Petrus Ferdinandi, domino de Ixar, etc.

            Lupus, Cesarauguste archiepiscopus

            Achonus de Focibus

            Johannes Eximini d'Urrea, etc.

            fuit clausum per Gundissalvum de Gradibus

---

* Sic: sc. hactenus.

C 899:60   (August 22, 1356)

[The king grants to Martinus Eximin the authority to
set and receive the fines to be paid by the Jewess
Maria for having converted to Judaism from Islam, and
for committing adultery with Jews while she was yet
a Muslim.]

Translated on pp.351-2.

...Tenore presentis damus et concedimus vobis domino Martio

omne ius quod habemus seu habere possumus aut debemus super

Mariam iudeam qui fuit sarracena, tam pro eo quia nuper derelicta

secta perfidi Mahometi abraicam legem assumpsit, quam occasione

adulterii quod ut dicitur commisit cum iudeis, ipsa existente

sarracena, quam ratione aliorum criminum per ipsam ut asseritur

commissorum. Dantes et concedentes vobis dicto Martio plenariam

potestatem et facultatem componendi cum dicta sarracena pro

illa peccunie quantitate pro qua melius secum poteritis convenire,

et recipiendi ac vestris utilitatibus licite et impune applicandi

omne quod ex dicta compositione habere poteritis,...necnon absol-

vendi et diffinendi iudeam ipsam a predictis et aliis quibuslibet

criminibus per ipsam qualitercumque commissis, ac si per nos lit-

teratorie dicta absolutio eidem fieret. Mandantes,...

C 899:230   (January 9, 1357)

[The king revokes the privilege of immunity from royal taxes on the aljama previously granted to Muslims working on the aljafería of Zaragoza.]

See pp.213-214, 426-427.

... Considerantes inquam nos enim minus immemores prouisionis preinserte et ob inportunitatem poscentium ac supplicantium concessisse aliquos franchitates, tam verbo quam aliter (signanter: Mahocmat Ballestero, et Audalazia Aterer, et quibusdam aliis sarracenis aljame pertacte), intencionisque nostre non fuerit nec existat franchitates aliquas concessisse verbo uel aliter--preter franchitates dictis magistris sarracenis concessas--in preinserte prouisionis nostre prejudicium et etiam lesionem; idcirco, attentis predictis, necminus ad humilem supplicationem per dictam aljamam propterea nobis factam, volentesque circa indempnitatem et reparationem al[jame] predicte, qui propter mortalitates preteritas et aliter ob diuersa et intolerabilia onera expensarum sive exactionum regiarum, que supportare habet, ad maximam inopiam et diminutionem bonarum [et] personarum est deducta, et ut per sufficientes et industriosas personas aljama ipsa in eius regimine et aministratione [sic] melius prosperare valeat, ut conuenit, prouidere concessionem uel prouisionem nostram preinsertam iuxta sui serie cum presenti confirmandum ducimus, eamque ab omnibus in concusse* exsequi volumus et etiam obseruari, quibusvis qu[ ]iis, prouisionibus, ac concessionibus per nos (ut pertangitur) in con-

---

* Sic: two words; sc. inconcusse.

trarium, uerbo uel aliter quomodolibet, predictis Mahocmat et Au-
dallaziz uel aliis--preterque dictis magistris--factis, quas presentibus reuocamus, obsistentibus nullo modo. Mandantes Gubernatori et Justicia sic Aragonie, ac Merino Cesarauguste, ceterisque aliis universis et singulis officialibus nostris, presentibus et futuris, uel eorum loca tenentibus, quod preinsertum mandatum nostrum et etiam huiusmodi compleant effectualiter et exse-
queantur ut superius continetur et non contraveniant aliqua ratione.
In cuius rei testimonium presentem fieri iussimus nostro pendenti
sigillo munitam.

Datis Cesarauguste, nona die Januarii, anno a nativitate Domini
m ccc l septimo, nostrique regni vicesimo secundo.

C 901:113   (July 18, 1357)

[The king grants safe-conduct through his dominions
for Muslims travelling to Mecca from Navarre.]

See pp.292ss.

Petrus, etc. Dilectis et fidelibus universis et singulis procuratoribus, gubernatoribus, justiciis, merinis, suppraiuttariis, vi-
cariis, et baiulis, necnon guardianis, portulariis, siue custodi-
bus passuum et rerum prohibitarum, ceterisque o[f]ficialibus et
subditis, ac etiam aliis servitoribus, amicis seu devotis nostris
quibuslibet, tam in terra quam in mari ubilibet constitutis, ad
quos presentes pervenerint, salutem, etc. Cum Mahoma Alcordoueri
et Abdella Tunici, sarraceni Tudele, regni Nauarre, cum uxoribus,
filiis, et familia [sic] suis, qui inter omnes numero nouem sunt,
apud partes ultramarinas pro visitando Mecca impresentiarum [?]
accendant, nosque contemplaconem [sic] illustris regis Navarre
sororii nostri carissimi tanquam fratris, dictos sarracenos et
eorum uxores, natos, atque familiam ac peccuniam et animalia, res,
bona que deferant secum, dum tamen res prohibitas non existant,
sub nostris regali guidatico, protectione, et custodia de speciali
gratia cum presenti duxerimus admittendos. Ideo vobis nostris
officialibus et subditis et unicuique vestrum dicimus, et mandamus
firmiter et expresse vos servitores, amicos, et deuotos nostros,
attente rogantes quatonus prefatos sarracenos et eorum uxores et
filios cum familia, peccunia, animalibus, et aliis omnibus bonis seu
rebus que secum deferant, ut prefertur, transire, yre [sic], ett
redire per omnia loca terre et dominationis nostre, tam in terra

videlicet quam in mari, totaliter permittatis salue periter et
secure, nullum eis vel alicui eorum in personis vel rebus distur-
bium, dampnum, seu impedimentum vel iniuriam aut molestiam ir-
rogando seu irrogari vel fieri per aliquem permittendo; quinimo
provideatis eisdem si opus fuerit et inde fueritis requisiti de
securo transitu et conductu. Presentes vero, quos post duos annos
volumus non valere, per illum vestrum cui in redditu predictorum
fuerint ultim presentate percipimus [sic] retineri.

Datis Cesarauguste, xviii die Julii, anno a nativitate Domini m ccc
l vii.

C 903:107   (October 4, 1359)

[The king grants to a favorite the price of a Muslim slave recently captured and worth thirty-seven pounds {of Barcelona}.]

See pp.49-56.

Petrus, etc. Ffideli scriptori officii thesaurarie nostre

Hugueto Cardona, ordinato ad vendendum sarracenos hiis diebus

captos per nobilem Bernardum de Capraria cum certis galeis

armatis, seu alii cuicumque ad recipiendum pretia ipsorum

sarracenorum deputato, salutem et gratiam. Quia ffidelis de

domo nostra Guillelmus ça Calui, ballistarius Barchinone,

emit in encanto facto de dictis sarracenis quendam vocatum Ma-

fumetus Algazu, pretio triginta septem librarum barchinonensium,

et nos eidem Guillelmo dictum pretium gratiose concessimus cum

presenti, propterea vobis dicimus et mandamus quatenus ab ipso

Guillelmo dictas triginta septem libras minime petatis seu etiam

exigatis, recuperando presentem loco apoche et mandati. Nos

enim mandamus magistro rationali curie nostre seu alii cuicum-

que a vobis de premissis compotum recepturo quatenus tempore

nostri ratiocini vobis vel exhibente presentem dumtaxat [?]

predictam in nostro regali compoto non postponat.

C 903:175   (November 27, 1359)

[To meet its debts, which are overwhelming, the aljama of Játiva is allowed to levy taxes and imposts exactly like those imposed by the Christian universitas, and to keep the money derived therefrom for the payment of debts.]

Translated on p.218.

Nos Petrus, etc. Compatientes inopie et paupertati ad quas vos, aliama sarracenorum civitatis Xative et singulares eiusdem, propter molem nimiam debitorum ad quem obligati existitis et tenemini estis deducti, propter quem, nisi per nos de subscripta et aliis debitis provisionibus, favoribus, et gratiis vobis provideretur, possetis de facili ad destructionem irreparabilem pervenire, idcirco supplicationibus vestris nobis propterea factis benigniter inclinati, tenore presentis concedimus vobis quod per quattuor annos a datis presentium in antea computandos, ut vestris debitis satisfacere facilius valeatis, possitis inter vos imponere et ordinare omnes illas et similes impositiones et eisdem modo, via, et forma quibus universitas christianorum dicte civitatis eas ex nostri licencia imposuit atque levat, quas quidem impositiones vendere et arrendare si volueritis cuivis possitis, et eas exigi et levari facere per tempus superius. expressatum, et peccuniam inde ex eis exeuntem liceat vel convertere in solutionem et satisfactionem vestrorum debitorum predictorum. Mandantes,....

C 903:203   (December 1, 1359)

[The king confirms a privilege of 1202 guaranteeing the right of the Muslims of Lérida to be tried only by officials of the aljama, even in cases involving Christians and Jews.]

Translated on pp.140-141.

Nos Petrus, etc. Attendentes dudum nos subscriptam confirmacionem fecisse vobis aliame sarracenorum Ilerde cum nostra littera, nostro sigillo secreto munita, continente subse[quen]tis: Nos Petrus, Dei gratia Rex Aragonie, etc. Quia adelantati siue nuncii aliame sarracenorum Ilerde nostram adeuntes presenciam exhibuerunt nobis humiliter quoddam priuilegium illustrissimi Domini Petri, Regis Aragonie, proaui nostri, memorie recolende, sigillo suo appendicio in corrigia siue cordula cerui sigillatum, datum Cervaria, die veneris tertia die Septembris, anno Domini m cc ii, in quo inter cetera sequens clausula continetur:

Item, statuo quod quod* si aliquis christianus vel judeus querimonian habuerit de aliquo sarraceno Ilerde uel de alio sarraceno qui in Ilerde venerit, conqueratur çalmedine uel alcaydo constitutis inter aliamam sarracenorum Ilerde, et in posse ipsorum faciat directum, et non distringatur aliquis sarracenus pro curia christiana uel judaica nisi tantum per çalmedinam† uel alcayt constitutos inter eos.

Et licet inter dictos adelantatos et aliamam ac baiulum Ilerde lis seu questio diu mota fuerit sive ducta an videlicet per dicta verba clausule preinserte aliama predicta prorsus exi-

---

* Sic: bis, perhaps for quod quum?
† Manuscript has elmedinam.

meretur uel eximi debeat ab examine siue judicio baiuli Ilerde,

sic quod pro aliquo crimine seu delicto dictus baiulus Ilerde

nequeat procedere contra eos uel de eis civiliter aut criminaliter

se intromittere quouismodo, attamen nos considerantes quod dicta

aljama ab aliquibus citra temporibus qui ad depopulationem deuenit,

in tantum quod nisi per subscripte nostre provisionis remedium cep-

eretur destructioni irreparabili videtur proculdubio subjacere,

ideo pro reformatione et reparatione aljame predicte litem seu

questionem predictam tollere omnino volentes, dictamque clausulam

interpretantes ac etiam declarantes prouidemus et uolumus, dicte-

que aljame deliberate et de certa scientia concedimus cum presen-

ti quod de cetero predicta aljama et singulares ex ea pro et super

quocumque negotio ciuili et criminali directum faciant in posse

alcaydi uel çalmedine dicte aliame qui nunc sunt uel pro tempore

fuerint. Ita quod dictus baiulus Ilerde, qui nunc est uel alii

qui pro tempore fuerint, de dicta aljama uel singularibus eius

aut quibuslibet negotiis eorundem ciuilibus seu criminalibus intro-

mittere se non possint, quinimo predicti alcaydi uel çalmedina pre-

sentes et futuri per aut juxta eorum çunam inde justiciam reddant,

eosque puniant prout nouerint faciendum. Et hoc quidem sic fieri

uolumus et seruari quibusuis comissionibus, processibus, ac usibus

factis in contrarium aut quomodolibet exercitis obsistentibus nul-

lo modo. Et uolentes ulterius dictam aljamam nostris specialibus

prosequi gratia et fauore pro reformatione dicte aljame, declara-

tionem factam per inclitum infantem Petrum, Comitem Rippacurcie

et Montanarum de Prades, patruum nostrum carissimum, tunc locum

tenentem nostrum generalem in Cismarinis regnis et terris nostris,
de uel super exercitio jurisdictionis ciuilis dicte aljame et ade-
lantatorum ipsius cum carta sua, suo sigillo pendenti munita, que
datam fuit Ilerde, xvii die Januarii, anno a natiuitate Domini
m ccc l quinto, necnon omnia et singula priuilegia tam per predecessores nostros, reges Aragonie, recordationis eximie, quam per
nos memorate aljame et singularibus ipsius, quomodocumque indulta,
prout melius eis usi hactenus extiterunt iuxta eorum tenores aut
series cum presenti duximus confirmanda. Mandantes itaque per
presentem gubernatori nostro generali et eius uices gerenti in
Cathalonia, ac vicario et curie Ilerde, necnon dicto baiulo ciuitatis predicte, ceterisque officialibus et subditis nostris, presentibus et futuris, sub pena quingentorum morabetinorum auri,
nostro applicandorum errario, qui pena totiens comptatur quotiens
fuerit contrafactum, quatenus concessionem, interpretationem,
declarationem et confirmationem nostram huiusmodi teneant firmiter
et obseruent ac teneri et obseruari inuiolabiliter faciant nostri
officiales predicti et non contrafaciant aliqua ratione. Et ut
premissa majori robore fulciantur, juramus ad Dominum Deum, et
eius sancta quattuor euangelia temporaliter per nos tacta, predicta
omnia et singula tenere et obseruare perpetuo atque teneri et
obseruari facere prout latius de super continetur. Ceterum volentes hanc concessionem, interpretationem et confirmationem sepedicte
aljame effectualiter atque premniter [sic] obseruari, expressius
dicto baiulo presenti et futuro sub eadem pena precipimus quod dictus baiulus qui nunc est incontinenti, et alii qui post eum dicte

baiulie prehabuerunt officio, antequam officio ipso utantur,
jurent ad predicta sancta Dei euangelia Dei [sic:bis] que
continetur superius obseruare.   Et etiam uolumus quod dicti officiales et nuncii eorum prestent dictis alcaydo, çalmedine, et
adelantatis predicte aljame in exercenda eorum jurisdictionem
predictam consilium, auxiliu, et fauorem si et quando inde fuerint requisiti.   Est tamen intentionis nostre quod in quibuscumque
judiciis sive sententiis per dictos alcaydum, çalmedinam, et adelantatos dicte aljame quomodolibet facien[dis] seu promulgandis
atque in processibus propterea faciendis procurator noster fiscalis
Ilerde, presens et qui pro tempore fuerit, habeant pro parte nostra
et conseruatione jurium nostrorum necessario interesse; quiquidem
fiscalis partem nobis prouenientem ex inde nomine nostro recipiat,
de qua non renuatur thesaraurio respondere.   Concedentes per hanc
eandem predicte aljame ut si in quocumque voluerit litteram nostram
presentem in pergamino et sub sigillo majestatis nostre appendicio
in formam [sic] priuilegii, valeant obtinere, cum ad presens fieri
nequeat, eo quare* dictum sigillum non habemus in promptu.   In horum
autem testimonium presentem fieri et sigillo nostro secreto jussimus communiri.
Datis in loco Montessoni, ix die Nouembris, anno a natiuitate Domini m ccc quinquagesimo octauo.   Rex Petrus.
Idcirco ad supplicationem pro parte uestri dicte aljame nobis
suppliciter factam, confirmationem eandem in huiusmodi carta perga-
mina redigi, et nostre majestatis sigillo in pendenti jussimus

---

*Or quum.

communiri.

Datis Ceruaria, prima die Decembris, anno a natiuitate Domini

m ccc quinquagesimo nono, nostrique regni vicesimo quarto.

P. Canc.

Signum † Petri, Dei gratia Regis Aragonie, Valentie, Maiorica-

rum, Sardinie, et Corsici, Comitisque Barchinone, Rossilionis

et Ceritanie

Testes sunt Egregius Petrus, Comes Urgelli et Vicecomes Hugo,

                Vicecomes Cardene, Domicelli

                Ffrater Johannes, archiepiscopus Callaritanus

                Matheus Mercerii, camerlengus, et Berengarius de

                Palatio, milites

Sig†num Mathei Adriani, prothonotarii, sigilla tenentis dicti

domini regis, qui de mandato eiusdem hoc scribi fecit, cum raso

et rescripto: in v^a linea tantum; in xii^a quomodolibet; in xiii^a

in; et in xxi^a et qui; in xxvi^a prima die decembris et clausum.

C 903:263   (January 13, 1360)

[Owing to irregularities in the proceedings against them, two Muslims are pardoned for the rape of two Christian women after donating 1,800s to the Crown.]

See p.345.

Nos Petrus, Dei gratia, etc. Attendentes vos, Iuce Uzmin,

et Mahoma de Pedrola, sarracenos civitatis Ceserauguste, fore

delatos seu inculpatos quod vos tractastis cognoscere carnaliter

in fidei catholice opprobrium, nostreque dominationis contemptum,

duas feminas christianas, earum alteram vocatam Sanctiam, alteram-

que Mariam, conatus vestros faciendo cum effectu ut id ad effec-

tum totaliter pervenisset, super quo* ad instantiam et requisi-

tionem fiscalis nostri, vobis et dictis feminis captis existenti-

bus in posse nostri alguazirii, fuit contra vos et vestrum quem-

libet processem per inquisitionem legitimam de predictis, verum-

[tamen] quare contentis in processu inquisitionis prelibate et

hiis qui in ea fuerunt ministrata iudicialiter et producta

invenimus procedendis aliquos modos fraudulentos processisse con-

tra vos per aliquos officiales nostros, qui potius voracitate

cupiditatis quam iusticie zelo moti, contra vos minus debite

procedebant, et ex aliis iustissimis causis que nos ad hoc mover-

unt cum ratione, ideo ad humilem supplicationem aliquorum domes-

ticorum nostrorum et quare aljama sarracenorum dicte civitatis

nobis humiliter supplicavit quia vobis et ipsi aljame et singular-

ibus omnibus eiusdem predicta remittere ex nostri regali clementia

dignaremur, tenore presentis absolvimus, difinimus, remittimus, re-

---

*The following clause is an emendation by the scribe.

laxamus, et perdonamus vel dictis Iuce Uzmin et Mahoma de Pedrola et bonis vestris, ac universitati dicte aliame et singularibus eiusdem et etiam bonis eorundem perpetuo, omnem accionem,
questionem, petitionem, et demandam, omnemque penam civilem et
criminalem, et aliam quamcumque quam nos aut officiales nostri
nunc vel de cetero possemus contra vos seu alterum vestrum aut
bona vestra et vestrorum, seu dictam aljamam et singulares ex
eadem* et bona sua facere....

...Pro hac autem absolutione, difinitione, et remissione
dedistis et solvistis nobis mille et octingentos solidos jaccenses, quod dilectus consiliaris et thesaraurius noster, Bernar-
dus de Ulzinellis, miles, legum doctor, pro parte curie nostre
a vobis quitios habuit et recepit†. Mandantes,....

---

* Manuscript has eidem.
† Manuscript has recepuit.

C 903:282   (March 23, 1360)

[In accord with the express wish of the Aragonese
Cortes lately held in Zaragoza, the king allows that
the Muslims of Aragon may arrange legal documents
through any public notary, rather than only through
those appointed by the Crown specifically for Muslims,
as was previously the case.]

See p.94.

Nos Petrus, etc. Attendentes quod iuxta capitula quadam in

generali curia, quam Ceserauguste Aragonensibus celebra[vi]mus,

inter nos et brachia eiusdem curie inita, concessa, adque firmata,

omnes et singuli iudei et sarraceni civitatum, villarum et aliorum

locorum regni Aragonie possunt licite contractus suos, instrumen-

ta et alias scripturas publicas et auctoritaticas facere cum qui-

buscumque notariis, prout eorum placuerit volentati et de foro

dicti regni eis est licitum et indultum, idcirco ad supplicationem

humilem iuratorum et proborum hominum ville Burgie, tenor presentis

aljamis iudeorum et sarracenorum ville eiusdem ac omnibus et

singulis personis ex eis et quolibet earum, vigorem capitulorum

ipsorum licentiam et plenum posse conferimus, quod decetero con-

tractus suos et instrumenta et alias scripturas predictas, quas

habeant recipi et fieri inter se sive inter eos et christianos,

valeant in posse quorumcumque notariorum ville prefate voluerint

firmare, et eisdem per ipsos recipi et confici facere licite et

impune, prout per forum aragonensem eis est licitum et permissum;

inhibitionem sive inhibitionibus quibuslibet per nos eisdem iudeis

et sarracenis factis de non faciendo contractus, instrumenta, et

scripturas eorum nisi cum certis notariis sive personis, quibus per nos scribanie dictorum iudeorum et sarracenorum concesse

existunt aut substitutis ab eis--quas quantum ad hoc huius serie

revocamus--obsistentibus nullo modo.   Mandantes,....

C 903:290   (May 7, 1360)

[The king grants to a Muslim certain property in Tarazona which had once belonged to the Mudéjar's father,
but which is now in the possession of a Jew whom the
king suspects of treason.]

See p.69.

Petrus, etc. Cum ad supplicationem nobis pro parte Audalle de

Foxa, sarraceni commorantis in civitate Cesarauguste, conces-

s[er]imus eidem sarraceno sub conditionibus infrascriptis

quoddam ortale sive campum parietibus circum clausum, quem As-

sacus Aboraxa, iudeus, habebat et possidebat in orta civitatis

Tarrasone, quique fuerat Iuce de Foxa, patris dicte Audalla,

quo idcirco vobis dicimus et mandamus quatenus in casu quo dictus

iudeus nunc sit nobis rebellis et vasallus Regis Castelle, dic-

tum campum eidem Audalle visis presentibus liberetis, dum tamen

iamdictus campus ultra valorem ducentorum solidorum jaccensium

non ascendat.

   Intendimus vero quod dictus Audalla teneatur facere in

dicta civitate Tarrasone residentiam personalem, et solvere omnia

ónera ad que dictus campus ratione census fuerat obligatus ante-

quam dicta civitas fuisset nobis per regem Castelle indebite

occupata.

C 904:73   (May 10, 1360)

[The king confirms the sale by a Christian to a Muslim of property located within the morería of Zaragoza, and specifies the taxes to be paid on the property.]

See p.68.

Nos Petrus, etc. Quia pro parte Abdalaziz de Terrer, sarracenus [sic] ciuitatis Cesarauguste, fuit nobis humiliter supplicatum ut cum tibi uenditio subscripta facta fuerit cum instrumento publico, cuius tenor talis est--

Sea conoscida cosa a todos homens como yo, Pero Sanchez de Penya, Rector de Manchonis, certificado plenerament en todas cosas, de mi drecho [sic] vendo e de present liuro de dia e no de noch, segunt fuero de Aragon, e en corporal possession vos end pongo con esta present carta publica a vos Abdalaziz Aterrer, moro uecino de la ciudat de Çaragoça, es assaber unas casas e corral que yo he sitiadas en la ciudat de Çaragoça en la moreria de la dita ciudat, las quales casas e corral affruentan con casas de Mafomat Alorqui, et con casas e corral de Gil d'Almenara, e con el molino de Bardaxi, e con la carrera publica, assin como las ditas affrontaciones encierran e departen en darredor las ditas casas e corrall, assin aquellas a uos e a los uestros e a quien vos queredes vendo con todas sus entrades e sus exidas e sus aguas e sus derexos e pertinencias e melloramientos, quantos que han e hauer deuen, del çielo fasta en los abissos, sines retenimiento alguno mio e de los mios,e obligacion e mala uoz de toda persona venyent e contradizient; es a saber por precio de huytanta solidos jaccenses, de los quales con el Ali Fara ensemble me atorgo de uos seer bien entregament pagado e contento.

Porque laudo e perpetual la dita uendicion confirmo e
apruheuo, e quiero que uos, dito comprador, e quien uos queredes
de oy adelant hayades, tengades, e possidades las ditas casas
e corral franchas, ferras, liures, e quitas, sines mala uoz e
embargamiento alguno, por dar, uender, camear, empenyar, alienar,
possedir, espleytar, e por fer de aquellas a toda vuestra propria
uoluntat, assi como de cosa vuestra propria, segunt que mellor
e mas sanament e proueytosa puede seer dito, scripto, e pensado
e entendido, a proueyto e saluamiento e buen entendimiento vuestro
e de los uuestros e de qui vos queredes.

E por mellor segurança vuestra e de los vuestros e de qui
vos queredes, yo mismo me offrezco e me establezco seer fiança
de saluo de las ditas casas e corral, e de leal encorja, e prometo
las uos saluar e deffender aquellas de toda persona que en aquellas
o en partida de aquellas uos puziesse pleyto o question o mala uoz,
dius obligacion de mi e de todos mis bienes muebles e seyentes ha-
uidos e por hauer do quiere que sean trobades, assi temporales
como spirituales. Fecha carta en Taraçona, viii dias del mes de
Março, anno a natiuitate Domini millesimo ccc sexagesimo....
--dignaremur uendicionem predictam de regia benignitate confirmare,
potissime cum peratus existas sponte pro dictis domibus et currali
facere nobis ac nostris ac soluere perpetuo pro tributo annis
singulis amodo in festo Sancti Johaniis Babtiste, mensis Junii, duo-
decim denariorum jaccensium.

Idcirco supplicatione ipsa benigne suscepta, tenore presentis carte nostre uenditionem preinsertam cum onere uel retentione dicti tributi nobis et nostris perpetuo fiendi et soluendi annis singulis in dicto festo Sancti Johannis, ut prefertur, laudamus, approbamus, ratifficamus, et etiam confirmamus ac eidem auctoritatem nostram impendimus et decretum. Mandantes,....

Predicta carta non fuit expedita sub dicta forma, sed sub alia, inferius registrata.*

---

*I.e., at C 904:85ss, which is, however, identical in tenor and in all but a few sentences to the above, being basically just a condensation of it. Only two new facts are mentioned: the annual tribute of 12d is to be paid to the Mayor of Zaragoza; and the property was purchased by Sanchei de Penya himself only three years previously--April 17, 1357--from Petrus Martinus de Stella and Maria Peralta, his wife, who were both citizens of Montalbán.

C 904:139   (August 13, 1360)

[The king grants to a merchant of Lérida the right
to transport forty Muslims to "Saracen lands," and
specifies the procedures to be followed for certifying
and taxing their departure.]

See p. 303.

Nos Petrus Rex volentes vos, fidelem nostrum Bernardum Manresa,

mercatorem civitatis Ilerde, favore prossequi in hac parte,

tenore presentis concedimus vobis quod non obstante inhibitione

quacumque facta vel etiam facienda, et absque aliavis pene in-

cursu, possitis extrahere a regnis et terris nostris, et ad par-

tes ultramarinas sarracenorum seu alias quaslibet deportare seu

deportari facere, inibique dimittere*quadraginta sarracenos,

mares seu feminas, franchos et liberos a qualibet servitute,

quos tamen teneamini recolligere in plagia Barchinone. Mandan-

tes baiulo nostro Cathalonie generali, et custodes rerum prohibi-

tarum, ceterisque universis et singulis officialibus nostris et

subditis et dictorum officialium loça tenentibus, ad quos presen-

tes perverint, quod vos dictum Bernardum seu extrahentes pro vobis

sarracenos predictos non impediant in terra vel mari, quinimo

concessionem nostram huiusmodi inviolabiliter observando et

observari etiam faciendo, vos et eos ad quaslibet partes abire

et transire permittant franche et libere et quacumque contradic-

tione cessante.

    Et in extractione dictorum sarracenorum recuperet a vobis

dictus noster baiulus generalis presentes, nec eius pretextu ullus

major sarracenorum numerus extraheri valeat per quemcumque, si non

---

* Manuscript has dimutere.

particulariter extrahantur. Faciat idem baiulus illos notari in
dorse huiusmodi ad cautelam, et in finale extractione presente[s] re-
cuperari ex preallegata causa procuret. Pro quolibet [dictorum]
sarracenorum quos pretextu concessionis nostre presentis extrahere vos continget, teneamini nobis dare quindecim solidos barchinonenses, de quibus antequam ipsos sarracenos recolligatis teneamini dicto baiulo respondere ratione [sic] curie nostre seu
cui voluerit loco sui.

C 904:144   (August 26, 1360)

[The king grants permission for any Moroccan Muslims of Valencia who wish to return to their homeland and who are free of obligations in Valencia to depart under the tutelage of Jacob Arracani.*]

See p.306.

En Pere, per la gracia de Deu Rey d'Arago, al amat conseller

nostre en Pere Boyl, Batle General de regne de Valentia, salut

e gracia.   Com Iacob Berniça Arracani, del realme de Marrochs,

de voluntat nostra se'n deja menar tots aquells moros que

trobara esser ffranchs o quitis en regne de Valentie, qui pero

sien estats del dit realme de Marrochs e vullan que aquells

se'n puxen anar ab lo dit Benabrafim [sic] (e sens ell) salva-

ment e segura, per ço a vos dehim e manam que [a] aquells moros

que ell vos nomenara, qui franchs o quitis seran trobats en lo

dit regne, e son del realme dessus dit, façats guiatge e segur-

etat en nom, loch, e [   ] nostres, axi que per nenguns oficials

ne sotsmeses nostres no'ls puxen esser donat dampnatge en bons

ne en persones, ans de tot en tot se'n puxen anar salvament, quitia,

e segura, ab tots lurs bons e drapes, axi com dit es.

[Safe-conduct for Jacob Arracani himself:]

Nos en Pere, etc. Per tenor de la present guiam e en nostra

bona fe real asseguram tu, Iacob Abenmusse Rancan, moro, axi

que si deça vols tornar, aço puxes fer salvament e segura, ab

---

* Cf. Alarcón Santón, Documentos, p.311, #140bis.

ta companya e bens, manants ab aquesta mateixa letra a tots

e sengles officials e sotsmeses nostres, axi deça della mar

e encara en mar constituits, de qualsevol conditio s[i]en, que

servant aquest nostre guiatge te lexen venir e estar e tornar

salv e segur ab los bens e companyes tues, e que no't donen algun

dampnatge en persones ne en bens, si la nostra ira e indignatio

cobeien squinar.

C 905:62   (November 22, 1360)

[The king concedes to the Muslims of Benavento the privilege of constructing a mosque and a graveyard.]

See p.263.

... Tenore presentis concedimus gratiose, de certa scientia,

et consulte quod in castro seu loco [Benaventi] vel eius ter-

mino possint sarraceni ipsi, presentes videlicet et qui pro

tempore fuerint, mezquitam iuxta eorum sectam adorandum necnon

fossare ad corpora eorum sepeliendum de novo construere et habere

franche, quitie, et impune, absque tamen iuris prejudicio alieni.

Ita quod pretextu huius concessionis nostri seu gratie, cunctis

temporibus durat[ur]e, sarraceni jamdicti, tam mares videlicet

quam femine, in castro seu loco prefato nunc habitantes seu in

futurum habitaturi, construant de novo et construere valeant ac

tenere in ipso castro seu loco aut eius temino mezquitam et in

eo orare, necnon fossare et in ipso eorum corpora sepelire,

sine tamen alieni iuris prejudicio, ut prefertur....

C 905:176   (May 28, 1361)

[The Muslim women of Picasent are granted immunity from
enslavement for practising prostitution outside the districts in which they are licensed.]

Translated on p.350.

Nos Petrus, etc., volentes vos, dilectum consiliarium nostrum

Petrum Boyl, militem, cuius est locus de Pitaçen, gratia pro-

sequi et fauore, et ut sarraceni et sarracene habitantes in

dicto loco de Pitaçen seu eius terminis et ad ipsum declinantes

ab inquietatione et molestatione quas aliter possent incurrere

preseruentur, tenore presentis concedimus uobis et uestris her-

edibus, dominis dicti loci, per priuilegium speciale, quod--

aliquo seu aliquibus regni Valentie consuetudine, usu, foro, aut

çuna sarracenorum minime obsistentibus--alique sarracene dicti

loci seu ad ipsum locum declinantes, quamuis se non scripserint

seu scribi fecerint pro meretricibus in locis regalibus, dummodo

pro talibus in dicto loco de Pitaçen se scribi fecerint, undecum-

que sint non possint per nos seu officiales nostros, etiam si eas

inter eorum districtum meretricantes repererint, captiuari seu fis-

co regio aplicari. Mandantes per presentem gubernatori nostro

generali, necnon eius vices gerentibus, et baiulo generali, aliis-

que uniuersis et singulis officialibus dicti regni, presentibus et

futuris, ipsorumque locatenentibus, quatenus concessionem nostram

huiusmodi uobis inuiolabiliter obseruantes contra non ueniant

aut faciant, nec sinant per aliquos fieri quouismodo. ...

Datis Çaranyone, xxviii die Madii, anno a natiuitate Domini m ccc

lx primo.

C 905:205   (June 3, 1361)

[The king orders the construction of a judería and a
morería in Tarazona, each to be separated from the
Christian population by walls.   Those Christians now
living in what is to become the morería or judería
are to be moved and given property of comparable
value elsewhere.]

See p.64.

Nos Petrus, etc., volentes circa reparationem et statum tran-

quillum civitatis nostre Tarasone et eius habitatorum, preser-

tim iudeorum et sarracenorum, qui nomine regalie nostre exis-

tunt, prout officii nostri debitum id exposcit sedule intendere,

idcirco de industria et approbata fide vestrorum [sic], dilecti

et ffidelis nostrorum Blasii Fferdinandi de Heredia, militis,

Iusticie Aragonie, et Gueraldi de Spelunca, sui thesaurarii,

illustris Alienore, Regine Aragonie, consortis nostre carissime,

merite confidentes, vobis et utrumque vestrum insolidum huius

serie dicimus, committimus, et mandamus quatenus accedendo persona-

liter ad civitatem predictam Tirasone [sic] nomine et pro parte

nostre ordinetis intus civitate* dicte civitatis, vel in barrio

Sancti Michaelis, vel alia parte civitatis eiusdem ibi (scilicet,

ubi magis expediens videbitur) iuderiam, intus quam omnes et

singuli iudei in dicta civitate habitantes et habitaturi habitent

et habitare teneantur, segregando iuderiam ipsam per clausuram

parietum ab habitatoribus christianorum.

Similiter ordinetis morariam sarracenis dicte civitatis,

in illa videlicet parte qua vobis videbitur, in qua sarraceni

---

* Sic: sc. civitatem.

ipsi habitent et morentur.

Committentes vobis et utrumque vestrum insolidum quod si domos vel hedificia per vos noviter dictis judeis et sarracenis intus iuderiam vel moreriam conferrenda vel assignanda iam per nos vel commissarios nostros a nobis potestatem habentes vel alios aliis habitatoribus christianis dicti civitatis concessa vel assignata fuerint, suis concessionibus quibuscumque non obstantibus (imo eas ipso [sic] causa cum presenti cassamus* et irritamus† et pro non factis ipsas haberi volumus), possitis domos ipsas et hedificia dictis iudeis et sarracenis conferre et assignare et christianis ipsis quibus concessa extiterant alias domos vel hedificia in aliis locis dicte civitatis in compensationem earum eis concessarum concedere et conferre, de quibus concessionibus possitis eis et quibuslibet ex eis nomine nostro fier[i] facere publica instrumenta, et possessiones corporaliter [?   ] de eisdem, que nunc pro tunc cum presenti laudamus et approbamus et permittimus observare et observari facere.... Et vos et utrumque vestrum insolidum ipsos et quelibet eorum ad predicta servanda et tenenda per captiones personarum et occupationes bonorum et aliter, prout vobis videbitur, compellere possitis.... Mandantes,....

---

* Cf. cassus, "void."
† Cf. irritus, "null."

C 913:33   (September 16, 1366)

[The king seeks to place the aljama of Játiva and its inhabitants under special protection to guard them from harassment by Christians.]

Translated on pp.359-360.

Nos Petrus, etc. Cum spectet ad principum potestatem futuris

subditorum periculis precauere, et a calumpniantium viribus defen-

dere debiles et inermes, ut per sue prouisionis industriam con-

antem offendere retrahat a delicto, et oppressum liberet a malig-

no, nosque deceat inter ceteros intra nostri dominii limites de-

gentes, ac sub nostra generali vel speciali quauis protectione

constitutos, eo prestantius sarracenos in nostris ciuitatibus,

villis, ac locis comorantes legittime defensionis subsidio deffen-

sare, quo illos humilioris legis grauat condicio, ipsique sunt

magis thesauri regii speciales, idcirco tenore presentis carte

nostre, firmiter et cunctis temporibus valiture, eo videlicet quia

ut ecerto percepimus sarraceni raualli siue morarie ciuitatis Xat-

iue, tam in personis quam bonis, sepius a christianis male tractan-

tur, et cautius plus timeri soleant que specialiter imperantur que-

que generaliter iniunguntur, licet uos aliama sarracenorum dicte

ciuitatis eiusque singulares iam sitis sub nostra generali protec-

tione et guidatico constituti, tamen ad tuitiorem [sic] cautelam

constituimus, recipimus, ac ponimus sub nostra protectione, com-

anda, securitate, et guidatico speciali vos, dictam aliamam sera-

cenorum [sic] ciuitatis Xative, et singulares eius, tam vicinos

et habitatores raualli siue morarie dicte ciuitatis, quam alios

quoscumque in peytis, tributis, et aliis oneribus dicte aliame con-

tribuentes, ubilibet sint vel existant, scilicet uniuersaliter
uniuersos et singulariter singulos eorundem sicut si singulares
ipsi nominarentur uel exprimerentur hic nominatim, presentes per-
iterque futuros, cuiusuis sexus, gradus, status, etatis aut conditionis existant, necnon famulos et famulas isporum et cuiuslibet eorum, et omnia et singula bona mobilia et sedentia ac se
mouentia, res, et merces ipsorum et cuiuslibet eorundem, queque
sint uel fuerint, et ubicumque intra nostrum dominium sistentes
et sistencia, et ad ipsam aliamam uel dictos singulares, seu cum
eis contribuentes, aut aliquem ipsorum pertinentes et pertinentia
nunc et decetero quouismodo. Ita quod nullus de nostri confidens
gratia vel amore audeat seu presumat vos, dictam aliamam, aut
dictos singulares vestros, uel in dictis peytis, tributis, et aliis
oneribus contribuentes, ubique sint uel existant, seu aliquem ipsorum aut famulos uel famulas eorum, seu dicta bona, res, aut merces
eorum, uel aliqua ex eisdem inuadere, capere, ledere, detinere,
marchare, pignorare, emperare, aut.aliter dampnum aliquod uel malum,
iniuriam, tedium, seu ofensam uobis uel eisdem inferre, palam quomodolibet uel occulte, modo aliquo siue causa, culpa, crimine, uel
delictis, aut debitis alienis, nisi prius in vobis et eis facita
[sic] inuenta fuerit de directo, aut vos uel ipsi [ut] principales
uel fideiussorie super predictis fueritis obligati, nec etiam in
hiis casibus nisi in quantum forus, jus, aut ratio fieri hoc permittat. Mandantes huius serie gubernatori nostro generali, eiusque
vicesgerentibus, justiciis, baiulis, ceterisque vniuersis et singulis officialibus et subditis nostris, presentibus et futuris, qua-

tenus protectionem, comandam, et guidaticum nostrum huiusmodi
teneant in omnibus et per omnia firmiter et obseruent, et ab aliis
faciant inviolabiliter obseruari, et non contraueniant nec aliquem
contrauenire permittant aliqua ratione. Quicumque autem ausu temerario ductus contra presentem protectionem, guidaticum, et comandam venire presumpserit iram et indignationem nostram ac penam
quinquaginta auri morabatinorum, nostro erario applicandorum, se
nouerit absque remedio aliquo incurrisse, dampno illato primitus
et plenarie restituto; adicientes quod uos et quilibet ex uòbis eisdem casibus et in eisdem causis in penam presentis protectionis
censeamini incidisse in quibus quicumque alii vos vel aliquem ex
vobis, ut premittitur, offendentes inciderent, ipso facto ut utrin-
que equalitas obseruetur. Et ne aliquis possit ignorantiam presentis nostre protectionis guidatici, comande, et securitatis aliquam
allegare, iniungimus expresse dictis nostris officialibus et locatenentibus eorundem, quod ad requisitionem vestram, seu vestri
procuratoris, dictum nostrum guidaticum, protectionem, et securi-
tatem prout magis expediens fuerit faciant ipsi, si requisiti fuerint, diuulgare voce preconia, iuxta modum et formam superius
expressatos firmiter obseruandum. ...

C 913:91   (November 25, 1366)

[In an effort to stimulate the repopulation of the war-torn aljama of Azp, the king grants its inhabitants the privilege of chanting the çala and sounding a trumpet before their ceremonies.]

See p.266.

Nos Petrus, etc. Volentès dare locum et modum [per] que locus

noster de Azp infra regnum Valentie situatum, in quo plures sar-

raceni habitare solebant, quique propter occasionem guerre Castelle

ad depopulationem maximam est deductus, citius valeat populari,

necnon ad humilem supplicacionem vestri alamini, veterum, et aljame

ipsius loci prepterea nobis factam, vobis Alfaquino Almuhaden,

alamino, veteribus, atque aljame et singularibus eiusdem, presen-

tibus et futuris, perpetuo licenciam et facultatem plenariam con-

cedimus cum presenti, quod vos et vestrum singuli possitis licite

sine metu vel incursu alicuius pene cantare çala et signum facere

orationis ad sonum trompete sive nafil intus mezquitam loci jam-

dicti prout sarraceni civitatum Valentie et Xative cantare dictam

çala[m] et sonare dictum nafil utuntur in mezquitis eorundem.

Mandantes per eandem universis et singulis procuratoribus, etc.,....

C 968:56   (December 10, 1362)

[Dominic Luppus Sarnes is appointed rector of the aljama
of Zaragoza, with complete authority over it in all
matters except criminal jurisdiction.]

Translated on p.76.

Nos Petrus, etc. Considerantes quod inter aljamam sarracenorum

Cesarauguste propter comp[u]lsiones, districtus, et pignorationes

qui fuerint in eorum bonis mobilibus et sedentibus per officiales

diuersos occasione peytarum et solutionùm que per eos anno quo-

libet debent solui, necnon ob contentiones et jurgia super comp-

ertimentis peytarum exorta pluries inter eos, inquietudines, graua-

mina, vexationes, et dampna in tantum ut ecerto didiciums sepius

oriuntur quod nisi per regalem clementiam subueniatur celeriter de

remedio congruenti ad casum desolationis et destructionis aliama

ipsa penitus duceretur. Quamobrem circa ipsius aljame reparationem

prouidere volentes, de industria, suficientia, et legalitate vestri,

fidelis consiliari nostri, Dominici Luppi Sarnes, merini Cesarau-

guste, plenarie confidentes, reuocantes huius serie comissiones

quasuis super infrascriptis quibuscumque personis retrohactis tem-

poribus per nos factas, tenore presentis comittimus siue comendamus

uobis curam, regiminem, et administrationem aljame sarracenorum

predicte, et compertimentum peytarum, tributorum, et subsidiorum,

et aliarum exactioneum eiusdem, dum de nostra processerit volen-

tate. Ita quod vos sitis rector sive administrator dicte aljame,

et regatis ac aministretis [sic] eandem legaliter et prudenter,

et compertimenta peytarum, tributorum, subsidiorum, et aliarum

exactionum siue contributionum quarumlibet eiusdem quouis modo

fiendorum ordinetis sagaciter inter eos, sic quod quilibet
ipsorum in solutione quolibet tatxetur iuxta facultates quas
possidet, ut per regiminis vestri industriam dicta aliama, qui
in tanta necessitate consistit, valeat suscipere incrementum;
iniugendo sarracenis iamdictis per penarum impositiones vel
aliter prout debite faciendum fuerit quod ordinationem et compertimentum per uos super premissis faciendum teneant firmiter et
obseruent, vosque peytas et hactiones [sic] colligatis et recipiatis pro parte curie nostre seu exigi, colligi et leuari faciatis
ab aliama predicta, per quem vel quos volueritis loco vestri
ipsos sarracenos et bona eorum ad hoc compellendo, et per quos
volueritis distringendo et faciendo de peccunia peytarum, tributorum, et aliorum predictorum, cum ad manus uestras peruenerint
solutiones illis personis quibus fieri habebunt temporibus et
terminis statutis.   Quodque de omnibus et singulis causis et licti-
bus [sic] ciuilibus dictam aljamam et singulares eiusdem quouismodo tangentibus eos noscatis, easque prout de foro et ratione
faciendum fuerit fine debito terminetis.   Et insuper omnia alia
et singula exerceatis et faciatis que ad utilitatem et comodum
aljame predicte neccesaria sciueritis et fuerint opportuna.
Mandantes per presentes sarracenis predictis et singularibus eorundem quod uos dictum Dominicum pro rectore et administratore
aljame ipsius, et peytarum, tributorum, et aliarum contributionum
predictarum habeant et teneant, vobisque vel cui volueritis loco
vestri respondeant de eisdem erogandis et distribuendis per uos

illis quibus solui et distribui habuerint seu etiam erogari.

Iniungentes nichilominus gubernatori, justicie et baiulo generali

Aragonie, necnon collectoribus, aliisque uniuersis et singulis

officialibus nostris et judicibus quibuscumque delegatis ac etiam

delegandis quod vos, dictum Dominicum, habeant et teneant pro

rectore et administratore predicto. Et contra presentem commis-

sionem in premissis vel aliqui premissorum se intromittere modo

aliquo non attemptent. In ciuis rei testimonium presentem fieri

iussimus nostro sigillo munitam, datis in Montessono, x die

Decembris, anno a natiuitate Domini m ccc lx secundo.

C 982:132   (June 29, 1358)

[The king clarifies the relative proportions to be
provided by the Christian and non-Christian communities of Teruel in a recent troop levy for the war with
Castile.]

See p.176.

Nos Petrus, etc. Attendentes quod iuxta compertimentum factum

de numero equitum nobis concessorum per Generalem Aragonensem,

in curia generali per nos nuper aragonensibus celebrata pretextu

guerre Castelle, universitas civitatis et aldearum Teroli tenetur

facere sexaginta quinque equites parum plus vel minus, in quibus

comprehendi debent--videlicet in solutionem solidi seu stipendii

eorum--judei et sarraceni in dicta civitate Turoli commorantes,

idcirco ne propter solutionem huiusmodi per ipsos judeos et

sarracenos ex causa predicta fienda inter homines dicte civitatis

et aldearum questio aliqua oriri valeat seu insurgi, harum serie

dicimus declarandum quod quantitas per dictos judeos et sarracenos

in predictas solvendi ad rationem, videlicet centum quadraginta

sex peditum pro viro equite, deducatur de numero dictorum sexa-

ginta quinque equitum, et residuum dividatur inter dictam civitatem

et aldeas, per illum modum et forma[m] quibus contributiones per

eosdem facte et fiende sunt in similibus fieri ordinate, taliter

quod inter dictam civitatem et aldeas et judeos et sarracenos

predictos cumpleant numerum sexaginta quinque equitum predictorum.

Mandantes,....

C 986:20   (August 26, 1365)

[The king commands his Muslim subjects in Artana,
Eslida, and Espada to obey his cousin, the Count of
Ampurias, whom he has appointed Captain of Segorbe,
and to co-operate in the recovery of the city and
its castle. Cf. following entry.]

En Pere, etc., als alamins, veylls, i aliames dels moros de

Castre de Arcana, d'Eslida, i de la Serra d'Espada, i de tots

los altres castells i lochs de moros de aquells comarques,

als quals la present prevendra, gracia sua. Manam vos expressa-

ment sots pena de cors i de adi, que creegats i obeesonts [sic]

a nostre car cusi, lo Comte d'Ampuries, lo qual hauem fet Capita

de la ciutat de Sogorb, de tots aquelles coses que per nom nostre

i axi com a capita damunt dit vos dara e us manara per servey

nostre i per guarda i deffensio de la dita ciutat de Sogorb i

per cobrar i haver lo castell de la dita ciutat, lo qual haura--

Deus volent--dins breus dies.

Dada en lo setge de Murvedre, sots nostre segell secret, a xxvi

dies d'Agost, en l'any dela nativitat de nostre Senyor m ccc lx v.

Rex Petrus.

C 986:28   (August 31, 1365)

[The king enjoins his cousin from abusing the power
lately granted him as Captain of Segorbe, especially
in regard to exploiting the non-Christian population
there.]

Translated on p.341.

En Pere, etc., al egregi baro, en Johan, Comte d'Ampuries,

cavaller, cosi nostre molt car, Capita de Sogorb, saluta, etc.

Per altres nostres letres nos recordam qu'us hauem strict manat

que no us entremetats del homnes de Segorp, ni de lurs bens, sino

tansolament del fet dela guerra e del cobrament del castell.

Car segons havem entes vos i vestres alguatzirs hi continuats de

pendre alguns moros i juheus i lurs bens, de qu'ens maravellam

molt. Per qu'us deim i manam expressament i de nostra certa sci-

encia que contra los dits homnes--axi crestians com juheus i

moros--de Segorp enactament algun no façats, ne en res d'ells vos

entremetats, sino en los affers dela guerra tansolament. E aço

per res no mudets. Manants i proveins per aquesta mateixa letra

als comissariis i portars nostres, qualssevol que la son, que

no's entremetre en res deles dits homnes i sos bens, sino ence-

rar, demanar, hauer, i cobrar bens del Rey de Castella i de com-

panyes sues Castellanes, si n'i ha.

Dada en lo setje de Murvedro, sots nostre segle secret, a xxxi

dia de Agost, en l'any de la nativital de nostre Senyor m ccc lx v.

Rex Petrus.

C 986:43   (September 10, 1365)

[The king absolves the Muslims of Artana from the fealty
they have lately sworn to him, directing them henceforth
to have as their lord Rodrigo Diaç.]

Translated on pp.36-37.

Jassia vosaltres enquant lo castell de Artana i vosaltres mateixs

haguessets dats a nos i hagessets fet jura i homenatge al noble

i amat conseller i maiordom nostre, En Gilabert de Cencelles, ca-

valler, en persona nostra regonoxents esser homnes i vassalls

nostres propris..., empero, car en les Corts que ara novellament

havem tengudes als Valencians, los havem atorgat retre lurs cas-

tells i lochs que havien cobrats del Rey de Castells, e entre'ls

altres havem manat retre al noble i amat nostre, En Rodrigo Diaç,

cavaller, lo dit castell i vall de Artana, per ço, absolutes vos

de tot homenatge i jura de feeltat que havats fet a nos..., vos

deim i manam que tingats de aqui avant per senyor lo dit En Rodri-

go Diaç, e li façats homenatge i altres coses a que li erets ten-

guts ans qu'el dit castell fos occupat per lo Rey de Castella.

C 986:45   (September 12, 1365)   (Secret Seal)

[The king orders the queen's procurator to proceed with
an investigation pending against the Muslims of Eslida
only in accord with the prescriptions of the çuna, especially in regard to torture.]

See p.125, n.76.

...Segons que'ns han humilment demostrat los moros d'Eslida, vos

procehits i enantats contra alguns d'ells per crims dels quals

son inculpats, e no guardada lur çuna, segons la qual deuen esser

jutjats, alguns d'aquells hauets turmentats e volets posar a tur-

ment. Per que a supplicacio dels dits moros per aço a nos feta,

a vos deim e manam que contra los dits moros procehistats axi

en turmentar com en altre manera segons que per lur çuna trobarets

esser fahedor*, de guisa que contra çuna los dits moros no sian

agreviats....

---

* I.e., fiendum.

C 986:47   (September 1, 1365)

[The king confirms to the Mayor of Zaragoza sole jurisdiction over Muslims and Jews in civil cases between
them, or between them and Christians when the latter are
plaintiffs, in accord with a privilege granted in 1346
to a previous mayor.]

Cf. Chapter III, passim.

Petrus, etc. Dilecto consiliario nostro, Dominico Luppi Sarnes,

militi, merino civitatis Cesarauguste, salutem et dilectionem.

Dudum Johannes Çabata, pre[de]cessori vestro in officio merinatus

predicti, scripsisse recolimus cum littera nostra, continentie

subsequentis: Petrus, Dei gratia Rex Aragonie, etc., dilecto

de domo nostra Johanne Çapata, merino Cesarauguste, vel eius

locum tenenti, salutem et dilectionem. Cum quorundam fidedigno-

rum nostrorum fidelium rumore sedulo nobis noviter sit deductum

quia çalmedina civitatis Cesarauguste ac alii officiales et judi-

ces, tam ordinarii quam delegati, ipsius civitatis et aliarum vil-

larum et locorum merinatus predicti, jurisdictiones eis et cui-

libet eorum comissis [sic] plusquam eis ac officiis sibi commissis

liceat et sit deditum ampliare et pretendere, satagentes jurisdic-

tionem ipsius merinatus (officii vobis comissi)--cui omnes judei

et sarraceni in civitatibus, villis et locis predictis constituti

subiecti et submissi retroactis temporibus semper et actenus exti-

terunt--usurpare et infringere pro viribus non formidant, trahendo

ipsos et eorum quilibet indiferenter pro quibusvis causis et nego-

tiis civilibus ad judicium coram eis, quod nedum in ipsorum jude-

orum et sarracenorum, qui pro inde fatigantur cotidie indebitis

laboribus et expensis, grande dispendium et jacturam, set in ipsius

merinatus officii graviter prejudicium et diminutionem non modicum
cernitur redundare.   Idcirco ad ipsius jurisdictionis officii merinatus predicti, ipsorumque judeorum et sarracenorum predictorum
conservationem volentes prout convenit debite providere, cum unus-
quisque manere debeat in ea sorte qua vocatus est, et quod uni
deditum est alius non usurpet, promiscuisque act[ion]ibus rerum
offic[ ] non turbentur, set suo gradu quilibet sit contentus,
sit super premissis providendum duximus seu etiam ordinandum
quod de cetero vos de omnibus causis et negotiis civilibus quibuscumque inter j deum et judeum aut sarracenum et sarracenum civitatis, villarum et locorum predictorum motis et movendis ad invicem, seu inter judeum et sarracenum et e converso, ac de illis
qui inter christianum et judeum sive sarracenum mote sunt aut de
cetero movebuntur civiliter, dummodo ipsi judei et sarraceni rei
et non actores existant, quantumcumque judei et sarraceni ipsi
privilegiati fuerint sive franchi, vocatis qui evocandi fuerint,
cognoscatis easque decidatis et terminetis sive debite prout juste
et rationabiliter extiterit faciendum.
Mandantes et inhibentes per presentes çalmedine, ceterisque officialibus et judicibus supradictis civitatis, villarum, et locorum
predictorum, presentibus et futuris, quodammodo de cognitione causarum et negotiorum predictorum se nullatenus intromittant, quinimo judeos et sarracenos ipsos, etiam si privilegiati fuerint sive
franchi, et quoscumque litigantes cum eis in casibus supradictis,
ad examinem vestri dicti judici una cum processibus causarum et

negotiorum predictorum continue remittere non postponant.

Quoniam nos eis et eorum cuilibet super premissis omnem prorsus per pre[sentes] adimimus potestatem, quibusvis litteris seu
commissionibus a nobis seu gubernatore nostro generali, aliisque
gubernatoribus regni Aragonie seu vices gerentibus eorundem, sub
quacumque forma verborum concessis, ac etiam concedendis de cetero, nisi de provisione huiusmodi plenam et expressam ac de verbo
ad verbum fecerint mentionem, obsistentibus nullomodo. Mandamus
nichilominus per eandem omnibus et singulis judeis et sarracenis
predictis, presentibus et futuris, sub indignationis nostre pene
incursu, quod deinceps ad examinem judici alicui ex officialibus
seu judicibus supradictis, nisi ad vestrum et tenentem locum
vestrum, dumtaxat adire seu recurrere pro causis et negotiis predictis nullatenus non presumant. Nos enim vobis et dictis tenentibus locum vestrum super predic is tanquam ordinariis comittimus vobis plenariter vices nost as.

Datis Ilerde, iiii idus Novembris, anno Domini m ccc xl vi.

Quia cum potestatem similem vos in redictis habere providerimus
et velimus, ideo vobis dicimus et mandamus quatenus de causis et
questionibus predictis cognoscatis t aliter faciatis et possitis
facere quod dictus predecessor vester juxta preinserte littere
tenorem facere poterat et debebat.

Datis in obsidione Murvieteris, sub nostro sigillo secreto,
prima die Septembris, anno a nativitate Domini m ccc lx v.

C 986:66   (September 19, 1365)

[The king informs the qadi of Uxó that two Muslims of
the city who brought charges against Christian merchants
of Morella in the king's court failed to appear on the
day appointed for trial, thus seriously inconveniencing
the Christians. The qadi is to see that they appear
within three days to answer these charges, and to inform
them that if they fail to do so they will be tried in
absentia.]

Cf. Chapter III, passim.

Petrus, etc., ffideli nostro alcaydo castri de Uxone vel eius

locum tenenti, salutem et gratiam. Scire vos volumus quod Mi-

chael Geraldi, et Berengarium Johanis, mercatores ville Morelle,

fuerunt hiis diebus per nos citati ad requisitionem et instantiam

Ali Porro et Ffamet Ayton, sarracenorum loci de Uxone, certis de

causis per dictos sarracenos in nostri [sic] cancellaria proposi-

tis et allegatis, et quamvis dicti Miquael et Berengarius infra

terminum per nos eis prefixum cum littera citationis nostre comper-

uerint,   non tamen sarraceni convenientes predicti infra dictum

tempus, ne que post aliquantulo comparere voluerunt, dictos con-

ventos christianos laboribus et expensis vexando in ipsorum dampn-

num et prejudicium manifestum. Quare ad requisitionem et instan-

tiam dictorum conventorum propterea nobis factam, vobis dicimus,

comittimus, et mandamus quatenus, dictis Ali et Fameto per vos

vice et nomine nostris citatis, eosdem infra tres dies per vos

eis prefigendos ad presentandum se coram nobis in nostri audientia

pro stando juri querelantibus de eisdem ad nos remittatis de pre-

senti, ipsos [sic] nichilominus certificantes quod si infra dictum

terminum non comperuerint, ut prefertur, procederemus in predictis contra ipsos et eorum bona, justicia mediante, eorum absentia
in aliquo non obstante.

Datis in ville Murvieteris, xix die Septembris, anno a nativitate
Domini M CCC LX V.

C 986:90   (October 4, 1365)   (Secret Seal)

[The king grants permission to a subject to sell a
Muslim whom he captured in Castile to any person
and for whatever price he may wish.]

See pp.49-56, 389.

Nos, Don Pedro, etc. Por tenor de les presents atorgamos a vos,

noble i amado nostro, Don Pedro Ferrandez de Vallascho, que

sienes*miedo d'alguno podades vender un moro cativo vestro,

el qual aduxiestes de Castella, y el qual es nombrado Mahoma,

a qual quiere persona vos queredes, i por aquel precio que hauer

podredes, i fazer d'aquell todas vestras voluntades. Mandan-

tes con esta misma a todos i cada unos officiales i subditos

nostros presentes y avenideros que la present concession nos-

tra haian firme, tengan, observan y no hi contravingan por

alguna razon. En testimonio de la [qua]l cosa mandamo[s] que

la present con nostro siello secreto siellar.

Dada en Valencia, en iiii dias de Octobre, del anyo de la

natividat de noster [sic] Senyor m ccc lx v.

---

* Sic..

C 1072:162   (August 30, 1360)   (Secret Seal)

[Having granted the Muslims of Valencia the right to emigrate to North Africa, paying certain fees to the Crown, the king privately explains to the officials delegated to collect the monies involved that this grant is to be honored only until the money needed for an embassy to Granada is collected, and that it is not to be applied to Muslims implicated in the recent conspiracy of Cilim. The original grant was issued the same day, and is found at C 1072:161.]

See pp. 311-312.

Petrus, etc.   Ffidelibus de domo nostra Johanni Dolit et Fferario

Gilaberti, salutem et gratiam.   Licet cum alia littera nostra

data ut infra comissionem absolute [sic] vobis fecerimus super

decimandis sarracenis regni Valencie et recipiendis iuribus inde

prouentis, ipsisque iuribus conuertendis in illis usibus in qui-

bus fideles consiliarii nostri Berengarius de Codinachs, Magis-

ter Rationalis curie nostre, et Arnaldus Johannis, legum doctor,

cum eorum albaranis vobis duxerint iniungendum, tamen nostra est

intentio quod dicta comissione utamini quousque habeatis comple-

mentum peccunie neccessarie ad expeditionem ambaxate quam dilec-

tus consiliarius noster Petrus Bohil, miles, Baiulus regni Valencie

Generalis, debet facere ad Regem Granate, scilicet ad armamentum

unius galee et ad sumptus neccessarios ipso Petro et aliis qui

cum eo ibunt in ambaxatam predictam, et ad soluendum motubellum

[sic], usuram, et interesse, et alios sumptus qui fient in manu-

leuandis quantitatibus neccessariis ad predictam; volentes quod

usque ad complementum dictarum quantitatum ad predictam necessar-

ium et non aliter utamini comissione predicta.   Et etiam volumus

et intendimus quod ipsa comissione utamini quo ad sarracenos qui
non videantur principales in illa seditione et factione, qui ad
nutum cuiusdam perfidi sarraceni vocati Cilim nuper in regno
Valencie extitit suscitata.   Nos enim promittimus vobis in nostra
fide regia et juramus per Dominum Deum et eius sancta quattuor
euangelia corporaliter a nobis tacta quod dictam comissionem vestram non revocabimus, ne in ea supersederi mandabimus aut facié-
mus, nec aliquid impedimentum apponemus seu apponi permittemus,
donec de dictis quantitatibus ad predicta omnia neccessariis
habueritis complementum.

Data in monasterio Populeti, sub nostro sigillo secreto, xxx
die Augusti, anno a natiuitate Domini millesimo ccc lx.

C 1073:95   (July 8, 1361)

[The king prohibits absolutely witnessing or notarizing
Muslim legal documents or transactions by any but royal
officials, or those approved by the Crown, and appoints
the addressee to undertake an inquisition against those
usurping the Crown's prerogatives in the matter, regardless of their position.]

See pp.92-94.

Petrus, etc. Ffideli de consilio nostro Roderico de Altabasio,

jurisperito Ceserauguste, salutem, etc. Ex clamosa pluriumque

assertione nostris auribus est deductum quod quamvis sarraceni

quicumque degentes in locis partium vel [conventarum ?] Ceser-

auguste, Osce, et Burgie ac termini eiusdem, et aliis locis tam

nobilium, militum, infantionum et generosorum ac ordinum regni

Aragonie teneantur facere jus coram alcaldis, çalmedinis, vel

alfaquiris dictarum civitatum ac villarum regiarum, et aliquis non

sit vel esset ausus nec posset conficere instrumenta sarracenica

inter sarracenos, nisi solum alfaquiri et scriptores sarraceni

deputati per nos in locis pretactis [sic], in quorum possessione

fuerunt predecessores nostri et nos ac officiales nostri a tanto

tempore citra quod hominum memoria in contrarium non habetur,

verumtamen a pauco tempore citra in fraudem, lesionem, detrimen-

tum ac usurpationem regaliarum jurisdictionis ac jurium nostro-

rum aliqui nobiles, milites, generosi, infantiones et religiosi

habentes in locis eorum sarracenos in[h]ibent sarracenis in locis

suis degentibus ne eant ad faciendum jus coram dictis officialibus

nostris, ut tenentur, nec contractus aliquos sarracenicos faciant

cum eisdem, et quod peius est, nostram jurisdictionem (ut dicitur)

usurpando constituerunt et constituunt officiales in locis
eorum qui cognoscunt indifferenter de causis predictis et
utuntur dictis officiis, de quibus aliqui nisi ad id per nos
fuerint deputati uti non debent (ut dicitur), necque possunt.

   Quocirca volentes circa conservationem jurium et jurisdictionis nostre, prout convenit, providere volumus, vobisque
dicimus, comittimus, et mandamus quatenus accedendo personaliter
ac discurrendo per loca quecumque dicti regni tam nobilium quam
militum, generosorum vel infantionum, quam ordinum et religiosorum, prout vobis melius videbitur expedire, vocatisque procu-
ratore nostro fiscali et aliis evocandis, quos in premissis
delinquisse repperitis, fortiter et districte tam in bonis quam
in personis puniatis rigide, prout de foro et ratione ac etiam
de regni consuetudine inveneritis faciendum, procedendo breviter,
summarie, et de plano, sola facti veritate attenta, ut in causis
fiscalibus ac nostrum patrimonium tangentibus debet et est fieri
assuetum. Mandantes harum serie gerenti vices gubernatoris in
Aragonia, ac justicie regni eiusdem, supraiuttariis, et universis et singulis aliis officialibus et subditis nostris, vel dictorum officialium loca tenentibus, quod super predictis assistant
et tribuant vobis auxilium, consilium, et favorem, quotiens et
quando inde per vos fuerit requisiti. Nos enim vobis super predictis et incidentibus connexis aut dependentibus vel emergenti-
bus quomodolibet ex eisdem vices nostras plenas comittimus per
presentes.

Datis Ceserauguste, viii die Julii, anno a nativitate Domini m ccc
lx primo.

C 1203:178   (August 20, 1364)   (Secret Seal)

[In return for sums he has advanced the Court,
Faraig de Belvis is granted a female Muslim slave
estimated to be worth 300s.]

See pp.43ss, 55.

Petrus, etc. Dilecto consiliario nostro Domenico Luppi Sar-

nes, militi, merino Ceserauguste, salutem et dilectionem. Cum

nos Ffarayg de Belluis, menescalo domus nostre, queudam sarra-

cenam captivam, que in posse vestro existit, queque nobis com-

petit, et que trescentos solidos jaccenses dicitur valere,

duxerimus concedendam, propterea vobis dicimus et mandamus ex-

presse quatenus, dicto Ffarayg vobis restituente cautelas cum

quibus consimilibus quantitas sibi per nostram curiam debeatur,

vel etiam maioris si sarracena ipsa majoris valoris existit,

eandem sarracenam tradatis dicto Ffarayg vel cui voluerit loco

sui. Quamobrem nos per presentem mandamus magistro rationali

curie nostre, vel alii sic cuicumque a vobis de predictis

competenter audituro, quod vobis sibi tempore vestri ratiocinii

restituente cautelas, huiusmodi de eadem sarracena nullam vobis

faciat questionem, vobis jurante quod dicta sarracena non valet

nisi trescentos solidos supradictos.

Datis Cesarauguste, sub nostro sigillo secreto, xx die Augusto,

anno a nativitate Domini m ccc lx iiii.

C 1204:63   (April 8, 1365)

[The king accepts back into his service the Muslims
of Castro and Alfandequiella, and responds to demands
made by them as pre-conditions of their return.]
English paraphrase on pp.367-8.

A tuyt sia manifest que nos, En Pere, etc., esguardants que

vosaltres, moros del castell de Castre i de l'Alfangeguella [sic],

qui, per maluats consells enganats, contra nos i la nostra corona

vos erets rebellats i alçats i donats al Rey de Castella, nostre

publich enemich; ara conexents vostra error i penedints de aque-

lla, cobejets de tot vostre cor exir de la dita vostra error i

tornar a nostra senyoria i obedencia, e sobre aço, ab aquella

humilitat que havets pogut, hajats a nos demanada venia i perdo

de ço que mal haviets fet, i encara per tal que en nostra fe

siats pus escalfats i pus volenterosament i pus coratjosa estiats

per mantenir nostra honor, nos haiats supplicat qu'us deguessem

atorgar alcunes gracies contengudes en los capitols deius escrits.

Per ço, nos volents seguir la carrera de nostres predecessors,

qui tots temps han anat benignament i misericordiosa envers lurs

sotsmeses, i qui moltes vegades envers aquells qui lur miseri-

cordia demanauen aquella misericordia han davant posada a ven-

jança, e cobejants enquant divinalment nos promes resemblar aquell,

lo loch del qual tenim en terra, qui diu que no vol la mort del

pecador, mas que's convertesca i viua, aquells capitols hauem vists

i regoneguts [sic], i apres hauda deliberacio en nostre consell,

los hauem otorgats i proveits segons que en la fi [sic] de cascun

de aquells es contengut. La tenor dels quals Capitols i de les
provisiones a aquells fetes es aytal:

Molt alt i molt poderos princep i senyor: a la vostra molt
excellent senyoria suspliquen i demanen los moros i aljama de
Castre i l'Alfandeguella, los quals, molt poderos Senyor, volen
venir a la vostra merce i benignitat, si'ls prometets les coses
infraseguentes i en los presents Capitols contengudes.

Primerament demanen los moros dels damuntdits lochs a vos,
molt poderos Senyor, que com ells sien talats i cremats i malme-
nats per captivitat de aquells, com n'i haj[a] catius alguns, que
placia a la vostra benignitat i senyoria que'ls façats franchs
i quitis de totes coses que'ls damuntdits moros sien tenguts pagar
a v anys, i que'ls confermets totes franquicies i libertates i
altres qualssevol privilegis que per Don Pedro de Xerica los era
estat confermat en temps antich, segons que ells ho tenen ja ordenat i han acostumat fer; i que ells puxen usar segons lur çuna;
i que nengu crestia no puxa entrar testimoni contra moro.
¶ Plau al Senyor Rey que sia servat ço qui antigament era acostumat.

Item demanen que negun official no puxa entrar en la lur
terra, sino que romanga lo merimperi axi com solia, i que no paguen
delme ni primicia, sino axi com han acostumat fer d'açi entras, i
que puxen cridar la çala axi com solian, i que no paguen sino de deu
barcelles de blat o de deu rones [?] una, axi com solien; com
los altres drets sien franchs, axi com raims, garafes, fig[uere]s,
i ortanta i ferraia; que la puxen dar francha i puxen penre la her-

encia que'ls pervenra en tot loch del regne d'Arago, i que
ells ho haien a dar semblantment segons que solien.

¶ Plau al Senyor Rey segons que era acostumat abans que lo dit
castell fos pres per lo Rey de Castella.

Item demanen que si nengu moro se'n volia passar en terra
de moros i venia ço del seu, que haja a pagar la deena part de
tot ço que venra, i que los que's volran mudar dins lo regne, si
venian ço del lur que sien franchs; i que los dits moros puxen
cobrar tots deutes que'ls fossen deguts de compres i de vendes
en tot lo regne, i que puxen cobrar ço del lur d'aquells qui
entraren fermançes per catius, los quals se'n passaren en Arago;
i que les termens i los erbatges estiguen segons que solien de
primer.

¶ Plau al Senyor Rey que ço per la de passar en terra de moros
i de vendre ço del seu i de la franquicia i de les termes i erbatges que's faça axi com antigament fou acostumat en temps de
Don Pedro.

Item demanen que sien franchs tots los catius que se'n passaren del una part a l'altra, i que sien absolts de tots crims que
haien fets o comeses en la senyoria del Senyor Rey; i que nengu
crestia ne juheu no puxa poblar ab ells; i que no sien tenguts de
pagar çofra al castell, ne a la senyoria, i que ells puxen usar
axi com lo Castell de Eslida fa, i que no sien tenguts de dar
gallina ne neguna cosa sino ab sos deners, i que no'n puxen esser
forçats.

¶ Plau al Senyor Rey.

Item demanen que de totes les damundites coses los façats
carta publica, e'ls observets segons que vostre pare i vostre
avi feu totes les damuntdites coses, i que totes les cartes que
per la dita raho se faran per Castre i per l'Alfaneguella, que
totes les los façats franques, com ells hajen prou que fer;
i que per nengu temps no paguen sisa ni cavalleria.
¶ Plau al Senyor Rey a tres anys.

Item demanen que tot l'erbatge de tot lo terme sia de la
aljama, segons que solien usar i acostumar, i forns i molins, que
tot sia franch, i apres de les v anys nolen senyor pagar i usar
i acostumar, segons que solien; i que nengu catiu que vingue de
nengun altre loch no puxe esser escorcollat per nengu si no es
de la senyoria, sidonchs no ere catiu del Senyor; i que nengu
no sia tengut per catiu si testimoni no'n ha moro; i que ells
puxen metre alami.
¶ Plau al Senyor Rey, empero que ells paguen la retinença del
castell.

On com se pertanga de bon princep servar les coses que
atorga, prometem en nostra fe reyal a vosaltres, dits moros, i
encara juram per Deu i per los sants iiii evangelis de nostres
mans corporalment tocats que los dits Capitols i les coses i
aquells contengudes segons que nos damunt los hauem atorgats
i proveits tenrem i observarem nos i noṡtres succeidors, i
null temps no hi contravindrem per neguna raho.
Manants,....

C 1206:138   (October 8, 1365)   (Secret Seal)

[The king concedes to the aljama of Játiva the right
to appoint and remove its own qadi, but stipulates that
this is not to affect the position of the current qadi,
Faraig de Belvis.]

Translated on p.85.

Ffideli nostro bajulo civitatis Xative necnon aljame sarracenorum

eiusdem civitatis salutem et gratiam.   Licet pridem provisionem

sive mandatum infrascriptum fecerimus cum littera nostra continen÷

tie subsequentis:

Nos Petrus, Dei gratia Rex Aragonie, etc.   Attendentes sicut

perpendimus pro aljama sarracenorum civitatis Xative secundum

zunam et xaram eorum per nos seu alios alcadius elegi non debere

nisi solum ad cognitionem dicte aljame, et talis qui in dicta

zuna et xara sit intelligens et expertus; attendentes etiam nos

de dicta alcadia dicta aljama insciente et contra dictam çunam

et xaram, de quibus non eramus immemores, providisse, et ob hoc

nobis aljama prefata humiliter suplicasse ut pro observatione dic-

te çune et xare et utilitatis dicte aljame super hiis dignaremur

eidem de subscripto remedio providere, idcirco tenore presentis

concedimus dicte aljame et placet nobis ac providemus quod possit

dictum alcadium eligere et eum removere quando et quotiens ei vi-

debitur expedire.   Quiquidem alcadius lites* inter sarracenos dic-

te aljame absque aliquo salario decidere habeat et etiam terminare;

de divisionibus vero habitatorum prout erat usitaticum antiquitus

duos denarios pro libra habeat et non ultra, et de instrumentis

---

* Manuscript has littes.

debiti qui receperit ac fecerit inter sarracenos quattuor denarios recipiat pro quolibet instrumento. Mandantes,....

Attamen quia nostra fuit et est intentio propter provisionem
preinsertam non derogare in aliquo jure Ffaraig de Bellvis, menescalli nostri, qui diu est ex nostri concessione ipsum alcadii officium obtinebat, propterea vobis dicimus et mandamus expresse
et de certa scientia quatenus eidem Ffaraig et eius substituto in
dicto alcadii officio, quamdiu eidem fuerit vita, respondeatis et
responderi faciatis de juribus assuetis dari et solvi pro officio
memorato, littera suprainserta in aliquo non obstante. Post vero
eius decessum ipsam litteram volumus observari juxta sui seriem et
tenorem. Datis Valentie, sub nostro sigilli secreto, viii die Octobris, anno a nativitate Domini mccclxv.

C 1534:150   (October 15, 1358)

[The king suggests to several Valencian aljamas that they make a "gift" to the queen of certain sums of money of which she is in need.]

Cf. Chapter V.

Cum illustris Alionora, Regina Aragonie, consors nostra carissima, per suas litteras rogando vobis scribat ut in auxilium emptionis sive luitionis per dictam reginam factarum de valle de Seta ac de aliis castris, locis, et vallibus que nobilis Comitissa Terrenove et Jaufridus de Jamvilla, pupillus seu eius tutor, a nobis pro certa peccunie quantitate tenebant pignori obligata, queque ad dictam reginam premissa de causa noviter pervenerunt subvenire velitis, idcirco nos, quem huiusmodi tangit negotium, habemus pro bono et volumus, vosque rogamus quatenus dicte regine predictis precibus annuatis, significantes vobis quod donum quod prefate regine in [?] premissorum feceritis placidum et acceptabilem habebimus veluti si nobis propr[io] factum esset, potissime [ut]* castra et loca jamdicta post mortem dicte regine ad nos et coronam regiam reverti debeant ac devolvi.

Datis Barchinone, xv die Octobris, anno a nativitate Domini millesimo trecentesimo quinquagesimo octavo.

Dominus Rex III

Dirigitur aliame sarracenorum Vallis de Seta.

Similes fuerunt directa [sic] infrascriptis, videlicet, juratis et probis hominibus castri et loci d'Alcoy, juratis et probis hominibus de Gorga, aliame sarracenorum de Bartaxell, aliame sarracenorum

---

* Manuscript has in.

de Xirillent, aliame sarracenorum de Trauadell.

C 1569:74   (November 12, 1360)

[The queen intervenes to correct abuses of the Muslim
aljama of Elche by the Jewish public notary there.]

See pp.292-294.

La Regina d'Arago, Tudriu del alt Infant en Marti, fill nostre
molt car: Com a nos sia stat donat a entendre que Iuceff Aben-
cavarell, juheu de Elx, qui te l'offici de torcimana a los moros
de Elx, fa moltes coses no degudes en lo dit seu offici, fahent-
se pagar e reembre los moros del dit loch de [correduçes ?] de
tot ço que la aljama dels dits moros ven, la qual cosa antigament no era acostumada, segons que per part de la dita aljama es
stat proposat devant nos, i altres coses diverses de que la dita
aljama es oprimiguda. E nos de totes les dites coses vullam
haver clara informacio, per ço que sobre aquelles puxem provehir
per justicia. Per ço, a vos de la fe de la qual confiam commenam
e manam que vista la present de totes les dites coses diligentment
e ab veritat nos en certifiquats, ço es lo dit Iuceff com ne en
qual manera se ha en fet lo dit seu offici de torcimania e en l'offici del testimoni e de la scrivania, e quins salaris o drets per los
dits seus officis han acostumats de hauer o de reebre antigament
ell e aquells qui han regit aquells. E hauda per vos clara certifi-
cacio de les dites coses, nos è la nostra cort volem que'n infor-
mats de continent prescrit clarament e vertadera, per ço que hauda
vostra informacio nos en les dites coses façam ço que justicia
requerat. E aço volem que per res no mudets.

Dada en Barchinona, a xii de Novembre del any de la natiuitad del Senyor m ccc lx.

Ffuit missa al fell nostro Berenger Togores, cavaller alcayt
del castell de Crevillen.

C 1569:75   (December 12, 1360)

[The queen intervenes against Domingo Lull, the
Bailiff of Elche and Crevillente, who has committed
various abuses against a prominent Muslim of Elche
in financial matters regarding the aljama.]

See p.89.

Na Alienora, regina, tudriu, etc., al fel nostre en Domingo

Lull, batlle e procurador dels lochs de Elix [sic] e de Crivilen,

qui son del dit Infant, salutem e graciam. Per part de Mahomet

Alfoll, moro habitador del dit loch de Eltx, havem novellament

entes que vos contra us c custum antigament usat en lo dit loch

demanats* al dit Mahomet que us deye donar en cristianesch trans-

lat del manual o compte seu, que ell ha fet e ordonat de la

cullita dels rendes e drets del dit loch (que colli despuis qu'en

Garcia de Loriç, cavaller, Governador del Regne de Valencia, pres

lo dit loch a amans del Senyor Rey tro per tot l'any de m ccc l

ix), de la qual collita o administraço es tengut de comptar ab

vos. Encara diu lo dit moro que ell dins lo temps de la sua admini-

straço ha donades a vos, e a alcuns de manament vostre, certes

quantitats de moneda, dels quals vos, jassia que moltes vegades

vos [h]aja request, no li volets fer apocha ne cautela ab que li

sien preses en† compte. Item diu que en lo dit temps de sa adminis-

traço ell bestrach alcuns quantitats de moneda per manament vostre

en talayes e escoltes necessarias al dit loch, les quals messions

apres foren comptades en l'alfarda que'ls moros del dit loch fa[h]-

eren, e'l çollidor [sic] de la dita alfarda ha reebudes dels dits

---

* Manuscript has demenats.

† Manuscript has em.

moros los dits messions. E vos vedats e hauets fet ser manament
al dit collidor de la alfarda que no deye donar al dit Mahomet
los dits messions que ha fetes, segons que diu. E encara mes
diu que vos hauets preses d'ell xix cafiços de civada per a ops
vostre e de vostres besties, sens que no feu aforada entre vos
ne ell en temps que la reebes. E, request per lo dit moro que
li tornets la dita civada, nou* volets fer, allegant que li darets
preu de cascun caffiç x solidos, de la qual cosa lo dit moro no's
ten per grent [?], car mes ama que li tornets la dita civada o
justa extimatio per aquella. Super les quales coses ha request
humillment e supplicat a nos que sobre aquells li deguessem de
remeyde justicia provehir.

Per que nos, la dita supplicaço benignament reebuda, a vos
dehim e menam que observets al dit supplicant lo us e custum del
dit loch de Elix antigament acostumat e observat en los altres
collidors en donar lo manuall o compte de lur collita en arabich,
ne per aquesta raho lo constrenguats, si husat no es de ordonar
lo dit compte o manuall en crestianesch, ans volem que li observets lo custum axi antigament observat en aytalls coses; si
vos empero hauets necessari que'l dit compte sia transladat en
crestianesch per raho de vostres comptes, fets aquell trasladar
a messions de la cort e no del dit moro (si, empero, açi se deu
fer, ne si los [   ] procuradors aço hauien acostumat). Encara
vos menam que encontinent façats al dit supplicant apoch e apochs
o altres cautelas bastantes o necessaries per al retiment de ses

---

* Contraction of no ho.

comptes de totes e sengles quantitats de deners o altres qu'us

haia donades o a altre en nom vostre e per vos.

E merevellam nos molt de vos e us en reprenem que, si axi

es, que vos deveguts a algu de fer apochs de com que reebets per

raho de vestro offici. Semblantment vos manam que les dites

messions que ha fetes en los escoltes e tayales, les quales ja

son stades tallades in compte de la dita alfarda, si empero a vos

sera cert que les dites messions sien per ell stades fetes, en-

continent les li façats [tornar] per lo collidor de la dita alfar-

da. O si vos aquelles hauets reebudes encontinent e de fet les

li tornats o restituiscats. E encara los dits xix brafiços de

civada segons que d'ell los reebes e si pus ladonchs no foren entre

vosaltres aforats, manam que li paguets per brafiç segons que en

lo temps d'ara valra en lo dit loch. Guardant vos curosament que

lo dit moro per les rahons damunt dites o per alguna d'aquellas

no haja a tornar a nos per colpa vestra. Car certificam vos que nos

de vostres bens li fariem satisfer en les messions, dans, e intere

esses que per aquesta auria fetes. E no res menys vos punirem axi

com trespasador de nostres manaments.

Dada en Barchinona, a xii dies de Decembre, en l'any de la nativitat

de nostre Senyor m ccc lx.

C 1569:92   (May 20, 1360)

[The queen intervenes to protect the aljama of Elche
from certain unjust demands being made upon it as a
result of the sale of its taxes for three years to
a local Christian.]

See pp.220, 225.

Na Alienora, Domina, Tudriu, etc. Al feel nostre En Domingo

Lull, batlle dels lochs de Eltx e Crevillen, que son del dit

Infant, o a son loch tinent, salutem et gratiam. Per part de

la aliama dels moros* del dit loch de Eltx nos es estat humil-

ment demonstrat que vos a instantia d'En G. Bosch, vehi de

Eltx, forçats la dita aliama a pagar a aquell quinque mille

centum sexaginta solidos, sex deners, reyals de Valencia, los

quals la dita aliama a li es tenguda donar (segons diu) per

rahon de una venda que la dita aliama a li feu feta, en temps

que'l dit loch era del alt Infant Don Johan, de tota la sosa que

dins iii anys ladonchs vinents se colliria en lo dit loch, a

rahon de m solidos e pugesa† per guantar; per la qual rahon ell

paga viii^m solidos [= 8,000s] a la dita aliama per los ii anys

primers vinents, e la dita aliama en los dits ii anys liura tan-

ta sosa al dit G. Bosch que munta (a la dita rahon) a ix^m l ii

solidos [= 9,052s] reyals de Valencia, axi que d'aquests ii anys

munta la sosa mes que ell ne havien pagat primer, m lii solidos

[= 1,052s], los quals reebe Berengar Romeu, ladonchs collidor

de la dita aliama per lo dit Infant. E que lo darrer any paga lo

dit G. Bosch iiii^m solidos [= 4,000s] primers en lo comançament

---

* Manuscript has <u>moreos</u>.
† Cf. modern Catalan <u>pujança</u>, "increase."

del dit derrer [sic] any, los quals liura a Mahomet Alfallugi,
moro de Eltx, collidor ladonchs per lo dit Infant, axi que la
dita aliama non reebe res.

E ara lo dit Guillem Bosch enten a demanar e hauer de la
dita aliama la dita quantitat e mes avant, per que a nos han
humilment supplicat que sobre aço lus deguessem de justaça
provehir. Nos empero, la dita supplicacio benignament reebuda,
a vos deym* e manam que appellats devant vos los dits Berengar
Romeu e Mahomat Alfallugi; si atrobarets que ells hagen reebudes les dites quantitats, e que sien romases en ells, forçats
aquells e cascun d'ells a tornar o restituir aquelles, e satisfer el dit G. Bosch en ço que degut li sera legitimament. E'l
sobreplus, si res hi sobrara, pergats a vostres mans per part
nostra en paga de ço que la dita aliama nos deu de temps passat.
E en altra manera, appellats aquells que faran a apellar, façats
en e sobre les dites coses a cascuna de les dites partes compliment de justicia sumariament e de pla, e sens pleyt, solament
la veritat del fet considerada. Com nos ab la present sobre
aquestes coses e altres d'aqu'en dependents e emergents vos com-
anam totes nostres veus.
Dada en Zaragoza, a xx dies de Maig, en l'any de la nativitat
de nostre Senyor m ccc lx.

---

* I.e., dehim.

TYPES OF CHANCERY REGISTERS CITED IN THIS STUDY

Registers in the series	bearing numbers	record information for the years
Commune	683-725	1355-1366
Gratiarum	858-913	1336-1367
Officialium	964-971	1352-1365
Diversorum	980-986	1355-1365
Venditionum	993-996	1353-1368
Curie	1067-1076	1353-1365
Sigilli Secreti	1148-1212	1355-1366
Secretorum	1293	1355-1374
Peccunie	1326-1342	1355-1366
Guerre Castelle	1379-1388	1356-1368
Pacium et Treguarum	1394	1357-1362
Armate	1401-1404	1354-1379
Castrorum	1462-1466	1348-1386
Demandarum	1472-1474	1346-1365
Inquisitionum	1494	1359-1371
Profertarum	1505-1506	1359-1368
Cenarum	1517-1518	1347-1386
Princeps Namque	1519	1361-1369
Pro Eleanora	1534-1537	1348-1377
De la Reina	1566-1573	1348-1377
Exercitum	1498-1499	1351-1375
Del Infante	1607-1613, 1649-50, 1676, 1707, 1734, 1801	1361-1366

GLOSSARY

A list of all the words in this study likely to be unfamiliar
to English readers would constitute an analytical index. The
aim here is simply to provide general definitions for key words.
Each of these words is defined more specifically within the text.
Latin words which occur in standard reference works are excluded,
as are designations of Christian officials which may be found in
standard texts of Spanish history, and words which occur infrequent-
ly or in contexts of minor importance.

adelantati elected officials governing Mudéjar communities, roughly
           corresponding to Christian jurados; see pp.72ss.

aljafería a converted Muslim stronghold used as a royal palace by
          Aragonese monarchs; the most important aljafería was in
          Zaragoza

aljama the corporate municipal body of Mudéjares; roughly com-
          parable to the Christian universitas

amin the principal financial officer of the aljama; see pp. 88ss.

çabiçala the prayer leader of the aljama; see p.74, n.41.

çala Muslim public prayer; loosely, the call to prayer

çalmedina the "mayor" of the morería (q.v.); see pp. 87-88.

cavallería war tax to support cavalry units

carnicería Muslims' meat market; see pp.95ss.

cena originally, a feudal duty of hospitality, but in this study
      it refers to a standard tax: see p.196 and tax tables

çofra a tax, either on wood or payable in wood for the needs of
      a castle

convivencia literally, "living together": Castilian designation for
      the interrelation of the various medieval Iberian religious
      and ethnic groups

çuna Islamic law (Romance for sunna)

exaricus a Mudéjar farmer; see pp. 40-41

faqi the legal officer of the aljama

fiancer   Catalan for fidejussor, q.v.

fidejussor co-signer of a loan or guarantor of a business venture

geneta   designation for Muslim cavalry units; loosely, a style of horsemanship modeled after these

judería   the Jewish quarter of an Iberian city

jurats   Catalan designation for jurados, or, loosely, the adelantati, q.v.

maravedí   see morabetí

merino   Christian municipal official; roughly, the "mayor"

morabetí(n) property tax; see pp.196, 199

morería   the Muslim quarter of an Iberian city; see pp.64 ss.

Mudéjar   a Muslim living under Spanish Christian domination

mustaçaf   the market official of the aljama; see p.101

peyta   standard tax on aljamas, usually a head tax

qadi   the chief judicial official of the aljama and generally its most powerful officer; see pp.74ss

qa'id   a military leader: see p.77, n.49

ravale   literally, "suburb"; loosely, the Muslim quarter or the morería

sueldo   unit of currency: see note p.25 loosely, "salary"

scribanus court-appointed notary: see p.92 et ss.

sisa   general war tax, collected principally in rural Valencia

torcimana translator for a Muslim aljama; see p.94, n.116

xara   Islamic customary law (shari'a), as distinct from çuna (q.v.), Islamic religious law

Sources: unpublished

Archive of the Crown of Aragon. Chancery Registers, numbers 683-
725, 898-913, 964-971, 980-986, 993-996, 1067-1076, 1148-
1212, 1293, 1326-1342, 1379-1388, 1394, 1401-1404, 1462-1466,
1472-1474, 1494, 1498-1499, 1505-1506, 1517-1519, 1533-1537,
1545, 1548-1549, 1566-1573, 1607-1613, 1649-1650, 1676, 1707,
1734, 1801.

Archive of the Crown of Aragon. Royal Patrimony Registers, numbers
337-352, 467-488, 642-644, 682, 687-688, 781-784, 921, 990-997,
1675, 1693-1694, 1704-1711, 1719, 1784-1786, 1788-1789, 1791,
1799, 1801, 1803, 1805, 1809, 1812-1813, 1972, 2402-2403, 2462-
2473, 2517-2518, 2603, 2604, 2637, 2911

Sources: published

Alarcón Santón, M. and R. García de Linares, Los documentos árabes
diplomáticos del Archivo de la Corona de Aragón. Madrid-Granada, 1940.

Bofarull y de Sartorio, Manuel de, Rentas de la antigua Corona de
Aragón, in Colección de documentos inéditos del Archivo general
de la Corona de Aragón, Próspero de Bofarull y Mascaró, ed.,
XXXIX. Barcelona, 1871.

Carreras y Candi, Francesch, "Ordinacions urbanes de bon govern a
Catalunya," Boletín de la Real Academia de Buenas Letras de
Barcelona, XI (1923-1926), 293-335, 365-431, and XII (1926-
1928), 37-63, 121-153, 189-208, 286-295, 368-380, 419-423, 520-
533.

Código de las Costumbres escritas de Tortosa, D. Ramón Foguet and
José Foguet Marsal, eds. Tortosa, 1912.

Colección de documentos inéditos del Archivo general de la Corona
de Aragón, Próspero de Bofarull y Mascaró et al., eds. 41 v.
Barcelona, 1847-1910.

Cortes de los antiguos reinos de Aragón y de Valencia y principado de
Cataluña, Real Academia de la Historia, ed. 26 v. Madrid, 1899.

Crònica general de Pere III, el Cerimoniós, dita comunament Crònica
de Sant Joan de la Penya, Amadeu-J. Soberanas Lleó, ed.
Barcelona (?), 1961.

Crònica de Pere el Cerimoniós, in Les quatre grans cròniques, Ferran
Soldevila, ed. 1003-1225. Barcelona, 1971.

Font Rius, José Ma., <u>Cartas de población y franquicia de Cataluña.</u>
I. Textos. Escuela de Estudios Medievales, XXXVI. 2 v. Madrid-
Barcelona, 1969.

<u>Fori antiqui Valentiae</u>, Manuel Dualde Serrano, ed. Escuela de Estudios
Medievales, XXII. Madrid-Valencia, 1950-1967.

<u>Furs de València</u>, Germà Colon and Arcadi Garcia, eds., in <u>Els Nostres</u>
<u>Clàssics</u>, 101. Barcelona, 1970.

González Hurtebise, Eduardo, <u>Libros de tesorería de la Casa Real de</u>
<u>Aragón</u>. I. Barcelona, 1911.

Gubern, Ramón, <u>Epistolari de Pere III</u>, in <u>Els Nostres Clàssics</u>, 78.
One volume to date. Barcelona, 1955.

Ramos y Loscertales, José Ma., "Documentos para la historia del derecho
español: Fuero concedido a Calatayud por Alfonso I de Aragón en
1131," <u>Anuario de Historia del Derecho español</u>, I (1924), 408-
416.

_____, "Textos para el estudio del derecho aragonés en la Edad Media:
Recopilación de Fueros de Aragón," <u>Anuario de Historia del Derecho</u>
<u>español</u>, II (1925), 491-523.

Tilander, Gunnar, <u>Los Fueros de Aragón según el manuscrito 458 de la</u>
<u>Biblioteca Nacional de Madrid</u>. Lund, 1937.

_____, "Fueros aragoneses desconocidos promulgados a consecuencia
de la gran peste de 1348," <u>Revista de Filología española</u>, XXII
(1935), 1-33, 113-152.

<u>Usatges de Barcelona i Commemoracions de Pere Albert</u>, Josep Rovira i
Ermengol, ed., in <u>Els Nostres Clàssics</u>, 43-44. Barcleona, 1933.

Villanueva, Joaquín Lorenzo and Jaime, <u>Viage literario a las iglesias</u>
<u>de España</u>. 22 v. in 11. Madrid, 1802-1851.

Zurita, Jerónimo, <u>Anales de la Corona de Aragón</u>, Angel Canellas López,
ed. 4 v. Zaragoza, 1973.

Secondary works

<u>L'Almoina reial a la cort de Pere el Cerimoniós</u>. Poblet, 1969.

Aunós Perez, Antonio, <u>El derecho catalan en el siglo xiii</u>. Barcelona,
1926.

Batlle Gallart, Carmen, <u>La crisis social y económica de Barcelona a</u>
<u>mediados del siglo xv</u>. 2 v. Barcelona, 1973.

Boronat y Barrachina, Pascual, <u>Los Moriscos españoles y su expulsión</u>.
2 v. Valencia, 1901.

Bru i Vidal, Santiago, "El Morvedre dels temps de Pere el Cerimoniós,"
VIII Congreso de Historia de la Corona de Aragón, II (1969), 1,
203-210.

Brunschvig, Robert, "Urbanisme médiéval et droit musulman," Revue des
Etudes Islamiques, XV (1947), 127-155.

Burns, Robert Ignatius, "Christian-Islamic Confrontation in the West:
The Thirteenth-Century Dream of Conversion," American Historical
Review, LXXVI (1971), 1386-1434.

_____, The Crusader Kingdom of Valencia: Reconstruction on a Thir-
teenth-Century Frontier. 2 v. Cambridge, Mass., 1967.

_____, "How to End a Crusade: Techniques for Making Peace in the
Thirteenth-Century Kingdom of Valencia," Military Affairs, XXXV
(1971), 142-148.

_____, "Immigrants from Islam: the Crusaders' Use of Muslims as
Settlers in Thirteenth-Century Spain," American Historical Review,
LXXX (1975), 21-42.

_____, "Irrigation Taxes in Early Mudéjar Valencia: the Problem of the
Alfarda," Speculum, XLIV (1969), 560-567.

_____, Islam Under the Crusaders: Colonial Survival in the Thirteenth-
Century Kingdom of Valencia. Princeton, 1974.

_____, "Journey from Islam: Incipient Cultural Transition in the
Conquered Kingdom of Valencia," Speculum, XXXV (1960), 337-356.

_____, "Le royaume chrétien de Valence et ses vassaux musulmans
(1240-1280)," Annales, économies, sociétés, civilisations, XXVIII
(1973), 199-225.

_____, Medieval Colonialism: Postcrusade Exploitation of Islamic
Valencia. Princeton, 1975.

_____, "Social Riots on the Christian-Moslem Frontier: Thirteenth-
Century Valencia," American Historical Review, LXVI (1969), 378-
400.

Cabezudo Astraín, José, "Noticias y documentos sobre moriscos,"
Miscelánea de estudios árabes y hebraicos, V (1956), 105-117.

Cagigas, Isidro de las, Los Mudéjares, in Minorías étnico-religiosas
de la Edad Media española, III, IV. 2 v. Madrid, 1948-1949.

_____, "Problemas de minoría," Hispania, X (1950), 506-538.

Caro Baroja, Julio, Los moriscos del reino de Granada: ensayo de
historia social. Madrid, 1957

Carrère, Claude, Barcelone, centre économique à l'époque des difficultés
1380-1462. 2 v. Paris, 1967.

Circourt, Albert de, Histoire des Mores mudejares et des morisques
ou des arabes d'Espagne sous la domination des chrétiens. 3 v.
Paris, 1845-1848.

Colin, Georges S., "Notes sur l'arabe d'Aragon," Islamica, IV (1929), 159-169.

Coroleu, José, "Código de los Usajes de Barcelona: Estudio crítico," Boletín de la Real Academia de la Historia, IV (1884), 85-104.

_____, "Glosario de las voces desusadas en el vocabulario jurídico moderno y con más frecuencia empleadas en la antigua legislación catalana," Boletín de la Real Academia de la Historia, LI (1907), 393-410.

Del Treppo, M., I Mercanti catalani e l'espansione della Corona Aragonese nel secolo xv. Naples, 1968.

Doñate Sebastiá, José Ma., "Salarios y precios durante la segunda mitad del siglo xiv," VII Congreso de Historia de la Corona de Aragón, II (1962), 420-1.

Dufourcq, Charles, L'Espagne catalane et le Maghrib, xiiie et xive siècles, de la bataille de Las Navas de Tolosa (1212) à l'avènement du sultan mérinide Abou-1-Hasan (1313). Paris, 1966.

Duran Sanpere, Agustín, "Los esclavos en la ciudad hasta el siglo xv," Barcelona Divulgación Histórica, II, 94-99.

Ewert, Christian, Islamische funde in Balaguer und die Aljaferia in Zaragoza. Berlin, 1971.

Fernández y González, Francisco, Estado social y político de los mudéjares de Castilla. Madrid, 1866.

Ferrandis e Irles, Manuel, "Rendición del Castillo de Chivert," Homenaje a D. Francisco Codera, 26-33. Zaragoza, 1904.

Font y Rius, José Ma., "Franquicias urbanas medievales de la Cataluña Vieja," Boletín de la Real Academia de Buenas Letras de Barcelona, XXIX (1961-1962), 17-47.

Forey, A.J., "Cena Assessments in the Corona de Aragón: The Templar Evidence," Gesammelte Aufsätze zur Kulturgeschichte Spaniens, XXVII (1973), 279-288.

Garces Ferra, Bartolomé, "Intervención de las autoridades catalanas en una presa de moros disputada al reino de Valencia," Boletín de la Real Academia de Buenas Letras de Barcelona, XXIV (1951-1952), 239-247.

García Sanz, Arcadio, "Mudéjares y moriscos en Castellón," Boletín de la Sociedad castellonense de Cultura, XXVIII (1952), 94-114.

Gazulla, Faustino D., "La redención de cautivos entre los musulmanes," Boletín de la Real Academia de Buenas Letras de Barcelona, XIII (1928), 321-343.

Gimenez Soler, Andrés, El poder judicial en la Corona de Aragón, in Memorias leída en.la Real Academia de Buenas Letras de Barcelona. Barcelona, 1901.

Glick, Thomas F., and Oriol P. Sunyer, "Acculturation as an Explanatory Concept in Spanish History," Comparative Studies in Society and History, XI (1969), 136-154.

_____, "The Ethnic Systems of Premodern Spain," Comparative Studies in Sociology, I (1977), in press.

González Palencia, A., "Carta de esclavitud voluntaria," Revista de archivos, bibliotecas y museos, XXXVII (1917), 347-356.

Gras de Esteva, Rafael, Catálogo de los privilegios y documentos que se conservan en el archivo reservado de la Cuidad de Lérida. Lérida, 1897.

Grau Monserrat, Manuel, "Mudéjares castellonenses," Boletín de la Real Academia de Buenas Letras de Barcelona, XXIX (1961-1962), 251-275.

Gual Camarena, Miguel, "Mudéjares valencianos, aportaciones para su estudio," Saitabi, VII (1949), 165-199.

_____, "Los mudéjares valencianos en la época del Magnánimo," IV Congreso de Historia de la Corona de Aragón, I (1959), 467-494.

_____, Vocabulario del comercio medieval. Colección de aranceles aduaneros de la Corona de Aragón (siglos xiii y xiv). Tarragona, 1968.

Guichard, Pierre, "Le peuplement de la région de Valence aux deux premiers siècles de la domination musulmane," Mélanges de la Casa de Velázquez, V (1969), 103-158.

Halperin-Donghi, Tulio, "Les morisques du Royaume de Valence au xvie siècle," Annales, économies, sociétés, civilisations, XI (1956), 154-182.

Hamilton, E.J., Money, Prices, and Wages in Valencia, Aragon, and Navarra (1351-1500). Cambridge, Mass., 1936.

Hillgarth, Jocelyn, The Spanish Kingdoms, 1250-1516. I. 1250-1410: Precarious Balance. London, 1976.

Hinojosa, Eduardo de, "Mezquinos y exaricos. Datos para la historia de la servidumbre en Navarra y Aragón," Homenaje a D. Francisco Codera, 523-531. Zaragoza, 1904.

Iglesias Fort, José, "El fogaje de 1365-70," Memorias de la Real Academia de Ciencias y Artes de Barcelona, XXXIV (1962), 249-356.

Janer, Florencia, Condición social de los moriscos de España. Madrid, 1857.

Küchler, Winfried, "Besteuerung der Juden und Mauren in den Ländern der Krone Aragons während des 15. Jahrhunderts," Gesammelte Aufsätze zur Kulturgeschichte Spaniens, XXIV (1968), 227-256.

Lacarra y de Miguel, José, Aragón en el pasado. Madrid, 1972.

Lapidus, Ira M., _Muslim Cities in the Later Middle Ages_. Cambridge, Mass., 1967.

Liauzu, Jean-Guy, "La condition des musulmans dans l'Aragon chrétien aux xie et xiie siècles," _Hespéris-Tamuda_, IX (1968), 185-200.

Longas, Pedro. _Vida religiosa de los moriscos_. Madrid, 1915.

Lopez de Meneses, Amada, _Documentos acerca de la Peste Negra en los dominios de la Corona de Aragón_. Zaragoza, 1956.

_____, "Una consecuencia de la Peste Negra en Cataluña: el Pogrom de 1348," _Sefarad_, XIX (1959), 92-131, 321-364.

_____, "Documentos culturales de Pedro el Ceremonioso," _Estudios de Edad Media de la Corona de Aragón_, V (1952), 669-771.

_____, "Florilegio documental del reinado de Pedro IV de Aragón," _Cuadernos de Historia de España_, XIII (1950), 181-190; XIV (1950), 183-197; XV (1951), 170-179; XVI (1951), 160-171; XVII (1952), 167-176; XVIII (1952), 161-172; XIX (1953), 165-172; XX (1953), 165-173.

López Ortiz, José, "La jurisprudencia y el estilo de los tribunales musulmanes en España," _Anuario de Historia del Derecho español_, IX (1932), 213-248.

Lourie, Elena, "Free Moslems in the Balearics under Christian Rule in the Thirteenth Century," _Speculum_, XLV (1970), 624-249.

Luttrell, Anthony, "Los Hospitalarios en Aragón y la Peste Negra," _Anuario de Estudios Medievales_, III (1966), 498-514.

Macho y Ortega, Francisco, "Condición social de los judéjares aragoneses (siglo xv)," _Memorias de la Facultad de filosofía y letras de la Universidad de Zaragoza_, I (1923), 137-319.

_____, "Documentos relativos a la condición social y jurídica de los mudéjares aragonese," _Revista de ciencias jurídicas y sociales_, V (1922), 143-160, 444-464.

Martínez Ferrando, J. Ernesto, _El Archivo general de la Corona de Aragón_. Madrid, 1958.

_____, _Indice cronológico de la Colección de documentos inéditos del Archivo de la Corona de Aragón_. Barcelona, 1958.

_____, "Repoblación en los territorios de la Corona de Aragón," _VII Congreso de Historia de la Corona de Aragón_, I (1962), 143-187.

Masía de Ros, Angeles, _La Corona de Aragón y los estados del norte de Africa_. Barcelona, 1951.

Mateu y Llopis, Felipe, _Glosario hispánico de numismática_. Barcelona, 1946.

Mateu y Llopis, Felipe, La moneda española. Barcelona, 1946.

_____, "Para el estudio del monedaje en Aragón, Tortosa y Lérida en el siglo xiv," Martínez Ferrando, archivero. Miscelánea de estudios dedicados a su memoria, 315-322. [n.p.], 1968.

Millás Vallicrosa, José Ma., "Ceduletes en árab vulgar d'origen aragonès," Estudis Universitaris Catalans, XII (1927), 59-64.

Miret i Sans, J., "La esclavitud en Cataluña," Revue hispanique, XLI (1917), 1-109.

Mut Remola, Enrique, La vida económica en Lérida de 1150 a 1500. Lérida, 1953.

O'Callaghan, Ramón, Los códices de la catedral de Tortosa. Tortosa, 1897.

_____, "Homenaje prestado por los moros de la aldea al Abad del monasterio de Benifazar," Anales de Tortosa, III (1888), 55-57.

Oliver, Bienvenido, Historia del derecho en Cataluña, Mallorca, y Valencia. 4 v. Madrid, 1876-1881.

Pedregal y Fantini, J., Estado social y cultural de los mozárabes y mudéjares españoles. Seville, 1898.

Piles Ros, Leopoldo, Estudio documental sobre el Bayle General de Valencia. Valencia, 1970.

_____, "Situación económica de las aljamas aragonesas a comienzos del siglo xv," Sefarad, X (1950), 73-114.

Pons Guri, J.M., "Un fogatjement desconegut de l'any 1358," Boletín de la Real Academia de Buenas Letras de Barcelona, XXX (1963-1964), 323-498.

Ramos y Loscertales, José Ma., El cautiverio en la Corona de Aragón durante los siglos xiii, xiv, y xv. Zaragoza, 1915.

Ribera Tarrago, Julian, Disertaciones y opúsculos. 2 v. Madrid, 1928.

_____, "La nobleza árabe valenciana," in Disertaciones y opúsculos, II, 214-247.

Roca Traver, Francisco A., "Un siglo de vida mudéjar en la Valenica medieval (1238-1338)," Estudios de Edad Media de la Corona de Aragón, V (1952), 115-208.

Russell, J.C., "The Medieval Monedatge of Aragon and Valencia," Proceedings of the American Philosophical Society, CVI (1962), 483-504.

Saavedra, E., "Discurso sobre la literatura aljamiada," Memorias de la Academia española, VI (1878), 1-56, 103-190.

Sanz, J.M., "Alarifes moros aragoneses," Al-Andalus, III (1935), 63-89.

Setton, Kenneth M., Catalan Domination of Athens, 1311-1388. London, 1975.

Sevillano Colóm, F., Valencia urbana a través del oficio de mustaçaf. Valencia, 1957.

Tasis i Marca, Rafael, Pere el Cerimoniós i els seus fills, in Biografies catalanes, VII. Barcelona, 1962.

Torres Balbás, Leopoldo, "Actividades de los moros burgaleses en las artes y oficios de la construccion (siglos xiii-xv)," Al-Andalus, XIX (1954), 197-202.

Torres Fontes, Juan, "Los mudéjares murcianos en el siglo xiii," Murgetana, XVII (1961), 57-90.

Ureña y Smenjaud, R., and A. Bonilla y San Martín, Obras del Maestro Jacobo de las leyes, jurisconsulto del siglo xiii. Madrid, 1924.

Valls Taberner, F., Estudis d'historia jurídica catalana. Barcelona, 1929.

Verlinden, Charles, L'Esclavage dans l'Europe médiévale. Vol.I. Péninsule ibérique-France. Brugge, 1955.

_____, "Esclaves fugitifs et assurances en Catalogne (xive-xve siècles)," Annales du midi, LXII (1950), 301-328.

_____, "La grande peste de 1348 en Espagne. Contribution à l'étude de ses conséquences économiques et sociales," Revue belge de philologie et d'histoire, XVII (1938), 103-146.

Vilar, Pierre, "Le déclin catalan du Bas Moyen-Age. Hypothèses sur sa chronologie," Estudios de Historia Moderna, VI (1956-1959), 3-68.

Vincke, Johannes, "Königtum und Sklaverei im aragonischen Staatenbund während des 14. Jahrhunderts," Gesammelte Aufsätze zur Kulturgeschichte Spaniens, XXV (1970), 19-113.